W. E. B. Du Bois

on Race and Culture

W. E. B. Du Bois
on Race and Culture

Philosophy, Politics, and Poetics

Edited by

Bernard W. Bell,

Emily Grosholz,

and James B. Stewart

Routledge
New York and London

Published in 1996 by

Routledge
29 West 35th Street
New York, NY 10001

Published in Great Britain in 1996 by

Routledge
11 New Fetter Lane
London EC4P 4EE

Printed in the United States of America
Design and typography: Jack Donner

Library of Congress Cataloging-in-Publication Data

W. E. B. Du Bois on Race and Culture edited by Bernard Bell, Emily Grosholz, and James Stewart
     p.   cm.
Includes bibliographical references and index.
ISBN 0–415–91556–2. — ISBN 0–415–91557–0 (pbk.)
1. Du Bois, W. E. B. (William Edward Burghardt), 1868–1963—Philosophy. 2. Race. 3. Race relations. 4. Pluralism (Social sciences) 5. Minority women—social conditions. 6. Pan-Africanism. I. Bell, Bernard W. II. Grosholz, Emily, 1950–   . III. Stewart, James B. (James Benjamin), 1947–   .
E185.97.D73C76   1996
305.896'073'0092—dc20
                                                                    95–52028
                                                                        CIP

Contents

Ackowledgments

This volume is dedicated especially to all who have labored to understand the interplay of race and culture and have drawn particular inspiration from the life and writings of W. E. B. Du Bois. The genesis of this collection was a conference entitled "The Thought of W. E. B. Du Bois," held at the University Park campus of Penn State University in March 1992. For us, the editors, the generous support provided by the Departments of African and African American Studies, English, History, Philosophy, Political Science and Speech Communication, as well as the College of the Liberal Arts, the Equal Opportunity Planning Committee, the Institute for the Arts and Humanistic Studies, the Office of Research and the Graduate School, the Office of Undergraduate Education, the Paul Robeson Cultural Center and the Rare Books Room confirmed the potential importance of developing a monograph to explore further the contours of Du Bois's thinking on race and culture.

A project of this magnitude could not have been completed without the dedicated assistance of many individuals. The support of the clerical and technical staff of the Departments of English and Philosophy and the Office of Educational Equity proved invaluable. Special thanks is due to Jody Auman and Missy Price in the Department of English and Beth Ondo in the Department of Philosophy. Top quality research assistance is always a critical ingredient in the success of any major publication venture. Susan Searls, Carol Davenport, and Carolyn Carey not only rendered highly professional research support, they also willingly undertook the massive task of copy editing the galley proofs. Finally, our editor, Maureen MacGrogan, has been helpful throughout the process as have several other members of the Routledge organization.

Each of the editors has received special inspiration and support from family and friends. Bernard Bell recognizes the inspiration and support of his sister, Gwendolyn Bell, and that neither this nor any other of his scholarly efforts would have been possible without the loving sacrifices and support of his wife, Carrie. Emily Grosholz acknowledges the support and encouragement of her husband, Robert Edwards, and their children Benjamin, Robert, William Jules-Yves and Mary-Frances. For James Stewart, the opportunity to experience and observe the efforts of his three daughters Talibah, Lorin, and Jaliya to develop their own individual identities in a world where the color line still conditions human interaction has been a special inspiration.

Editors' Introduction

The raging ethnic conflicts and genocidal wars in the former Union of Soviet Socialist Republics and the former Yugoslavia, as well as in South Africa, India, Sri Lanka, and Burundi, justify the reexamination by contemporary scholars of the prophetic voice of W. E. B. Du Bois. His prophecy that "the problem of the twentieth century is the problem of the color line,—the relation of the darker to the lighter races of men in Asia and Africa, in America and the islands of the sea," has in large part been fulfilled. Also, the correlative problem of double-consciousness, the struggle of peoples to reconcile the tension between their national or political and ethnic or cultural identities, has become a major problem in the emerging new world order. Contemporary dialogue in the academy and media concerning the increasing educational, political, and philosophical influence throughout the American educational system of multiculturalism in general, and of Afrocentrism in particular, also often refers to the provocative ideas of W. E. B. Du Bois on race and culture. In this context, Emily Grosholz convened a conference at The Pennsylvania State University in 1992 on "The Thought of W. E. B. Du Bois."

A product of that conference, this collection of essays is a multivocal response to the politics, philosophy, and rhetoric of W. E. B. Du Bois's social construction of race. The four essays in the first section, "The Question of Race," appropriately begin the examination of what Du Bois called the problem of the color line by focusing on the evolution of his ideas on race and culture. Each of these essays includes a close reading of the definition of race in "The Conservation of Races," an explanation of the relationship of race, culture, and history, and a response to controversial readings of Du Bois's concept of race, especially that of Kwame Anthony Appiah. The complementary essays by

Lucius Outlaw and Bernard Boxill directly contest Appiah's readings, whereas the essay by Robert Gooding-Williams contests Outlaw's and Appiah's responses to Du Bois. And Bernard Bell's essay takes off from Appiah's account, before analyzing the evolution of Du Bois's rhetorical use of the racial and cultural sign of double-consciousness in his earliest unpublished and published fiction.

Outlaw contextualizes his "'Conserve' Races?: In Defense of W. E. B. Du Bois" by reminding us that both the major contemporary challenges to social order and the administration of justice in the United States result in part from racial and ethnic demographic changes that are increasing the number of people of color in the population. But many people consider "claims for justice framed in terms that valorize race or ethnicity" as the resurgence of "anachronistic, divisive, and socially disruptive particularist sentiments" that had supposedly been displaced by the "'self-evident' universalist conceptions and principles" on which the United States was founded and on which its claim to be "the historically paradigmatic, distinctively modern, democratic, Liberal nation" was based. Paradoxically, even those committed to valorizing race and ethnicity in their continuing struggle against institutionalized white supremacy and for justice with dignity are also often committed to "the complex of modern white Liberal principles" that advocates "that all persons be treated as having a shared *essential* identity as human beings, without regard to a person's race or ethnicity."

Outlaw's thesis is that, contrary to Appiah's reading of "The Conservation of Races," Du Bois's 1897 speech to the American Negro Academy (a new organization of black intellectuals) set forth an important approach to an understanding of race in a racially and ethnically pluralistic, democratic society. Outlaw's analysis convincingly explains how Du Bois understands race as a cluster concept: "'race' refers to a group of persons who share and are distinguished by several properties taken disjunctively such that 'each property is severally sufficient and the possession of at least one of the properties is necessary." The key to Appiah's reading of "The Conservation of Races," then, is his interpretive strategy of isolating and analyzing each of the elements in Du Bois's definition of race individually, rather than taking them as "a cluster of . . . biological and cultural . . . elements that together comprise the definition." The major premise of Outlaw's text is that Du Bois's definition of race is a political project which "involves prescribing norms for the social reconstruction of identity and for self-appropriation by a particular people suffering racialized subordination to the end of mobilizing and guiding them in efforts of emancipatory social transformation."

In "Outlaw, Appiah, and Du Bois's 'The Conservation of Races,'" Robert Gooding-Williams addresses three of Outlaw's objections to Appiah's argument that Du Bois's definition of race did not transcend nineteenth-century scientific concepts: first, Outlaw's objection to Appiah's assumption that Du Bois believes "that families are joined by biology ... and not by acts of choice"; second, his opposition to Appiah's rejection of Du Bois's "common history" criterion as circular reasoning; and third, Outlaw's argument that Appiah misrepresents Du Bois's essay as an attempt to define a "heritable racial essence" by a set of several properties taken conjunctively rather than disjunctively.

Although Appiah is right, according to Gooding-Williams, that "The Conservation of Races" fails to transcend the perspective of the nineteenth-century, he is wrong to suggest that the essay fails to repudiate "the claim of the racial sciences to explain the spiritual and cultural differences between the races." In particular, Gooding-Williams concurs with Outlaw's reading of Du Bois's nonbiological explanation of group spiritual differences and use of the language of race as a political project. Gooding-Williams concludes with the argument that Du Bois's explanation of nonbiological group spiritual differences in "The Conservation of Races" is a prolegamenon to the representation of black historical strivings and spirituality in *The Souls of Black Folk*. This antiphonal pattern of voices continues throughout subsequent essays in this collection as well as in the evolution of Du Bois's thoughts on African American double consciousness and the problem of the color line.

The philosophical voice of Bernard Boxill, in his essay "Du Bois on Cultural Pluralism," contrasts with the more political voice of Outlaw. Influenced by the pragmatism of William James, Du Bois, according to Boxill, "was clear that race was not a classification given by nature or reality, but was carved out by human beings to suit their purpose, which in this instance was to find laws that could be used to enhance human progress." Because of the limited abilities of individuals, however, progress is always the product of group cooperation. Assuming that culture gives people their most basic preferences and ideals, Boxill argues that Du Bois's position implies that a race of people with common impulses and strivings will have a common culture. And he concludes that Du Bois's assumption "that the cultural group he called a race was a group with a common history" is a reasonable one.

Contrary to Anthony Appiah's claim that Du Bois "fell back on a biological definition of race," Boxill argues for a more charitable interpretation of Du Bois's views. His major line of argument is that, rather than the claim of a common history committing Du Bois to a biological conception of race, "What is essential is that the group inherit a common way of life that has developed over generations." After examining Appiah's claim that Du Bois's theory was tainted by racist assumptions and premises, Boxill shows how Du Bois's view that each cultural group had something to teach the world "led him to affirm that the juxtaposition of different cultural groups in culturally plural societies gave such societies unique opportunities to learn from each other."

Although Du Bois's theory of cultural pluralism indicates that racial unity is necessary for progress, Boxill stresses that "it also maintains that the progress of the races is interdependent because every race has something to learn from, and to teach, every other race." At the dawn of the twentieth century Du Bois believed that under certain conditions the problems of cultural diversity, such as group conflicts, could be managed not by a melting pot amalgamation but by each cultural group striving together to advance. In this regard, Boxill argues, both Du Bois and Booker T. Washington saw segregation as an opportunity. "Washington saw segregation as an opportunity to develop Black Capitalism. Du Bois rejected this proposal because his study of Marx had led him to the conclusion that capitalism was corrupting. He saw segregation as an opportunity to develop a cooperative black economy."

According to Boxill, the issue between Du Bois and Washington was over whether work was sufficient for moral improvement. Washington thought it was; Du Bois thought the teachings of a Talented Tenth were also necessary. Comparing Du Bois's theory of a Talented Tenth to the elitist theories of other major philosophers, Boxill reveals that like Locke rather than Plato, Du Bois advocated "that the elite had to save the majority by teaching it how to live morally." However, unlike Locke's elite, the Talented Tenth was expected "to share with other cultural groups the insights they had sifted and developed out of the raw material of their own culture." Unlike Plato's philosopher kings, Du Bois's black Talented Tenth was also expected only "to fashion a morality out of the customs of the common people." Boxill thus argues that Du Bois believed that his theory of cultural pluralism was the solution to the problem of the color line. "A cooperative society pioneered by the African American community could, he argued, lead the world out of the chaos of the collapsing capitalistic system. Its example would be a gift of American blacks to world civilization, and the vindication of his case for cultural pluralism."

Despite the apparent flaws in Du Bois's optimistic thinking, especially his underestimation of "the power of the economy to corrupt even the teachers," Boxill is sympathetic to Du Bois's assumption "that probably some of the principles of the moralities of every culture are objectively valid." He offers this assumption as the foundation of Du Bois's "democratic and cosmopolitan view that the process of discovering the best way to live relied on the input of all cultural groups." Boxill, anticipating the tone of Bell's concluding essay in this section, is equally sympathetic and optimistic about Du Bois's claim that American blacks each had a double-self, and were confused by the contradiction of double aims, for Du Bois "only said that these aims were 'unreconciled'; he never said that they were unreconcilable." Du Bois also "spoke positively of the American Negro's longing 'to merge his double self into a better and truer self.'"

Bernard Bell's "Genealogical Shifts in Du Bois's Discourse on Double Consciousness as the Sign of African American Difference" has two aims. The first is to trace the historical origins and discursive shifts in Du Bois's ideological construction of double consciousness as a sign of African American racial and ethnic difference, and the second is to analyze its dialectic and dialogic use as a theme and trope in the unpublished "A Fellow of Harvard" and the published "Of the Coming of John." After identifying the distinctive rhetorical, dialectal, and dialogical discourse and outlining the probable origins of the concept in European romanticism and psychology, Bell analyzes Du Bois's first articulation of his theory and trope of double consciousness in "The Conservation of Races." He argues that "the distinctiveness of African American double consciousness is the residual African spirituality expressed in African American folk and formal art." Turning to the originary sites of Du Bois's classic definition of double consciousness in "Strivings of the Negro People" and "Of Our Spiritual Strivings," Bell also contends that double consciousness was "not the fate of all ethnic immigrants or hyphenated Americans.... Rather, it was the complex double vision of Americans of African descent whose humanity and culture had been historically devalued and marginalized by people of European and British descent." Politically and rhetorically, double consciousness, is for Bell, "a dialectic and a dialogic process in American society between the bearers, on one hand, of residually oral sub-Saharan African cultures and, on the other, of industrialized Western print cultures."

Bell's analysis of Du Bois's unpublished incomplete narrative drafts of "A Fellow of Harvard" and published narrative "Of the Coming of John" in *The Souls of Black Folk* illuminates two important aspects of the nature and function of double consciousness as a sign of difference. First, as a sociopsychological and sociocultural process, double consciousness is the dynamic by which Americans of African descent of all classes strive to discover and realize their full potential, their rights and responsibilities, as human beings and American citizens. Second, as a sociohistorical product, double consciousness is the unnecessary, tragic consequence of the pent-up anger and hatred of many Americans of African descent struggling to overcome the barriers and agents of institutionalized racism. Racism thus frustrates the attainment of justice with dignity by African Americans, in the pursuit of their democratic right to the equal economic, cultural, and political opportunities necessary to reconcile the tensions of their biracial and bicultural heritage.

Though Du Bois's famous dictum that the problem of the twentieth century is the problem of the color line indicates that the philosophical analysis of race was his central concern, he was also well aware of how the social construction of class and gender bore heavily upon a society already unbalanced by racism. Like Frederick Douglass before him, Du Bois was keenly interested in women's suffrage and the status of women, not only because he saw instructive parallels between the oppression of women and that of African Americans, but also because he was distressed by the effects of the double scourge of sexism and racism on African American women. In his sociological studies, his political polemic, his philosophical reflections, and the prophetic romances of his fiction, he sought to portray and understand the special sufferings and heroism of women of color. This aspect of Du Bois's work is taken up in section two, "The Question of Women."

In her essay, "The Margin as a Center of a Theory of History: African-American Women, Social Change, and the Sociology of W. E. B. Du Bois," Cheryl Townsend Gilkes observes that up until recent years, European and American sociology had tended to view gender and race as subsidiary issues. Du Bois's insistence on the importance of the color line, and his awareness that the status of women was central to human emancipation, makes him a significant early twentieth-century forerunner of contemporary socio-political thought. And much of what he has to say about both the suffering and the activism of African American women can, Gilkes maintains, provide guidance for current feminist theory as it tries to come to terms with the complexities of race and class.

Gilkes points out that in a great variety of writings, both scientific and literary, Du Bois showed that African American women might experience their suffering as a source of meaning which could provide them with a special perspective on American society and, indeed, on the political reconfiguration of the globe. In particular, they would have a disenchanted vantage on male elites, corrupted by domestic or colonialist politics, who might try to avoid including women in the process of liberation. And African American women would not be misled by the mystifying "worship of women" that pacified so many upper-class white women, since they had long been forced to labor, and were also regarded as sexual prey. Indeed, they were often provoked to an especially forceful counter-activity: Du Bois "saw the social movements of black women as a redemptive response to that suffering," a response on the one hand spiritual and transcendent, and on the other closely linked to concrete social reality.

Du Bois, always sensitive to the economic dimension of social change, often noted that black women played a significant emancipatory role simply by virtue of working, "fighting for their daily bread like men; independent and approaching economic freedom." The presence of black women as domestic workers in so many white households, Du Bois further observed, contributed to the Africanization of American culture and also, as a bitter consequence of concubinage, led to the thorough mixture of black and white blood. (On this point Du Bois does not seem to do justice to the social reality of rape.) The cultural challenge became a political challenge in the lives of monumental figures like Harriet Tubman and Mary Ellen Pleasants. The suffrage of African American women, Du Bois concluded, is important because they are human, because they are women, and because they are black. Gilkes counsels anyone worried about the underdevelopment and failures of feminist theory to consult the extensive writings of Du Bois on the "paradoxical situation of black women in the United States."

By contrast, Joy James, in her essay "The Profeminist Politics of W. E. B. Du Bois with Respects to Anna Julia Cooper and Ida B. Wells Barnett," sees greater tension in the relation of Du Bois's opposition to racial oppression and his opposition to injustice against women. She argues that, while Du Bois clearly held that women should be emancipated, he had certain difficulties working with and acknowledging the importance of African American leaders like Ida B. Wells Barnett and Anna Julia Cooper. Though he held quite progressive positions on gender equality, sexual violence, and women's suffrage, his pronouncements on African American women treated the category more often than the individuals who constituted it. In his many autobiographical works, for instance, he has very little to say about the intense intellectual and practical activity of particular African American women. James takes this as evidence that his support for feminism existed uneasily with an unreflective acceptance of male privilege and dominance.

An advocate for greater access to higher education for African Americans and an outspoken critic of Booker T. Washington, Anna Julia Cooper was, theoretically and politically, an obvious ally for Du Bois. But Du Bois often failed to acknowledge his indebtedness to her ideas, and occasionally even quoted her words without mentioning her name. The interesting and complex interaction between the ideas of the two intellectuals, turning especially on the nature and function of elites, has thus been lost to view. Similarly, Du Bois's account of his own political organizing makes almost no mention of the courageous efforts of Ida B. Wells Barnett in her international campaign against lynching. Nor does he acknowledge the significance of her exclusion from the group which would develop the NAACP. James concludes that Du Bois recorded in his memoirs the general features of the struggle of African American women, while obscuring the full contribution of their leadership.

This tendency noted by James may explain why Du Bois's most touching and urgent meditations on the question of women occur in his literary works. For poetry traditionally deals with the universal, not the particular. The chief protagonists, it may be argued, of both *Dark Princess* and *The Quest of the*

Silver Fleece are women, or types of womanhood, whose wisdom, suffering, and moral growth organize and redeem the lives of those around them. In his essay "Du Bois's Passage to India: *Dark Princess*" Arnold Rampersad argues that this novel does not deserve its critical neglect. Among other things, the novel draws upon a serious and long-standing interest in the history and culture of India that distinguishes Du Bois from most other American intellectuals of his day, black or white. The cosmopolitan vision that led Du Bois to promote the pan-Africanism discussed in the last section of this book also led him to seek in the brown peoples of India allies in social change, and in their culture an alternative to the Greco-Roman tradition of Europe and America.

The Indian princess who figures as the heroine of the book combines intellectual accomplishment and civilized refinement with a moral purity that has as its object the alleviation of suffering in the underclass, both American and Indian. This allows Du Bois to reflect, as did Martin Luther King in later years, on the parallel status of untouchables and blacks, though Du Bois's understanding of social remedy differed greatly from that of King and Gandhi. But the spiritual revolution that lifts the princess from her royal prejudices to true understanding has as its midwife the mother of her black American lover—"a poor but mighty, purposeful mother," who lives in a cabin in rural Virginia. Rampersad argues that in this figure Du Bois sees that "the black woman is the world's metaphor, born out of violation and shame, but then recuperated as the living symbol of the interrelationship of the races."

In the fictional political alliance of American blacks, Indians, and representatives of other Third World countries that forms the backdrop for the romance of the Indian princess and her lover, Rampersad sees Du Bois as an accurate prophet who foresaw the Bandung Conference of 1955, which aimed to establish African-Asian neutrality in the midst of the Cold War. By implication, he also recommends Du Bois's "romance" to those interested in a politics of liberation that is truly international and cosmopolitan.

Emily Grosholz, in her essay "Nature and Culture in *The Souls of Black Folk* and *The Quest of the Silver Fleece*," sees Du Bois's fictional progress against a metaphysical, rather than political or sociological, background. Metaphysical assumptions, however, may prove to have practical consequences, for good or ill. Here she examines the way the opposed terms nature and culture organize the oppositions and conflicts that move the action in Du Bois's novel *The Quest of the Silver Fleece*. Throughout the book, the heroine Zora is identified with nature, as is woman in contrast to man, and black in contrast to white. This classification seems to work both against and for Zora: it gives her an abiding home in a natural setting, a swamp whose creatures are familiar to her, and at the same time seems to underlie the childhood prostitution into which her amoral mother forces her.

Zora's life blossoms as her romance with a young man develops; she does not go over to the side of culture, but begins to unify the two terms in her own life through a complex series of integrations that involve work, learning, and love. This process is interrupted when her lover rejects the stormy nature with which she must be connected, and retreats into the artificial, corrupt culture of urban Washington. But when his sterile dreams collapse and he returns to the countryside, he rediscovers in Zora a conduit to the life of the body, the secrets of lost Africa, and effective political activity. As Zora and her lover prepare to marry at the end of the "romance," they present a kind of concrete schema of what the unification of opposing terms might look like, a vision of the future in which nature and culture, black and white, and man and woman are brought into stable relationship.

That schema, which surfaces again in some of the narratives in *The Souls of Black Folk*, can among other things provide a positive version of the "double consciousness" discussed in the first section of this book. For double consciousness is both a scourge and a gift. When the opposed terms cannot be set in any intelligible relationship, as happens when metaphysics, politics, and economic structures work to sunder them, double consciousness leads to tragedy. Bernard Bell analyzes that sundering in "Of the Coming of John." But *Dark Princess* and *The Quest of the Silver Fleece* imagine different worlds, where what is sundered can be brought into a relationship that is not only intelligible, but creative. Fictive, romantic, and idealistic those worlds may be, but they are the counterpart to Du Bois's quite earthbound conviction that America's struggle with the diversity of its people is the place not only of its suffering, but also of its greatness. Insofar as we have recognized, named, and overcome that internal strife, we provide an example for the world that the world very badly needs, as we move toward a global community in which difference cannot be avoided or spurned.

The essays in the third section, "The Question of Pan-Africanism," explore the application of Du Bois's ideas to the promotion of social change, human progress, and the eradication of inequalities among groups. One of the common themes in this section is Du Bois's involvement in efforts to promote pan-African unity. In many respects, the ideology and praxis of Pan-Africanism, at its inception as a formal movement, constituted an effort to extend domestic notions of race and culture into an international milieu. As Du Bois observed, as late as the 1920s Pan-Africanism was still an American rather than an African idea.

The processes that helped transform Pan-Africanism into an African movement also forced Du Bois to reconsider the strategies he had previously advocated to address the plight of African Americans. He became increasingly convinced that the eradiction of racism and its effects required a coordinated international strategy. Thus when Du Bois rejoined the administrative structure of the NAACP in the 1940s he attempted to resurrect the Pan-African movement.

Pan-Africanists were spurred by practical as well as ideological considerations in pursuing African unity. They carefully observed the global trend toward regional and international confederations, and sought to insure that such alliances would not further disadvantage peoples of African descent. In this context the delegates at the Fifth Pan-African Congress in 1945 made their demand for independence for Black Africa conditional on the extent to which "it is possible in this One World for groups and peoples to rule themselves subject to inevitable world unity and federation."

The essays by Manning Marable and Segun Gbadegesin provide complementary perspectives on Du Bois's efforts to promote Pan-Africanism. Marable, in "The Pan-Africanism of W. E. B. Du Bois," gives a comprehensive overview of the political dynamics that shaped the contours of Du Bois's Pan-Africanist advocacy. He locates the impetus for Du Bois's growing involvement in efforts to transform the ideology of Pan-Africanism into political reality in his long-standing "commitment to a democracy, defined by the realization of racial equality and social justice for all social groups and classes within the society." From this vantage point, Marable argues that "Pan-Africanism . . . was merely the concrete political expression of Du Bois's intellectual commitment to eradicate racism, colonialism, and all structures of exploitation." Marable locates the origins of Du Bois's commitment to Pan-Africanism in his undergraduate experience at Fisk University, "which first awakened Du Bois's lifelong identification with African culture." His intellectual interest in African history developed concurrently with his efforts to establish a Pan-African political movement. As Marable observes, "throughout the first two decades of the twentieth century, he was one of the few American scholars who encouraged others to take an active interest in the cultural, economic and political history of African people."

Gbadegesin disentangles various strands in the concept of Pan-Africanism and identifies three distinct interpretations, in his essay "Kinship of the Dispossessed: Du Bois, Nkrumah, and the Foundations of Pan-Africanism." The first interpretation, pan-Negroism, emphasizes solidarity based on either a phenotypical or socio-historical notion of race. Pan-humanism, the second interpretation, extends the kinship of the oppressed to include peoples of color other than those of African descent. The third is pan-continentalism, which focuses specifically on the unity of African states in the struggle against colonial exploitation. Gbadegesin finds that all three interpretations exist in Du Bois's writings, but that Du Bois's emphasis changes over time, as does that of the overall movement. Specifically, there is a shift away from pan-Negroism toward pan-humanist and pan-continentalist constructions. Gbadegesin argues that the shift from pan-Negroism to pan-continentalism is associated with a "shift of agenda from the struggle against colonial exploitation to the post-colonial struggle for unity and development."

Both Marable and Gbadegesin identify Kwame Nkrumah as the major torch bearer of Du Bois's pan-Africanist legacy, most notably in his efforts to effect the equivalent of a United States of Africa, an initiative that went beyond even Du Bois's vision. In this context, Gbadegesin asserts that "the vision of Du Bois inspired the subsequent activities of Kwame Nkrumah, who, together with George Padmore, organized the Manchester Pan-African Congress of 1945."

In the third essay of this section, "Culture, Civilization, and Decline of the West: The Afrocentrism of W. E. B. Du Bois," Wilson J. Moses also acknowledges Nkrumah as perpetuator of Du Bois's vision; but his evaluation of Du Bois's and Nkrumah's Pan-Africanism is very different from those of Marable and Gbadegesin. Moses insists that Du Bois exhibited a long-standing preference for authoritarian forms of leadership and authority that can be traced to "his youthful homage to the 'unbending righteousness' of Alexander Crummell." According to Moses, "Du Bois's fascination with the strong man, the political or military leader who could bend nations to his will . . . was a recurrent theme in his work." Nkrumah, Moses asserts, fit Du Bois's model of the ideal strong leader. But Moses decries Nkrumah's leadership style and characterizes Nkrumah as "an increasingly ruthless dictator." He extends his critique to Du Bois himself, whom he describes at one point as a "pan-African chauvinist with a penchant for the theatrical" who had the "problem of controlling his authoritarian emotions in observance of egalitarian niceties and democratic protocols."

Moses argues further that there is a consistent "Afrocentric" theme in Du Bois's writings that enabled him to synthesize his conception of Pan-Africanism with his advocacy of socialism. This "Afrocentrism" was manifested through Du Bois's reinterpretation of his earlier views of African history, allowing him to pay increasing homage to the contributions of ancient Africans to global civilization. These tendencies are seen by Moses as being in conflict with Du Bois's interest in articulating a coherent conception of the advancement of culture and civilization. Moses concludes that "Du Bois's theory of history from beginning to end was tied up with the problem of power and authority," such that "individuals must always be subordinated to collective goals and racial destiny."

Is it possible to reconcile these apparently opposed views of Du Bois's Pan-African agenda? The essay by James B. Stewart, "In Search of a Theory of Human History: W. E. B. Du Bois's Theory of Social and Cultural Dynamics," although it does not address the Pan-Africanism issue directly, offers one possible path of reconciliation. Stewart attempts to correlate Du Bois's concepts of culture, civilization, progress, and development as they were articulated at different points in his life. The specific focus on "civilization" connects directly with one thrust of the Pan-African movement. The resolutions that emerged from the 1921 and 1927 Pan-African Congresses, which had Du Bois's imprimatur, included calls for "modern education for all children" and "the treatment of civilized men as civilized despite differences of birth, race or color." Since Du Bois's major statement on the evolution of culture and civilization was published in the 1940s, there is an obvious continuity of concern with this issue.

Du Bois's most comprehensive statement of his views of the progression of civilizations is in an obscure, co-authored review of the multi-volume history of civilizations authored by sociologist Pitrim Sorokin. Stewart examines this essay in detail, linking its focus to that of a 1904 article in which Du Bois articulates a four-stage model of general societal development. The model developed by Du Bois can accommodate the "Afrocentric" analysis of the functioning of African villages which Moses discusses as well as Marxist constructs. And it reflects the fact that in the end, Du Bois was not so much concerned with celebrating the historical contributions of peoples of African descent to world civilization as he was with insuring that there would be opportunities to contribute an alternative vision of the future.

Du Bois's concern, in the latter stages of his life, was with what he saw as the "leveling of culture patterns" resulting from the continuing expansion of monopoly capitalism. From this vantage point Pan-Africanism constituted a means by which to take advantage of economies of scale, i.e. to allow peoples of African descent to make a larger contribution to global civilization collectively than would be possible through efforts of individual collectives. This idea is relevant to contemporary efforts to establish regional and extra-regional federations throughout the world. Du Bois saw the effects of a Pan-African movement as beneficial not only to people of African descent but to all who have an interest in the values identifed by Marable—democracy, equality and social justice.

The

Question

of Race

"Conserve" Races? | **1**

In Defense of W. E. B. Du Bois[1]

Lucius Outlaw

> There is, of course, nothing more fascinating than the question of
> the various types of mankind and their intermixture.
>
> W. E. B. Du Bois[2]

PROBLEMS INVOLVING "THE COLOR LINE"

Race and ethnicity continue to be among the most vexing problems in
American life. At present there is no widely shared consensus in answer to the
questions of whether, and if so how (and if not, why not), consideration
should be given to the race and/or ethnicity of a person, or to a racial/ethnic
group, when deciding questions having to do with the preservation, creation,
or distribution of important resources, awards, and sanctions. Nor is there a
settled consensus among persons in the various natural and social sciences in
answer to questions of whether, and if so how (and if not, why not), it is possible to characterize and classify racial and ethnic groups, and thereby identify
individuals with precision as members of a particular racial or ethnic group,
on the basis of real, objective, shared features, in rigorous accordance to the
most settled norms governing the production and validation of empirical
knowledge. Without a consensus secured by knowledge of this kind, it seems,
adjudicating the vexing questions of race and ethnicity in political, social, and
economic life cannot be accomplished with the guidance of secure, general
principles based on such knowledge that insure a just and democratic liberal
nation-state in which the play of invidious notions of race and ethnicity are
curtailed as much as is possible.

Still, persons and groups continue to be identified, and to identify themselves, as particular races and/or ethnie (ethnic groups). As a nation-state deliberately composed of diverse peoples, the United States of America has a long and continuing history of being deeply troubled by practices and orientations involving value-laden, often invidious conceptualizations of race and ethnicity. As W. E. B. Du Bois predicted, what he characterized as "the problem of the color line"—problematic relations involving persons distinguished, initially, by skin-color as constituting or belonging to distinct races—has been a major problem throughout the twentieth century. And though there is a clear record of substantial achievements in recent decades in addressing and resolving some of the difficulties involving race and ethnicity in the realms of social, judicial, political, and economic life, challenging problems remain that prevent the realization of more complete social peace and harmony with justice. We are experiencing yet another period of heightened tensions and social conflict in which claims for justice are framed in terms that valorize race or ethnicity in various ways. We desperately need, then, settled and widely shared knowledge regarding the empirically and socially appropriate identification of persons and groups, knowledge that will assist us in devising and institutionalizing norms to help in fashioning, maintaining, and legitimating well-ordered, stable, and just political communities within which individual and shared lives can be nurtured.

Why has this knowledge been so difficult to achieve and legitimate? In significant part it is because the term "race" has been employed to cover a combination of distinctively different, yet supposedly linked, factors thought to constitute raciality: on the other hand, inherited biological characteristics, and on the other, a particular history of origin—generally associated with a specific geographic setting—and of continuity via cultural traditions (e.g., language, arts and literatures, religion, forms of life in general). Similarly, "ethnicity" has often been employed to conceptualize and thereby distinguish groups of persons primarily in terms of shared cultural factors (practices, traditions, histories, sites of origin and occupancy). In both cases, the collections of factors are thought to combine so as to determine a distinctive racial or ethnic identity, objectively and subjectively, of a group of people, and to be key to the meaningfulness, authenticity, and legitimacy of their lives, individually and as a group. Moreover, many of the particular groups thought to be a race involve many persons who very often do not live their lives in intimate relations with all those who are members of the race, but in smaller, local populations of sub-race ethnies that continue to develop and evolve in their own right, in some cases in spaces and times quite different from the site of origin and "home" of the parent-race. In this case, as well as for racial groups generally, the factors thought to define the race are subject to variation.

Thus, the efforts to characterize a group of people by a combination of complexes of varying biological and cultural factors, and to refer to this combination in a coherent and precise way using a single, stable term ("race," "ethnie"), are especially difficult—particularly if, as noted, these efforts are to satisfy various scientific norms for objective and valid empirical reference. (The difficulties are increased when the terms "race" and "ethnic group" are used interchangeably, as they often are.) Hence, it becomes difficult to understand and deal in a settled way with all of the nuances and complexities of challenging situations in which race and ethnicity are contested issues, and difficult to do so in ways that will facilitate the achievement of the consensual understandings needed to achieve stable, lasting social peace and harmony on the basis of principles of democratic justice, especially when it is proposed that justice be achieved by taking race and/or ethnicity into account in positive ways.

Many persons argue that valorizations of race and/or ethnicity are morally and politically inappropriate, and that taking these matters into account when making evaluative judgments may well have the further consequence of either promoting or sanctioning the return of disruptive, anachronistic sentiments and conceptions concerning *groups*, conceptions that had been delegitimated and replaced by universalist (as opposed to group-relative, particularist), "self-evident" conceptions of and principles concerning *individuals*. Such conceptions and principles, as in "All Men are created equal," are foundational to the political organization of the United States as a distinctively modern, democratic, and Liberal nation. For these persons, neither race nor ethnicity should have any constitutive role in the formulation of ideals and principles for justice and social order, nor in conceptions of "human being" even though, anthropologically, it might be appropriate to acknowledge that there are different races and ethnies.

For other persons, however, racial and ethnic differences are fundamentally constitutive of human beings, and each member of a particular race and/or ethnie shares the group's defining characteristics, more or less, and is substantially identified (and identifiable) by these characteristics. Therefore, race and ethnicity, in important instances, must be taken into account when formulating basic principles by which to order social life. And for many people who continue to suffer invidious discrimination leading to diminished life-chances and quality of life because of practices rationalized by reference to their race and/or ethnicity, embracing notions of race and/or ethnicity in struggles against these conditions are an important aspect of their efforts to achieve freedom and justice with dignity. Such struggles have been made necessary by a long history of failure on the part of empowered persons of socially dominant ethnies of the white race who supposedly have been applying principles to all persons "without regard for race, creed, color, sex, or national origin." From the outset, however, America was structured, with the assistance of complex doctrines of white racial supremacy, into a racialized, hierarchic nation-state (further complicated by other relations like class and gender hierarchies among others). For some persons, then, at the heart of racism, invidious ethnocentrism, and sexism are serious inadequacies in the notion of the human being at the core of modern, Liberal political principles: abstract "Man" is insufficient for conceptualizing and referring to the full range of important factors that characterize persons, individually and socially. And, in an ethnically and racially diverse nation-state with continuing legacies of invidious ethnocentrism and racism, justice, it is argued by some, can be neither properly conceived nor practically achieved without consideration to race and ethnicity.

But *proper* consideration is imperative if society is to achieve and maintain social order and justice rather than descending into chauvinism and fratricide. And this requires a shared widespread commitment to the proposition that in important contexts, and for important purposes, all persons must be regarded as having a shared *essential* identity as human beings, race or ethnicity notwithstanding, that is, each citizen must have access to fair and equal opportunities to acquire resources critical to the realization of well-formulated plans for life, liberty, and the pursuit of happiness, and must enjoy equality before the law as well as all of the rights, privileges, and responsibilities of free citizens. Of course, working out and realizing practically, in a coherent and socially viable way, multiple commitments to diverse and seemingly divergent principles that favor individuality without regard to race and/or ethnicity and also favor regard for ethnicity and race (or gender, or sexual orientation) is a most demanding task which, unfinished, adds to the potential explosiveness of the complexities and tensions of contemporary American social life.

We continue to be challenged, then, to reconsider and possibly transform the ways in which many of us have come to think of ourselves and of this nation. Political movements which seek identity and recognition, and thereby respect and empowerment, for racial and ethnic groups, as well as political movements that are grounded in affirmations of the common humanity of all peoples, and thereby regard all persons as in essence "the same" and to race and/or ethnicity as inappropriate, confront us with two agendas that are so difficult to reconcile that they threaten social and political unity. This threat is enhanced as demographic changes in the country confirm a continuing increase in the numbers of "peoples of color" in the population.[3] A cover story in *Time* magazine a few years ago explored in a poignant way several of the critical issues involved in this historic demographic shift: "Someday soon, surely much sooner than most people who filled out their Census forms ... realize, white Americans will become a minority group. Long before that day arrives, the presumption that

the 'typical' U.S. citizen is someone who traces his or her descent in a direct line
to Europe will be part of the past."[4]

This increasing "coloring" of Americans is prompting major changes in the
nation and posing serious challenges to social ordering and the administration
of justice. In virtually every area of social, political, economic, and private life,
empowered persons and groups—and others hoping to become empowered—
continue their organized efforts to secure, maintain, and then rationalize what
has been gained (or threatened with loss) for persons in their racial and/or
ethnic groups. Herein lies the potential for much social conflict, a great deal of
it already realized.

Can the tensions and conflicts involving race and ethnicity, and the subsequent threats to social order and political unity, be avoided or resolved, or at
least substantially reduced—if not completely eliminated—while allowing for
the recognition, celebration, and even nurturing of racial and ethnic differences? Only if appropriate principles and related practices can be achieved,
and widespread, institutionalized consensus in support of them secured, as a
framework that will structure social life overall. This will require, of course,
substantial alterations to the fundamental conceptions, values, and practices
that constitute the ideologically and politically dominant consensus regarding
notions of the person and of appropriate forms of political life and that have
helped to define and shape modern American life. Foremost among these is the
principle that race and ethnicity not be taken into account in determining or
recognizing the fundamental being and worth of a person or group of persons,
nor in deciding who is or can be a citizen, or what rights a citizen enjoys.
Substituting for this a principle with explicit commitments to raciality and
ethnicity in achieving social justice, and in understanding the historical and
social being and worthiness of a person, while preserving past achievements
won with the assistance of modern, individualist principles, is a major challenge. Doing so will require re-conceptualizations of race and ethnicity that are
compatible with revised principles of justice intended to aid in the realization
of a well-ordered and stable, racially and ethnically diverse, society.

RETHINKING "RACE"

What might be expected from the anticipated rethinking of "race"?[5] Hopefully, at the very least, a contribution to critical thought might be expected in
terms of understandings that assist in guiding the way to the resolution of
difficulties and, thereby, to the promotion and practical realization of
"progressive" or "emancipatory" social evolution. In other words, we expect
the development of forms of shared understanding and forms of social practice free of epistemologically untenable conceptualizations and of morally
inappropriate valorizations of race. The persistence of struggles involving race

present those of us who are committed to critical thought and emancipatory practice with several problems to which we must attend. First off, there is the need to engage in a critical review of our informing traditions of thought and practice, to investigate the extent to which these traditions have failed to accommodate race appropriately in failing to provide compelling understandings of ourselves, individually and collectively, and of social reality generally. Such understandings are needed in efforts to mobilize persons and groups to undertake the social renovations required to achieve the emancipatory possibilities latent in situations in which race is problematic.

Second, there are the difficulties, noted earlier, to be met in requiring stability and precision in *race* as a concept that can combine, in a coherent and stable way, biological and cultural factors definitive of a race (if there are such), while both sets of factors are subject to variation across time and space. A review of efforts by natural philosophers of the seventeenth, eighteenth, and nineteenth centuries, as well as by subsequent natural and social scientists, to identify various races leads one to conclude, first, that racial characteristics are only partially a function of biological systems and processes, and second, that what relations there are between biological and cultural factors are not of a mechanical, deterministic sort. Rather, in complex interplay with complex systems of environmental, cultural, and social factors, biological factors provide not yet fully understood boundary conditions and possibilities that affect the development of the relatively distinctive gene pools of various geographically and/or socially relatively isolated, self-reproducing, relatively distinct cultural groups. These pools of genes, conditioned by social and cultural factors (normed practices), help to determine (the process of) "raciation": that is, processes by which members of a group come to share, more or less (that is, with relative frequencies of occurrence), "statistically covarying" biologically-determined properties along with shared cultural repertoires. Hence, the development of "geographical races."[6]

"Race," then, would best be understood as a cluster concept which draws together under a single word references to biological, cultural, and geographical factors thought characteristic of a population. Accordingly the characterization of particular races should be done as "indefinitely long disjunctive definitions" in which definitely racial features are not to be understood as being "severally necessary and the entire set of necessary properties . . . jointly sufficient."[7] An example of defining a race by combining characteristics disjunctively would be as follows: "The African race is made up of persons who are descended from at least one African parent; who have dark, *or* brown *or* light-colored skin; tightly curly *or* straight-hair; a broad, flat *or* narrow nose; other physical characteristics that are such-and-such; *or* was born and socialized into a social, cultural world characteristic of African or African descended peoples; *or* ...." Further any definition of "race" is, to a great extent, a function of the interplay of prevailing norms and strategies: on one level, those drawn from everyday life in which ideas, attitudes, and valuations of "race" are elements of common sense, and on another, those constituted by the discursive rules of communities of "experts" (that is, "sciences"). In both cases the elements and strategies of the definition are always subject to challenge and change. "Racial" categories and valorizations, then, though they refer, in part, to biological characteristics, are socially determined rather than simple descriptions of "natural kinds" or populations of individuals who are what they are necessarily by virtue of definitive intrinsic properties which are "severally necessary and jointly sufficient" to constitute their racial essence.[8] Hence, "race" refers to heterogeneous complexes of socially normed biological and cultural characteristics. And the biological features referred to when making racial distinctions are always *conscripted* into projects of cultural, political, and social construction. They are never simply given.

Michael Omi and Howard Winant, in their *Racial Formation in the United States*,[9] provide an insightful and revealing review of some of the history of changes in the meaning and political deployment of "race" in America. They analyze race as a "formation," rather than as either, in their words, a "fixed, concrete and objective" "essence" or a "mere illusion" to be eliminated in an ideal social order. The meaning of "race," they argue, is socially determined and changes as a result of social struggle, and hence is irreducibly political and must be understood as "*an unstable and 'decentered' complex of social meanings constantly being transformed by political struggle.* ..."[10] The strength of this view of "race" is that it makes it possible to understand the investments of often contested interests involved in notions of race, and to join this understanding to an account of social evolution that takes account of learning.[11] Social learning regarding race, assisted by critical social thought, might well provide resources by which to move beyond racism to a socially productive pluralist democracy without an unnecessary abstract, reductionist individualism that promotes an amorphous universalism.

Still to be explored are the meanings of race in terms of the lived-experiences of persons who are identified, and who identify themselves, as members of a racial group, particularly persons who have experienced invidious discrimination and subordination in America's racialized social hierarchy. Though biological and other sciences have shown that the complexes of characteristics thought to determine raciality do not constitute an unvarying *essence* that is determinable and constitutive of "natural kinds," this does *not* mean that, thereby, there is no real referent for the term "race," nor that the term is without positive social significance, even though it has been employed in rationalizations of injustices against racial "others." What must be explored is the possibility of appreciating the integrity of those who see themselves through the prism of "race," without taking racial characteristics to be a heritable essence shared equally by all members of a given race. We need not commit the error of concluding that, as a way of achieving enlightened thought which will guide us to fuller social emancipation for peoples oppressed because of their race, all regard for race must be eliminated.

Such elimination, I think, is both unlikely and unnecessary. By all means, the invidious, socially unnecessary forms and consequences of thought and practice associated with race ought to be eliminated to whatever extent possible if, in the U.S. in particular, we are to be successful in achieving further democratization in a multi-ethnic and multi-racial society in which public discourse that valorizes racial and ethnic cultural groups is once again an important aspect of intellectual, social, cultural, economic, and political life. Understandings of race and ethnicity that contribute to the learning and social evolution vital to democratic justice and to stability and order in racially and ethnically diverse societies could be of major significance and are much needed by many of us as we struggle to find ways through the maze of "the politics of identity difference."[12] What is a major concern for many, myself included, is the formulation of a cogent and viable concept of race that will be of service to the non-invidious conservation of racial and ethnic groups—a formulation, and the politics it facilitates, that also avoids the quagmire of chauvinism. W. E. B. Du Bois's 1897 essay "The Conservation of Races" is an important example of how one might work at such an understanding of race and for a long time has been, for me, a rich resource in this regard.[13] However, in making the case for drawing on Du Bois as a resource I feel compelled, first, to defend him against strong criticisms advanced by Kwame Anthony Appiah.[14]

IN DEFENSE OF DU BOIS

My dissatisfaction with Appiah's analysis of Du Bois's theory of "race" in "Conservation. . ." (and in another essay by Du Bois published in the August 1911 issue of *Crisis* magazine) moved me to return to it for yet another close reading and serious consideration. According to Appiah, Du Bois's argument-strategy in "The Conservation of Races" is the antithesis of the "classic dialectic of reaction to prejudice," the thesis of which is a denial of difference. Du Bois's strategy involves "the acceptance of difference, along with a claim that each group has its part to play; that the white race and its racial Other are related not as superior to inferior but as complementaries; that the Negro message is, with the white one, part of the message of humankind."[15] Importantly, Du Bois's strategy rests on the understanding that race is not determined by biological factors alone:

Although the wonderful developments of human history teach that the grosser physical differences of color, hair and bone go but a short way toward explaining the different roles which groups of men have played in Human Progress, yet there are differences—subtle, delicate and elusive, though they may be—which have silently but definitely separated men into groups. While these subtle forces have generally followed the natural cleavage of common blood, descent and physical peculiarities, they have at other times swept across and ignored these. At all times, however, they have divided human beings into races, which, while they perhaps transcend scientific definition, nevertheless, are clearly defined to the eye of the Historian and Sociologist.

What, then, is a race? It is a vast family of human beings, generally of common blood and language, always of common history, traditions and impulses, who are both voluntarily and involuntarily striving together for the accomplishment of certain more or less vividly conceived ideals of life.[16]

Appiah, however, reads Du Bois as attempting—but not succeeding—to transcend a nineteenth-century biological essentialism typical of scientific and popular conceptions of race of the period, and as relying on this conception while engaging in "a revaluation of the Negro race in the face of the sciences of racial inferiority." What evidence does Appiah have for this interpretation? Du Bois's reference to "common blood": "for this, dressed up with fancy craniometry, a dose of melanin, and some measure for hair-curl, is what the scientific notion amounts to. If he has fully transcended the scientific notion, what is the role of this talk about 'blood'?... If Du Bois's notion is purely socio-historical, then the issue is common history and traditions; otherwise, the issue is, at least in part, a common biology."[17] However, Du Bois has not offered a definition that is intended as "purely socio-historical." Rather, as I read him, he seeks to articulate a concept of *race* that includes both socio-historical or cultural factors (language, history, traditions, "impulses," ideals of life) and biological factors (a *family* of "common blood"). It is crucial to determine just how Du Bois's characterization of race is to be understood, and this requires an understanding of the strategizing, as well as of the socio-historical goal and objective that it serves, that is part of the overall structuring project in which Du Bois's defining effort should be situated.

Appiah takes pains to analyze and evaluate *individually* each of the elements in Du Bois's definition, a strategy that is central to what I think results in Appiah's serious misreading of Du Bois. For example: Du Bois includes in his conception of race the idea that members of a racial group "generally" share a common language, but Appiah excludes this as "plainly inessential."[18] Du Bois speaks of a race as a "vast family," but Appiah sees this as clear evidence that Du Bois failed to move beyond a nineteenth-century scientific notion "which presupposes common features in virtue of a common biology derived from a common descent. . . ." Instead, Appiah counters, "A family can . . . have adopted children, kin by social rather than biological law. By analogy . . . a vast human family might contain people joined not by biology but by an act of choice. But it is plain that Du Bois cannot have been contemplating this possibility: like all of his contemporaries, he would have taken for granted that race is a matter of birth."[19] This is an odd claim, indeed, for three paragraphs later Appiah notes that Du Bois was a descendant of Dutch (as well as of African) ancestors. Yet Du Bois *identified* himself as a member of the Negro race. Was there no choice involved in his doing so? I do not find it "plain" that there was not. Rather, Du Bois, as I read him, was following particular social conventions in appropriating in his own way, with definite deliberation, an otherwise socially defined and often imposed racial identity linked to a particular line of his complex ancestry.

As for whether a common history "can be a criterion that distinguishes one group of human beings—extended in time—from another . . . ," Appiah claims "[t]he answer is no":

> [I]n order to recognize two events at different times as part of the history of a single individual, we have to have a criterion for identity of the individual at each of those times, independent of his or her participation in the two events . . . sharing a common group history cannot be a criterion for being members of the same group, for we would have to be able to identify the group in order to identify *its* history. Someone in the fourteenth century could share a common history with me through our membership in a historically extended race only if something accounts both for his or her membership in the race in the fourteenth century and for mine in the twentieth. That something cannot, on pain of circularity, be the history of the race. Whatever holds Du Bois's races together conceptually cannot be a common history; it is only because they are bound together that members of a race at different times can share a history at all.[20]

Appiah concludes that common history and traditions, and language, "on pain of circularity," "must go too" as criteria for defining race. But here, I think, Appiah is simply wrong: Du Bois's strategy would be circular (and viciously so) only if common history were the *only* criterion. As one criterion among others taken severally, however, its use is not circular, and need not be ruled out.

Without common history and traditions (and language), Appiah has Du Bois left with common descent, impulses, and strivings as the remaining factors to provide a socio-historical definition of race. Since common descent is tied to biology, and since Du Bois, according to Appiah, was after a "purely socio-historical" definition, common descent cannot be used as a criterion. Common impulses and strivings are all that is left. However, Appiah claims that these cannot be criteria by which to place a person into a racial group but, if detected, can only be what he terms "a posteriori properties":

> If, without evidence about his or her impulses, we can say who is a Negro, then it cannot be part of what it is to be a Negro that he or she has them; rather, it must be an a posteriori claim that people of a common race, defined by descent and biology, have impulses, for whatever reason, in common. Of course, the common impulses of a biologically defined group may be historically caused by common experiences, common history. But Du Bois's claim can only be that biologically defined races happen to share, for whatever reason, common impulses. The common impulses cannot be a criterion of group membership. And if that is so, we are left with the scientific conception.[21]

On the basis of this critical, eliminative analysis of the elements of Du Bois's definition of race, each considered individually, Appiah concludes that what remains of Du Bois's criteria is inadequate to support his effort to define race in a purely socio-historical way. Further, he claims that the notion of a common group history conceals a "superadded geographical criterion": "group history is, in part, the history of people who have lived in the same place."[22] The conclusion to be drawn, then, is that Du Bois's criterion "actually . . . amounts to this: people are members of the same race if they share features in virtue of being descended largely from people of the same region. Those features may be physical . . . or cultural." Du Bois's definition of race supposedly founders on a tension which "reflects the fact that, for the purposes of European historiography . . . it was the latter [cultural features] that mattered; but for the purposes of American social and political life, it was the former [shared physical features of a geographical population]."[23]

Appiah is right: Du Bois's effort to give an account of race does harbor a tension. However, he is wrong in thinking that the tension resulted from conflicts between two different agendas: one involving European historiography, the other the demands of American racialized social and political life. What Appiah has failed to note is that there were not two *different* agendas. With regard to race and Africans, Europe (Britain, France, Belgium . . .) and America shared an agenda: the enslavement and exploitation of Africans and the African continent. The histories of two-continent, transatlantic Europe-to-America racism make abundantly clear that invidious notions of African peoples *as a race* covered both physical features and culture-making and involved putative causal linkages between biology and culture; that is, the cultural achievements of African and African-descended peoples were deemed unequal to those of peoples of the white race *because* of the biologically determined, "natural" limitations of the African race. The tension in Du Bois's conception, in my reading of his essay, is a function of his attempt to capture in the same term reference both to changeable cultural factors (hence, Du Bois's focus on the historical and sociological) and to physical features, themselves varying as a consequence of race-mixing and of descent with modification, or evolution, as explained by Charles Darwin. What is especially significant, I think, something overlooked by Appiah, is that Du Bois's effort to give an account of race in "Conservation" is one of many arresting examples of his courageous intellectual independence and brilliant creativity during an era when it was not yet been widely accepted that the long-standing notions of the specific, biologically determined, fixed "nature" or "character" of each race had been falsified.

Appiah also examines the approach to race in Du Bois's 1911 *Crisis* essay and 1940 *Dusk of Dawn* and concludes that Du Bois was involved in an "impossible project," one in which he "took race for granted" and attempted to "revalue one pole of the opposition of white to black" in the "vertical hierarchy" of the received concept of race by "rotating the axis" through a "'horizontal' reading" of race. For Appiah, such a project confines one within the "space of values" inscribed by the notion of race. The way out? "Challenge the assumption that there can be an axis, however oriented in the space of values, and the project fails for loss of presuppositions."[24] For Appiah, this is where Du Bois should have ended up since the logic of Du Bois's argument

> leads naturally to the final repudiation of race as a term of difference and to speaking instead "of civilizations where we now speak of races." The logic is the same logic that has brought us to speak of genders where we spoke of sexes, and a rational assessment of the evidence requires that we should endorse not only the logic but the premises of each argument.... One barrier facing those of us in the humanities has been methodological. Under Saussurian hegemony, we have too easily become accustomed to thinking of meaning as constituted by systems of differences purely internal to our endlessly structured *langues*.... Race, we all assume, is, like all other concepts, constructed by metaphor and metonymy; it stands in, metonymically, for the Other; it bears the weight, metaphorically, of other kinds of difference.
>
> Yet, in our social lives away from the text-world of the academy, we take reference for granted too easily. Even if the concept of race *is* a structure of oppositions ... it is a structure whose realization is, at best, problematic and, at worst, impossible. If we can now hope to understand the concept embodied in this system of oppositions, we are nowhere near finding referents for it. The truth is that there are no races: there is nothing in the world that can do all we ask "race" to do for

us. The evil that is done is done by the concept and by easy—yet impossible—
assumptions as to its application. What we miss through our obsession with the
structure of relations of concepts is, simply, reality.[25]

And what is the "reality" that is missed by the notion of race? According to
Appiah, it is culture: "Talk of 'race' is particularly distressing for those of us
who take culture seriously. . . . What exists 'out there' in the world—communities of meaning, shading variously into each other in the rich structure of
the social world—is the province not of biology but of hermeneutic understanding."[26] I agree that hermeneutic understanding is of major significance
to the ordering of social life. And adherence to the most rigorous prevailing
standards for confirming or falsifying empirical hypotheses leads to the
conclusion that there are no fixed and invariant biological connections to the
production of cultural worlds that would support a definition of race in
which biological factors are seen as the ultimate determinants of culture-
production.

But none of this was lost on Du Bois *even in the nineteenth century*. As I
read Du Bois, he was *deeply* committed to "taking culture seriously." Indeed,
he was concerned to "rotate the axis" defining the "scale of values" in the
concept of race from vertical and hierarchic to horizontal and egalitarian,
thereby making it more appropriate to a pluralist democracy of diverse races
and ethnic groups each of which had a "message" to offer to civilization. The
"messages," for Du Bois, are manifested in cultural achievements, the forms
and meanings of which are relative to life-worlds that are "generally" popu-
lated by persons who, historically and sociologically, tend to share, more or
less, certain physical characteristics that become valorized, and come to function socially and historically, as partially constitutive of the race. His was an
effort to make room in the "space of values" for a positive valorization and
appreciation of the cultural achievements of peoples of African descent, and
of other groups: "Manifestly some of the great races of today, particularly the
Negro race, have not as yet given to civilization the full spiritual message
which they are capable of giving."[27]

Du Bois, however, in setting out what he thought to be the defining characteristics of a "race," did not think that biological characteristics causally
determined cultural and moral (historical and sociological) characteristics. In
a very important sense, as I read him, Du Bois took care not to characterize a
race by regarding the defining features (physical characteristics, geography,
cultural practices and traditions) as essential and invariant and, when taken
together, as severally necessary, connected conjunctively, and, collectively,
jointly sufficient.[28] Appiah seems to interpret Du Bois as having considered
races as natural kinds, each constituted and distinguished by an invariant

"heritable racial essence"[29] that was to be kept "pure" by limiting interracial breeding.

Certainly, there were notable proponents of supposed scientific accounts of race advanced during the nineteenth century who did think of races in this way. But it was not the point of Du Bois's effort. To read Du Bois in this way would be to overlook—or to disregard—the possibility that his notion of race is best read as a *cluster* concept: that is, as referring to a group of persons who share, and are thereby distinguished by, several properties taken *dis*junctively: that is, "each property is severally sufficient and the possession of at least one of the properties is necessary."[30] How else to make sense of Du Bois's *explicit* concern to have his account of race be conditioned by attention to history and sociology and, as well, to the work of Charles Darwin? For, he argues,

> so far as purely physical characteristics are concerned, the differences between men do not explain all the differences of their history. It declares, as Darwin himself said, that great as is the physical unlikeness of the various races of men their likenesses are greater, and upon this rests the whole scientific doctrine of Human Brotherhood.[31]

What is particularly disturbing about Appiah's analysis and his subsequent conclusions is that he fails to take up Du Bois's effort to "rotate the axis" of the "space of values" within which groups of persons are defined as comprising supposedly opposed races except to say that by challenging its presuppositions, Du Bois's project is exposed as "impossible." But this is to seriously misconstrue Du Bois's project. It is *not* simply—or even primarily—an effort devoted to definition and taxonomy. Rather, it is a decidedly *political* project, as Winant and Omi argue definitions of race tend to be, which is very much concerned with altering the negative valorizations of the Negro race. To this end Du Bois's project involves prescribing norms for the social reconstruction of personal and social identities and for self-appropriation by a people suffering racialized subordination, which norms were to aid in mobilizing and guiding members of the race in their efforts to realize emancipatory social transformation leading, ultimately, to a flourishing humanism. According to Du Bois, "the history of the world is the history, not of individuals, but of groups, not of nations, but of races." Of especial importance to Du Bois was how peoples of the African race would develop and contribute their message to world history along with the messages of other races. The answer to this question, he said, "is plain: By the development of these race groups, not as individuals, but as races. . . . For the development of Negro genius, of Negro literature and art, of Negro spirit, only Negroes bound and welded together, Negroes inspired by one vast ideal, can work out in its fullness the great message we have for humanity."[32]

I take this to be one of the motivating assumptions, part of the very grounding, of "The Conservation of Races," which was prepared and read by Du Bois as the second of the Occasional Papers of the newly formed American Negro Academy (devoted to promoting intellectual activity among black folk in defense against racist attacks).[33] Though the purposes of a definitional project do not guarantee its adequacy, having a sense of Du Bois's overall project is nonetheless crucial to understanding what is involved in his effort to characterize a race. In this case, then, it is not accurate to say, as Appiah does, that Du Bois simply "took race for granted," since he goes to such lengths to try and characterize a race. Appiah is right, however, in noting that Du Bois's effort to define "race" does involve a tension. But I disagree with his judgment as to its source: it emerges from Du Bois's effort to have "the unit of classification . . . be the unit of identification."[34]

Du Bois seeks to mobilize and galvanize black folk (certainly the "talented tenth" among them) into a scientifically informed, politically astute and effective force to combat oppressions that were rationalized with pernicious valorizations that had been inscribed in the notion of race. Crucial to this endeavor would be a sense of shared identity growing out of the recognition and appropriation of commonalties of a geographic race (history, language, culture more generally). Of particular importance, it was Du Bois's judgment that American Negroes were accepting much too quickly American ideals of brotherhood while forgetting what he thought to be "the hard limits of natural law," evident to the those who study history appropriately, that govern human associations: it is groups, not individuals acting on their own, that make history:

> Turning to real history, there can be no doubt, first, as to the widespread, nay, universal, prevalence of the race idea, the race spirit, the race ideal, and as to its efficiency as the vastest and most ingenious invention for human progress. We, who have been reared and trained under the individualistic philosophy of the Declaration of Independence and the laisser-faire [sic] philosophy of Adam Smith, are loath to see and loath to acknowledge this patent fact of human history. . . . We are apt to think in our American impatience, that while it may have been true in the past that closed race groups made history, that here in conglomerate America *nous avons changer* [sic] *tout cela*—we have changed all that, and have no need of this ancient instrument of progress. This assumption of which the Negro people are especially fond, can not be established by a careful consideration of history.[35]

Still, in turning to "real history" Du Bois was mindful of the troubling tensions involved in the effort to forge a racial identity in the context of a nation-state that required of its citizens a defining identity as "American":

> Here, then, is the dilemma, and it is a puzzling one, I admit. No Negro who has given earnest thought to the situation of his people in America has failed, at some time in life, to find himself at these cross-roads; has failed to ask himself at some time: What, after all, am I? Am I an American or am I a Negro? Can I be both? Or is it my duty to cease to be a Negro as soon as possible and be an American? If I strive as a Negro, am I not perpetuating the very cleft that threatens and separates Black and White America? Is not my only possible practical aim the subduction of all that is Negro in me to the American? Does my black blood place upon me any more obligation to assert my nationality than German, or Irish or Italian blood would?[36]

This dilemma, Du Bois went on to say, gave rise to "incessant self-questioning" on the part of persons of African descent that produced vacillation and contradictions which, in turn, contributed to stifled coordinated action, shirked responsibilities, inattention to various enterprises of the race, and, of particular importance to Du Bois, to a situation in which "the best blood, the best talent, the best energy of the Negro people cannot be marshaled to do the bidding of the race." Du Bois felt compelled to ask whether the situation was right, rational, or good policy, whether black folks in America have a different and distinct *mission* as a race or whether "self-obliteration [is] the highest end to which Negro blood dare aspire?"[37]

In a society structured by white racial supremacy and the subordination of black folk, such questions were, and are, of major import. And the appropriateness of answers given cannot be determined simply by assessing their adequacy according to norms of logical rigor. Rather, it is the end-in-view, the overall project as well as the means chosen for completing it, that is at issue. For Du Bois, the project involved the historical development and well-being of a relatively distinct group of people who suffered oppression at the hands of persons of various ethnies of a particular race. And for him both that development and the well-being required a strategically crucial form of self-understanding that resolved the dilemma, solved the existential "riddle," which he characterized elsewhere as a form of "double consciousness":

> Here, it seems to me, is the reading of the riddle that puzzles so many of us. We are Americans, not only by birth and by citizenship, but by our political ideals, our language, our religion. Farther than that, our Americanism does not go. At that point, we are Negroes, members of a vast historic race that from the very dawn of

creation has slept, but half awakening in the dark forests of its African fatherland.[38]

The riddle resolved, it would then be possible to achieve the needed concerted and coordinated efforts, *on the part of black people themselves*, by which the race might advance in its own behalf, but which would also help bring about the realization of interracial humanism:

> as a race we must strive by race organization, by race solidarity, by race unity to the realization of that broader humanity which freely recognizes differences in men, but sternly deprecates inequality in their opportunities of development.
>
> For the accomplishment of these ends we need race organizations.... Let us not deceive ourselves at our situation in this country ... our one haven of refuge is ourselves, and but one means of advance, our own belief in our great destiny, our own implicit trust in our ability and worth.[39]

For Du Bois, in order to understand human history and be thus informed in attempting to structure the making of the future through organized effort, the focus of such understanding must be the racial group, the "vast family" of related individuals. While individuals are, of course, necessary components of social groups, and must never be lost sight of when analyzing and assessing human ventures, they are neither sufficient for accounting for social groups, nor self-sufficing and thus able to account for their own existence and well-being. Du Bois's critical insight is a significant one: namely, that the commitment to laissez-faire individualism in certain traditions of modern Liberal political philosophy is important but not adequate for providing a full and appropriate understanding of human beings. Survival of individuals is tied inextricably to the well-being of the individual's natal group; and the well-being of this group requires the concerted action of its individual members, action, to a significant degree, predicated on and guided by shared, self-valorizing identities defined, to some extent, in terms of the group's identifying bio-social and cultural racial (or ethnic) characteristics. These are both constituted by and are constitutive of the group's cultural life-world. It is the racial/ethnic life-world that generally provides the resources and nurturing required for the development of an individual's talents and accomplishments. And it is these that Du Bois sees as the distinctive contributions particular persons can make and offer up to be shared by human civilization more generally. Thus, he argues, must the African race, through its ethnies and, by extension of his argument, all races and ethnies, be "conserved."

Appiah, then, is right when he argues that what is at the heart of the matter, "What exists 'out there' in the world—communities of meaning, shading variously into each other in the rich structure of the social world—is the province not of biology but of hermeneutic understanding."[40] The appreciation of the cultural creations of whatever person or racial/ethnic group is an endeavor of hermeneutical understanding. But who are the persons, individually and collectively, that make up the socio-historical, anthropological bases of "communities of meaning" that are to be understood in terms of various systems and traditions of meaning-configurations (literature, music, dance, art, etc.)? How do such communities cohere and persist in and across times and spaces as self-reproducing populations? If there are no relevant occasions when we can use appropriately "race" and/or "ethnicity" as holding-notions by which to capture complexes of characteristics in terms of which to identify the persons constituting such a community, particularly when the members of a given community *do* share physical as well as historical and cultural characteristics, how ought we to describe them and their socio-historical, cultural lifeworld? Since there are various geographically situated groups that are composed of persons who are collectively more or less similar physiologically and culturally so as to be relatively distinct from other groupings of persons, groups that seem appropriate candidates for being designated races and ethnies, how are they to be identified?

There is an important footnote in Appiah's "The Uncompleted Argument" in which he argues against a claim set forth in an essay by Masatoshi Nei and Arun K. Roychoudhury,[41] that "their work shows the existence of a biological basis for the classification of human races; what it shows is that human populations differ in their distributions of genes. That *is* a biological fact. The objection to using this fact as a basis of a system of classification is that far too many people don't fit into just one category that can be so defined."[42] Appiah's objection is central, I think, to understanding why he is so determined to eliminate "race" as a notion for classifying, certainly for characterizing, persons into or in terms of biologically constituted racial groupings: that is, "too many people" don't fit into just one racial category. But, if this claim is true, and I am convinced that it is, how can this show that all racial classification is thereby inappropriate? I think it cannot. It might well just mean that an additional racial or sub-racial category may be needed for such persons.

However, I think the problems that Appiah is concerned with here are not simply those of racial taxonomy and philosophical ontology. It is, instead, the vexing issue of *the politics of identity*: with which race does a person identify when their parents are persons of *different* races? Are the social conventions appropriate which require such persons to identify in terms of the race or ethnicity of one of their parents? Would the situation be better if the person involved were allowed to choose? Would it be better if such issues were regarded as irrelevant, if not morally inappropriate? For Appiah, and for "many people," as it is even for those of us who have parents thought to be of the same race, this is more than an issue of philosophical semantics in racially hierarchic societies which continue to engage in efforts to promote and sustain forms of racial supremacy. In this context, racial categories take on the various valorizations of the hierarchy and affect the formation and appropriation of identities as well as affect, in significant ways, a person's life-chances.

That this was the case for Du Bois and motivated much of his life's work is well known. Still, it is important to note the way in which Du Bois endeavored to *choose* and *fashion* his racial identity, at least consciously to embrace, re-interpret, and re-valorize an identity that was partly proscribed for him by prevailing conventions for applying a racial category/characterization to any person one of whose ancestors, of whatever generations, was thought to be of the Negro race. Many people of mixed racial parentage have done as Du Bois without, at the same time, under-representing their ancestry by disregarding the raciality of their non-Negro ancestors: that is, they have chosen an identities defined in terms of one line of parental ancestry while acknowledging the other line as a constitutive aspect of the complexly constituted persons they are. Depending on the person and circumstances, such a choice may be more or less difficult. However, often such choices are made unnecessarily difficult by the efforts of racists and chauvinists to proscribe an identity and identification on the basis of their commitments to an erroneous notion that the character, personality, and capacities of individuals are determined by a heritable, fixed, racial essence shared in the same way by all members of the race, which essence also determines the culture-making of the race. To the contrary, personal and social identities, in being formed and appropriated, *always* involve socially conditioned personal choices as well as meaning-configurations that are socially articulated and made available to the individual, sometimes socially imposed on the individual. Our identities, then, are never a result of simply acknowledging some identity-determining heritable raciality. Rather, identities are ongoing projects of configurations of often contested meanings and values relative to which our bodies, in racialized societies especially, are often made the sites at which the meanings and values cohere phenomenologically, and skin color, for example, is made both a supposed self-evident sign and symbol of these socially constituted meanings and values.

Again, Appiah is certainly right in noting, "Few candidates for laws of nature can be stated by reference to the colors, tastes, smells, or touches of objects. It is hard for us to accept that the colors of objects, which play so important a role in our visual experience and our recognition of everyday objects, turn out neither to play an important part in the behavior of matter nor to be correlated with properties that do."[43] However, it seems to me that in advancing this important metaphysical insight Appiah then fails to appreciate another crucial fact, in large part, I think, because he harbors a commitment to an unarticulated, unreviewed, and thus uncritically held metaphysical realism: that the colors of objects are very important *to us* and to our valuation and utilization of things in everyday life, to the routine, meaningful organization of everyday life. Aesthetic traditions provide the norms through which color appreciation is developed and exercised. Likewise, the "laws of nature" cannot themselves settle questions regarding what import and value, if any, phenotype and morphology ought to have for human beings. It is utterly crucial that "race," as a way of referring to biologically *and* socio-culturally and historically constituted, varying groupings of persons, be uncoupled from any presumptions of such groupings having been constituted by an unchanging, heritable, race-defining biological essence. Nonetheless, we must, I think, still be mindful of how group-based phenotypes (and, in important instances, genotypes as well, as when two persons who are considering sexual sharings leading to biological reproductions might need to be mindful of the potential for problematic genetic consequences in offspring) do figure in the normed aesthetics and somatic imaging of social life. But let us, as well, be committed to continuing to work to revise the forms of politics that are assisted by ontologies and aesthetics of invidious, essentialist, biologized notions of race.

There are many more people, myself included, for whom a racial identity is not a particularly complicated matter, nor a matter whose importance is settled by the rigor of a definition made possible by clear lines of biological descent, the evidence for which is a compelling set of physical criteria. It is, rather, in significant part, the important and still pressing business of getting on in stable, just, harmonious ways within and among racially and ethnically complex societies of many "communities of meaning." And for many of us the continued existence of discernible racial/ethnic communities of meaning is highly desirable, *even if, in the very next instant, racism and invidious ethnocentrism in every form and manifestation were to disappear forever.* However desirable such a situation may be, I am certain this is not about to become a reality, though I still hope for and work toward its realization as much as this may be practically possible.

Like Du Bois, I am convinced that *both* the struggle against racism and invidious ethnocentrism, as well as the struggles on the part of persons of various races and ethnies to create, preserve, refine, and, of particular importance, to share their "messages" or cultural productions with other humans, require that we understand how the constantly evolving groups we refer to as "races" can be "conserved" in democratic political communities which value and promote cultural pluralism constrained by Liberal principles. As many persons in America continue to struggle to consolidate the realization of justice with harmony in areas of our collective life in which raciality and ethnicity are at issue in important and appropriate ways, I remain unconvinced that we must give up on the notion of race, the difficulties of definition and ugly legacies of racism notwithstanding. The challenge is to find ways to conserve a revised understanding of race that is both socially useful and consistent with a revised notion of democratic justice that is appropriately balanced between recognizing and valuing racial and ethnic cultural groupings and preserving the best achievements of modern Enlightenments and the political revolution of Liberalism.

Du Bois, in my judgment, was one of the foremost thinkers in modern history to see into these complex issues with near full clarity, and to have had the disciplined courage, fortitude, and near genius to wrestle, in promising ways, with the seemingly intractable and *always* potentially divisive and destructive "problem of the color line." What he has offered, I think, is particularly worthy of, and rewards, close and careful reading and consideration. His efforts are an invaluable aid to the pursuit of understandings that might help to guide social praxis that will, it is to be hoped, get us through the difficulties involving race and ethnicity. The need is compelling. For even as I write, "problems of the color line" are being played out in projects of genocide and mass destruction in the former nation-state of Yugoslavia and in Rwanda—just two examples from among far too many others that are ready-to-hand.

Those horrible living lessons are not, however, the inevitable fate of our striving to conserve races and ethnic groups. There are other examples of successful multi-racial, multi-ethnic unity-in-diversity throughout this nation and others—in local communities, institutions, and organizations of various kinds—that validate my hope. Learning from these examples, I think, will provide resources that can assist us as we continue the struggles to rescue ourselves from a distorted fate made much too probable by our own doings which, unless corrected, might well be 'the fire next time' that will be our undoing.

NOTES

1. A much earlier version of this essay was prepared for and presented as On W. E. B. Du Bois's "The Conservation of Races" during the Symposium on Racism and Sexism: Differences and Connections, hosted by the Department of Philosophy of Georgia State University, Atlanta, Georgia, on May 3–4, 1991. Revised versions have been the basis of subsequent lectures at numerous colleges and universities, and one was presented during the Pennsylvania State University conference on "The Thought of W. E. B. Du Bois" on March 21, 1992, and subsequently circulated in the *SAPINA Newsletter* (Bulletin of the Society for African Philosophy in North America) 4, no. 1 (January–July 1992): 13–28. This essay is a revision, several times over, the last being rather extensive, of that read at the Pennsylvania State University conference. Special thanks to Bernard Bell, Emily Grosholz, and James Stewart for their careful reading

of an earlier draft and for their especially helpful comments and suggested improvements.

2. W. E. B. Du Bois, "The Concept of Race, in *Dusk of Dawn: An Essay Toward an Autobiography of a Race Concept"* (New York: Schocken Books; 1968 [1940]), 103.

3. For provocative discussions of some of the challenges see Arthur M. Schlesinger, Jr., *The Disuniting of America: Reflections on a Multicultural Society* (New York: W. W. Norton & Company, 1992), and Charles Taylor and Amy Gutman, *Multiculturalism and "The Politics of Recognition,"* (Princeton: Princeton University Press, 1992).

4. William A. Henry III, "Beyond the Melting Pot," *Time* 135, 15 (April 9, 1990): 28.

5. While from here on I shall refer almost wholly to race—much though by no means all—of what I shall say applies to ethnicity as well. For I consider ethnic groups as being, for the most part, subsets of racial groups, and the constitution and characterization of ethnic groups mostly a function of cultural characteristics.

6. When we refer to races we have in mind their geographically defined categories, which are sometimes called geographical races, to indicate that while they have some distinctive biological characteristics they are not pure types. Michael Banton and Jonathan Harwood, *The Race Concept* (Praeger: New York, 1975), 62.

7. David L. Hull, "The Effect of Essentialism on Taxonomy Two Thousand Years of Stasis (I)," *British Journal for Philosophy of Science* 15 (1965): 322–23.

8. See T. E. Wilkerson, "Natural Kinds," *Philosophy* 63 (1988): 29–42; John Dupré "Wilkerson on Natural Kinds," *Philosophy* 64 (1989): 248–51; Leroy N. Meyer, "Science, Reduction and Natural Kinds," *Philosophy* 64 (1989): 535–46; and John Dupré, "Natural Kinds and Biological Taxa," *The Philosophical Review* 90, no. 1 (January 1981): 66–90.

9. Michael Omi and Howard Winant, *Racial Formation in the United States,* (New York and London: Routledge & Kegan Paul, 1986). Other especially helpful texts are Michael Banton, *The Idea of Race* (Boulder, Colorado: Westview Press, 1977) and Michael Banton's and Jonathan Harwood, *The Race Concept* (New York: Praeger, 1975).

10. Omi and Winant, 68–69.

11. For an example of such a notion of social evolution see Jürgen Habermas, "Historical Materialism and the Development of Normative Structures" and "Toward a Reconstruction of Historical Materialism," in *Communication and the Evolution of Society,* trans., Thomas McCarthy, (Boston: Beacon Press, 1979), 95–177.

12. For a provocative discussion of the politics of difference and identity-recognition, see Charles Taylor, *Multiculturalism: Examining the Politics of Recognition,* ed. Amy Gutman (New Jersey: Princeton University Press, 1994).

13. The Du Bois text used for this discussion is reprinted in Howard Brotz, ed., *African American Social and Political Thought, 1850–1920* (New Jersey: Transaction, 1992), 483–92.

14. Anthony Appiah, "The Uncompleted Argument: Du Bois and the Illusion of Race," in *"Race, Writing, and Difference,* ed. Henry Louis Gates, Jr. (Chicago: The University of Chicago Press, 1986), 21–37. Appiah revised and extended his argument against Du Bois as "Illusions of Race" in *In My Father's House: Africa in the Philosophy of Culture* (New York: Oxford University Press, 1992), 28–46.

15. Appiah, "The Uncompleted Argument . . . ," 25.

16. Du Bois, "The Conservation of Races," in Brotz, 485, emphasis added.

17. Appiah, "The Uncompleted Argument . . . ," 25–26.

18. Appiah, "The Uncompleted Argument . . . ," 26.

19. Appiah, "The Uncompleted Argument . . . ," 26.

20. Appiah, "The Uncompleted Argument . . . ," 27.
21. Appiah, "The Uncompleted Argument . . . ," 28.
22. Appiah, "The Uncompleted Argument . . . ," 29.
23. Appiah, "The Uncompleted Argument . . . ," 29.
24. Appiah, "The Uncompleted Argument . . . ," 36.
25. Appiah, "The Uncompleted Argument . . . ," 35–36.
26. Appiah, "The Uncompleted Argument . . . ," 36.
27. Du Bois, "The Conservation of Races, in Brotz," 487.
28. David L. Hull, "The Effect of Essentialism on Taxonomy . . . ," 318.
29. See Appiah, "In My Father's House," 39.
30. David L. Hull, "The Effect of Essentialism on Taxonomy," 323. For example, given several groups of features A (heritable physical features), B (shared cultural practices), C (linked if not quite common histories and traditions, which have their beginnings in), D (a common site of origin which accounts, in significant part, for the shared physical features), which are shared by members of a group in a limited number of patterned combinations, necessarily one feature, any one, (say B) plus several others (C *or* A *or* . . . D) would be sufficient to identify a person as a member of a particular race.
31. Du Bois, "The Conservation of Races," in Brotz, 484–85.
32. Du Bois, "The Conservation of Races," in Brotz, 487.
33. On March 5, 1897, the one-hundred-twenty-seventh anniversary of the Boston Massacre where Crispus Attucks, who was believed to have been a mulatto, was the first to die, eighteen black men assembled in the District of Columbia's Lincoln Memorial Church to formally inaugurate the American Negro Academy. This date was chosen because it recalled an event especially sacred to the Negro . To the men who planned the meeting, Attucks death in 1770 was a symbol of the patriotic and heroic role black Americans played in the creation of the United States. Consequently, they felt it appropriate that a black society formed to encourage intellectual activity among blacks, and to defend them from vicious assaults should begin its public life on this day. Alfred A. Moss, Jr., *The American Negro Academy: Voice of the Talented Tenth* (Baton Rouge and London: Louisiana State University Press, 1981), 35. Du Bois was one of the eighteen founding members of the Academy.
34. David L. Hull, "The Effect of Essentialism on Taxonomy," 322.
35. Du Bois, "The Conservation of Races," in Brotz, 485.
36. Du Bois, "The Conservation of Races," in Brotz, 488. However, one might, as did Du Bois, have to take up the socially enforced choice of defining one's racial identity, in part, by *either* matrilineal or patrilineal descent, though for Appiah doing so requires that one drastically underrepresent the biological range of one's ancestry (Appiah, "The Uncompleted Argument," 26.)
37. Du Bois, "The Conservation of Races," in Brotz, 488.
38. Du Bois, "The Conservation of Races," in Brotz, 488–489.
39. Du Bois, "The Conservation of Races," in Brotz, 489.
40. Appiah, "The Uncompleted Argument . . . ," 36.
41. "Genetic Relationship and Evolution of Human Races," *Evolutionary Biology* 14 (1983).
42. Appiah, "The Uncompleted Argument," 37, note 10.
43. Appiah, *In My Father s House,* 39.

Outlaw, Appiah, and Du Bois's "The Conservation of Races"

2

Robert Gooding-Williams

INTRODUCTION

Lucius Outlaw's treatment of Du Bois's "The Conservation of Races" proceeds by way of a critique of K. A. Appiah's interpretation of that essay.[1] My evaluation of Outlaw's response to Du Bois and Appiah has two parts. First, I shall proffer a reconstruction of Appiah's argument regarding Du Bois's definition of 'race.'[2] In the course of this reconstruction, I will address three of Outlaw's objections to Appiah's argument. Second, I will sketch a reading of "The Conservation of Races" that, *pace* Appiah and Outlaw, identifies the theoretical focus of Du Bois's essay as a question of explanation, not of terminological definition.[3] On the basis of this reading, I shall argue that "The Conservation of Races" can be interpreted as a sort of philosophical prolegomenon to *The Souls of Black Folk*.

APPIAH'S ANALYSIS OF DUBOIS'S DEFINITION

Du Bois defines 'race' in the following passage:

> What, then, is a race? It is a vast family of human beings, generally of common blood and language, always of common history, traditions and impulses, who are both voluntarily and involuntarily striving together for the accomplishment of certain more or less vividly conceived ideals of life. ("CR," 485)

Du Bois claims, moreover, that there exist eight "distinctly differentiated races," each of which, one assumes, satisfies his definition. These are: "the Slavs of eastern Europe, the Teutons of middle Europe, the English of Great Britain and America, the Romance nations of Southern and Western Europe, the Negroes of Africa and America, the Semitic people of Western Asia and Northern Africa, the Hindoos of Central Asia and the Mongolians of Eastern Asia" ("CR," 485).

Now as I see it, Appiah's interpretation of Du Bois's definition of 'race' assumes that this definition is meant to identify a set of criteria that can be used to know whether it is or is not the case that two individuals belong to the same race. (This is a reasonable assumption, since Du Bois makes explicit reference to the problem of identifying "criteria of race differences" ("CR," 484).) To be more precise, Appiah assumes that Du Bois's definition is intended to characterize a set of individually *informative,* necessary, and jointly sufficient conditions that can be applied to determine (to ascertain) whether or not two individuals are both Slavs, both Teutons, both English, etc. (When I speak of a condition that is "individually informative," I have in mind a criterion, the successful application of which as a source of information does not presuppose the successful application of some *other* criterion to acquire the same information. The point of my use here of this caveat will become clear in the course of my discussion of Appiah's treatment of Du Bois's "common history" criterion.) Appiah's argument proceeds by way of an analysis of each of the conditions Du Bois mentions in his definition of 'race'. The goal of his argument is to establish that a claim he attributes to Du Bois— namely, the claim to have transcended the nineteenth-century scientific conception of race—is false. According to Appiah, Du Bois, far from transcending this conception, "relies on it" (Appiah, 25).

Appiah, in essence, conceptualizes Du Bois's definition of 'race' as asserting the following:[4] Two individuals, x and y, are members of the same race if, and only if, they (a) share a language *and* (b) belong to the same "vast family" *and* (c) are of a "common blood" *and* (d) share a "common history" (which Appiah does not distinguish from having common traditions) *and* (e) have common impulses and strivings.

Regarding the criterion of a common language, Appiah notes that it is *not* the case that two individuals are members of one of Du Bois's eight races only if they share a language. Consider, for example, that there are pairs of persons belonging to the "Romance" race, such that one of them speaks French and the other Spanish or Italian. From this, it follows that sharing a language is not a necessary condition of membership in one of Du Bois's races. This, I take it, is what Appiah has in mind when he writes that "[t]he claim that a race generally shares a common language is . . . plainly inessential" (Appiah, 26).

What about the criteria of a "vast family" and a "common blood"? For Appiah, both of these criteria signify a notion "of shared ancestry" (Appiah, 26). Thus, he argues, Du Bois's definition of 'race' does not fully transcend the scientific definition, as the latter "presupposes common features in virtue of a common biology derived from a common descent" (Appiah, 26). Still, Du Bois's definition is not reducible to the concept of a common ancestry, since "there are many groups of common ancestry—ranging from humanity in general to narrower groups such as the Slavs, Teutons, and Romance people taken together—which do not for Du Bois constitute races" (Appiah, 26–27). At best, then, Du Bois's references to a "vast family" and to a "common blood" identify a necessary condition for determining whether two individuals belong to the same one of his eight races, but not a condition that is by itself sufficient for making such a determination.

Now Outlaw, though he offers no criticism of Appiah's treatment of Du Bois's "common language" criterion, objects to Appiah's assumption that, in speaking of races as families, Du Bois is supposing that families are joined by biology—that is, by common ancestry—and not by acts of choice. In criticizing this assumption, Outlaw argues that Du Bois himself, though biologically linked to both Dutch and African ancestors, *chose* to identify racially with the latter (Outlaw, 32). What, however, does this argument establish? Even if Outlaw's biographical assertion is accurate—even if, in other words, Du Bois did at some time make a choice of the sort Outlaw attributes to him—it does not follow that, for theoretical purposes, Du Bois has repudiated the notion that families, racial families included, are joined by biology and not by acts of choice. Du Bois's text, moreover, with its suggestion that families are biological units bound by "blood," seems *prima facie* to support Appiah's assumption:

> The final word of science, so far, is that we have at least two, perhaps three, great families of human beings—the whites and Negroes, possibly the yellow race. That other races have arisen from the intermingling of the blood of these two. ("CR," 484)

There are other passages in "The Conservation of Races" that can be read as supporting Appiah's view.[5] It seems to me, nonetheless, that Du Bois's position is not, as Appiah suggests, unequivocal. Indeed, in the second part of this essay, I will argue that Du Bois's use of the expression "vast family" to define "race," when considered carefully and in context, suggests that he rejects the notion that all racial families are bound together by a "common blood." This is not to say, as Outlaw perhaps would wish to say, that Du Bois believes that families are joined by acts of individual choice; yet it is to suggest, *pace* Appiah, that while Du Bois thinks that racial families are, largely, "blood unities," he still allows for the possibility that there exist *some* racial families whose unity is an effect of "social rather than biological law" (Appiah, 26).

Let me turn now to Appiah's treatment of Du Bois's "common history" criterion. Here, again, Appiah's argument is straightforward: one cannot determine whether two individuals belong to a particular race by establishing that the history of that race is the history of a race to which each of them belongs, unless one can appeal to criteria *other* than "common history" to determine whether these individuals belong to that race. Supposing, however, that such criteria are available, the appeal to "common history" becomes redundant. As Appiah puts it:

> sharing a common group history cannot be a criterion for being members of the same group, for we would have to be able to identify the group in order to iden-tify *its* history. Someone in the fourteenth century could share a common history with me through our membership in an historically extended race only if some-thing accounts for his or her membership in the race in the fourteenth century and for mine in the twentieth. That something cannot, on pain of circularity, be the history of the race." (Appiah, 27)

In response to this argument, Outlaw proffers a second objection to Appiah's analysis of Du Bois's definition of 'race': "here, I think, Appiah is simply wrong: the strategy would be circular (and viciously so) only if common history were the *only* criterion. As one criterion among others taken severally, however, its use is not circular" (Outlaw, 33). As far as I can tell, this is the only place in Outlaw's essay in which he offers a reason for his earlier expressed complaint that Appiah analyzes and evaluates "*individually* each of the elements in Du Bois's definition" (Outlaw, 32). But Outlaw's reason misses the logical force of Appiah's argument. As I have already claimed, Appiah's argument establishes that the successful use of "common history" as a crite-rion of racial discrimination will always be redundant. In other words, the successful use of this criterion will *always* presuppose that one has available some *other* criteria (or criterion) for determining whether the individuals in question are members of the same race. In a sense, then, Outlaw is right: if I have some other criteria permitting me to establish that two individuals, A and B, belong to the Teutonic race, then, having established their racial identi-ties, I can validly infer, without pain of circularity, that the history of the Teutonic race is the history both of A's race and of B's race (thus, a "common (racial) history") and hence, again, that each of them is a Teuton. Since, however, I have established that both A and B were Teutons, *prior to* my successful application of the "common history" criterion, this criterion cannot be a criterion I used, or, generalizing, that Du Bois used, actually to establish that A and B belonged to the Teutonic or any other race, supposing that this had not already been established.

According to Appiah, "Du Bois' reference to a common history cannot be doing any work in his individuation of races" (Appiah, 27). Here, Appiah states the conclusion of the argument I have been attempting to summarize: because Du Bois's use of a "common history" criterion is at best redundant, this criterion cannot be an *informative* element of the definition Du Bois (or anyone) actually uses to ascertain whether two individuals are members of the same race.[6] Since Appiah has already established that sharing a language is not essential to that definition, what remains for him to consider is the "common impulses and strivings" criterion, presumably in order to determine whether *this* criterion, *in conjunction with* Du Bois's appeal to a notion of common ancestry, constitutes a set of conditions that are individually informative, necessary, and jointly sufficient to do the work of individuating races.

Unfortunately, there is no help here. The appeal to "common impulses and strivings," Appiah argues, is based on historical evidence, the availability of which assumes the possibility of individuating races. For example, historical inquiry that discovers that all Negroes share certain impulses and strivings presupposes that, prior to such inquiry, it is possible to say who is and who is not a Negro. Thus, Appiah infers, the criterion of "common impulses and strivings" cannot be a part of the definition of 'race' used by Du Bois and the historians on whom he relies to do the individuating work which historiography takes for granted.

In Appiah's view, the criterion by which Du Bois does in fact distinguish racial groups is a modification of the "common ancestry" criterion, and thus a version of the scientific (biological) conception of race:

> How, then, is it possible for Du Bois' criteria to issue in eight groups, while the scientific conception issues in three? The reason is clear from the list. Slavs, Teutons, English, Hindus, and Romance peoples each live in a characteristic geographical region. (American English—and, for that matter, American Teutons, American Slavs, and American Romance people—share recent ancestry with their European "cousins" and thus share a relation to a place and certain languages and traditions.) Semites and Mongolians each inhabit a rather larger geographical region also. Du Bois' talk of common history conceals his superaddition of a geographical criterion: group history is, in part, the history of people who have lived in the same place. *The criterion Du Bois actually uses amounts to this: people are members of the same race if they share certain features in virtue of being descended largely from people of the same region.* Those features may be physical—hence Afro-Americans are Negroes—or cultural—hence Anglo-Americans are English. (Appiah, 28–29, emphasis mine)[7]

Strictly speaking, Appiah should have written that people (or two individuals) are members of the same race, if, *and only if,* they share certain features in virtue of being descended largely from people of the same region. Du Bois's criterion, in other words, defines a necessary and not only a sufficient condition of race-membership: in contrast to what we saw in regards to the "common language" criterion, it does not appear that there are pairs of persons whom Du Bois would have recognized as members of some one of his eight races but who prima facie fail to satisfy the criterion of individuation he *seems in fact to exploit.* A signal virtue of the criterion Appiah suggests Du Bois tacitly and "actually" uses, which distinguishes that criterion from Du Bois's *stated* definition of 'race' as Appiah interprets it (again, common language, common ancestry, common history, and common strivings), is that it provides a plausible explanation of Du Bois's eightfold classification of human races. This virtue needs to be borne in mind, I believe, in evaluating Outlaw's third objection to Appiah's treatment of Du Bois's stated definition.[8]

In essence, Outlaw's third objection is that Appiah incorrectly represents Du Bois as attempting to define a "natural kind," or "heritable racial essence," by identifying a set of individuating conditions that are "severally necessary, connected conjunctively, and, collectively, jointly sufficient" (Outlaw, 38). Outlaw gives two reasons for this objection. The first is that Appiah, in reading Du Bois in this way, disregards the possibility that Du Bois's notion of race "is best read as a *cluster* concept: that is, as referring to a group of persons who share, and are thereby distinguished by, several properties taken *dis*junctively: that is, 'each property is severally sufficient and the possession of at least one of the properties is necessary'" (Outlaw, 38). The second reason is that reading Du Bois as attempting to define a natural kind cannot make sense of "Du Bois's *explicit* concern to have his account of race be conditioned by attention to history and sociology, and, as well, to the work of Charles Darwin" (Outlaw, 38).

Outlaw's first reason amounts to the proposal that Du Bois's stated definition of 'race'—viz., his answer to the question "What, then, is a race?"—should be read as asserting the following proposition:

> Two individuals, x and y, are members of the same race if, and only if, they (a) share a language *or* (b) belong to the same "vast family" *or* (c) are of a "common blood" *or* (d) share a "common history" *or* (e) have common impulses and strivings.

The obvious problem with this proposal is that it, no less than Du Bois's stated definition as Appiah interprets it lacks precisely the virtue possessed by Appiah's hypothesis as to the definition and criterion which Du Bois *actually uses* to distinguish racial groups. To put the point more precisely, Outlaw's proposal does not explain Du Bois's eightfold classification of races. Suppose, for example, that we consider "shared language" to be one of Outlaw's severally sufficient conditions of membership in the same race. From this supposition it would follow that the English-speaking Negroes of America and the English-speaking non-Negroes of Great Britain and America belonged to the same race—which they do not, according to Du Bois's eightfold classification (Appiah, 27). Or suppose that we considered "common blood" or "shared ancestry" to be a sufficient condition. On this view, we should have to say, as Appiah intimates (Appiah, 27), that contrary to Du Bois's classification scheme the Slav and Teuton peoples taken together constitute a race. (Du Bois ["CR," 486] implies that Slavs and Teutons alike are descended from "the white variety of mankind.") As for "common history," we have already seen that this criterion, by itself, cannot do the work of individuation, and so cannot be one of Outlaw's severally sufficient conditions. The suggestion that "common impulses and strivings" constitute such a condition would be, finally, implausible, as this would entail that any time two individuals shared an impulse and a striving, e.g., a passion for liberty and a striving for justice, they would be members of the same race.

As regards Outlaw's second reason, I am not sure that it is accurate, though it does raise an important issue. As I read Appiah, he *is* claiming that Du Bois's stated definition is intended to individuate racial kinds. But he appears also to be claiming that Du Bois envisions those kinds, *not* as "natural" and "heritable" essences such as a nineteenth-century biologist might investigate, but as essences that are in some sense "sociohistorical." Du Bois fails, Appiah argues, (a) because he does not articulate a coherent sociohistorical conception of a racial kind, and (b) because he depends on a conception of a racial kind (the conception which accounts for his eightfold classification of races) that, in fact, is biological and not sociohistorical. Still, it seems to me, a weaker statement of the issue Outlaw's second reason raises may be valid. While it seems to be false that Appiah's reading cannot make sense of Du Bois's intention to situate his account of race in relation to history and sociology, it may be true that Appiah has not done justice to the point of that intention. It is to this possibility that I shall direct my attention in the next section of this essay.

EXPLANATION AND DEFINITION IN "THE CONSERVATION OF RACES"
Consider, then, the following passages from the "The Conservation of Races":

> The final word of science, so far, is that we have at least two, perhaps three, great families of human beings—the whites and Negroes—possibly the yellow race.

That other races have arisen from the intermingling of the blood of these two. This broad division of the world's races which men like Huxley and Raetzel have introduced as more nearly true than the old five-race scheme of Blumenbach, is nothing more than an acknowledgement that, so far as *purely physical characteristics* are concerned, the differences between men do not *explain* all the differences of their history. . . .

Although the wonderful developments of human history teach that grosser physical differences of color, hair and bone go but a short way toward *explaining* the different roles which groups of men have played in Human Progress, yet there are differences—subtle, delicate and elusive, though they may be—which have silently but definitely separated men into groups. While these *subtle forces* have generally followed the natural cleavage of common blood, descent and physical peculiarities, they have at other times swept across and ignored these. At all times, however, they have divided human beings into races, which, while they perhaps transcend scientific definition, nevertheless, are *clearly defined to the eye of the Historian and Sociologist.*

If this be true, then the history of the world is the history, not of individuals, but of groups, not of nations, but of races, and he who ignores or seeks to override the race idea in human history ignores and overrides the central thought of all history. ("CR," 484–85, emphases mine)

Du Bois praises the work of Huxley and Raetzel, because it shows that physical racial differences—the province of science—do not explain "all the differences of their [men's] history." Du Bois develops this insight when, in the next paragraph, he writes that "the grosser physical differences . . . go but a short way in explaining the different roles which groups of men have played in Human Progress," by which I take him to mean, roughly, "go but a short way in explaining historical differences," or, more exactly, "in explaining the different roles different groups of men have played in the progress of human history." Now human history ("the history of the world"), Du Bois claims, is the history of the "groups of men" we call 'races'. Moreover, he insists, a race *plays a role* (is "a factor") in history, just to the extent that it delivers itself of its own distinctive *spiritual message*:

"Manifestly some of the great races of today—particularly the Negro race—have not yet given to civilization the full spiritual message which they are capable of giving. . . . For the development of Negro genius, of Negro literature and art, of Negro spirit, only Negroes, bound and welded together, Negroes inspired by one vast ideal, can work out in fullness the great message we have for humanity. We cannot reverse history; we are subject to the same laws as other races, and if the Negro is ever to be a factor in the world's history—if among the gaily colored banners that deck the broad ramparts of civilization is to hang one uncompromising black, then it must be put there by black hands...." ("CR," 487)

For Du Bois, it appears, explaining the "different roles" of different races is a matter of accounting for the distinct spiritual messages by which these races—the Negro race included—acquire an eminent historical significance. The "subtle forces" to which he refers, powers that can sweep across the "natural" cleavages separating physical races, seem to be the causes he thinks explanations of spiritual messages and of the division of human beings into races should identify. What, then, does Du Bois have in mind when he speaks of "subtle forces"?

The answer to this question is present, I believe, in the following paragraph:

> The question now is: What is the real distinction between these nations? Is it the physical differences of blood, color and cranial measurement? Certainly we must acknowledge that physical differences play a great part, and that, with wide exceptions and qualifications, these *eight great races* of to-day follow the cleavage of physical race distinctions; *the English and Teuton represent the white variety of mankind*; the Mongolian the yellow; the Negroes the black. Between these are many crosses and mixtures, where Mongolian and Teuton have blended into the Slav, and other mixtures have produced the Romance nations and the Semites. *But while race differences have followed mainly physical race lines, yet no mere physical distinctions would really define or explain the deeper differences—the cohesiveness and continuity of these groups. The deeper differences are spiritual, psychical differences—undoubtedly based on the physical, but infinitely transcending them. The forces that bind the Teuton nations are, then, first, their race identity and common blood, secondly and more important, a common history, common laws and religion, similar habits of thought and a conscious striving together for certain ideals of life.* ("CR," 486, emphases mine)

Here, again, Du Bois proclaims that the physical differences between races cannot explain the spiritual differences which, previously, he described as role differences. In order to explain spiritual differences, he suggests, one must appeal to the "more important" and non-physical "forces"—the "subtle forces" to which he earlier referred—namely, "a common history, common laws and religion, similar habits of thought and a conscious striving for certain ideals of life" ("CR," 486). The case of the Teutonic race is instructive here, since, from a physical or biological perspective, there is nothing to distinguish the Teutons from the English: they both represent, without mixture, "the white variety of mankind." The nations which make up the

Teutonic race (and here, Du Bois includes the German, the Scandinavian, and the Dutch ("CR," 486)), *like* those which make up the English race, are bound together by a physio-biological "race identity and common blood" constituting them as white. The spiritual differences separating the English from the Teutons (to which Du Bois alludes when he writes "The English nation stood for constitutional liberty and commercial freedom; the German nation for science and philosophy" ["CR," 487]) cannot be a function of this "white" identity, since the English and the Teutons have this identity in common; rather, these differences derive from the differing causal efficacies of different (English and Teutonic) histories, different (English and Teutonic) laws and religion, different (English and Teutonic) habits of thought, etc. The spiritual message and "difference" of the Teutonic nations is in a sense "based" or founded "on" a physio-biological "race identity and ... blood," in that this message and difference is borne, upheld and sustained in the world by individuals and groups that are physically "white."[9] And yet, since physical "whiteness" plays no causal role in explaining the content of the Teutonic message and difference, Du Bois can view Teutonic spiritual identity as "infinitely transcending" the physio-biological racial identity of its bearers. The subtle historical, legal, and religious forces producing the spiritual differences between the Englishman and the Teuton have, here, "divided human beings into races," as it is precisely these forces that have constituted the Teutonic and the English races as distinct entities.

By rejecting the view that the physical differences between races explain their spiritual differences, Du Bois repudiates one of the most influential claims put forth by the racial sciences of the nineteenth century: namely, that physical racial differences explain the spiritual (psychological), social and cultural differences distinguishing different racial groups.[10] For Du Bois, spiritual differences have historical, social, and cultural causes (law, religion, etc.) that are themselves not causally reducible to biological racial differences. Thus, he can characterize these causes as having acted independently of biological racial facts, that is, as having "*swept across and ignored*" what he calls "the natural cleavage of common blood, descent, and physical peculiarities." ("CR," 483, emphasis mine)

Reading Du Bois as making a theoretical break with one of the *explanatory* commitments of nineteenth century racial science lets us see his *definition* of 'race' from a perspective somewhat different from those of Appiah and Outlaw. Consider this definition, once again:

> What, then, is a race? It is a vast family of human beings, *generally* of common blood and language, *always* of common history, traditions and impulses, who are both voluntarily and involuntarily striving together for the accomplishment of

certain more or less vividly conceived ideals of life. ("CR," 485, emphases mine)

In reconsidering this definition, I want to draw attention to Du Bois's distinct uses of the terms 'generally' and 'always'. 'Generally', as distinct from 'always', can mean the same as 'usually'. What is usually the case, moreover, need not be the case *always*. The claim that the members of a race are "generally" of the same blood suggests that common blood, like common language, is, to use Appiah's word, "inessential" to membership in the same race. Just as two individuals can be members of the Romance race, yet not speak the same language, so too can two individuals be members of some race, yet not be of the same "blood" and descent—or so Du Bois *himself* seems to imply. That Du Bois *should have wanted* to imply this should come as no surprise, since, we have seen, he claims explicitly, in the paragraph immediately preceding his definition, that the "subtle forces" separating human beings into races, though they have "*generally* followed the natural cleavage of common blood, descent and physical peculiarities ... have at other times swept across and ignored these" (emphasis mine). Though Du Bois begins his definition of 'race' by invoking the biological notion of a family, his use of the term 'generally' in this context, both before and after that invocation, suggests the view that at least *some* racial families are not "blood unities."

No less surprising is Du Bois's claim that the members of a given race *always* share a history, traditions, impulses and strivings, since he has already told us that racial differences, "while perhaps they transcend scientific definition, nevertheless, are clearly defined to the eye of the Historian and Sociologist." The *point* of Du Bois's definition, this last statement suggests, is to offer an alternative to the scientific (physio-biological) definition of 'race' by providing a thoroughly historical and sociological definition. Du Bois's use of 'generally' to qualify "common blood" implies that, strictly speaking, "common blood" is not one of a set of individually *necessary* and jointly sufficient conditions for determining whether two individuals are members of the same race. His use of 'always' to qualify *only* what the historian and the sociologist see—common history, common traditions, common impulses, and common strivings—suggests that none of the members of this set is a physio-biological phenomenon, and that x and y are members of the same race if, *and only if,* they share in common a history, traditions, impulses *and* strivings (though *not only if* they share a common blood and a common language).[11]

I can summarize the claim I am making by saying that Du Bois's definition of 'race', his references to a "vast family" and "common blood" notwithstanding, seems intended to represent race as a phenomenon that is *in essence* social, historical, and nonbiological. I am *not* claiming, however, that Du Bois's definition, thus understood, does the "work of individuation" he wants it to do. With respect to this question, Appiah's objections to Du Bois's appeals to common history, common impulses, etc. seem decisive. It is important, nonetheless, to see precisely *what* definition of 'race' Du Bois is proposing, so that we can clarify the motivation that probably prompted it. This motivation begins to come into view when we notice that Du Bois's reference to the forces that explain the spiritual and psychical differences between races—that is, to "common history, common laws and religion, similar habits of thought and conscious striving for certain ideals of life"—can reasonably be read as glossing and fleshing out the reference in his definition of 'race' to common history, traditions, impulses and strivings. It seems, in other words, that Du Bois has formed a definition of 'race'—"*always* of common history, traditions and impulses, etc."—consisting precisely of the elements he later represents as explaining the spiritual differences between races. In effect, he has attempted to adjust his definition of 'race' to his explanation of spiritual differences between races by intimating that, for the purposes of the historian and the sociologist, 'race' can be defined without reference to biological facts and, therefore, without implicating the racial sciences' biological explanations of spiritual differences, which explanations he repudiates.

I am suggesting, then, that Du Bois's sociohistorical and stated definition of 'race' (as I have interpreted it) draws its motivation from a theoretical belief in the possibility of nonbiological explanations of spiritual differences between the races. As we have seen, however, this definition, the elements of which cannot do the work of individuation, is *not* the definition Du Bois uses to do that work. The definition Du Bois uses, because it represents shared physical *and* cultural attributes as the effects of common descent, *contradicts* his explicit rejection of the view that biological racial differences explain the spiritual and cultural differences between races. Appiah is right, then, to maintain that Du Bois, in the definition of 'race' he actually but tacitly uses in "The Conservation of Races," fails to transcend the perspective of nineteenth-century racial science; he is wrong, however, to suggest that Du Bois, in this same essay, has not overtly repudiated the claim of the racial sciences to explain the spiritual and cultural differences between the races (Appiah, 29–30).[12] Regarding this issue, Outlaw correctly claims that Du Bois, in "The Conservation of Races," did "not think that biological characteristics causally determined cultural and moral . . . characteristics" (Outlaw, 38).

Du Bois's tacit dependence on a scientific definition of 'race' reflects the fact that he cannot, on the basis of his sociohistorical and stated definition—"*always* of common history, traditions and impulses, etc.,"—draw the distinctions he wishes to draw. Had the stated definition (as I have interpreted it) done the work Du Bois wished it to do, he would not have needed to rely tacitly on a scientific and biological definition, and so there would have been no contradiction between the definition of 'race' he actually uses and his explanation of the spiritual and cultural differences between the races. All this said, of course, we may still wonder why Du Bois believed he needed *any* definition of 'race' to support his explanation of spiritual differences, be it biological, sociohistorical, or something else. After all, if spiritual differences are the differences which matter (Du Bois ["CR," 486] describes them as the "deeper differences"), and if the causes which explain these differences act independently of biological racial differences, why not scuttle the language of race altogether? Why not speak "of civilizations where we now speak of races" (Appiah, 35)?

Outlaw sees correctly, I think, that explaining Du Bois's commitment to the language of race requires that we consider the political work which this language is doing for Du Bois. Du Bois's project "is a decidedly *political* project. . . . Du Bois's project involves prescribing norms for the social reconstruction of personal and social identities and for self-appropriation by a people suffering racialized subordination" (Outlaw, 39). For Du Bois, the political mobilization of African Americans (in part, through the formation of the American Negro Academy) required the rhetorical mobilization of such signifiers as 'Negro' and 'race' because these signifiers were the signifiers in terms of which African Americans comprehended themselves as a subordinated group. So while Du Bois could have produced a nonbiological explanation of group spiritual differences, *absent* any talk of race, he continues that talk for political purposes, and, in order to rationalize it, states a definition of 'race' consistent with a nonbiological explanation of group spiritual differences. Still, to the extent that Du Bois seems not to use *this* definition (to do the work of individuation), and appears to rely instead on one congenial to the nineteenth-century racial sciences, he demonstrates his inability fully to reconcile the rhetorical requirements of his politics and the theoretical implications of a nonbiological explanation of group spiritual differences.

Let me conclude this essay by considering briefly the connection between the theoretical focus of "The Conservation of Races" and Du Bois's representation of black spirituality in *The Souls of Black Folk*. The theoretical focus of the former, I have been arguing, is Du Bois's claim that spiritual differences between the races can be explained on a nonbiological basis, that is, by appeal to such causal factors as *common history, common laws and religion, similar habits of thought and a conscious striving for certain ideals of life*. What, however, are the implications of this thesis for Du Bois's understanding of the spiritual life of the American Negro? Du Bois hints at an answer to this question, when, in "The Conservation of Races," he discusses the Negro's status in America:

If we carefully consider what race prejudice really is, we find it, historically, to be nothing but the friction between different groups of people. . . . [I]f now this difference exists touching territory, laws, language, or even religion, it is manifest that these people cannot live in the same territory without fatal collision; but if, on the other hand, there is substantial agreement in laws, language and religion; if there is a satisfactory adjustment of economic life, then there is no reason why, in the same country and on the same street, two or three national ideals might not thrive and develop, that men of different races might not strive together for their race ideals as well, perhaps even better, than in isolation. Here, it seems to me, is the reading of the riddle that puzzles so many of us. We are Americans, not only by birth and citizenship, but by our political ideals, our language, our religion. Farther than that our Americanism does not go. At that point we are Negroes, members of a vast historic race that from the very dawn of creation has slept but half awakening in the dark forests of its African fatherland. ("CR," 488–89)

Considered in light of Du Bois's earlier identification of the causal factors that account for the spiritual differences between the races, this passage implies that the spiritual distinctiveness of the American Negro is an effect of his *history,* his *habits of thought,* and his *conscious striving for certain ideals of life.* Neither American *religion* nor the political ideals embodied in American *law* can help to explain the distinctive character of Negro spirituality, Du Bois suggests, since these factors account only for the "Americanism" in Negro life, which, he seems to believe, expresses nothing of what is unique in the Negro's spiritual message. The destiny of the American Negro, he insists, "is *not* absorption by the white Americans ... not a servile imitation of Anglo-Saxon culture, but a stalwart originality which shall unswervingly follow Negro ideals" ("CR," 487–88).

In a sense, *The Souls of Black Folk* takes up the phenomenon of Negro spirituality, just at the point at which "The Conservation of Races" puts it aside. The opening chapter of *Souls,* "Of Our Spiritual Strivings," is a revision of an essay that Du Bois published in 1897, the same year he delivered "The Conservation of Races" to The American Negro Academy.[13] In this chapter, he begins to sketch what, in the book's "Forethought," he describes as "the spiritual world in which ten thousand thousand Americans live and strive."[14] To be more precise, Du Bois uses the first chapter of *Souls* to represent African American spirituality as drawing its character and mold from the post-Emancipation history of blacks in America. Indeed, the narrative of "Of Our Spiritual Strivings" mentions almost all of the major themes which Du Bois later takes up in *Souls*—the aftermath of emancipation, progress, economic hardship, physical freedom, despair, and the sorrow songs—and so provides a preview of his treatment of the historical formation of black spirituality in the remainder of the book.[15] We cannot be surprised, then, that Du Bois himself characterizes this chapter as prefiguring the portrait and song he has yet to flesh out: "And now what I have briefly sketched in large outline let me on coming pages tell again in many ways, with loving emphasis and deeper detail, that men may listen to the striving in the souls of black folk."[16]

Besides placing African American spirituality in an historical context, "Of Our Spiritual Strivings" brings to light the Negro's conscious striving for certain ideals—Du Bois mentions explicitly the ideals of physical freedom, political power, and education—as well as some of the tendencies or "habits" of thought that belong to the history of the Negro's striving: "Whisperings and portents came borne upon the four winds: Lo! we are diseased and dying, cried the dark hosts; we cannot write, our voting is in vain, what need of education, since we must always cook and serve? And the Nation echoed and enforced this self-criticism...."[17] In keeping with the argument of "The Conservation of Races," Souls' first chapter represents the Negro's history, his conscious striving for certain ideals, and, to a lesser extent, his habits of thought, as the causal forces which have lent a unique identity to his spiritual life. We should not be surprised that this chapter makes no reference to law or religion—two of the "more important" factors that, we have seen, "The Conservation of Races" identifies as contributing to the constitution of group spiritual identities—since, again, these forces account for the Negro's Americanism, not for his spiritual distinctiveness.[18]

"The Conservation of Races" provides a philosophical prolegomenon to The Souls of Black Folk, because it offers a theoretical promise that Du Bois only begins to fulfill in what eventually became the opening essay of Souls. This promise is to show that the distinctive character of Negro spirituality admits of a nonbiological explanation that highlights the history, the conscious ideals, and the tendencies of thought which have given form to African American spiritual development. In attempting to make good on the promise of his prolegomenon, Du Bois suggests that the Geisteswissenschaften, no less than the Naturwissenschaften, are indispensable to the study of African-American black folk.[19]

NOTES

1. For Outlaw's essay, "'Conserve' Races?: In Defense of W. E. B. Du Bois," see pp. 19–55 of this volume. (My critique here of Outlaw's essay is based on a draft sent to me by the editors. I do not address revisions in the substance of Outlaw's argument made after he read this critique.) This essay is a response to Appiah's "The Uncompleted Argument: Du Bois and the Illusion of Race," which appears in 'Race,' Writing, and Difference, ed. Henry Louis Gates, Jr. (Chicago: University of Chicago Press, 1986), 21–37. (An expanded version of Appiah's article appears as chapter 2 of In My Father's House [New York: Oxford University Press, 1992].) All references to

these essays, indicated in each case by the last name of the author, will be included in the text. My references to "The Conservation of Races" cite the text of that essay which appears in *Negro Social and Political Thought*, ed. Howard Brotz (New York: Basic Books, 1966), 483–92. All of these references, abbreviated in each case as "CR," will be included in the text.

2. Here, and throughout this essay, I use the convention of single quotes (as in 'race') when I mention a word but do not use it.

3. Outlaw (32) argues that Appiah misconstrues Du Bois's project. It is a political project, says Outlaw, and "*not* simply—or even primarily—an effort devoted to definition and taxonomy." My point will be that there is a question of explanation that is related to Du Bois's political project, and that this question can be distinguished from the question of definition on which Appiah and Outlaw concentrate.

4. The particular formulation which follows is mine, and does not appear in Appiah's essay. But it is, I believe, faithful to the logical trajectory of his argument.

5. For example, Du Bois seems to be employing the biological conception of a family again, when, a few paragraphs later, he begins to tell the story of the formation of racial groups:

    > The age of nomadic tribes of closely related individuals represents the maximum of physical differences. They were practically vast families, and there were as many groups as families. As families came together to form cities the physical differences lessened, purity of blood was replaced by the requirements of domicile. . . . ("CR," 486)

    Let me suggest, furthermore, that Du Bois, in representing races as families and families as biological entities, is paying homage to the views of Alexander Crummell, the first president of the organization—The American Negro Academy—to which Du Bois first presented "The Conservation of Races" in 1897. (For a similar view, see Eric Sundquist, *To Wake the Nations: Race in the Making of American Literature* [Cambridge: Harvard University Press, 1993], 517.) In *Africa and America*, originally published in 1891, Crummell included an essay entitled "The Race-Problem in America." In that essay, he wrote that "Races, like families, are the organisms and the ordinance of God. . . . Indeed, a race *is* a family." (*Africa and America* [New York: Negro Universities Press, 1969], 46.). A close examination of "The Race-Problem in America" suggests that, in many ways, it provided the framework for Du Bois's thinking in "The Conservation of Races." Crummell's claim that "race is the key to history" (which Crummell attributes to Lord Beaconsfield), his talk of racial cohesion and continuity, and his use of the rhetoric of "conservation" (he speaks of race as possessing a "conserving power which tends everywhere to fixity of type") all find clear echoes in Du Bois's later essay (see, e.g., *Africa and America*, especially 46–9). It is noteworthy, finally, that on Wilson Moses's account, Crummell, in the discussion that ensued in the immediate aftermath of Du Bois's delivery of his paper to the Negro Academy, seems to have reiterated the biological and organicist conception of families and races he espoused in 1891, and to have supposed that this conception was consistent with Du Bois's talk of families and races in his paper. See Wilson Moses, *Alexander Crummell: A Study of Civilization and its Discontents* (New York: Oxford University Press, 1989), 264–65.

6. Appiah, as I read him, reinforces his insight as to the redundancy of the "common history" criterion when, in *In My Father's House* he draws on an analogy from John Locke's *Essay Concerning Human Understanding*: "Locke's view was that two souls at different times were, in the philosopher's jargon, 'time slices' of the same individual if the later one had memories of the earlier one. But, as philosophers since Locke have

pointed out, we cannot tell whether a memory is evidence of the rememberer's identity, even if what is 'remembered' really did happen to an earlier person, unless we know *already* that the rememberer and the earlier person are one" (32, emphasis mine).

7. Here, it is worth noting that Du Bois's use of a geographical criterion may, as does much else in his essay (see 5 above), reflect the influence of Alexander Crummell. Cf. Crummell, *Africa and America*, 46.

8. Outlaw also suggests a fourth objection that I do not take up in the body of this essay. This objection concerns Appiah's claim that there is a tension in Du Bois's stated definition of race, which tension is due to the fact that, for the purposes of nineteenth-century European historiography, cultural differences between groups mattered, whereas in American social and political life physical differences mattered (see Appiah, 19). Outlaw acknowledges a tension in "Du Bois's effort to give an account of race," but claims that Appiah has misdiagnosed the source of that tension (Outlaw, 34). Outlaw himself gives two separate alternative accounts of this tension, the relationship between which is not clear to me (see Outlaw, 34, 37).

9. Similarly, I read Du Bois's claim in the first chapter of *The Souls of Black Folk*, that "Negro blood has a message for the world" (Du Bois, *The Souls of Black Folk* [New York: Bantam, 1989], 3), as asserting that "biological" Negroes are the bearers of a message, not that the character and content of that message is dictated by a biological racial identity. It is worth noting, here, that Du Bois's reference to a message borne by Negro blood involves a slight alteration of a similar claim he made in an essay—"Strivings of the Negro People," *The Atlantic Monthly* (August 1897): 194–198—that he wrote in the same year that he delivered "The Conservation of Races" to The American Negro Academy (see David Levering Lewis, *W. E. B. Du Bois: Biography of a Race* ([New York: Henry Holt, 1993], 194–201). The first chapter of *Souls* is a revised version of the *Atlantic Monthly* essay. In the earlier piece, Du Bois's remark about Negro blood reads as follows: "Negro blood has yet a message for the world" (for this point, see Sundquist, 486).

10. For careful and historically informed discussions of these matters, see Michael Banton, *Racial Theories* (Cambridge: Cambridge University Press, 1987), especially chapter 2, and Robert Miles, *Racism* (London: Routledge, 1989), 30ff.

11. For a similar interpretation of Du Bois's stated definition, see Tommy L. Lott, "Du Bois on the Invention of Race," *The Philosophical Forum* 24, nos. 1–3 (Fall–Spring 1992–93): 167.

12. See, too, Appiah, *In My Father's House*, 34.

13. See note 9 above.

14. See W. E. B. Du Bois, *The Souls of Black Folk*, xxxi.

15. For more on the first chapter of *Souls* and its relation to Du Bois's conception of history, see my "Philosophy of History and Social Critique in *The Souls of Black Folk*," *Social Science Information* 26, 1 (1987): 99-114.

16. Du Bois, *The Souls of Black Folk*, 9. For two discussions of *Souls* as a "singing book," see Sundquist, 490 and Houston Baker, Jr., *Modernism and the Harlem Renaissance* (Chicago: University of Chicago Press, 1987), 58–68.

17. Du Bois, *The Souls of Black Folk*, 7.

18. By the time he wrote "On the Faith of the Fathers," which is the tenth chapter of *Souls*, Du Bois seems to have modified his conception of the role of religion in shaping a distinctively African American spiritual identity. In contrast to the view that seems to inform "The Conservation of Races" and "Of Our Spiritual Strivings," the perspective adumbrated in this later essay emphasizes the African origins and character of Negro religious life. ("Of the Faith of the Fathers" is a revision of "The

Religion of the American Negro," *New World: A Quarterly Review of Religion, Ethics, Theology* [December 1900]: 614–25.)

19. To be sure, we *can* find a few passages in *Souls* (as well as in some of Du Bois's subsequent writings) that seem to tie Negro psychology to Negro biology (see, e.g., *The Souls of Black Folk*, 139–40; see also, on this point, Adolph Reed's provocative interpretation of the early Du Bois as a neo-Lamarckian social scientist in Reed's "Du Bois and Progressive Era American Thought," *Studies in American Political Development* 6 (Spring 1992): 132–37, esp. 135). These passages notwithstanding, the prevailing and all but pervasive tendency of Du Bois's book is his attempt to put the "spiritual world" of the American Negro in social and historical perspective. It is this tendency, moreover, that accounts for *Souls'* richness as a sociohistorical portrait of black people's lives.

Du Bois on Cultural Pluralism | 3

Bernard R. Boxill

Early in his career Du Bois became convinced that a close study of society and history would contribute greatly to the progress of black people. This conviction pulled him in different directions. Sometimes it led him to emphasize that a careful collection of facts was necessary to framing and implementing social policy to improve the condition of black people. This approach showed the influence of Gustav von Schmoller, with whom Du Bois had studied at the University of Berlin. Schmoller was one of the leaders of the German historical school of economics that depreciated the search for scientific laws of economics, and called instead for a systematic collection of facts to support ameliorative social policy.[1] The effect of his teaching on Du Bois is clear in Du Bois's early work, "The Study of Negro Problems."[2] In that essay, although Du Bois emphasized that "social reform" required a study of the "history and condition of American Negroes," he left it an open question whether such a study would "eventually lead to a systematic body of knowledge deserving the name of science. . . . "[3] But Du Bois had too speculative and fertile a mind to remain trapped in Schmoller's pedestrian empiricism. Thus he often expressed the belief that the study of society and history would assist black progress by revealing scientific laws that black people could use for their advancement. This idea is the main premise of the essay, "The Conservation of Races."[4]

In "The Conservation of Races," Du Bois proposed, "It is necessary . . . in planning our movements, in guiding our future development, that at times we rise above the pressing, but smaller questions of separate schools and cars, wage discrimination and lynch law," and lay down "on a basis of broad knowledge and careful insight, those large lines of policy and higher ideals" that will form the "guiding lines" of future black progress.[5] This proposal was an implicit criticism of Schmoller's approach. Du Bois was saying that piece-meal, ameliorative social reform was not enough; "large lines of policy" were also necessary. And he was clear that such policy would have to be based on the scientific laws that Schmoller said either did not exist, or could not be discovered. Thus, after calling for his "large lines of policy," he warned that "all human striving must recognize the hard limits of natural law."[6]

Du Bois was not referring to the kind of "law" Marxists and others claim to have discovered and which enable them to predict the course of history. William James, his favorite teacher at Harvard, had exposed the fallacies in the search for such laws in his refutation of Herbert Spencer's "laws of history." As James concluded, "It is folly . . . to speak of the 'laws of history' as of something inevitable, which science has only to discover, and whose consequences anyone can then foretell but do nothing to alter or avert."[7] The laws of science, James emphasized, were "conditional."[8] They predicted what would happen if something else happened, and therefore they put humanity in a position to control its future. Given that Du Bois wanted to put black people in a position to control their future, he naturally shared James's view of the nature of scientific laws. The laws he sought as a basis for his large lines of policy were necessarily conditional. They were laws of human progress that predicted that people advance if they do certain things, and fail to advance if they do certain other things.

Two further tenets of pragmatism entered Du Bois's conception of the laws of progress. According to pragmatism, the categories or classifications in terms of which scientific laws are stated are not given to us by nature or real-ity, but are rather made by us. James illustrated this point with the example of the constellations. "We carve out groups of stars in the heavens," James observed, and "call them constellations."[9] Further, pragmatism argues that we make classifications to suit our purposes. James made this generalization from the case of the constellations. He wrote, "We carve out everything, just as we carve out constellations, to suit our human purposes."[10] Du Bois was follow-ing these pragmatic tenets when he sought his laws of progress. For example, he complained that Americans were especially prone to overlook the fact that races are the units of progress. As he wrote, "We, who have been reared and trained under the individualistic philosophy of the Declaration of Independence and the laissez-faire philosophy of Adam Smith, are loath to see and loath to acknowledge this patent fact of human history. We see the Pharaohs, Caesars, Toussaints and Napoleons and forget the vast races of which they were but epitomized expressions."[11] But he was clear that race was not a classification given by nature or reality, but carved out by human beings to suit their purpose, which in this instance was to find laws that could be used to enhance human progress. As he put it, the "race idea" was an "invention" for "human progress."[12]

But what is the principle according to which people are carved out into races? The principles which determine the classifications found in statements of scientific laws are determined by the purpose for which the laws are sought. Consequently, given that Du Bois's purpose was to find laws of progress, it seems that the principle according to which he classified people into races would be that the members of a race are especially able or likely to make progress together. Let us see if Du Bois's conception of a race satisfies this principle.

Du Bois described a race as "a vast family of human beings, generally of common blood and language, always of common history, traditions and impulses, who are both voluntarily and involuntarily striving together for the accomplishment of certain more or less vividly conceived ideals of life."[13] The central idea in this account is clearly that the members of a race have in common history, traditions and impulses, and strive together for the realization of the same ideals; these are the only characteristics that Du Bois says are "always" true of races. Assuming that culture gives people their most basic preferences, as well as their ideals, the claim that a race of people have common impulses and strive together for the realization of the same ideals implies that they have a common culture. But culture and traditions are always the product of a long historical development. Accordingly, Du Bois made the reasonable assumption that the cultural group he called a race was a group of people with a common history.

Now, progress implies change and change for the better; this change for the better arises from human beings continuously increasing their ability to control their natural and social environment rather than from nature becoming spontaneously more bountiful or responsive, or from human beings becoming spontaneously more benevolent. Human beings increase their ability to control their natural and social environment by deepening their understanding of nature and society, and by inventing ever more efficient ways to control nature and ever better ways to organize society. But human abilities are too limited for one individual to make much headway in understanding nature and society all by himself. Thus progress is never the work of an individual but is always the product of a number of individuals who cooperate, or at least divide their labor. The specialization this involves is essential to the invention that is similar, essential to progress. Further, when people cooperate or divide their labor they may do different things, but their actions are directed to one major end, though this end may not be equally clear to all of them. Thus progress implies a unity of aims or ideals among the people who make progress. One last point about progress deserves mention: progress depends on accumulation as well as cooperation. Our knowledge of nature and society, and the stock of strategies and techniques we have for controlling nature and organizing society, derives from the fact that each generation passes on its stock of knowledge and inventions to the next.

If this account of progress is correct, Du Bois's conception of a race satisfies the principle that the members of a race are especially able and likely to make progress together. As I argued, his conception of a race is that it is a group of people with a common culture. But a group of people with a common culture satisfies the conditions identified above as essential to progress: its members have a common way of life and therefore are conditioned into a division of labor; and they tend to share similar aims and ideals. It may be objected that these conditions for progress are so vague that they can be satisfied by almost any group of people. But Du Bois's view was that progress is possible, or at least most rapid, if there is wholehearted agreement on definite aims and ideals, and a relatively unforced division of labor, and that these conditions are found only found among people with a common culture. Indeed, if, as I argued, people with a common culture tend to be people with a common history, they probably have already made considerable progress together. A group of people have a common history if they have inherited their common way of life from a long series of ancestors who faced common problems together, and passed on their way of handling these problems—their way of life—to their descendants, usually with adjustments and amendations; and as I noted, one of the conditions of progress is that earlier generations pass on their stock of knowledge and insights to later generations.

Du Bois's conception of race suggests that racial unity is an important law of progress. For if the members of a race are especially able and likely to make progress together, then it seems that people who take advantage of this fact by coordinating their efforts with others of their own race are likely to enhance their progress.[14] This law does not make the true but empty claim that progress requires unity and coordination of effort. It makes the substantive and plausible claim that the unity required for progress depends on similarities of outlook and sentiment that have been shaped by a common history and deepened and matured over eons, and consequently that people cannot simply will these similarities, but must find themselves moved and bound by these similarities independently of their wills.

This theory is not nationalistic. Nationalistic theories claim that each nation should be a state. On the grounds that cultural groups are nations, such theories claim that each cultural group should be a state. Du Bois's theory argues, on the contrary, that although the members of each cultural group must strive together to make progress, in certain circumstances different groups should share the same state. This followed from his view that each cultural group has something to learn from, and to teach, every other cultural group.

Du Bois's theory is also not a form of liberalism. Some forms of liberalism claim that people have rights to pursue their conception of the good, and that if governments respect those rights, each state is likely to contain many cultures. Others add that different cultural groups in the same society can learn to tolerate and respect each other, and even that the variety of lifestyles in culturally plural societies helps make life in such societies more interesting and pleasurable than life in culturally homogeneous societies. But none make Du Bois's bold claim that, because each culture has something to teach other cultures, people are obligated to cultivate the moral and aesthetic insights that are contained in their culture. This claim supported his call to blacks to "maintain their race identity." According to Du Bois, blacks "have a contribution to make to civilization and humanity which no other race can make," and consequently they have a "duty" to "maintain their race identity until this mission of the Negro people is accomplished, and the ideal of human brotherhood has become a practical possibility."[15] His theory therefore calls for a deepening of cultural particularities simultaneous with the broadening of these particularities by insights from different cultures. In the end, Du Bois envisages a cosmopolitan world culture to which every race has made an essential contribution.

Du Bois first sketched this theory in several essays at the turn of the century. It is a beautiful and optimistic theory, deeply coherent and based on the egalitarian premise that what are called the races of mankind are equally rational, equally capable of morality, and equally capable of teaching and learning from each other. Moreover, this egalitarianism is bolder and more honest than the evasive egalitarianism assumed in the theories of cultural relativism that were just beginning to compete with the evolutionary theories of culture dominant at the turn of the century. I present, criticize and defend Du Bois's theory in this essay. In sections one and two, I defend it against two important criticisms; in sections three and four, I describe its main outlines; and in section five, I suggest some of the signigicant difficulties that it faces.

PLURALISM AND RACISM

Du Bois's theory is open to a potentially fatal objection. In his day and ours, races were and are commonly conceived to be biologically defined. Because his theory associated race and culture, it may seem to endorse the racist view that important biological differences between the races determine their historical and cultural differences. It is true that he attempted to define race in social, cultural and historical terms. But Kwame Anthony Appiah has argued that, although Du Bois made such an attempt, he failed, and fell back on a biological definition of race.[16] I will now show that many considerations suggest a more charitable interpretation of Du Bois's views.

One of Appiah's main arguments is that Du Bois's claim that races have a common history commits him to a biological conception of race. This argument may seem to have force. I described a group of people as having a common history if they inherit their common way of life from a long series of ancestors. If this is correct, then, supposing that people are biologically related to their ancestors, it may seem that Du Bois's conception of race must be biological. But my account of a common history in terms of common ancestry is only a manner of speaking. In fact, having a common ancestry is neither necessary nor sufficient for a group of people to have a common history. What is essential is that the group inherit a common way of life that has developed over generations. Suppose, for example, that living in a certain region induces total sterility among humans, although the people of that region do not leave it because it is otherwise a paradise. Such people, call them the "Steriles," can still preserve their way of life by adopting large numbers of infants from all the biological races of mankind that inhabited parts of the globe favorable to human fertility. Apart from being human, the members of any generation of Steriles would not be biologically related to each other, nor to the preceding generations from which they learned and inherited their way of life. Yet on my account they would have a common history, and on Du Bois's conception of race would constitute a race. Now suppose that one of the infants who the Steriles adopted had brothers and sisters that were not adopted. On the account of race that I have attributed to Du Bois, when that infant grew up it would not share a common history with, or be of same race as, its brothers and sisters; although it would, of course, be biologically related to them.

Appiah's suspicions are aroused by Du Bois's claim that races were "generally of common blood." These suspicions can be allayed. The example of the Steriles is only a logical possibility designed to make the analytical point that having a common history does not entail being related biologically. Normally, people with a common history are "generally of common blood." It does not follow, however, that being of common blood is a necessary part of having a common history. To see this, let us make the reasonable assumption that over the eons, differences in climate and other natural forces associated with differences in geographical location cause people living in different parts of the world to develop the striking but superficial physical differences that are mistakenly said to make them of different blood. The same natural forces that thus divided human beings into groups of peoples of "common blood" also presented each such group with a common set of opportunities and obstacles to deal with in its struggle to survive. Supposing that this led to the development of common repertoires of techniques, habits and beliefs, it follows that people of "common blood" will tend to have common histories in the sense that during the longest periods of their struggles to survive they struggled to survive with common repertoires of techniques, habits and beliefs. This conjectural history shows how Du Bois could rightly say that races are "generally of common blood," and at the same time consistently deny that common blood was any part of having a common history.

But if people of common culture and history are only "generally" of common blood, why does Du Bois so often use skin color—blood—to track, and as a marker for, culture? There are at least two reasons. The first is that culture is persistent.[17] Human beings tend to be drawn to those with a familiar culture and appearance, and to be wary of those with alien cultures and appearances. Since different races tend to differ in both physical appearance and culture, it follows that the members of each race will tend to stick together and to form families with each other, even when members of other races are in relatively close proximity. Now, the first things we learn are generally from our families. We learn the things our families teach us explicitly and intend that we learn, and, perhaps more importantly, we also learn things from our families that our families may not intend that we learn. But the things we thus learn from our families are part of the culture of our families. Consequently, the first things we learn are part of the cultures of our families. Further, the things we learn first set broad limits on how we understand and interpret the things we learn later. Since the things we learn first are the culture of our families, it follows that the culture of our families sets an ineradicable seal on the things we learn later. Although this suggests that acculturation may often be only a veneer, it obviously has no truck with the racist view that biology determines culture. But it gives us theoretical reasons for supposing that race may track culture more reliably than easily acquired facades of culture, and consequently that classifying people into races may be useful, although the real aim is to classify people into cultures.[18]

Du Bois's second reason for using skin color as a marker for culture is pragmatic, and stems from his conception of a race as a group of people who are especially likely to make progress together. Given white racism, people prevent black people from making progress with them, and it seems that black people had better not think of themselves as being of the same race as white people.

It may be objected that this discussion only shows that Du Bois need not have thought that biological differences between groups of human beings determined their historical differences, but that in fact he thought that this was the case. His claim that different races have different impulses may be cited in support of this objection, for different impulses may seem to imply different biologies. But this claim does not support the objection. Impulses are not instinctual reactions to bare physical stimuli—not like jerking a hand away from a hot object. They may be spontaneous, but it does not follow that they are unlearned. It only follows that some of the things we learn can become so intrinsic to our personalities that they lead us to do some things spontaneously. As the previous paragraph suggests, certain parts of culture are among the things so learned. Consequently, I stand by my earlier view that Du Bois's claim that different races have different impulses only commits him to the view that different races have different cultures.

But Du Bois said that scientists have acknowledged that "so far as purely physical characteristics are concerned, the differences between men do not explain all the differences of their history."[19] This may seem to allow that biological differences determine some cultural and historical differences between people, and consequently that, although Du Bois defined the races in terms of their cultural and historical differences, his views are still contaminated with racism. But in the passage cited Du Bois was only revealing that even the biologists of the period, who were naturally inclined to explain historical differences with biological differences, were being forced to concede that their preferred way of explaining history was a failure. He was not committing himself to the view that historical differences were determined by biological differences.

Indirect evidence that Du Bois would have rejected the biological determination of culture comes from another consideration. As I noted earlier, progress is a cumulative process consisting of the regular and continuous transmission of ideas beliefs and strategies from generation to generation. There are two ways to explain how this occurs. The first is that insights are transmitted from generation to generation through a process of inculcation and imitation; the older generation deliberately teaches its techniques and insights to the younger generation, and independently of this the younger generation tends to imitate the habits and ways of life of the older generation. On this account, only groups can possibly make progress. If there were no groups, there could be no progress, because being solitary, no one would be in a position either to teach or to learn from others. Rousseau stated this argument forcefully. As he observed, if individuals lived solitary lives in the state of nature, then if one of them "made some discovery, he was all the less in a position to communicate it as he did not recognize even his children. The art perished with the inventor; there was never education nor progress, generations multiplied uselessly . . . as each one of them always started at the same point."[20]

The second possible way in which insights could be transmitted from generation to generation is through biological inheritance. If people who discover better ways of doing things could pass on their insights to their children biologically, there would be a transmission, and presumably an improvement of techniques from generation to generation. Now, of course, this Lamarckian theory has been thoroughly discredited: people do not pass on their insights biologically; they pass on their insights by inculcation. But the important lesson for us here is analytical rather than factual. If insights could be passed on biologically, they would not have to be taught to younger generations, nor would younger generations have to learn them by imitating older generations. But this is to say that if insights could be passed on biologically, they could be passed on from generation to generation even if people did not live in groups. Consequently, supposing that progress depends on the transmission of insights from generation to generation, it follows that there could conceivably be progress even if people did not live in groups. But as we saw, Du Bois insisted that progress took place only in groups. This implies that he would have denied that insights could be passed on biologically, and that he probably would have resisted racist views of the biological determination of culture.

But the clearest point in my favor is that Du Bois explicitly argued that attempts to define race in biological terms were hopeless. Thus after listing the physical characteristics that biologists use to divide people into races, he concluded that " Unfortunately for scientists . . . these criteria of race are most exasperatingly intermingled. Color does not agree with texture of hair, nor does color agree with breadth of the head."[21]

I conclude that, although Du Bois allowed that cultural and historical differences tend to coincide with differences of "blood," he succeeded in providing a conception of race that was historical and cultural, and that he was not committed to the view that biological differences between human beings determine differences in either their histories or their cultures. Further, although his law of progress stated that the unity required for progress must be based on similarities that are given rather than merely willed, it does not make the racist claim that these similarities are similarities of "blood," and that people of the same color must unite simply because they are of the same color. We can therefore proceed with our analysis of Du Bois's theory of cultural pluralism with no qualms that it rest on racist foundations.

PLURALISM AND ECONOMIC DETERMINISM

As we have seen, Du Bois argued that the people of each cultural group should strive together to develop the distinctive insights of their culture both to advance and to teach the people of other cultures. But it may be objected that a culturally plural society that is democratic, relatively affluent and economically integrated will inevitably be a "melting pot." This objection stems from what can be termed "economic determinism," and it may seem an especially difficult problem for Du Bois, for he laid down as a necessary condition of cultural pluralism that there be "a satisfactory adjustment of economic life."

Economic determinism comes in both a liberal and a Marxist form. The liberal form is more crass than the Marxist form. It assumes *homo economicus*. It says that we are all profit maximizers, and that culture is only a set of habits and beliefs developed and acquired because they are means to the end of maximizing profit.[22] If this is true then, cultural differences will rapidly disappear once people are integrated into the same economic system. In the same economic system one particular set of habits and beliefs will be the best means to the end of profit maximization. Presumably all groups can learn what that set of habits and beliefs is, and given that all groups are profit maximizers, it follows that all groups will acquire that set of habits and beliefs, that is, that all groups will acquire the same culture. If one group has an initial advantage over the others, these others will quickly learn from it, that is, they will assimilate its culture. So cultural differences will disappear unless the group with the initial advantage practices educational and economic discrimination to prevent the other cultural groups from learning the habits and beliefs necessary to maximize profit. Given that Du Bois condemned such forms of discrimination, it would follow that cultural differences would not last long in the kind of society he recommends.

But we are not all profit maximizers, or at least we need not all be profit maximizers. The desire to maximize profit is not a fact about human beings as such. It is a fact about some human beings in some cultures. In some cultures a lot of people tend to be profit maximizers. In other cultures few people are. Efforts to stir economic development in certain parts of the world routinely run into this fact.

It may seem that people must be profit maximizers because they usually respond to economic incentives and constraints. This conclusion is mistaken. I admit that people usually respond to economic incentives and constraints. I also admit that people often act rationally when they respond to economic incentives. Money is a means to securing many ends, and since it is rational to seize the means to one's ends, it is usually rational for people to respond to economic incentives. It does not follow, however, that they are profit maximizers. This would follow if they sacrificed their other ends in order to maximize their profit. But in that case it would no longer be true that people acquire money as a means to securing their ends.

It may be argued that money tends to become an end itself because it is a means to so many ends. This argument must be taken seriously: Plato, Mill and Marx all seem to endorse it. Plato decided to call the third part of the soul the "money-loving" part because most of its "appetites" are "most easily satisfied by means of money."[23] Marx wrote that "money, since it has the property of purchasing everything, of appropriating objects to itself, is, therefore, the object par excellence."[24] And Mill postulated the general psychological principle that when a means like money is closely associated to the ends for which it is a means, it tends to become desired "as a part of the end itself."[25]

But these texts do not say that money inevitably replaces the ends for which it was originally a means. Mill simply observes that money *sometimes* replaces the ends for which it was originally a means. And read in context, the remarks of Plato and Marx suggest at most that in some societies money *tends* to become the dominant end of some people. Thus in Plato's ideal republic, only the members of the merchant or producing class of the city are money-lovers; the members of the soldiering and learned classes are lovers of honor and wisdom. And since Marx is speaking of capitalist society, it is also fair to assume that he is only saying that in the culture of that society is money the object *par excellence*.

Further, Plato and Marx are both mistaken insofar as they suggest that in a commercial society—the merchant class for Plato, and the capitalist society for Marx—everyone tends to become a money-lover. The proof of this is the persistence of racial discrimination in commercial societies. Thomas Sowell has long urged an infamous theory, invented by his mentor Milton Friedman, that the market will eliminate racial discrimination. I do not need to go into the details of this theory. Its central idea is that since people generally have to pay for indulging the taste for racial discrimination, in a free market, those who refrain from indulging that taste will save money.[26] Thus if most people were profit maximizers, racial discrimination would disappear in a free market. But racial discrimination has not disappeared even in commercial societies with relatively free markets.

Some theorists argue that there is profit in racial discrimination.[27] They are right. Racial discrimination helps to keep whites as a group better off than blacks as a group. But it does not follow that most people are profit maximizers. If people were profit maximizers they would not be concerned with maintaining such racial inequality. Each person would be concerned with maximizing his own profit, and this concern would lead to the disappearance of racial discrimination. So the fact that racial discrimination keeps whites as a group better off than blacks as a group shows that many people prefer something else to maximizing their profit. What they thus prefer is the hegemony of whites over blacks. But this preference—racism—is a cultural trait.

Let us now consider the Marxist version of economic determinism. It does not say that we are profit maximizers, but it says that economics determines culture. Marx and Engels think that this is obviously true. As they argue in "The German Ideology," "What they [individuals] are, therefore, coincides with their production, both with what they produce and with how they produce. The nature of individuals thus depends on the material conditions determining their production."[28] This argument has an aura of plausibility, but it begs the question. I concede that what people are—i.e., in large part the culture they have—has to fit in some sense with how they produce their means of subsistence. If it did not, they could not produce their means of subsistence and consequently would soon cease to exist. But this concession is not a concession to economic determinism. Even if our culture must fit with how we produce our means of subsistence, culture, not economics, may be ultimately determinant, since culture may determine just how we produce our means of subsistence. Of course, economic determinism denies this. It claims that how we produce our means of subsistence is somehow forced on us by the physical conditions in which we find ourselves. This is grotesquely false. Two different sets of people in the same environment need not produce their means of subsistence in the same way. Indeed they may produce their means of subsistence in radically different ways even when they are not subjected to any forces. In such case the differences in how they produce their means of subsistence will depend on their cultural differences.

Marx says, "The way in which men produce their means of subsistence depends first of all on the nature of the actual means of subsistence they find in existence and have to reproduce."[29] This passage may seem to suggest that he is not an economic determinist because it says that the way people produce their means of subsistence depends only "first of all," and so perhaps not entirely, on the "actual means of subsistence" people find in existence. But it underestimates the role of culture, too. Marx talks as if "the actual means of subsistence" is some kind of brute fact that is the same for people of all cultures. This is false. To some people pork is a means of subsistence; to others, it is taboo. To some oil is a sticky mess. To others it is a means to produce fertilizer and a million other things. And these differences depend on cultural differences.

Someone may protest that I appealed to something like the Marxist theory that economics determines culture when I argued that race, history and culture tend to coincide. This would be a misunderstanding. I argued that the races develop different cultures because they contend with different natural forces. This does not imply that material conditions or natural forces "determine" production or culture. Further, my argument is compatible with the notion that culture helps to steer production in one direction rather than another.

I maintain that, like the liberal version of economic determinism, the Marxist version of economic determinism is false, and therefore cannot prove that economic integration will inevitably lead to cultural assimilation. People can be integrated into the same economic system and yet remain culturally different. Indeed, their cultural differences will tend to influence the development of the economic system in different ways.

PLURALISM AND CONFLICT

The above conclusion suggests that different cultural groups in the same society are likely to come into conflict. This is the worry of some recent critics of multiculturalism. *The Disuniting of America: Reflections on a Multicultural Society* is the title of a recent book by Arthur M. Schlesinger Jr. This worry is not unfounded. Culture is not simply ethnic food and dress. These are only the superficial expressions of culture. Culture is the set of attitudes and beliefs, many inchoate and unarticulated, that lie behind judgments of right and wrong, of good and evil. Consequently, when different cultural groups live side by side in apparent peace, this may only be because they do not draw out the full implications of their cultural differences. If they did, they would probably come into strong disagreements about morality, law, education, politics and economics.

Du Bois was well aware of this danger. He was clear that not every culturally plural society is likely to be peaceful. If the cultural groups in a society disagreed on "territory, laws, language or even religion," he thought it was "manifest" that these people "cannot live in the same territory without fatal collision."[30] On the other hand, he believed that culturally different groups could live and thrive peacefully in the same society if certain conditions were satisfied. In his own words, "if ... there is substantial agreement in laws, language and religion; if there is satisfactory adjustment of economic life, then there is no reason why, in the same country and on the same street, two or three great national ideals might not thrive and develop, that men of different races might not strive together for their race ideals as well, perhaps even better, than in isolation."[31] The condition of a common language is especially important. If people can speak the same language, they can understand one another, and consequently are more likely to reach compromises that resolve their conflicts than if they cannot speak the same language and cannot understand one another.

But misunderstanding is not the only cause of conflict between groups. If different groups want the same thing, but cannot all have it, they may come into conflict even if they understand each other perfectly. Of course, the conflict need not erupt into open fighting. Weak or insecure groups may wisely decide not to press their claims; or if all groups are manifestly of equal strength, a stalemate may ensue. In such cases, however, the conflict is only temporarily submerged. Indeed, there are thinkers like Thomas Hobbes and Martin Delany who believe that people are likely to do what they think they ought to do only when this serves their interests. Such thinkers deny that people or groups of people are likely to avoid conflict just because they share a morality; they maintain that where the self-interests of people or groups conflict, only a fear of a loss to their self-interest will keep people or groups in peace. That was why Hobbes argued that people will be at peace only if they had a common power over them to keep them in awe, and why Delany argued that blacks will avoid white domination only when a powerful black nation arises to countervail the power of white nations.[32]

Du Bois certainly rejected the view that human beings are moved by moral considerations only when these considerations serve their interests. Consider, for example, his claim that every race has a "Talented Tenth" whose function is to teach the others how to live.[33] Since he meant that the "Talented Tenth" had to teach the others how to live morally, this would make no sense if people did not have the capacity to act outside of efforts to secure what they believe to be in their self-interest. Or consider that in the earlier part of Du Bois's career one of the crucial points that put him in opposition to Booker T. Washington was that he was a firm follower of Frederick Douglass's view that moral suasion of the white majority was an essential means to black elevation. Again, this would make no sense if people do not have the capacity to act other than to try to secure what they believe to be in their self-interest. It may be objected that after studying Marx, Du Bois lost confidence in moral suasion. But, as I will show, Du Bois only became more clear about the limits of moral suasion after studying Marx. Throughout his career he continued to believe that people could be moved by moral considerations, and moreover that such considerations do not merely track the autonomous development of the economic structure of societies as the Marxists maintain, but can actually direct that development.

But, of course, people can disagree bitterly and violently even if they are powerfully moved by moral considerations. Moral considerations do not always lead people to agree. On the contrary, because they can lead people to feel justified and righteous they may lead to especially intractable and violent disagreements. This can happen even when people share a common morality, but it is especially likely where people have different moralities. This seems to raise a particularly grave difficulty for Du Bois's claim that peaceful, culturally plural societies are possible, for he believed that different cultures embody different moralities.

But even groups that have different moralities can learn to resolve their conflicts in a mutually acceptable way; one of the groups may convert the other to its way of thinking, or both of them may change how they think and converge on the same set of moral principles and assumptions. Consequently, even if different cultural groups have different moralities, culturally plural societies need not be condemned to permanent conflict. But this bland conclusion conceals some of Du Bois's most interesting and controversial views on the nature of morality.

Unlike the moral relativists, Du Bois believed that moral principles are in some sense objective. Moral relativism says that, although the basic rules and assumptions of different cultural groups are likely to be different and indeed incompatible, all moralities are equally valid. Moral relativism does not say that morally based conflicts between different cultural groups are irreconcilable. It allows that such conflicts can be resolved because it allows that one group can persuade the other to share its moral views. When this happens, however, the relativist is committed to saying that all that has happened is that one group has changed its moral views. In particular, he is committed to denying that the group that has changed its moral views has learned anything truer or better. But Du Bois not only insisted that different cultural groups could learn from each other; he believed that they could learn something truer and better from each other. He spoke of this learning as bringing the world "nearer and nearer that perfection of human life for which we all long, that 'one far off Divine event.'"

Du Bois's conception of morality must also be distinguished from that of the moral pluralist, who also says that moral principles are objective. Moral pluralism maintains that there are several independent and equally basic moral principles. It is often contrasted with monistic theories which state that there is only one basic moral principle.[34] Now it may seem that a pluralistic moral theory can always be turned into a monistic theory by taking the various moral principles it claims to be basic, and using conjunctions to combine them into one principle. But moral pluralism says that this cannot be done because moral principles are not only independent and equally basic, but also often incompatible. There are many different kinds of moral pluralism, but the kind that concerns us here emphasizes the deep differences and incompatibilities between the moralities of different cultures taken as a whole. The major contemporary defender of this view is Isaiah Berlin. Following Machiavelli, Vico and Herder, Berlin insists that, though "objective," the values of different cultures differ "in some profound, irreconcilable ways, not combinable in any final synthesis."[35]

Berlin's moral pluralism greatly resembles the moral pluralism of William James, who, as I noted earlier, was Du Bois's favorite teacher at Harvard. James insists that ultimate moral principles are plural. "The elementary forces in ethics," he writes, "are probably as plural as those of physics are. The various ideals have no common character apart from the fact that they are ideals."[36] And like Berlin, he believes that the search for a synthesis of moral principles is a dangerous undertaking. Berlin rejects the very idea of such a synthesis as "conceptually incoherent," and describes the search for it ominously as the search for a "final solution."[37] James the pragmatist is characteristically more flexible. He thinks that the only "path of peace" for mankind is the continual invention of ways to satisfy an ever widening array of ideals and principles.[38] But, though he is clear that this is an overall improvement, he is equally clear that it is nevertheless always "tragic" because along the way, some ideals must always be "butchered."[39]

Du Bois's view of morality differs from those of both James and Berlin. He does not reject the very idea of a final synthesis of moral principles. On the contrary, he hailed the synthesis of the moralities of different cultures as that "perfection of human life" and that "one far off Divine event" which he believed to be the goal of history. Nor does this language suggest that he thought that such a synthesis must be tragic. It is true that he claimed that American blacks each had a "double self," and were confused by the "contradiction of double aims."[40] But he only said that these aims were "unreconciled;" he never said that they were irreconcilable.[41] Further, he spoke positively of the American Negro's longing to "merge his double self into a better and truer self," and urged the development of Negro "traits and talents" so that "some day on American soil two world-races may give each to each those characteristics both so sadly lack."[42]

Berlin describes the view that moral principle can be synthesized as the rationalistic and the Platonic.[43] Du Bois's moral theory is rationalistic to the extent that it refuses to countenance the possibility that valid moral principles could be incompatible. But it is not Platonic or even rationalistic in any stronger sense. Du Bois believed that moral truths are discovered as a people reflects on its particular historical experiences. It was this that sustained his insistence that different peoples discover different moral truths. If he believed that morality was rationalistic in the sense of being an a priori discipline like mathematics, he could not have been so insistent. Kant also argued that peoples only come to appreciate moral truths as a result of their historical experiences. But his view was that "reason could have suggested" these moral truths to people "even without so many sad experiences."[44] Du Bois's view of morality was not rationalistic in this weaker sense either. He followed his teacher James in holding that experience was absolutely necessary if moral principles were going to be discovered, and consequently, as James put it, that ethics must to some extent "wait on the facts."[45]

It is particularly illuminating to compare Du Bois's claim that every culture contains important and distinctive moral insights with Mill's arguments in favor of experiments in living set out in *On Liberty*. In that work Mill maintains that unless people harm others they should be allowed to live as they choose. Some of his arguments justify only toleration. I have in mind the passage where he says that a person's "own mode of laying out his existence is best, not because it is best in itself, but because it is his own mode."[46] But Mill's well-known "experiments in living" argument stresses that allowing others to live as they please can contribute to the discovery of a way to live that is objectively best. Thus Mill wrote that "it is important to give the freest scope to uncustomary things, in order that it may in time appear which of these are fit to be converted into customs."[47]

Mill's argument on the value of experiments in living may not seem easily applicable to Du Bois's theory that there are probably objectively valid principles in the morality of every culture. Mill's argument was that freethinkers, eccentrics and intellectuals should be permitted to conduct their experiments in living. But freethinkers, eccentrics and intellectuals are not cultural groups. How then can his argument support Du Bois's theory? The main idea is that cultures are experiments in living. They are, of course, not so in every sense. In an experiment proper someone deliberately puts certain things together in order to see what will happen. A society is not an experiment in that strict sense. Although a society is made up of institutions and practices, no one deliberately puts every element of these together, not even Plato's philosopher kings. Further, although people may deliberately make changes in their institutions and practices, they do not usually do so just to see what will happen. They do so because they believe that the changes will make their lives better. Still, it is useful to think of a society as kind of experiment, for people do learn from the results of the changes that are introduced, and on that basis they introduce further changes, if they are able.

It may be objected that few cultures have encouraged experiments in living, but I doubt that any culture has succeeded in altogether suppressing human inventiveness. Further, as I noted earlier, cultures are always the products of long evolutions. This compensates for the tendency of cultures to suppress experiments in living.

But there is an important gap in the argument. Since the members of a culture persist over many generations, and a people that persists over many generations must have followed at least some elementary moral principles, it is a safe bet that every culture will have some elementary moral principles embedded in its mores and customs. But these principles—for example, that children have to be educated and violence restrained—are likely to be the same for all cultures, and Du Bois's claim is that every culture has hit on some distinctive and valuable moral insight. The view that ethics is an experimental science does not easily support this claim. Recall that according to that view, people cannot hope to find out how to live by thinking more carefully about the implications of self-evident moral principle; they must guess and experiment. Now, suppose that they guess wrong; the further evolution of their culture may very well be an elaborate compounding of their initial error.

It may be objected that they will quickly discover their mistake because in effect they put their guesses about how to live to the test of experiment. But this is not the way that experiment works. There is no such thing as a decisive experiment. Even if the results of an experiment seem to confute a conjecture, observers with an interest in the conjecture being true can always maintain its truth by inventing saving hypotheses. This has happened many times in the history of the physical and social sciences. If ethics is indeed an experimental science it is likely to be even more common there, given the scope and complexity of ethics, and the interests people obviously have in some ethical system being true rather than others.

No one who has read Rousseau's "Discourse on the Origin of Inequality" can fail to be impressed with the terrible possibility, and indeed likelihood, that having made one bad guess about how to live, a people may spend the rest of its history in ever more tortuous, immoral and unsuccessful attempts to justify or cover up its original mistake. And it cannot be argued that through dissenters like Rousseau even bad cultures will have something to teach other cultures, for really bad cultures will have suppressed dissent.

The difficulties I have pointed to afflict all experimental sciences. The only way to offset them is to have a class of educated, independent scientists who are free to express their views about the results of experiments. This is the way Mill solved the analogous difficulty that the experiments in living he urged might not be properly interpreted. He was clear that while experiments in living may turn up innovations that are better than the customs in force, they may also turn up, and are perhaps more likely to turn up, innovations that are worse. If people tended to imitate bad innovations, encouraging experiments in living could be counterproductive. Mill avoided this difficulty partly on the ground that "the average man" tended to imitate good innovations rather than wicked ones when he had the alternatives clearly before him. But he also maintained that the average man needed an intellectual and moral elite to conduct experiments in living and to set the alternatives clearly before him.[48]

Du Bois also appealed to an intellectual and moral elite to solve the difficulty that cultures may not produce important and valuable insights on how to live. He believed that in every race, which is to say, in every cultural group, there were a number of gifted people— the "Talented Tenth"—who have the function and duty to teach the remaining ninety percent "how to live," or the "meaning of life."[49] This Talented Tenth is analogous to Mill's intellectual elite, whose function it is conduct experiments in living and to judge if they reveal better ways to life that the majority should be persuaded to adopt.[50] But the analogy is importantly imperfect. Mill thought that only the experiments in living conducted by the elite could throw up useful ideas about how to live. Du Bois thought that the experiments in living conducted by common people were possible sources of insight for the Talented Tenth. With that proviso, the roles of the Talented Tenth and Mill's intellectual elite are remarkably similar. Du Bois's idea seemed to be that although every culture contains important moral insights, every culture can also contain false views on how to live, and the valid insights can be undeveloped and inchoate. To separate the wheat from the chaff, and to find and develop these insights, the Talented Tenth had to examine the culture of their group, to reflect on it, and to sift through it. Otherwise, the ninety percent could be corrupted by the inevitable flaws and blind alleys in their own culture.

Now, Du Bois believed that in the natural order of things every cultural group had an elite to teach it better—its Talented Tenth—although this natural order could be interrupted by outside interferences.[51] He could therefore consistently argue that in every culture that is autonomous a set of traditional practices and institutions develops that can be fairly described as tested by experience, and as improved in the light of that experience. This does not imply that every culture is all good simply because it has survived.[52] But it does suggest that Du Bois had well-considered grounds for claiming that there are probably some objectively valid principles in the morality of every culture.[53]

The above discussion emphasizes the role of experience in the elaboration of a morality. But the elaboration of a complete morality is also, of course, partly philosophical. The Talented Tenth must have criteria for choosing among the innovations thrown up by experiments in living, and the discovery or construction of such criteria is a philosophical task. That Du Bois would have concurred is evident from his criticism of the social policies Booker T. Washington recommended.[54] I take this criticism to be an example of Du Bois's view of the work of the Talented Tenth. Washington urged, famously, that black people should pursue economic security by acquiring technical skills and deemphasizing higher education and agitation for political rights. Du Bois objected that this strategy was likely to leave blacks in poverty because no people could advance economically if its political rights were not secure. This objection is open to challenge. It may be argued that groups like the Jews have advanced economically while their political and civil rights were being violated, though it could be argued in Du Bois's favor that such groups were never economically secure. But Du Bois had a second and more philosophical argument against Washington. He argued that even if Washington's strategy enabled blacks to become well off, it would fail more generally because it would make them into money-makers. And his criticism of the life of the money-maker is philosophical. He believed that a money-maker—presumably someone whose main aim in life is to become wealthy or economically secure—was certain to be dishonest, and that in any case his life was likely to be poor, even if we consider only his pleasure.

But teaching the ninety percent of their own cultural group how to live was only half the work of the Talented Tenth. The other half of their work was to share with other cultural groups the insights they had sifted and developed

out of the raw material of their own culture. This work was partly philosophical. Different cultures employ different concepts, and in extreme cases
comprise different conceptual worlds. There is no a priori reason to believe
that all such worlds are equal in any or all respects. Some may enable us to
organize experience and understand each other better than others, or more
likely, each may have some advantages, and yet be deficient in other ways.
One of the great contributions a diversity of cultures can offer to a complete
theory of morality is the opportunity for a philosophical exploration of their
different conceptual worlds. Still, the work of the Talented Tenth also relies on
the experience of average people. The conceptual worlds that they study are
the product of average people experimenting with ways of thinking and living.

THE TALENTED TENTH

It is fair to ask why Du Bois thought that black people would become money
makers if they were only taught the technical skills necessary to get a job and
earn a living. Washington did not recommend that black people devote all their
time and effort to becoming rich, and he did not think less of morality than did
Du Bois. Indeed, part of his argument for blacks learning technical skills that
would get them jobs was that steady honest and skilled work was moralizing.[55]
On this point he was certainly right. To become moral we need to develop
dispositions to behave morally, and steady, skilled, responsible work is surely
among the most important ways in which we develop such dispositions. But
Du Bois agreed that such work was necessary for moral improvement.[56] The
issue between him and Washington was over whether it was sufficient for
moral improvement. Washington seemed to think that it was. Du Bois maintained that the teachings of a Talented Tenth were also necessary.

Work cannot be sufficient for moral improvement because not all work is
moralizing. Mindless, repetitive, back-breaking work, work that leaves no
time for leisure or for reflection, is demoralizing. I think Washington knew
this. That was why he wanted blacks to become skilled. But he did not see that
society tends to change so that many people become confined to such work.
First, as Adam Smith noted famously, people are led as by invisible hands to
an ever increasing division of labor; and one usual result of an increasing division of labor is that some work is mindless, repetitive, and intellectually stulti-
fying. Second, as Rousseau emphasized, once a division of labor is introduced,
large economic inequalities tend to emerge,[57] and large economic inequalities
lead to the less well-off being confined to mindless, repetitive, mind crippling
work, while the very rich often do not work at all.

Political philosophers who understand that society tends to change spontaneously in ways that can be degrading for the majority usually also argue that
an elite should design, or at least control, society to prevent such changes.

Plato is the most famous example of such a philosopher. One may suppose that Marx is the exception, but he is not. Marx implies that an elite, who in his view form the Communist Party, would have to control the economy in a socialist society to prevent a relapse into the degradation of capitalism. Of course, he also predicts that at some point the majority could be trusted to run things, but he has no theory to justify this prediction. Mill spelled out, far more clearly than Marx, the implications and advantages of participatory democracy; but he was just as anxious to find ways to ensure that the wise few got a privileged hearing. Indeed, for Mill, the justification of participatory democracy is not that the masses have any insights to offer about how things should be run, but that the activity of participating will help to make them better people. Finally, even Rousseau, to whom we tend to turn to for extreme egalitarian measures, makes his concession to the wisdom of the few. For in Rousseau's hands, though the laws must be ratified by the people, they must be devised by the wise legislator.[58]

Du Bois's theory of the Talented Tenth differs from these concessions to wisdom. He never argued that the Talented Tenth should control the economy. He argued that the Talented Tenth should teach the majority. At first he seemed to think that this teaching could be successful despite the corrupting influence of the kind of work the majority had to do. This has not been a popular position in the history of political philosophy, but it was upheld by at least two famous philosophers: Socrates and John Locke.

Socrates tried to teach his fellow citizens how to live, just as Du Bois thought the Talented Tenth had to teach the masses. Socrates thought that this strategy for moral improvement would work because he had an extremely intellectualized conception of moral motivation. Du Bois's position was different. Here it is more illuminating to compare him to Locke. Locke understood that the economy tends naturally to the degradation of the majority.[59] Here he anticipated both Marx and Adam Smith. The big difference between these three philosophers is that while Marx railed against the degradation of the majority, and Adam Smith worried about it, Locke accepted it. Locke's theory of justice implied that unless the economy is designed and controlled in a way that violates principles of justice, large economic inequalities are likely to arise through a series of transactions each of which is perfectly just. Assuming that justice is the first virtue of societies, which should not be violated for other concerns, it follows that manipulating the economy to prevent the degradation of the majority may be wrong. In this eventuality, the only legitimate way left to prevent the degradation of the majority was for the elite to teach it its moral lessons.

At first Du Bois seemed to envisage a similar role for the Talented Tenth. He did not embrace Locke's theory of justice; certainly he would not have objected to designing the economy so as to prevent the emergence of large inequalities that degrade the poor. Perhaps he fell back on Locke's idea that the elite had to save the majority by teaching it as a temporary expedient because he saw no prospects of the black Talented Tenth's controlling the black community.

When he wrote *Dusk of Dawn* in 1940, however, he was absolutely clear that the economy had to be intelligently designed and controlled to make people better morally. Of course the black Talented Tenth had no more power to control the economy blacks faced in 1940 than they did in 1903, but Du Bois thought that this problem could be solved.[60]

One reason for his optimism was that continued racial segregation had forced blacks into an economy that was to some degree separate from the larger economy. Du Bois saw this as a opportunity for reforming the economy of the black community. As he put it, "We are now segregated largely without reason. Let us put reason and power beneath this segregation."[61] His theory must be distinguished from that of Booker T. Washington, who saw segregation as an opportunity to develop Black Capitalism. Du Bois rejected this proposal because his study of Marx had led him to the conclusion that capitalism was corrupting. He saw segregation as an opportunity to develop a cooperative black economy. "Rail if you will against the race segregation here involved and condoned," Du Bois wrote, "but take advantage of it by planting secure centers of Negro co-operative effort."[62]

Although Du Bois was persuaded and deeply impressed by much of Marx's social theory, he had reservations about some of its crucial aspects. In particular, he denied that it could fully explain racial oppression in the United States. As he put it, "the Marxian philosophy is a true diagnosis of the situation in Europe in the middle of the 19th Century. . . . But it must be modified in the United States of America and especially so far as the Negro group is concerned."[63] The main problem was that the working class in America was not uniting, as the Marxian philosophy predicted it would. Indeed, Du Bois maintained that there was not "the slightest indication that a Marxian revolution based on a united class-conscious proletariat is anywhere on the American far horizon."[64] In Du Bois's view, part of the reason for the disunity of the working class was the "large development of a petty bourgeoisie within the American working class."[65] Another closely related reason was the relentless racism of the white workers which kept black workers out of labor unions and in the worst jobs. Particularly disturbing about this latter development was that it was not due to ignorance. The exclusion of blacks by the white working class was motivated by material self-interest and was perfectly rational given that end. As Du Bois put it, "the bulk of American white labor is neither ignorant or fanatical. It knows exactly what it is doing and means to do it."[66]

This presented Du Bois with a dilemma. On the one hand, he was convinced by Marx's arguments that capitalism was moribund and corrupting. On the other hand, he could not follow Marx in assigning leadership to the working class in the declining days of capitalism because the working class was dominated by the white working class, and the white working class was racist and materialistic. Du Bois thought that his theory of cultural pluralism showed the way out of this dilemma. A cooperative society pioneered by the African American community could, he argued, lead the world out of the chaos of the collapsing capitalistic system. Its example would be the gift of American blacks to world civilization, and the vindication of his case for cultural pluralism. "The emotional wealth of the American Negro, the nascent art in song, dance, and drama can all be applied," he wrote, "not to amuse the white audience, but to inspire and direct the acting Negro group itself. I can conceive no more magnificent nor promising crusade in modern times. We have a chance here to teach industrial and cultural democracy to a world that bitterly needs it."[67]

Du Bois knew that history had no mechanism to assure that leadership would fall to the group that would use it best. In particular he understood that blacks might fail to create a cooperative society because they could yield to the temptation to enter into, or to imitate the doomed capitalistic system of white society. This was another reason why he saw segregation as in some ways a blessing: it effectively prevented blacks from fully merging into and accepting the decaying and corrupting capitalist system of white society.[68]

But what about the temptation to imitate white capitalism, and to reproduce capitalism within the black community—the temptation to which Washington yielded so completely? Du Bois believed that the special work of the black Talented Tenth was to prevent this from happening. He understood that they had no power at their disposal, and that they would have to depend on persuasion. But he thought this was for the best. "A nation," he admitted, can depend on force to implement a "co-operative commonwealth." But "in the long run force defeats itself. It is only the consensus of the intelligent men of good will in a community and in a state that can really carry out a great program with absolute and ultimate authority. And by that same token, without the authority of the state, without force of police and army."[69] So although Du Bois came to see that the moral salvation of the people depends on the intelligent control of the economy, he also continued to believe that the Talented Tenth could persuade the people to change their economy for their own moral salvation. His distance from Plato therefore remains. Education, not power, is the master key to moral salvation. In the end the Talented Tenth must teach the majority. Thus, speaking of "the mass of people" who may not accept the cooperative idea, Du Bois wrote, "these people . . . must be taught.

They must be taught in long and lingering conference, in careful marshalling of facts, in the willingness to come to decision slowly and the determination not to tyrannize over minorities.... They must be patiently taught to understand."[70]

Du Bois had two reasons for believing that the Talented Tenth could succeed in its mission. The first was that there was no powerful and entrenched capitalist class in the black community to counter its teachings. The second reason is more provocative. Rightly or wrongly Du Bois believed that African culture was communalistic. Given his view, already mentioned, that culture was remarkably persistent, he therefore believed that American blacks had latent dispositions to be cooperators. The echoes and basic impulses of their communal African past lingered, partly because of the inertia of culture, and partly because of segregation and outside threats. In the African communal group, he wrote,

> ties of family and blood, of mother and child, of group relationship, made the group leadership strong.... In the case of the more artificial group among American Negroes, there are sources of strength in common memories of suffering in the past; in present threats of degradation and extinction; in common ambitions and ideals; in emulation and the determination to prove ability and desert. Here in subtle but real ways the communalism of the African clan can be transferred to the Negro American group.[71]

This gave him hope that the teachings of the black Talented Tenth would not fall on deaf ears. He was no cockeyed optimist. It will be, he admitted, "a real battle. There are chances of failure." But, "there are also splendid chances of success."[72]

CONCLUSION

I have tried, mainly, to present and clarify Du Bois's theory. But clearly Du Bois raises many questions. I am wary of his view that individuals are duty bound to reject assimilation, though I am aware that the issue is debatable, and I doubt that his reliance on moral suasion is justified. Appiah would surely object that the cultural unity of Africa it appears to rely on is false. Orthodox Marxists will also surely object to his reservations about the proletariat being the best class to lead the society when capitalism collapses: they are clear that the proletariat will destroy capitalism, and that it then will and ought to lead society. I share Du Bois's reservations on this point. Marx's arguments that capitalism will inevitably collapse deserve serious attention, whether or not they prove ultimately to be sound. But he gave no arguments that deserve serious attention to support his further claims that after the collapse of capitalism the proletariat would inevitably take over leadership of the society and, moreover, that it ought to do so. Du Bois's opposing view is therefore salutary. It reminds us that history is not programmed to bring about our good, but at best gives us opportunities that we can take advantage of to secure our good.

Orthodox Marxism can, however, raise a more serious objection to Du Bois's theory. Du Bois proposed that the Black Talented Tenth should persuade the black community to skip the capitalist stage and develop a cooperative economy. There is a tradition in Marxist thought to support this proposal, started by Marx himself. Toward the end of his life, Marx suggested that Russia could skip the capitalist stage of society and build communism directly using the communitarian village system as a basis. But orthodox Marxism takes the view that no society can skip capitalism on its way to communism. This view is summarized in Marx's claim that "the country that is more advanced industrially only shows, to the less advanced, the image of its future."[73] The main argument in favor of this view is that conditions must be ripe for communism to be possible, and that they ripen only in capitalism. The history of attempts to skip the stage of capitalism and to establish socialism in underdeveloped economies suggest that this argument may be sound. If this is indeed the case, Du Bois's proposal seems to have been a mistake.

A related mistake vitiated the original version of his theory of cultural pluralism. That version suggested that the Talented Tenth could teach and educate the masses even if the economy kept them unemployed, poor and miserable. Later on, when Du Bois came to more fully appreciate that a capitalist economy could be corrupting, he proposed that the Talented Tenth persuade the black community to set up a noncorrupting cooperative economy. But if the material conditions were not ripe for such an economy, the second proposal was hardly advance on the first. Both of them underestimated the power of the economy to corrupt even the teachers.

When he was an old man of eighty-three, Du Bois admitted this sadly: "The majority of the American Negro intelligentsia. . ." he wrote, "shows symptoms of following in the footsteps of western acquisitive society, with its exploitation of labor, monopoly of land and its resources, and with private profit for the smart and unscrupulous in a world of poverty disease, and ignorance, as the natural end of human culture." As he also admitted, he had hoped that this temptation would be countered by an "inner Negro cultural ideal . . . built on ancient African communism, supported and developed by memory of slavery and experience of caste, which would drive the Negro group into a spiritual unity precluding the development of economic classes and inner class struggle." But this was not to be. The "loosening of outer discriminatory pressures," he lamented, only allowed blacks to "ape the worst of American and Anglo-Saxon chauvinism, luxury, showing off, and social climbing."[74]

But a part of his theory remains intact. Material conditions may place limits on what the Talented Tenth can do: the Talented Tenth cannot make the majority moral in impossible conditions, and it cannot cause society to skip stages. But material conditions are never sufficient to make people moral or to usher in new and better forms of society. They may make such developments possible, but some class or group must make them actual. Although the Talented Tenth are certainly not incorruptible, Du Bois's theory is correct that, when they are democratically restrained, they are humanity's best bet to bring about better societies and higher moralities—as soon as material conditions make this possible. To oppose this is to deny that art and intelligence are necessary for moral improvement, and to indulge in the wishful thinking that humanity will blunder into utopia. Du Bois's theory is not an objectionable form of elitism. As I have emphasized, he insisted that the Talented Tenth not have the power to make people change the ways in which they lived.[75] He thought that it was better that they influence others simply by their teaching. If this is objectionable elitism then so was Socrates's mission to educate his fellow citizens. One last possible objection is that Du Bois was wrong to conjecture that the elaboration of a complete morality is a democratic process which depends on the input of all cultural groups. But the egalitarianism that grounds this conjecture is a warning that we must never abandon it.

NOTES

1. Good discussions of Schmoller and his school are in Henry William Spiegel, *The Growth of Economic Thought*, (Durham: Duke University Press, 1991), 424–27, and, in greater detail, Joseph Schumpeter, *History of Economic Analysis* (New York: Oxford University Press, 1954).

2. W. E. B. Du Bois, "The Study of the Negro Problems," in W. E. B. Du Bois, *The Seventh Son: The Thought and Writings of W. E. B. Du Bois*, ed. Julius Lester (New York: Vintage Books, 1971) I: 229–47.

3. Du Bois, "Negro Problems," 241, 229.

4. Du Bois, "The Conservation of Races," in *The Seventh Son*, I: 176–87

5. Du Bois, "The Conservation of Races," 176.

6. Du Bois, "The Conservation of Races," 176, 177.

7. William James, "Great Men and their Environment," in William James, *The Will to Believe and Other Essays in Popular Philosophy* (Dover Books, 1956), 244.

8. James, "Great Men and their Environment," 244.

9. William James, "Pragmatism and Humanism," in *The Moral Philosophy of William James*, ed. John K. Roth (New York: Thomas Y. Crowell Company, 1969) 318.

10. James, "Pragmatism and Humanism," 318.

11. Du Bois, "The Conservation of Races," 178.

12. Du Bois, "The Conservation of Races," 178.

13. Du Bois, "The Conservation of Races," 178.

14. This point is, of course, repeated in Du Bois' works.

15. Du Bois had another reason for being wary of cultural assimilation. He worried that it would encourage blacks to be servile and imitative. Their destiny, he wrote, is not a "servile imitation of Anglo-Saxon culture," but a "stalwart originality which shall unswervingly follow Negro ideals."

16. Anthony Appiah, "The Uncompleted Argument: Du Bois and the Illusion of Race," in *"Race," Writing and Difference*, ed. Henry Louis Gates, Jr., 21–37. Houston A. Baker's "Caliban's Triple Play," 381–95 in the same volume, is a response. The debate was continued in Anthony Appiah's "The Conservation of 'Race,'" in *Black American Literature Forum* 23 (Spring 1989): 37–60. Particularly useful discussions are Tommy Lott, "Du Bois on the Invention of Race," *The Philosophical Forum*, 24, 1–3, (Fall–Spring 1992–93): 166–87, and Lucius Outlaw, "On W. E. B. Du Bois's 'The Conservation of Races'" in this volume. Much of Appiah's original essay is reprinted as Chapter 2, "Illusions of Race," in Kwame Anthony Appiah, *In My Father's House* (New York: Oxford University Press, 1992).

17. See the essays "Of the Faith of the Fathers" and "The Sorrow Songs," in *The Souls of Black Folk*, ed. John Edgar Wideman (New York: Vintage Books, 1990).

18. Forty years later, Du Bois conceived of races as biological categories. But while he called for racial unity, he still did so on the ground that races were also culturally distinctive, rejecting the idea that there were significant biological differences between the races. See "The Revelation of Saint Orgne the Damned," in *The Education of Black People: Ten Critiques 1906–1960*, ed. Herbert Aptheker (New York: Monthly Review Press, 1973), especially 121, where he says, "There are certainly no biological races in the sense of people with large groups of unvarying inherited gifts and instincts thus set apart by nature as eternally separate," and 125, where he argues that "through cooperation, education and understanding the cultural race unit may be the pipe line through which human civilization may extend to wider and wider areas to the fertilization of mankind."

19. Du Bois, "The Conservation of Races," 177.

20. Jean-Jacques Rousseau, "Discourse on Inequality," in Jean-Jacques Rousseau, *The First and Second Discourses*, ed. Victor Gourevitch (New York: Harper Torch Books, 1986), 166.

21. Du Bois, "The Conservation of Races," 177.

22. See George Stigler, "Economics or Ethics?" in *Tanner Lectures on Human Values*, ed. S. Murrin (Cambridge: Cambridge University Press, 1981), 2: 188.

23. Plato, *The Republic*, trans. G. M. A. Grube (Indianapolis: Hackett Publishing Company 1974), 581A.

24. Karl Marx, *Early Writings*, trans. and ed. T. B. Bottomore (New York: McGraw Hill, 1963), 189, 190.

25. J. S. Mill, "Utilitarianism", in J. S. Mill, *Utilitarianism, Liberty and Representative Government*, (New York: E. P. Dutton, 1951), 45.

26. Thomas Sowell, *Race and Economics* (New York: David McKay, 1975), 165.

27. See Sowell, *Race and Economics*.

28. "The German Ideology," in *Karl Marx: Selected Writings*, ed. David McLellan (Oxford: Oxford University Press, 1977), 161.

29. Marx, "The German Ideology," 161.

30. W. E. B. Du Bois "The Conservation of Races," in *The Seventh Son*, I: 182.

31. Du Bois, "The Conservation of Races," 182.

32. The case of Hobbes is well known. See Chapter 13 in Thomas Hobbes, *Leviathan*, ed.

Michael Oakeshott (Oxford: Basil Blackwell, 1947). Delany's theories are presented in *The Condition, Elevation, Emigration and Destiny of the Colored People of the United States* (Salem, Mass.: Ayer Publishing Company, 1988). I have discussed the case of Delany and his relation to Hobbes in "Two Traditions in African American Political Philosophy," *The Philosophical Forum* 24, nos. 1–3 (fall–spring 1992–1993).

33. W. E. B. Du Bois, "The Talented Tenth," in *The Seventh Son*, I: 385.

34. The paradigmatic example of a pluralistic theory is the theory of W. D. Ross. A good example of a monistic theory is the act utilitarianism of Henry Sidgwick or J. J. C. Smart. See W. D. Ross, *The Right and the Good* (Oxford: Clarendon Press, 1930); Henry Sidgwick, *The Methods of Ethics*, 7th ed. (Indianapolis: Hackett Publishing Company, 1981); and J. J. C. Smart and Bernard Williams, *Utilitarianism: Far and Against* (Cambridge: Cambridge University Press, 1973). For general discussion, see Thomas E. Hill, Jr., "Kantian Pluralism," in *Ethics*, 102, no. 4 (July 1992): 743–62.

35. Isaiah Berlin, "The Pursuit of the Ideal," in Isaiah Berlin, *The Crooked Timber of Humanity* (New York: Vintage Books, 1992), 10.

36. William James, "The Moral Philosopher and the Moral Life," in *The Moral Philosophy of William James*, ed. John K. Roth (New York: Thomas Y. Crowell Company, 1969), 181.

37. Berlin, "The Pursuit of the Ideal," 13, 15.

38. James, "The Moral Philosopher and the Moral Life," 184.

39. James, "The Moral Philosopher and the Moral Life," 185, 182, 183.

40. Du Bois, "Of Our Spiritual Strivings," in *The Souls of Black* Folk, 9.

41. Du Bois, "Of Our Spiritual Strivings," 10.

42. Du Bois, "Of Our Spiritual Strivings," 9, 14.

43. Berlin, "The Pursuit of the Ideal," 5, 6.

44. Immanuel Kant, "Idea for a Universal History," in *Kant's Political Writings*, ed. Hans Reiss (Cambridge: Cambridge University Press, 1991), 47.

45. James, "The Moral Philosopher and the Moral Life," 186–7.

46. J. S. Mill, *On Liberty and Other Writings* (Cambridge: Cambridge University Press, 1989), 67.

47. Mill, *On Liberty and Other Writings*, 67.

48. Mill, *On Liberty and Other Writings*, 66.

49. See "The Talented Tenth," in *The Second Son*, 381. Other strikingly elitist essays are "Of the Wings of Atalanta," and "Of the Training of Black Men," in *The Souls of Black Folk.*

50. See "The Talented Tenth," 386.

51. Du Bois was well aware of the mistake that supposes that those that survive—the fit— are necessarily the best. See "Of the Sons of Master and Man," in *The Souls of Black Folk*, 119, 120.

52. This point is made eloquently in "Of the Training of Black Men," in *The Souls of Black Folk*, 82. Du Bois extended it in a defense of democracy. See "The Revelation of Saint Orgne," 119, where he says that "life as any man has lived it, is part of that great reservoir of knowledge without use of which no government can do justice."

53. See "Of Mr. Booker T. Washington and Others" in Lester, I: 354–66.

54. See his comments in "Development Since Emancipation," in *The Negro and the South*, ed. Herbert Aptheker (New York: Carol Publishing Co. 1970), 73.

55. "Education and Work" in Lester, I: 574–575.

56. "Second Discourse" in Jean-Jacques Rousseau, *The First and Second Discourses and Essay on the Origin of Languages* ed., trans. and annotated Victor Gourevitch (New York: Harper Torchbooks 1986), 179.

57. J. J. Rousseau, *The Social Contract and Discourses*, trans. G.D.H. Cole, (New York: Dutton & Co, 1950), Book II, Chapter 7, 41.

58. See, for example, John Locke, *Essay Concerning Human Understanding* (Oxford: Oxford University Press, 1975), 707–708.

59. Du Bois's endorsement of the leadership of a Talented Tenth was more qualified in 1940 than in 1903. See, for example, "The Immortal Child," in Du Bois, *Darkwater* (New York: Kaus, 1975), 193–217. But, as will be clear, the endorsement persisted in *Dusk of Dawn.*

60. W. E. B. Du Bois, *Dusk of Dawn*, (New York: Schocken Books, 1940), 215.

61. Du Bois, *Dusk of Dawn*, 215.

62. Du Bois, "Marxism and the Negro Problem" in *The Second Son*, II: 295.

63. Du Bois, "Marxism and the Negro Problem," 295.

64. Du Bois, "Marxism and the Negro Problem," 295.

65. Du Bois, "Marxism and the Negro Problem," 295.

66. Du Bois, "Dusk of Dawn," 219.

67. Du Bois, "Dusk of Dawn," 190.

68. Du Bois, "Dusk of Dawn," 220.

69. Du Bois, "Dusk of Dawn," 213.

70. Du Bois, "Dusk of Dawn," 219.

71. Du Bois, "Dusk of Dawn," 219.

72. Karl Marx, *Capital* (New York: International Publishers, 1987) I: 8–9. Marx explicitly denies that a society can "clear by bold leaps" the "successive phases of its normal development."

73. W. E. B. Du Bois, *The Autobiography of W. E. B. Du Bois* (New York: International Publishers, 1963), 392–393.

74. Early in his career, Du Bois had some Millian reservations about democracy for "undeveloped people." See, for example, "Of the Sons of Master and Man," in *The Souls of Black Folk,* 128. By the time he wrote *Darkwater*, however, he was an uncompromising democrat. See "Of the Ruling of Men," in *Darkwater*, 134–59.

Genealogical Shifts in Du Bois's Discourse on Double Consciousness as the Sign of African American Difference

4

Bernard W. Bell

How valid and viable today is W. E. B. Du Bois's nineteenth-century discourse on double consciousness as the sign of African American racial and cultural difference? Had Du Bois "considered the issue of gender," states historian Darlene Clark Hines, "instead of writing, 'One ever feels his twoness,' he would have mused about how one ever feels her 'fiveness': Negro, American, woman, poor, black woman."[1] Prominent white feminists like Catherine MacKinnon and black feminists like bell hooks contend that patriarchy is the central problem in the social construction of contemporary human identities. Clearly, inquiries into processes of subject construction and the politics of differences, as critic Joan W. Scott reminds us, should examine "the relationships between discourse, cognition, and reality, the relevance of the position or situatedness of subjects to the knowledge they produce and the effects of difference on knowledge."[2] Although race, ethnicity, gender, and class are interrelated major forces in the construction of human subjects, history has vindicated Du Bois's prediction that the problem of the twentieth century is the problem of the color line. Contemporary global ethnic conflicts also suggest that the correlative problem or sign of double consciousness will be central to identity formations in the twenty-first century.

Although sensitive in different degrees to the historical representation of the black subject as male, Ralph Ellison, Larry Neal, Robert Stepto, Berndt Ostendorf, Henry Louis Gates, Jr., Mary Helen Washington, Barbara Johnson, and this author are but a few of the many artists, scholars, and critics who have reformulated the rhetoric, dialectics, and dialogics of Du Bois's double consciousness to map the quest in contemporary literary criticism for a truth that acknowledges and synthesizes the souls and art of black folk.[3] As a student of Sterling A. Brown and an African American revisionist theorist of the relationship between vernacular and literary traditions, I will not, however, in this essay focus exclusively on Du Bois's contemporary impact on cultural studies, critics, and workers. Rather, I will first trace the historical origins and discursive shifts in Du Bois's ideological construction of double consciousness as the sign of African American racial and ethnic difference. Secondly, I will analyze its dialectic and dialogic use as a theme and trope in two of his earliest narratives in which the protagonists are represented as "epitomized expressions" of African Americans: the unpublished "A Fellow of Harvard," and the published "Of the Coming of John."

Since Aristotle's *Rhetoric*, Plato's *Phaedrus* and *Gorgias* and, more recently, Bakhtin's *The Dialogic Imagination*, the distinction between rhetorical, dialectical, and dialogical discourse have been a topic of contention among their different advocates. In "Dialogics as an Art of Discourse in Literary Criticism," Don Bialostosky provides the most lucid and cogent explanation of these distinctions that I have found useful for my examination of Du Bois's discourse on double consciousness. In Bialostosky's account,

> dialectic concerns impersonal relations among terms that are independent of those who hold them—relations of confirmation and contradiction, antithesis and synthesis, and the like. Rhetoric concerns relations of practical agreement and disagreement among persons—relations that may be effected, despite ideological differences in the formation of consensuses among divergent interests and parties. Dialogics concerns the relations among persons articulating their ideas in response to one another, discovering their mutual affinities and oppositions, their provocations to reply, their desires to hear more, or their wishes to change the subject . . . dialectic aims at discovering the truth of ideas or theses, rhetoric at determining the decisions of people, and dialogics at articulating the meaning of people's ideas, our own and those of others. As dialectic strives for conviction on a question and

rhetoric for persuasion of an audience, dialogics strives for comprehensive respon-
siveness and responsibility to the consequential person-ideas of a time, culture,
community, or discipline—that is, for the fullest articulation of someone's ideas
with the actual and possible ideas of others.[4]

For our examination of the shifts in Du Bois's discourse on double consciousness, the most important distinction here is between dialectics and dialogics.
Although both are interpretive strategies that involve oppositional forces, the
former signifies the dynamics of a historical process of inquiry for a truth that
synthesizes partial views and the latter the dynamics of a rhetorical process
that acknowledges and articulates different voices.

Etymologically, according to the *Oxford English Dictionary*, consciousness
is derived from Latin *conscius*, which denotes "knowing something with
others, knowing in oneself." Its linguistic origin thus suggests an epistemological relationship among language, knowledge, and power. Its first literary attes-
tation in English as internal knowledge or conviction occurred in 1632. As an
ontological concept inscribed in British philosophical discourse of 1678 with
the suffix "ness," it signified "the state or faculty of being and volition."[5]

In "W. E. B. Du Bois and the Idea of Double Consciousness," Dickson D.
Bruce, Jr. perceptively identifies the two main sources that probably influenced
Du Bois's use of the term.[6] The first was the product of European
Romanticism and American Transcendentalism, and the second was a product
of the emerging field of psychology. In 1843, for example, Ralph Waldo
Emerson used the term "double consciousness" in "The Transcendentalist" to
explain the dialectic tension between the self and the world, the soul and
Nature. "The double consciousness plaguing *The Transcendentalist*," Bruce
writes, "summarized the downward pull of life in society—including the
social forces inhibiting genuine self-realization—and the upward pull of
communion with the Divine; the apparent chaos of things-as-they-are and the
unity of Nature comprehended by universal law; and the demanding, cold
rationality of commercial society and the search for Truth, Beauty and
Goodness—especially Beauty—that ennobled the soul."[7] Although it is also
probable, as critics contend, that both Emerson and Du Bois were familiar
with the reference in Goethe's *Faust* to "Two souls, alas! Reside within my
breast," Du Bois's use of the allusion is distinctively African American, as
Wilson J. Moses reveals in "The Poetics of Ethiopianism."[8]

The *O.E.D.* identifies the rise of double consciousness as a diagnostic term in
psychological discourse in 1882 as "a condition which has been described as a
double personality, showing in some measure two separate and independent
trains of thought and two independent mental capabilities in the same individual." But the term actually appeared as early as 1817 in a psychological case

study of Mary Reynolds entitled "A Double Consciousness, or a Duality of Person in the Same Individual."[9] In 1890, as Arnold Rampersad has noted, William James, who possibly introduced the term to Du Bois at Harvard, explored the idea of double consciousness in *The Principles of Psychology*, and in the English translation of the 1893 German text of psychologist Oswald Kulpe the term is defined as a "general derangement of memory" that "is characterized by the existence of a more or less complete separation of two aggregates of conscious processes, which alternate at certain intervals or can be called up in irregular sequence by favourable conditions. The two aggregates are oftentimes of entirely opposite character."[10] As an idea and a term double consciousness is therefore derived from philosophical discourses on European Romanticism and American Transcendentalism, as well as from medical and psychological discourses on personality disorders that Du Bois probably encountered and from which he probably appropriated the phrase as a student at Harvard between 1888 and 1890 or the University of Berlin between 1892 and 1894.

Why and how, then, is double consciousness the sign of the distinctiveness of African American culture and character, and not merely of the potential for disorder and pathology, as in the dominant European and American discourses, of particular individuals? In "The Conservation of the Races," a speech he presented in March 1897 as a founding member of the American Negro Academy, a newly formed organization of black intellectuals, Du Bois first articulated his African American transformation of double consciousness in his ostensibly masculinist theory of racial and national identity:

> Here, then, is the dilemma and it is a puzzling one, I admit. No Negro who has given earnest thought to the situation of his people in America has failed at some time in life, to find himself at these cross-roads; has failed to ask himself at some time in life: what, after all, am I? Am I an American or am I a Negro? Can I be both? Or is it my duty to cease to be a Negro as soon as possible and be an American? If I strive as a Negro, am I not perpetuating the very cleft that threatens and separates black and white America? Is not my only possible practical aim the subduction of all that is Negro in me to the American? Does my black blood place upon me any more obligation to assert my nationality than German, or Irish, or Italian blood would? It is such an incessant self-questioning and the hesitation that arises from it, that is making the present period a time of vacillation and contradiction for the American Negro; combined race action is stifled, race responsibility is shirked, race enterprises languish, and the best talent, the best energy of the Negro people cannot be marshaled to do the bidding of the race. . . . Have we in America a distinct mission as a race, a distinct sphere of action and an opportunity for race development, or is self-obliteration the highest end to which Negro blood dare aspire?[11]

Here double consciousness is implicitly ascribed to Negroes who have given earnest thought to their racial, national, and, in a more modern cultural construction, ethnic identity as a people in America.

With a disdain for racial demagogues and a resolve for moral uplift, Du Bois rhetorically combines a biological, patriarchal, and social definition of race in this appeal to the "Talented Tenth"—the exceptionally gifted and morally qualified male and female black cultural elite—to choose racial solidarity over racial assimilation in realizing "that broader humanity which freely recognizes differences in men, but sternly deprecates inequality in their opportunities of development."[12] But the tension between rhetorical and dialectical discourses is apparent in this speech because, as Outlaw persuasively argues elsewhere in this collection, Du Bois's "The Conservation of Races" is "a decidedly *political* project . . . which is very much concerned with altering the negative valorizations of the Negro race."

It is apparent by his references to blood in this speech, a year after the *Plessy v. Ferguson* Supreme Court decision and two years after Booker T. Washington's Atlanta Cotton Exposition speech, both supporting separate-but-equal racial policies, that with this audience of black intellectuals Du Bois stresses biological as well as spiritual and cultural factors in explaining "the riddle" of the racial distinctiveness of African Americans. "We are Americans, not only in birth and by citizenship, but by our political ideals, our language, our religion. Farther than that our Americanism does not go," he states. "At that point we are Negroes, members of a vast historic race that from the very dawn of creation has slept, but awakens in the dark forests of its African fatherland."[13] In other words, despite the survival of Africanisms especially in the Deep South through the anthropological process of syncretism, in late nineteenth-century America, most Americans of African descent were born in the United States, spoke a dialect of American English, subscribed to the democratic ideal, and believed that God endowed all people with inalienable rights to life, liberty, and the pursuit of happiness. The faith of black Americans in a transcendent truth, which at times and in different ways was both a curse and a blessing, is of paramount importance in our intraracial as well as interracial struggle against all forms of domination.

If Negroes are Americans by birth, geography, ideals, language, and religion, what, then, are the criteria that define African American difference for Du Bois? "We are the first fruits of this new nation, the harbinger of that black tomorrow which is yet destined to soften the whiteness of the Teutonic today," Du Bois lyricizes. Using the language of dialectics in stressing African spirituality over Teutonic nationalism and American materialism, he underscores the distinctive complexity of his transformation of double consciousness by identifying the presence of African Americans and their three general cultural traits and gifts to America that were apparent to him as well as to Alexander Crummell, Anna Julia Cooper and other black intellectuals by 1897: "We are that people whose subtle sense of song has given America its only American music, its only American fairy tales, its only touch of pathos and humor amid its money-getting plutocracy."[14] Moving beyond a superficial, essentializing concept of racial and national identity, Du Bois engages in a radical, racialized counter-discourse to the hegemonic ideology of white supremacy that subordinates the will and well being of blacks individually and collectively to those of the dominant group.

Despite the complicity and disingenuity of too many of those "who have been reared and trained under the individualistic philosophy of the Declaration of Independence and the laissez-faire philosophy of Adam Smith," Du Bois states in "The Conservation of Races," "The history of the world is the history, not of individuals, but of groups, not of nations, but of races, and he who ignores or seeks to override the race idea in human history, ignores and overrides the central thought of all history." In an effort to reconcile the biological and sociocultural tensions in his definitions of race, he elaborates:

> Although the wonderful developments of human history teach that the grosser physical differences of color, hair and bone go but a short way toward explaining the different roles which groups of men have played in human progress, yet there are differences—subtle, delicate, and elusive though they may be—which have silently but definitely separated men into groups. . .which, while they perhaps transcend scientific definition, nevertheless, are clearly defined to the eye of the historian and sociologist.[15]

Race, he continues, may be thus defined biologically and socioculturally as

> a vast family of human beings, generally of common blood and language, always of common history, traditions, and impulses, who are both voluntarily and involuntarily striving together for the accomplishments of certain more or less vividly conceived ideals of life. . . . But while race differences have followed mainly physical race lines, yet no mere physical distinctions would really define or explain the deeper differences, the cohesiveness, and continuity of these groups. The deeper differences are spiritual, physical, differences—undoubtedly based on the physical, but infinitely transcending them."

Equally as important as the deeper yet transcendant spirituality of racial differences for Du Bois is the message that, in the nineteenth century, "the whole Negro race has not as yet . . . given to the world. . . . For the development of

Negro genius, of Negro literature and art, of Negro spirit, only Negroes bound and welded together, Negroes inspired by one vast ideal, can work out in its fullness the great message we have for humanity."[16] Clearly, then, the distinctiveness of African American double consciousness is a dynamic, rather than merely static and essentialist, residual African spirituality expressed in "the great message" of African American folk and formal art.

"The Talented Tenth," Du Bois's first call for a black "aristocracy of talent and character" to inspire and lead the self-liberating struggle of the most socially exploited and marginalized class of black Americans, was published in 1903 in *The Negro Problem*. Edited by Booker T. Washington, this was a collection of essays by "representative" black American leaders of the period.[17] In his essay, Du Bois boldly proclaimed that the mission of the Talented Tenth was to be the messengers of moral integrity, racial justice, and social equality for black Americans, and that the mission of black Americans was to be the crusaders for spiritual and social change in the world. In 1948, influenced by subsequent ideological, technological, and geopolitical developments, as well as by the unrelenting criticism of his apparent advocacy of cultural elitism, Du Bois, in an address to the Grand Boule, a national black social fraternity, reformulated his earlier concept of the Talented Tenth and of blacks as a group. "This group," he explained, "was not simply a physical entity, a black people, or people descended from black folk. It was, what all races really are, a cultural group.... 15,000,000 men and women, who for three centuries have shared some common experiences and common suffering; and have worked all those days and nights together for their own survival and progress; that this complex of habits and manners could not and must not be lost. It must be conserved for the benefit of the Negro people themselves, and for mankind."[18] Thus Du Bois argues that the principal defining characteristic, mission, and message of a people is the cultural expression of their shared struggle for survival.

It is important to remember that Du Bois's thoughts and feelings on double consciousness, race, and nationalism were shaped at the end of the nineteenth century. As Arnold Rampersad notes, Du Bois probably drew on the psychology and philosophy of his teachers and time, including the orthodox religious philosophy of James McCosh at Fisk and the pragmatism and phenomenology of William James at Harvard.[19] Profoundly impressed by German nationalism and culture while studying in Germany between 1892 and 1894, he was startled by an imperious, aristocratic professor's remark in a lecture on America: "*Die Mulattin sind niedrig! Sie fühlen sich niedrig!*" [Mulattoes are inferior; they feel themselves inferior.] Reflecting on this period at ninety, Du Bois writes: "I began to feel that dichotomy which all my life has characterized my thought: how far can love for my oppressed race accord with love for the oppressing country? And when these loyalties diverge, where shall my soul find refuge?"[20]

It was also in a solitary ritual celebration, of his twenty-fifth birthday, that he sought to resolve his sociocultural and sociopsychological dualism. "I am firmly convinced that my own best development is not one and the same with the best development of the world and here I am willing to sacrifice," he writes in his posthumously published autobiography. "That sacrifice to the world's good became too soon sickly sentimentality. I therefore take the world that the Unknown lay in my hands, and work for the rise of the Negro people, taking for granted that their best development means the best development of the world."[21] For Du Bois, the age of social Darwinism and disinterested scientific truth culminated in the 1890s with the "separate but equal" *Plessy v. Ferguson* Supreme Court decision; the triumph of hegemonic white nationalism and Jim Crow law; the rape, lynching, and disenfranchisement of many thousands of blacks, especially in the Deep South; and the resurgence after the Spanish-American War of American military, economic, and cultural domination of non-white peoples in several nations.

Five months after addressing the American Negro Academy, Du Bois shifted his rhetoric on double consciousness in the publication of "Strivings of the Negro People," a more poetic description of the complex fate of being a black American for a primarily white audience, in the August 1897 issue of *Atlantic Monthly*. This essay, shifted again slightly to sharpen the nuances of its personal and political tone, appears as "Of Our Spiritual Strivings" in the multivoiced *The Souls of Black Folk*. After introducing his classic racialized metaphor of the veil in describing his initiation, in primary school into the world of color prejudice and discrimination, and after discovering that he was "shut out from their world by a vast veil" that engendered contempt and longing for the "dazzling opportunities" beyond the veil, Du Bois provides us with his equally classic, often quoted definition of double consciousness:

> After the Egyptian and Indian, the Greek and Roman, the Teuton and Mongolian, the Negro is a sort of seventh son, born with a veil, and gifted with second-sight in this American world—a world which yields him no true self-consciousness, but only lets him see himself through the revelation of the other world. It is a peculiar sensation this double consciousness, this sense of always looking at one's self through the eyes of others, of measuring one's soul by the tape of a world that looks on in amused contempt and pity. One ever feels his twoness—an American, a Negro; two souls, two thoughts, two unreconciled strivings; two warring ideals in one dark body, whose dogged strength alone keeps it from being torn asunder.
>
> The history of the American Negro is the history of this strife,—this longing to attain self-conscious manhood, to merge his double self into a better and truer self.

> In this merging he wishes neither of the older selves to be lost. He would not
> Africanize America, for America has too much to teach the world and Africa. He
> would not bleach his soul in a flood of white Americanism, for he knows that
> Negro blood has a message for the world. He simply wishes to make it possible
> for a man to be both a Negro and American, without being cursed and spit upon
> by his fellows, without having the doors of Opportunity closed roughly in his face.

The end of the black American's strivings, Du Bois continues, is "to be a co-worker in the kingdom of culture, to escape both death and isolation, to husband and use his best powers and his latent genius".[22]

Clearly, in each of the shifts in these texts, African American double consciousness was not the fate of all ethnic immigrants or hyphenated Americans. Rather, it was the complex double vision of Americans of African descent whose humanity and culture had been historically devalued and marginalized primarily by people of European and British descent, but occasionally with the complicity of members of their own racial or ethnic group. African Americans were both people of mixed African ancestry and nonpeople to the majority of whites; we were a fundamental part of American society, yet segregated apart within it. We were among the first people to build the nation, but twentieth-century America only began reluctantly in the 1950s and 1960s to redress the violations of our civil rights as full first-class citizens.

African Americans—especially Southerners, intellectuals, artists, and professionals—were therefore impelled by a complex combination of custom, law, circumstances, and choice to function primarily on two levels of a pervasively, perversely, and paradoxically racialized reality. Although it is true that our human personalities are complex and contradictory, our attitudes as black Americans toward racial integration and separatism were largely determined by the degree of alienation from or faith in the principles and practices of the ruling class of white Anglo-Saxon and Euro-American Protestants.[23]

For Du Bois, then, double consciousness was a mythic blessing and a social burden: an ancestral gift for making sense of the mystery of life in the cosmic scheme of things, a product of institutionalized racism, and a dialectic and a dialogic process in American society between the bearers, on the one hand, of residually oral sub-Saharan African cultures and, on the other, of industrialized Western print cultures. It is, for most contemporary African Americans, the striving to reconcile one's ancestral African and diasporic slave past—however remote, mythic, or spiritual—with one's American present; one's sense of being a subject with that of being an object, of being an outsider with that of being an insider; and one's socially and historically ascribed status and identity with one's socially and culturally constructed status and identity.

Rather than a sociocultural conflict that has been inevitably internalized as incipient personal pathology, African American double consciousness thus signifies a biracial, bicultural state of being in the world, an existential site of socialized cultural ambivalence and emancipatory possiblities of personal and social transformation, and a dynamic epistemological mode of critical inquiry for African Americans.

Although on the surface both "The Conservation of the Races" and "Of Our Spiritual Strivings" illuminate the paradox, dualism, and dialectic of the experiences of black Americans, of being "an outcast and a stranger in mine own house," the differences in the moral and political tone of the two discourses reflect the primary racial differences in their audiences. While adhering to the nineteenth-century masculinist convention of privileging the male pronoun as the generic marker for representing both sexes, "Of Our Spiritual Strivings" distinctively racializes the metaphor of the veil and the multiple leitmotifs of sight and insight, visibility and invisibility, slavery and freedom. By metaphorically encouraging the reader's participation in the public discourse on race, the rhetorical and dialectic tension in the text is fore-grounded in its representation of the sociopsychological and sociocultural differences and struggles between the worlds of whites and non-whites.

"In 'Strivings,'" historian Thomas C. Holt contends, "blacks are not so much aliens as alienated. It is not cultural difference but cultural disfranchise-ment that shapes their struggle."[24] Actually, cultural and racial differences inscribed in eighteenth- and nineteenth- century legal statutes as "black codes" and implemented in juridical decisions reinforced the hegemonic power of the white ruling class, fostered anxiety and paranoia about chal-lenges to that power, and perpetuated until the 1960s the paradoxical political and cultural disfranchisement of black American citizens. Johnson's *The Autobiography of an Ex-Colored Man*, Toomer's *Cane*, Wright's *Native Son*, Ellison's *Invisible Man*, Baldwin's *Go Tell it on the Mountain*, and Morrison's *Beloved* readily come to mind as improvisational variations on Du Boisian themes and tropes of double consciousness.

An apparent revision of Du Bois's metaphor of double consciousness and of sociologist Robert E. Park's 1928 theory of the marginal man as a racial and cultural hybrid or Creole, socialized ambivalence, as defined in 1937 by anthropologist Melville J. Herskovits in *Life in a Haitian Valley*, is the anthro-pological adjustment to the sociopsychological conflict that results from the contradictory imperatives of European and African cultural traditions primar-ily in colonial and neocolonial situations.[25] In the United States, this ambiva-lence is expressed both in the mixed emotions of many Americans of African descent about ideologies of social integration, cultural assimilation and black cultural nationalism, and in our shifting identification between white and black cultural systems as a result of institutionalized racism. Double vision, an apparent rewriting in 1964 of Du Bois's metaphor by Ralph Ellison in *Shadow and Act*, is a fluid, ambivalent, laughing-to-keep-from-crying perspective toward life, as expressed in the innovative use of irony and parody in African American folklore and formal art.[26]

Much of this irony and parody was and is a creative way of managing the legacy of systemic American racism. Although there is no valid scientific evidence of a biological relationship between culture and race, as Anthony Appiah argues in "The Uncompleted Argument: Du Bois and the Illusion of Race," it is nevertheless the perception of biological and cultural differences (color, hair, religion, language, beliefs, and values) ascribed to and socially inscribed as race in popular and formal texts by the white American majority that served as the principal basis for the social subjugation, exploitation, and exclusion of African captives and African Americans.[27] More than mere prejudice, as sociologist William J. Wilson reminds us, racism is "an ideology of racial domination or exploitation that (1) incorporates beliefs in a particular race's cultural and/or inherent biological inferiority and (2) uses such beliefs to justify and prescribe inferior or unequal treatment for that group."[28]

Historically, the increasing demand for cheap labor in the United States led to the construction of political and racist acts in the late seventeenth century and the reification of a racist ideology by the late nineteenth century that—in paradoxical contravention of the letter and spirit of the Declaration of Independence, the Constitution of the United States, and the Bible—restricted or nullified the civil rights of non-white persons and immorally devalued our human rights as subjects. *De facto* and *de jure* racism clearly prevented the equal participation of blacks in the dominant white cultural and literary discourse, so that our need for empowering symbols and values had to be satisfied and sustained by the resourcefulness, resilience, and creativity of our indigenous ethnic group.

"What seems clear upon reading the texts created by black writers in English or the critical texts that responded to these black writings," as literary critic Henry Louis Gates brilliantly demonstrates in a recent study that illuminates the kinship of the trope of double consciousness to the Yoruba and African American trickster and toast traditions of Eshu Elegbara and the Signifying Monkey,

> is that the production of literature was taken to be the central arena in which persons of African descent could, or could not, establish and redefine their status within the human community. Black people ... had to represent themselves as 'speaking subjects' before they could even begin to destroy their status as objects, as commodities, within Western culture. In addition to all of the myriad reasons

for which human beings write books, this particular reason seems to have been paramount for the black slave.[29]

It is in this racially and ethnically specific context that we can best understand the shift from the rhetoric and dialectics of Du Boisian double consciousness in his speeches and essays to the dialectics and dialogics in two of his contemporaneous narratives.

A close examination of Du Bois's earliest unpublished and published fiction, "A Fellow of Harvard" and "Of the Coming of John," reveals that they are semi-autobiographical narratives which illuminate the socialized ambivalence of the writer's dialectic and dialogic use of the sign of double consciousness. "A Fellow of Harvard" is the incomplete unpublished manuscript of a novel. It consists of fragments of three versions. The first is a two-page plot outline, dated Berlin, 7 December 1892, in which the idea of double consciousness is expressed intratextually in the romantic tension between the idealism and spirituality of the self and the provincialism and materialism of the world. The author/narrator describes the nameless hero as "a Western boy of N. E. ancestry—somewhat eccentric from childhood." His eccentricity, like Du Bois's, is his driving ambition to excel intellectually and psychologically to become "a fellow of Harvard" even though his local school committee awards him a prize for a year at "x—coll." Supported by a hometown church that encourages him to enter the ministry, he leaves the college in disgust with its "narrowness" before graduation and "writes a capital brochure which secures him aid at Harvard where he enters as a junior." Intertextually and dialogically, the correlation between the voices of the author/narrator and the nameless protagonist in this fragment, and between the voices in this fragment and the divergent views we hear in Du Bois's autobiographies and *The Souls of Black Folk* indicate that they are morally, culturally, psychologically, and politically close, although temporally and spatially distant.

Also like Du Bois, the protagonist struggles with uneven success to maintain his fellowship status, and manages to receive a European fellowship. In Europe, he is not a good student, but becomes "an avowed socialist" and returns to America without completing his thesis. His efforts to find a teaching position are unsuccessful, except at "a Southern Negro school where his eccentricities get him [in] trouble with the blacks & his radicalism with the whites." After completing and publishing his thesis with "brilliant success," he secures and loses another college position because his politics and "ideals clash with the mammonism & materialism of his surroundings." After his dismissal and the ridicule his published masterpiece receives, "He already [a] monomaniac becomes hopelessly insane and dies 'a fellow of Harvard.'"[30] In the plot outline, then, Du Boisian double consciousness is clearly more of a personal and artistic emancipatory effort than a group sociopsychological condition, and more of a curse than a blessing to the semi-autobiographical, fictive, non-conforming, African American idealist and political radical of the Victorian era.

The second fragment is eight pages of a multi-voiced chapter in which the protagonist, George Smith, is a "smart but odd" sixteen-year-old boy whose father and small-Western townsmen wonder if he will apply his genius to a trade or a profession as a livelihood. Du Bois employs conventional dialogue in black dialect for the parents and interior dialogue for George, dramatizing in stylized standard English the implied author's support for liberal college education over industrial education as the better preparation to attain full freedom, literacy, dignity, and civil rights for post-Reconstruction black Americans.

Expressing sympathy for industrial education in the major generational and educational conflict in both the plot and black communities of that era, a member of the local chapter of the locomotive engineers states in frustration, "No sooner a workman make himself respectable than off his sons go to the kid gloved professors or to college. Education is a good thing—a good thing of course, but somehow it don't work out right. If we could educate our sons for farmers or for tradesmen—it would be all right, but that's just what they won't be—and I'm blessed if I see my way out of the thing."

When asked by his father what he "goin' t' do for a living," George sinks into reflection and interior dialogue on the vagueness and flux of his plans for the future. "Now what a question to put to a sixteen year old boy, a living? The thought had scarcely occurred to him—yes it had occurred but not in that way, or no, not in that in 'living' there was a touch of the sordid, the shadow of a breathless scramble for bread—and he shrank from that—he feared it—it had no part in his dreams, in his great airy castles."[31] Grounded in the choice during the 1890s of the right educational path up from slavery as the horns of the dilemma of double consciousness and social stratification for blacks as individuals and as a group—this fragment ends abruptly with George's interior self-questioning.

The longest fragment of the three versions of "A Fellow of Harvard" is forty-seven handwritten pages and dated April 14, probably 1893. Du Bois's use of double consciousness in this narrative is clearly derived from the redemptive vestiges of African spirituality and the unredemptive impact of American racism and materialism. The first of seven planned but uncompleted chapters focuses on a Southern revival meeting that dramatizes the cultural syncretism of African and American belief systems and the economic exploitation and racial discrimination of sharecropping that divide the world and consciousness of John Johnson, the black protagonist. His "holy mission from his own flesh & blood . . . from a prophet of the high God"—from his African great-grandfather who was a legendary preacher and conjuror—was "to lead the people he loved into the promised land."[32]

Through description and dialogue, black myth-legend, music, and speech, Du Bois establishes the origins of African American spirituality in the rural Southern black revival meetings and the legacy of such blends of African and non-African religious beliefs and practices as Christian fundamentalism, goophering (i.e., conjuring, hoodoo, or mystical syncretic powers), and root healing or folk medicine. (As Zora Neale Hurston explains in *Mules and Men*, "Nearly all of the conjure doctors practice 'roots,' but some of the root doctors are not hoodoo doctors.")[33]

Du Bois begins the heteroglossic chapter with "a strange song rolling down the valley in rythmic [sic] cadence" to which a black sharecropper responds in dialect: "Reckon the big meetin's begun." As the voices of men, women, and children that begin in sorrowful cadence rise in powerful triumph and communion, an approaching church member responds, "Lord, but the spirrit [sic] seem to be a moving right pretty." Holding center stage in this spiritual drama of "simple true hearted folk" is the minister, whose enthralling chanted sermon and wounds-of-Jesus call to join the church establishes the dominant messianic motif of the narrative:

> there he hangs on the tree . . . I have seen his wounds . . . see from his side the crimson stream is rippling down the mountain . . . see it is pouring in the door, it is rushing thro the windows, can you not feel it, its warm hands are clasping at you O my little ones come to Jesus, come to Jesus here ye the song—[34]

In response to this call, the teenaged protagonist, John, and his even younger sister Tildy, "git religion."

But young John was still dissatisfied by the world about him. "From his cradle he had looked out upon a double world . . . a white one and a black one and the first meant to him all that was overbearing unfortunate and hateful, the second all that was lovable and dear to him." He was troubled, however, that "he could not trace this line throughout the world. Not only did the two worlds seem to grow together at the top when the sun glare[d] bright and rosy o'er the eastern hills and drank up the dew in the meadow of black & white, and washed Capt. Thornton & Sam Johnson and the black cow and George's dog—not only here was the world necessarily [?] one, but at other unexpected places the two worlds faded into one."[35] Most troubling was the thought that God was not "black and kinky haired," as he had learned from his mother's stories about his own mission as God's messenger and warrior, but white as in the Bible. Significantly, Du Bois represents John's mother Matilda as an exemplar of the emancipatory possiblities of double consciousness for her son and the community.

Throughout the chapter the color symbolism and dialectic between residual African cultural elements and Christian myth-legend reinforce the capacity of double consciousness to evoke the ambiguity and irony of the protagonist's experiences as a young American of African ancestry. The symbolism and voices we experience as readers are more dialectic than dialogic because the language situates the characters in a specific historical and ideological context that highlights interracial and intraracial class and color conflicts and proposes a synthesis of antithetical elements to achieve sociocultural emancipation and enlightenment by affirming a transcendant messianic truth. Taunted by the son of a white, post-Reconstruction plantation owner about his plans to go to Phillips Exeter Academy, to write books, and to become a Fellow at Harvard, John is motivated by personal pride and moral commitment to lead his people in their struggle for freedom, justice, dignity, and literacy. When his family is threatened with lynching because he beats Captain Thornton's son in a fight, it is through the emancipatory agency of his mother Matilda that he learns how his legendary African great-grandfather and she have sacrificed to provide him with the legacy of resources, spiritual and material, necessary for him to fulfill his mission as God's avenging messenger and his people's messiah.

After killing the white overseer who cut him with a whip, John's great grandfather, "William John Thoms, the grandson of the prince Chiawba of Africa," a powerful preacher, and a "goopher man" who "c'd heal the sick & no magic ever worked agin him," disappeared. But he left a legacy of courage, goopher charms, a written will, and crumpled instructions to locate a buried inheritance. "I remember his big form as he stod at the door," John's mother Matilda tells him in passing on her grandfather's patrimony; "he only hand this to father and said 'give it yo first granson, when he is ready to gird on the sword of God & go forth & smite his enemies."[36]

Following the instructions at midnight and using the goopher charms, John finds a grave containing a skeleton, an anvil, and two hundred dollars in gold and silver. Matilda then resolutely gives her son the hundred dollars in silver that she has saved to send him to school and "into the great wicked world for to fight for his people agin the hosts of the devil." Rather than closure, the final chapter leaves the reader with John telling his little sister Tildy that he is going over the mountain to the great city "to be a great man—perhaps a preacher, perhaps perhaps, a Fellow of Harvard."[37] The resolution of the racial and cultural conflicts is thus inscribed as an expected synthesis of masters of both the spoken and written word: the preacher and the professor.

Prefaced with an excerpt from a poem by Elizabeth Barrett Browning and three moving bars of music from a black spiritual, "Of the Coming of John" is Du Bois's most effectively developed short fictive orchestration of his turn-of-the-century motif of double consciousness. The stylization of black and white voices dramatizes the dominance for the implied author and the protagonist, John Jones, of the problem of the color line over problems of gender, class, and culture. As in the other thirteen chapters of *The Souls of Black Folk*, in which the story was published, the tension between dialectic and dialogic discourse in "Of the Coming of John" is apparent.

Although, as Frederic Jameson stresses in his reading of Mikhail Bakhtin, "the normal form of the dialogical is essentially an *antagonistic* one, and ... the dialogue of class struggle is one in which two opposing discourses fight it out within the general unity of a shared code," within the master code of the Christian religion, "the basic formal requirement of dialectical analysis is maintained and its elements are still restructured in terms of *contradiction*."[38] This reading of Bakhtin's theory of dialogics is also useful in interpreting "Of the Coming of John," which is ultimately a univocal rather than multivocal text in its deep structure. On this level the Du Boisian matrix of music, speech, and symbolism in the narrative illuminates the class and cultural as well as racial conflicts in the historical struggle of blacks for social equality with whites.

Anthropologically, the protagonist's identity crisis of double consciousness is dramatized by the triadic ritual process of his separation, liminality, and reintegration with his primary racial and ethnic community. The major racial, class, and cultural dualisms are constructed in the tragedies of two Johns: one black and the other white. Before the protagonist's separation from his hometown to pursue higher education, John Jones is accepted by both the white and black communities as a black, good-natured, respectful plough-hand and childhood playmate of John Henderson, the white, bigoted son of wealthy Judge Henderson. Socialized in the ethics of Jim Crow, they become conscious, in the liminal stage of their college educations, of radically different responses to continuing their traditionally structured system of social power and privilege. In their futile efforts to reintegrate with their communities they turn on, rather than to, each other. Their lives end tragically with murder and suicide after white John sexually assaults black John's sister, Jennie, a house servant to Judge Henderson.

The opening and closing episodes of the triadically structured narrative are situated in Georgia. Following the contrapuntal cultural and racial referents of the lyrical epigraphs, the first voice we hear is that of a first-person plural male narrator/observer. He introduces us to the multi-leveled ironies of the separate-but-equal community within a community of Southern white Jonestown, where he is a faculty member and the protagonist is a student on the black campus of Wells Institute. Speaking standard English with the authority and norms of the collective voice of the aspiring black middle class, the nameless narrator's discourse is disrupted and subverted by white voices of authority.

Judge Henderson and other white folk of the protagonist's hometown of Altamaha (Atlanta) paternalistically disapprove of higher education and social equality for John Jones—"'It'll spoil him,—ruin him,' they said"(167)—and other blacks. But for the Judge's white son John to go to Princeton is both desirable and good. "'It'll make a man of him,' said the Judge, 'college is the place'" (168). Although the coming home of both Johns to their "Southern village" was eagerly awaited with pride and hope, "neither world thought the other world's thoughts, save with a vague unrest" (168). In the closing episodes, about which I will later say more, an omniscient narrator assumes the authority of orchestrating the multiple black and white Southern dialect voices.

But it is in the climactic liminal episode in a New York opera hall that the protagonist experiences the inspirational beauty and harmony of the cultural synthesis of European folk and formal art in Wagner's *Lohengrin* and in the disruptive power of the Veil, Du Bois's classic metaphor for institutionalized racism, in the American North. Before he arrives in New York, however, we witness the protagonist's transformation in body and soul as a result of his college education and discovery of "the Veil that lay between him and the white world." Differences, restraints, and slights that he had felt natural, ignored, or laughed at as a boy in his hometown, such as the Jim Crow cars caused by "the color-line that hemmed in him and his," now evoked sarcasm and a vague bitterness from him (170). Ambivalent about his plans to return home to be a leader of his people, he welcomes the offer at graduation to travel North to sing spirituals during the summer vacation with the school quartet.

In New York he is so overwhelmed by the material elegance and cultural richness of the white world around him that he is swept into an opera hall with a young white couple, subsequently recognizing the male in the couple, beside whom he is seated in the hall, as his boyhood white playmate. Before suffering the indignity, injustice, and irony of being ejected because of his race at the angry insistence of the white John, the black John was enthralled by "a world so different from his, so strangely more beautiful than anything he had ever known, that he sat in dreamland, and started when, after a hush, rose high and clear the music of Lohengrin's swan. . . . A deep longing swelled in all his heart to rise with that clear music out of the dirt and dust of that low life that held him prisoned and befouled" (171).

Based on a German legend from the Middle Ages, *Lohengrin* was written to the composer's own libretto and established the Wagnerian organic style of the interplay of ethereal and earthly leitmotifs in his romantic operatic dramas. The transmutation of the embedded folk narrative text of *Lohengrin* into the aristocratic text of the opera captivates the protagonist and ironically dramatizes Du Bois's unconscious complicity in the pattern of transcultural appropriation by which the dominant culture revitalizes itself and perpetuates the single voice and values of a hegemonic class.

The changing movements and swelling harmony of *Lohengrin* stir the soul of the protagonist and make his identity crisis more acute. "If he could only live up in the free air where birds sang and setting suns had no touch of blood," he exclaims more plaintively than rebelliously, to himself and God. "Who had called him to be the slave and butt of all? And if he had called, what right had he to call when a world like this lay open before men" (172)? As the movement of harmony changes and grows fuller, "he felt with the music the movement of power within him. If he but had some master-work, some life-service, hard,—aye, bitter hard, but without the cringing and sickening servility, without the cruel hurt that hardened his heart and soul. When at last a soft sorrow crept across the violins, there came to him the vision of a far-off home,—the great eyes of his sister, and the dark drawn face of his mother" (172).

Hurrying from the hall and calling himself "'a natural-born fool,'" John immediately writes his family that he is coming home. On the train South, he seeks through interior monologue to reconcile the ironic tension of his double consciousness with a Biblical imperative: "Here is my duty to Altamaha plain before me; perhaps they'll let me help settle the Negro problems there,— perhaps they won't. 'I will go in to the King, which is not according to the law; and if I perish, I perish'" (172–73).

Distanced emotionally and intellectually, as well as spatially, from the orthodox Christian codes of Altamaha, the protagonist is unsuccessful in his effort to reintegrate himself with his primary community in the final episodes of the narrative. The abstract, impersonal, methodical tenor and tone of his coming-home speech at the Baptist church, in which he speaks of fostering a black unity that transcends religious and denominational antagonisms alienated him from his community and evokes the scorn of the folks in the Amen corner. "'Today,' he said with a smile, 'the world cares little whether a man be Baptist or Methodist, or indeed a churchman at all, so long as he is good and true. What difference does it make whether a man be baptized in a river or washbowl, or not at all? Let's leave all that littleness, and look higher'" (174).

The college educated John Jones no longer fit in. "He had come to save his people, and before he left the depot he had hurt them," he thinks, after being sent by Judge Henderson to his back door. "He sought to teach them at the church, and had outraged their deepest feelings. He had schooled himself to be respectful to the Judge, and then blundered into his front door" (175–76). On the surface level, John seems to accept the situation of hegemonic white rule. Judge Henderson reminds him that this means that "'in this country the Negro must remain subordinate, and can never expect to be the equal of white men. . . . By God! we'll hold them under if we have to lynch every Nigger in the land'"(176). Although in order to teach at the black school he acquiesces to the Judge's bigoted injunction to "'teach the darkies to be faithful servants and laborers as your fathers were'" (176), the protagonist is summarily dismissed and the school closed by the Judge after he discovers that John has appropriated the text of the French Revolution to subvert the rule of whites and revoiced the text of social equality and independence to empower his black students.

Du Bois ends his narrative of double consciousness on a paradoxical and Pyrrhic note with the spiritual and moral triumph, but physical and psychological defeat of the protagonist. Resolved to leave Altamaha after his dismissal by Judge Henderson, John Jones is enraged to find near the bluff of the sea his young sister, Jennie, struggling in the arms of Judge Henderson's bored, "little spoiled and self-indulgent," "headstrong" son, John Henderson. "He said not a word, but, seizing a fallen limb, struck him with all the pent-up hatred of his great black arm" (179). In utter despair he tells his mother that he is "'going away,—I'm going to be free'" (179), and he returns to the site of the fatal encounter in the pine trees high above the sea. Hearing the noise of galloping horses merging with "the faint sweet music" of the opera hall, the protagonist jumps into the sea, humming the "Song of the Bride"—"*Freudig geführt, ziehet dahin*"—and pitying "that haggard white-haired man, whose eyes flashed red with fury" as he rushed to lynch him (180).

That in the final resolution of his double consciousness by suicide the protagonist not only hums the German lyrics to a Wagnerian aria, but also pities his chief white antagonist, is both a paradoxical and Pyrrhic triumph of the romantic over the realistic and the spiritual over the material. This shift from rhetoric to dialectics and dialogics in Du Bois's discourse on the theme and trope of double consciousness foreshadows the dominant contradictions and complementarities in his subsequent texts, especially his messianic self-representation as an epitomized expression of the African American racial spirit in *Darkwater* and *Dusk of Dawn*.

We should thus celebrate Du Bois as the preeminent exemplar of the black scholar/activist whose life and legacy of double consciousness are a sociocultural and sociopsychological sign of the distinctive, complex fate of being an African American, especially a black intellectual or artist. As demonstrated by its resurgence in African American literary criticism,[39] Du Boisian double consciousness continues to be a vital and viable rhetorical sign: first, of the dynamics of continuity and change in the biracial, bicultural state of being in the world with others; second, of the existential site of socialized cultural ambivalence and the emancipatory possiblities of personal and social transformation; and third, of an epistemological mode of critical inquiry for interpreting the rich complexity of African American culture, especially literature.

NOTES

1. Darlene Clark Hine, "'In the Kingdom of Culture: Black Women and the Intersection of Race, Gender, and Class," in *Lure and Loathing: Essays on Race, Identity, and the Ambivalence of Assimilation,* ed. Gerald Early (New York: Penguin Press, 1993), p. 338.

2. "Experience," in *Feminists Theorize the Political,* ed. Judith Butler and Joan W. Scott (New York: Routledge, 1992), 28.

3. See Ralph Ellison, *Shadow and Act* (New York: Signet Book, 1966); Larry Neal, "And Shine On," in *Black Fire: An Anthology of African-American Writing* ed. LeRoi Jones and Larry Neal (New York: William Morrow and Company, 1968), 638–56; Robert B. Stepto, *From Behind the Veil: A Study of Afro-American Narrative* (Urbana: University of Illinois Press, 1979); Henry Louis Gates, Jr., *The Signifying Monkey: A Theory of African-American Literary Criticism* (New York: Oxford University Press, 1988); Berndt Ostendorf, *Black Literature in White America* (Totowa, N.J.: Barnes and Noble Books, 1982); Mary Helen Washington, ed. *Invented Lives: Narratives of Black Women 1860–1960* (Garden City, N.Y.: Anchor Press, 1987); Barbara Johnson, "Metaphor, Metonomy and Voice in *Their Eyes Were Watching God*," in *Black Literature & Theory*, ed. Henry Louis Gates, Jr. (New York: Methuen, 1984), 205–19; and Bernard W. Bell, *The Afro-American Novel and Its Tradition* (Amherst: University of Massachusetts Press, 1987).

4. *PMLA 108* (October 1986): 789.

5. *The Compact Oxford English Dictionary* (New York: Oxford University Press, 1971), 1: 522.

6. Dickson D. Bruce Jr., "W. E. B. Du Bois and the Idea of Double Consciousness," *American Literature*, 64 (June 1992), 229–309.

7. Bruce, "W. E. B. Du Bois and the Idea of Double Consciousness," 300–301.

8. See Bruce, "W. E. B. Du Bois and the Idea of Double Consciousness," 301–302. See also Johann Wolfgang Von Goethe, *Faust*, trans. Bayard Taylor (New: Arden, n.d.), 68; Werner Sollors, "Of Mules and Mares in a Land of Difference; or Quadrupeds All?" *American Quarterly* 42 (1990): 182; Joel Porte, "Emerson, Thoreau, and the Double Consciousness, *New England Quarterly* 41 (1968): 41, 50; W. E. B. Du Bois, "Strivings of the Negro People," *Atlantic Monthly* 80 (August 1897): 197; and Moses, "The Poetics of Ethiopianism: W. E. B. Du Bois and Literary Black Nationalism," *American Literature* 47(1975): 411–26. See also Shamoon Zamir, *Dark Voices: W. E. B. Du Bois and American Thought* for an interesting development of this point.

9. Samuel L. Mitchell, *Medical Repository* m.s. 3 (1817): 185–86. See also William S. Plumerm, "Mary Reynolds: A Case of Double-Consciousness," *Harper's* 20 (May 1860): 807–12.

10. O.E.D., 522; and Bruce, "W. E. B. Du Bois and the Idea of Double Consciousness," 303; and Oswald Kulpe, *Outlines of Psychology*, trans. Edward Bradford Titchener (New York: MacMillian, 1895), 217. See also Arnold Rampersad, *The Art and Imagination of W. E. B. Du Bois*, (Cambridge: Harvard University Press, 1976) 74.

11. "The Conservation of Races," in *The Seventh Son: The Thought and Writings of W. E. B. Du Bois*, ed. Julius Lester (New York: Vintage Books, 1971), 1: 182.

12. Du Bois, "The Conservation of Races," 183.

13. Du Bois, "The Conservation of Races," 182–83.

14. Du Bois, "The Conservation of Races," 183.

15. Du Bois, "The Conservation of Races," 178.

16. Du Bois, "The Conservation of Races," 178–81.

17. "The Talented Tenth," in *The Negro Problem: A Series of Articles by Representative Negroes of Today* (New York: James Pott & Co., 1903), 33–75. See also Lester, *The Seventh Son*, 385–403.

18. W. E. B. Du Bois, "The Talented Tenth: The Reexamination of a Concept," in *The Papers of W. E. B. Du Bois* 1803 (1877–1963) 1979, comp. Robert W. McDonnell, (University of Massachusetts, Amherst: Microfilming Corporation of America, 1981), reel 80: frame 1090,

19. Rampersad, *The Art and Imagination of W. E. B. Du Bois*, 74.

20. W. E. B. Du Bois, *The Autobiography of W. E. B. Du Bois: A Soliloquy on Viewing My Life from the Last Decade of its First Century* (New York: International Publishers, 1968), 165, 169.

21. Du Bois, *The Autobiography of W. E. B. Du Bois*, 171.

22. W. E. B. Du Bois, *The Souls of Black Folk: Essays and Sketches* (Greenwich, Conn.: Crest Book, 1969), 16–17. Subsequent references to this book will be identified parenthetically in the text.

23. As we are reminded by the responses of twenty black intellectuals and artists in Early, *Lure and Loathing*, (see n.d.) the consensus of contemporary critics acknowledges the validity but questions the viability of Du Boisian double consciousness. Some argue that it is no longer useful because it reduces the complexity and diversity of African American character to a schizoid male construct that reinforces racial stereotypes. Aside from the fact that those who dismiss the usefulness of double consciousness as a contemporary interpretive metaphor implicitly or explicitly acknowledge that racism was, if not is, a stifling dominant force in their lives, the statement that the significance of race in America is declining is, as the Rodney King case so tragically reminds us, at best a premature, if not a fallacious, assumption, and an unconvincing, if not illogical, conclusion.

24. Thomas C. Holt, "The Political Uses of Alienation: W. E. B. Du Bois on Politics, Race, and Culture, 1903–1940," *American Quarterly* 42 (June 1990): 304.

25. Melville J. Herskovitz, *Life in a Haitian Valley* (New York: Alfred A. Knopf, 1937), 295–96.

26. Ellison, *Shadow and Act*, 136–37.

27. Anthony Appiah, "The Uncompleted Argument: Du Bois and the Illusion of Race," in *"Race," Writing, and Difference*, ed. Henry Louis Gates, Jr. (Chicago: University of Chicago Press, 1976), 32.

28. William J. Wilson, *Power, Racism, and Privilege: Race Relations in Theoretical and Sociohistorical Perspectives* (New York: Free Press, 1976), 32

29. Gates, *The Signifying Monkey*, 129.

30. W. E. B. Du Bois, "A Fellow of Harvard," in *The Papers of W. E. B. Du Bois* 1803 (1877–1963) 1979, comp. Robert W. McDonnell, (University of Massachusetts, Amherst: Microfilming Corporation of America, 1981), reel 87: frame 756,

31. Du Bois, "A Fellow of Harvard," Frames 759 and 760.

32. Du Bois, "A Fellow of Harvard," Frame 783.

33. Zora Neale Huston, *Mules and Men: Negro Folktales and Voodoo Practices in the South* (New York: Perennial Library, 1970), 340.

34. Du Bois, "A Fellow of Harvard," Frame 766.

35. Du Bois, "A Fellow of Harvard," Frame 772.

36. Du Bois, "A Fellow of Harvard," Frames 780 and 781.

37. Du Bois, "A Fellow of Harvard," Frame 786.

38. Frederic Jameson, *The Political Unconscious: Narrative as a Socially Symbolic Act.* (Ithaca: Cornell University Press, 1981), 84–86.

39. In addition to the texts identified in n. 2, see Eric Sundquist, *To Wake the Nations* (Cambridge: Belknap Press, 1993); Denise Heinze, *The Dilemma of "Double Consciousness": Toni Morrison's Novels* (Athens: University of Georgia Press, 1993); and Sandra Adell, *Double-Consciousness/Double Bind: Theoretical Issues in Twentieth-Century Black Literature* (Urbana: Univerity of Illinois Press, 1994).

The

Question

of Women

The Margin as the Center of a Theory of History   5

African-American Women, Social Change, and the Sociology of W. E. B. Du Bois[1]

Cheryl Townsend Gilkes

During the first decades of this century, in a word of prayer before his students at Atlanta University, W. E. B. Du Bois petitioned:

> Give us grace, O God, to dare to do the deed which we well know cries to be done. Let us not hesitate because of ease, or the words of men's mouths, or our own lives. Mighty causes are calling us—the freeing of women, the training of children, the putting down of hate and murder and poverty—all these and more. But they call us with voices that mean work and sacrifice and death. Mercifully grant us, O God, the spirit of Esther, that we say: I will go unto the King and if I perish, I perish——Amen.[2]

In prayer, Du Bois identified multiple dimensions of oppression that demanded resistance and challenge and pointed to the simultaneous importance of gender, race, and class. At the heart of a prayer full of sociological

truth was a call to explore and interpret African American women's experience in American society.[3] W. E. B. Du Bois included women's lives in his
perspective on social change. For Du Bois the sociologist and activist, there
were "three great revolutions" at work in "the making" of the United States.
These revolutions involved women, labor, and black folk. In various writings,
he observed that black women embodied all three of these revolutions in their
historical roles in the family, the community, and the labor force.

This chapter offers a review of Du Bois's diverse writings on women and on
the importance of women's suffrage. Early in the history of sociology, W. E. B.
Du Bois emphasized that gender, race, and class intersected in the lives of
black women to foster an important critical perspective or standpoint. This
standpoint was translated into activism, progressive voting behavior, cultural
enterprise, and moral authority. Standpoint is a term currently used to point
out that "an oppressed group's experiences may put its members in a position
to see things differently" and therefore develop an alternate way of knowing
and acting in the world."[4] Although Du Bois did not use the term standpoint,
he developed a critique of black women's oppression. He identified black
women's suffering as a social fact that provided an important and distinct
angle of vision. Black women's roles made them an economic vanguard in
society. As agents of history and social change, they were especially empowered by their religious experience. In asserting the historical importance of
black women's collective political life, Du Bois evinced a view of black
womanhood as culture. The value of Du Bois's work rests both in his description of the black female experience and in his incorporation of that experience
into a larger theory of history, a theory that placed the situations of the most
rural and marginalized African Americans during and after slavery within the
interlocking webs of a world capitalist system characterized by "the color
line." Although Du Bois produced important empirical and historical analyses, his perspective on women must be gleaned from a wide variety of writings, most of which sociologists ignore because they are not perceived to be
systematic and formal theory.

African American women's lives highlighted a nexus of social problems.
Du Bois was critical of the subordinate sexual status, limited family role, and
economic dependency that the dominant culture enforced for all women. At
the same time, Du Bois pointed to the ways in which these limits particularly
and peculiarly oppressed black women. African American women had been
consigned to the social and moral margins of society and, because of their
experiences at these margins, they were vital to the process of progressive
social change and to the realization of a future United States as a multicultural social democracy. A single-minded reading of Du Bois's diverse writings—poetry, prose, fiction, empirical studies, litanies, editorials, essays,

parables, and jeremiads—points to the conclusion that, for Du Bois, black women represented a unique force for progressive change in the United States. Du Bois's insights anticipated the contemporary importance of standpoint and consciousness for the interpretation of women's history and for the practical implications of the intersections of race and class in women's experiences.[5]

EMERGENT DEMOCRACY AND THE MARGINS OF SOCIAL EXPERIENCE

Theories of society not only describe the structures and dynamics of particular nation states but they also, implicitly or explicitly, offer images of human progress and social change. These theories often take their shape from the assumptions thinkers hold about the nature and direction of social change. Although issues of class, race, and gender ought to be addressed, most early social theory only focused on class and not on gender or race. In spite of its prominence in American society, the problem of race relations was not accorded the same theoretical importance as were issues centered on class, change, and social structure. Critical theories that assumed the primacy of human action and enterprise in the process of social change often dismissed the issues of race and gender as subordinate to or derived from the problem of class. The result, according to Anthony Giddens, has been a neglect of gender and of racial-ethnic oppressions. Both structural functionalism and conflict theory attempt to address the grand issues of history, but the problems of race and gender are not central to the development of a general theory of either social action or history, enterprises Giddens and Mills warned should never have been separated.[6]

Du Bois began his sociological work on American society when Emile Durkheim and Max Weber, two of the most important "founders" of sociology, were at work in Europe. While studying in Germany, Du Bois heard Weber lecture and had an opportunity to study with the German economist Gustav Schmoller.[7] Du Bois received his Ph.D. in 1895, the same year in which Durkheim, the first French academic sociologist, published *Suicide* and just six years after Weber defended his dissertation. In 1899, four years after Durkheim published *Suicide,* Du Bois published *The Philadelphia Negro,* the first empirical community study in the history of American sociology.[8] Weber read and admired *Souls of Black Folk*, suggesting that it ought to be translated into German. In 1906, Weber edited a journal and included in it an essay by Du Bois.[9] Durkheim died in 1917 and Weber in 1920.[10] Thus, Du Bois began to address the major problems of democracy and inequality in American society when the basic problems of sociological thought were still being formulated and debated.

Sociology for Du Bois was a means to seek solutions to social problems. The problems of African Americans were central to his understanding of the dynamics and direction of the United States. Du Bois was an astute observer of the problems of African Americans and the societal contradictions with which they were inextricably bound. The practical side of his sociological imagination assumed that the problems and methods of sociology could be beneficial for African Americans particularly and for the society as a whole. The theoretical side was historical, seeking lessons for the future from the past. African Americans were deeply implicated in the formation and development of class structure in the United States. Their emancipation or liberation was necessary for social progress. Du Bois's vision of an expanding or emergent democracy included all of the voices on the social margins. However, he felt his responsibility was to articulate clearly the African American voice.

Early in his work, Du Bois developed a broad theory of history that concerned itself with the development of democracy and of American culture. He focused on describing and explaining the history of the United States' political economy. Society was the result of the human enterprise that challenged structures that restricted participation in this developing, emerging, or evolving democracy. Du Bois viewed American culture and political economy as unfinished human projects which every group played an historical role in "making"—a theme that comes through clearly in his emphasis in *The Gift of Black Folk*, on the role of African Americans in the "making of America."[11]

For overall social progress, Du Bois acknowledged the importance of all categories of human experience and their subsequent emancipations: "...women ... peasants ... laborers, [and the] ... socially damned."[12] These people were the key to the proper evolution of United States society as a model democracy; they were the central motive force in the making of America. The freeing of laborers, the freeing of women, and the freeing of black people were all unfinished developments essential to the progress of society. Black women, because of their gender, race,[13] and work role, contributed to the emergence of all three emancipations, thus providing both an important sociological case and a vanguard role for the society. Prior to current concerns about African American women, African American women's experience had long been a public problem and a shared concern of the black community.[14]

In spite of the silence of European-based social theory, race was an historical and structural problem in the development of United States political economy. The earliest American sociology focused on the problem of slavery from a conservative point of view that actually defended and apologized for slavery utilizing the prevailing critique of capitalism.[15] As the nineteenth century gave way to the twentieth, Du Bois made it clear that the central problem of history and social structure of the twentieth century would be "the problem of the color line." Writing in *The Souls of Black Folk*, he stated,

The problem of the twentieth century is the problem of the color-line,—the relation of the darker to the lighter races of men in Asia and Africa, in America and the islands of the sea. It was a phase of this problem that caused the Civil War; and however much they who marched South and North in 1861 may have fixed on the technical points of union and local autonomy as a shibboleth, all nevertheless knew, as we know, that the question of Negro slavery was the real cause of the conflict."[16]

Du Bois believed in the importance of an activist social science for the growth and development of democracy. Like other sociologists, he recognized the importance of the great transformation that gave rise to the political revolutions of the eighteenth century. He also saw these revolutions as a logical development in the course of human history—an outgrowth of the revolutionary process basic to social change. He pointed out that:

Democratic movements inside groups and nations are always taking place and they are the efforts to increase the number of beneficiaries of the ruling. In 18th century Europe, the effort became so broad and sweeping that an attempt was made at universal expression and the philosophy of the movement said that if All ruled they would rule for All and thus Universal Good was sought through Universal Suffrage.[17]

Emphasizing what more accepted sociologists found important to the development of sociological theory, Du Bois eventually connected the thought of Marx and of Freud to his thinking.[18] Du Bois's view, that the expansion of democracy was perhaps the central motive force in history, was quite similar to Marx's.

As the principal spokesman for the NAACP and editor of its magazine, *Crisis*, Du Bois oversaw the consciousness of black people for nearly thirty-five years. Within the pages of the *Crisis*, Du Bois expressed the thrust of the NAACP's program as a "fight" for political, economic, and social equality.[19] However, it was not the only struggle. Other "fields to conquer" included

the question of political rights for women, for the poor, for the unrepresented laboring millions throughout the world; there is the problem of economic justice in the distribution of income and in the democratization of the whole industrial process; and there is the question of caste and social class based on wealth and privilege. There is above all the question of peace and the cessation of imperial aggression on weaker peoples.[20]

Du Bois argued that the problem of the color line blocked the realization of any other kind of human emancipation. "In other words," he insisted

the color line today is hindering democracy; is stopping economic justice; and is
making real human contact impossible. . . . not simply by depriving colored folk of
these advantages, but by the fact that through this color discrimination, the majority of white folk are also kept from democracy in politics, industry and society."[21]

This expansion of democracy in the United States and the role of black
people in that expansion, was the "making of America." Such a view of
history mandated a detailed analysis of the African American experience. In
his examination of the historical role of black people and in his advocacy for
the disinherited, the central importance of the role of women in the politics,
economics, and social organization of black communities emerged. He
constructed a sociological perspective that accounted for the importance of
race in history. His observations of the particular situation of black people in
the United States led him to assert the importance of black women and men to
wider society. In spite of the accuracy of his perspective, Du Bois found
himself on the margins of mainstream sociological thought.

The origins of sociological theory lie in the attempt of students of political
economy to explain the massive social changes of European societies—
changes fueled by the industrial and political revolutions of the eighteenth and
nineteenth centuries—and to interpret their consequences for culture and
social organization. Since the major facts confronting thinkers such as Marx,
Weber, and Durkheim involved the social dislocation of European agricultural
laborers and their subsequent urbanization, the problem of social theory
became the problem of "the social institutions brought into being by the
industrial transformations of the past two or three centuries."[22] Since those
social institutions were dramatically shaped by the rise of capitalism and the
emergence of the class societies associated with capitalism, the problems of
sociology have been grounded in the questions surrounding social class and its
primary importance in the modern social order of advanced societies in
Europe.

As sociology developed in the United States, the historical particularity of
social analysis so critical to the perspectives of Marx, Weber, and Du Bois was
lost. The problem of social class and social change modulated into the problem
of socio-economic status and occupational ranking. In the United States, that
meant a principal preoccupation with the problems of a white, male labor
force. Furthermore, the European origins of sociological theory obscured the
problem of origins in the study of the political economy of the United States.
An adequate historical methodology was rooted in the Marxian tradition, a
tradition largely suppressed during the McCarthy era, further obscuring the
problem of class conflict. Since Du Bois eventually took Marx's sociological
perspective and its historical emphasis quite seriously, this further marginalized

him in society and as a sociologist. What C. Wright Mills calls "abstracted empiricism" and "grand theory" emerged from preoccupations with white male reality, especially in such areas as stratification, work, and occupations and professions.[23] This deepened the subordination of the problems of gender and race in the development of sociological theory.

Consequently, gender and race have been viewed as subsidiary problems in the study of society and subordinate issues in the development of sociological theory. Failing in several areas of concern, sociological theory has been particularly deficient in its attention to the "several sets of questions linked to human emancipation," of which racial oppression and gender are most prominent.[24] Although Giddens defines these questions with reference to the failure of Marx and Marxist writings, it is really the failure of sociologists to apply the historical method, so integral to Marxist analysis, to the United States that is responsible for the deficiency. Thus, in addition to the problems of human adjustment to nature and of the role of the state and its monopoly on violence, the problems of racial-ethnic oppression and of sexual oppression remain urgent and demanding issues.

For Du Bois, however, oppression always was the central issue. And like the sociologists of the early Chicago School,[25] Du Bois was quite impatient with "armchair" thinking.[26] However, his writings contain within them a critical sociology built upon his observations of African American women and their situation in the United States. By placing women at center stage in the drama of history, Du Bois is able to highlight the importance of African American women and men to democracy, social change, society, and history. His is a political sociology that specializes in historical perspectives on the nature of American culture. Taken together these insights add up to a coherent theory of history which assumes that progress takes the form of an ever expanding democracy, and regards progress as the result of human enterprise.

BEHIND THE VEIL: DUBOIS'S WRITINGS ABOUT WOMEN

A critical component of Du Bois's sociological thinking focused on African American women and their historical role in the United States. He recognized black women's suffering as a social fact, acknowledged their collective autonomy as a valuable social institution, and interpreted their experience as a significant social and historical force. His thinking about women was part of a political sociology and a descriptive analysis of the formation and emergence of American culture. And these women's lives were central to the larger project of human emancipation. The questions of human emancipation were precisely what concerned Du Bois when he focused on African American women. "In law and custom," Du Bois wrote, "our women have no rights which a white man is bound to respect."[27]

Over the course of his eighty-year career as a published writer, Du Bois wrote pieces that specifically addressed the problems of African American women. His early work as a newspaper correspondent from 1883 to 1885 for the *New York Globe* shows a sensitivity to the contributions of black women to community life.[28] As "exchange" editor of the *Fisk Herald* in 1885, Du Bois responded to an article on feminism by observing, "The column on woman's work is interesting, and a first rate woman's rights argument."[29] It was in the *Fisk Herald*, after becoming editor in chief in 1887, that Du Bois published his novel *Tom Brown*, a semi-autobiographical novel in which the protagonist is a woman school teacher.[30] In 1892 Du Bois published articles, "my Harvard daily themes," in a paper called the *Courant*, edited by Josephine St. Pierre Ruffin.[31]

This editorial relationship was highly significant. Josephine St. Pierre Ruffin was a suffragist, an early supporter of Ida B. Wells-Barnett, the founder of the Woman's Era Club (one of the earliest black women's clubs), and a prime mover in the black women's club movement.[32] It was Ruffin who provided the classic definition of a woman's movement from an African American women's perspective: she defined the black women's movement as a movement led by women for the benefit of women and men, and she invited men to join women's work and struggles.[33] The woman who offered the defining ideas of the black women's movement was one of Du Bois's earliest employers. According to Du Bois:

> Mrs. Ruffin of Charles Street, Boston ... was a widow of the first colored judge appointed in Massachusetts, an aristocratic lady.... She began a national organization of colored women and published the *Courant*, a type of small colored weekly paper which was spreading over the nation. In this I published many of my Harvard daily themes.[34]

Early in his career as a scholar and an activist, then, Du Bois was publicly associated with the woman whose conference call launched the most critical mobilization of African American women in the history of the United States.

Herbert Aptheker's survey of Du Bois's writings indicates that he contributed pieces on African American women and their work, literature, birth control, education, and politics to a variety of periodicals, and developed a substantial body of material during his tenure at the *Crisis*. He was friends with quite a few women leaders, including Jane Addams, Mary McLeod Bethune, and Florence Kelley, and a number of other active feminists. He openly supported women's suffrage precisely because he believed in the ultimate importance of women to the political liberation of African American people. The contact and consciousness with the organized public life of black women that began during his early years and continued throughout his lifetime, and Du Bois was socialized to include women and women's experience in his thinking. Du Bois's relationships with women need to be remembered when examining his writings about women.

"WEEPING AND WAITING": SUFFERING AS SOCIAL FACT

Du Bois maintained that African American women approached American society with a unique perspective, one that came from their suffering. He exclaimed in his 1887 novel, *Tom Brown at Fiske,* "It's hard to be a woman, but a black one—!"[35] One of Du Bois's most significant discussions of black women can be found in his essay, "The Damnation of Women." The essay was part of a larger work, *Darkwater: Voices from Within the Veil,*—a volume "of poems, essays, and sketches previously published in the *Crisis,* the *Independent,* the *Atlantic,* and the *Journal of Race Development* but here very considerably revised, changed, and expanded."[36]

In *Darkwater,* Du Bois offers a cogent political critique of leadership and its relationship to contemporary social problems. In "Of the Ruling of Men," he argues that twentieth-century leaders must be inclusive in their thinking and beliefs: "The persons, then, who come forward in the dawn of the 20th century to help in the ruling of men must come with the firm conviction that no nation, race, or sex, has a monopoly of ability or ideas."[37] For Du Bois the problem was complex, and first of all demanded respect for the ideas of people of all nationalities, all races, and of both women and men. He wrote, "no human group is so small as to deserve to be ignored as a part, and as an integral and respected part, of the mass of men."[38] He then referred specifically to the "twelve million black folk" who were "at the physical mercy of a hundred million white majority."[39] He argued that the denial of real political power and advancement crippled "the very foundations of all democracy and all human uplift."[40] Referring to elites as "consciously efficient minorities," he criticized their desire to restrict suffrage and argued that they did not need "less democracy" to maintain their position.[41] "However desperate the temptation," he declared," no modern nation can shut the gates of opportunity in the face of its women, its peasants, its laborers, or its socially damned."[42] Du Bois concluded on a note of outrage about the debate over woman suffrage and racism, saying:

> How astounded the future world-citizen will be to know that as late as 1918 great
> and civilized nations were making desperate endeavor to confine the development
> of ability and individuality to one sex,—that is, to one-half of the nation; and he
> will probably learn that similar effort to confine humanity to one race lasted a
> hundred years longer."[43]

His poetry also demonstrated the deep feeling with which Du Bois viewed the suffering of black women. In his poem "The Riddle of the Sphinx," he interprets the famous statue as a black woman sentinel listening to a "whistling wind" that represents "that soul-waking cry, . . . out of the South, —the sad, black South— . . . / Crying: 'Awake, O Ancient Race!' Wailing, 'O woman, arise!'"[44] Then follows Du Bois's explanation why the Sphinx, this "dark daughter," is unable to rise to challenge the source of this suffering:

> And crying and sighing and crying again as a voice
> in the midnight cries,—
> But the burden of white men bore her back and the
> white world stifled her sighs.[45]

He then angrily refers to the "white world's vermin and filth" as the source of African and African American oppression and suffering. Within the poem there is a critique of the internal politics of colonialism that challenges the complicity of native elites in the establishment of the color line, and a prediction that those same political forces may also "drag them down again." The process of undoing the evils of colonialism, according to Du Bois's imagery, would be advanced by a black man and woman who would "Bid the black Christ be born!" The poem ends on a note of hope, with a prayer to this "black mother":

> Then shall our burden be manhood,
> Be it yellow or black or white;
> And poverty and justice and sorrow,
> The humble and simple and strong
> Shall sing with the sons of morning
> And the daughters of even-song:
> > Black mother of the iron hills that ward the
> > blazing sea,
> > Wild spirit of a storm-swept soul, a-struggling
> > to be free,
> > Where 'neath the bloody finger-marks
> > thy riven bosom quakes,
> > Thicken the thunders of God's Voice and lo!
> > a world awakes![46]

For Du Bois, the suffering of black women provided them with a legitimate voice of challenge and, metaphorically, endowed them with the power to speak to God.

There are other pieces in which Du Bois asserts this power. In a vein similar to that of liberation theologians today, Du Bois insisted that God was a God of the disinherited and, as such, would appear in places where this suffering was taking place, challenging the oppressed to play a messianic role in the transformation of society. In four other pieces, "The Second Coming,"[47] "Jesus Christ in Texas,"[48] "The Call,"[49] and "Children of the Moon,"[50] he alludes to the sufferings of black women as the places where God and the Christ are revealed.

His parable, "The Call," is of particular interest because it clearly argues that the role of black women in society is a prophetic role. Prior to its inclusion in *Darkwater*, the essay was published in *Crisis* in 1911, under the title "The Woman."[51] Not only a rationalization for black women's participation in the public affairs of the community, the essay chides more privileged people for their failure to match the efforts of black women. God is imaged as "the King" who has come to "the Land of the Heavy Laden." At an initial call for "the Servants of the King," "there were a hundred-and-forty-four thousand, —tried men and brave . . . and women of wisdom and women marvelous in beauty and grace." Any one familiar with the Apocalypse (the biblical book of Revelation) will recognize this group as the chosen people— those expected to be in the heavenly elite. Perhaps this is a subtle critique of the talented tenth. These servants were too overwhelmed by enemies to fulfill their calling, so, "They hid their faces in dread silence and moved not." After the King calls three times a woman arrives at the throne, having abandoned her domestic drudgery, and responds, "'The servant of thy servants, O Lord.'" She receives the order, "'Go smite me mine enemies.'" After she has "lifted her eyes to the hills" and observed "the heathen whirling onward in their rage," obvious references to Psalms 121 and 122, she attempts to excuse herself from answering on the grounds that she is a woman. Of course God responds that she is clearly capable because she is "Mother of Men." She then attempts to use her age as an excuse, a response similar to that of Jeremiah, and that excuse is also rejected. Finally the woman insists, "Dear God I am black!" At this point in the story, Du Bois uses the device of a theophany to establish the moral authority of black women to speak to and for the community. He writes:

> The King spake not, but swept the veiling of his face aside and lifted up the light of his countenance upon her and lo! it was black.
>
> So the woman went forth on the hills of God to do battle for the King, on that drear day in the land of the Heavy Laden, when the heathen raged and imagined a vain thing.[52]

Various aspects of the story mirror the biblical stories of prophets and their calls and commissions to challenge society. At a time when the position of black women as leaders, particularly in religious bodies, was under severe attack, Du Bois's essay was a challenge to those male leaders, particularly religious leaders, whom he perceived to be more of a hindrance than a help. Like "The Woman," "The Call" was aimed at and reached a very large audience. However, Du Bois makes an additional allusion by retitling it "The Call" in *Darkwater* and placing it just after "Of the Ruling of Men" and immediately before "The Damnation of Women." Du Bois affirms the importance of black women's leadership by pointing to their experience as the basis for a divinely appointed mission to exercise power.

The "Damnation of Women" is a powerful piece.[53] It is a detailed exploration of the history and experience of black women in the United States with reference to their African background. The starting point of Du Bois's analysis is the experience of "four women of my boyhood"—his mother and two cousins, and a very deprived white woman. As the essay develops he also reflects on his African heritage in the person of the "far-off mother of my grandmothers." Du Bois moves from the particular to the general and places the experiences of these women in the contexts of world and American history in order to demonstrate the tensions between the African experience and that in the United States, and between the experiences of black women and white women. Du Bois also identifies a fundamental contradiction of American society and a modern world that wanted "healthy babies and intelligent workers," but

> refuse[d] to allow the combination and force[d] thousands of intelligent workers to go childless at a horrible expenditure of moral force, or we damn them if they break our idiotic conventions. Only at the sacrifice of intelligence and the chance to do their best work can the majority of modern women bear children. This is the damnation of women.[54]

This general contradiction affecting all women did not begin to describe the situation of black women. Excluded from the "worship of women" that characterized treatment of the good women, black women were "daughters of sorrow" whose particular experiences "the world must heed."[55] Those particular experiences range from the prehistoric to the contemporary.

Du Bois uses the particular experiences of the women he knows to move through a very specific outline of history. That outline begins with a statement of African cultural attitudes toward mothers specifically and women generally. While acknowledging that the life and work of African women was arduous, Du Bois appeals to ancient history to point out:

[T]hat the woman, though often heavily burdened, is in herself held in no small esteem among the Negroes is clear from the numerous Negro queens, from the medicine women, from the participation in public meetings permitted to women by many Negro peoples.[56]

The observations of anthropologists and travellers confirmed Du Bois's impressions of his "far-off mother of my grandmothers," whose sad songs mourned the loss of a world where "it is mothers and mothers of mothers who seem to count." He follows this cultural theme through into slavery where black people preserved the family in spite of the law. He points to advertisements for runaway slaves that mention the motivation for running away as being attempts to see mothers, wives, and other relatives. The assumptions concerning the women who survived slavery seemed to be that "nothing decent in womanhood" could emerge. Furthermore, people assumed that progress and development were impossible for black women given their history of suffering during slavery. Du Bois asked, and answered:

> Can all these women be vile and the hunted race continue to grow in wealth and character? Impossible. Yet to save from the past the shreds and vestiges of self-respect has been a terrible task. I most sincerely doubt if any other race of women could have brought its fineness up through so devilish a fire.[57]

Du Bois found the lack of protection for black girls and women and their transformation into breeders the most appalling aspects of slavery. He found it so devastating that he declared himself unable to "forgive, neither in this world or the world to come: [the white South's] wanton and continued and persistent insulting of black womanhood which it sought and seeks to prostitute to its lust."[58] The fierceness and singularity of this degradation was the index by which the status of the entire black community could be measured. He agreed with and cited Anna Julia Cooper's declaration: "Only the black woman can say 'when and where I enter, in the quiet, undisputed dignity of my womanhood, without violence and without suing or special patronage, then and there the whole Negro race enters with me.'"[59]

Du Bois juxtaposed the details of their suffering with black women's contribution to the community. It was this heroic response to suffering that Du Bois emphasized. He started, again, with his experience in Great Barrington, Massachusetts, and the life experience of "'Mum Bett,'" a freed woman who moved one white man to write: "Having known this woman as familiarly as I knew either of my parents, I cannot believe in the moral or physical inferiority of the race to which she belonged. The degradation of the African must have been otherwise caused than by natural inferiority."[60] Du Bois portrays her as paradigmatic of "such strong women that laid the foundations of the great Negro church of today." Other "such strong women" were Harriet Tubman, Sojourner Truth, and Mary [Ann] Shadd [Carey]. Out of slavery and into freedom, Du Bois declared, "the sacrifice of Negro women for freedom and uplift is one of the finest chapters in their history."[61] He believed passionately that "it is the five million women of my race who really count." He went on to detail their roles as teachers, churchwomen, settlement house workers, homemakers, and employees. All of this Du Bois saw as the outcome of their suffering.

The suffering of black women was a particular yet critical component of the suffering and injustice that was part of many American experiences, and it was a situation that demanded heroic and prophetic responses. The social movements of black women were a redemptive response to that suffering. Du Bois was not arguing a fundamental difference between women and men similar to the "moral superiority" theme that was part of white feminist ideology of the nineteenth century. Instead, Du Bois was making a sociological point: that black women's actions represented a situated response to social reality, what Patricia Hill Collins calls black women's standpoint.[62] Such a perspective was consistent with Du Bois's view that deprivation and oppression made all excluded groups, particularly laboring groups, women, and black people, a challenge to society. In the context of American political economy, the situation that offered the most comprehensive challenge was that of black women. American society, by the very facts of its history, was forced to reckon with black women and the social fact of their suffering as a motive force in the progress or development of the society.

"THE WORLD MUST HEED": BLACK WOMEN AS AN HISTORICAL FORCE

Du Bois viewed black women as a motive force in the progress and expansion of this emergent democracy. Du Bois concluded "The Damnation of Women" with an accounting of the way in which black women challenged traditions and structures that restricted all women. Noting that labor force participation represented a "clash of ideals and facts," Du Bois confronted the resulting problems with which black women coped, problems such as broken homes. He asked, "Is the cause racial?" and he answered, "No, it is economic."[63] Du Bois maintained that black women's economic independence changed the institution of the family by challenging its harem-like structure. He summarized the overall effect of black women's economic freedom."

> Indeed, here, in microcosm and with differences emphasizing sex equality, is the industrial history of labor in the 19th and 20th centuries. We cannot abolish the new economic freedom of women. We cannot imprison women again in a home or require them all on pain of death to be nurses and housekeepers.[64]

From this point, he focused on the universal implications of black women and their work, concluding:

> What is today the message of these black women to America and to the world? The uplift of women is, next to the problem of the color line and the peace movement, our greatest modern cause. When, now, two of these movements—woman and color—combine in one, the combination has deep meaning.[65]

Du Bois expands our understanding of this "deep meaning" in his 1924 book *The Gift of Black Folk*.[66] Du Bois demonstrates in this much ignored document that the black experience itself is central to the material and cultural development of the United States as an industrial democracy. The presence of black people was a redemptive element in a history of violence, economic exploitation, and ideological contradiction.

The Gift of Black Folk was written during the height of the American nativist movement to restrict immigration. Membership in the Ku Klux Klan was the largest ever in United States history and cultural racism was a part of the dominant popular racial ideologies. Du Bois countered that America's pluralism was one of its strengths. What we now call diversity was to Du Bois's way of thinking a force for the society's development. Nativists mobilized around their white protestant identities when they perceived southern and eastern European immigration and black urban migration as challenges to their dominance. Du Bois believed their fears were unfounded. As part of his anti-nativist argument, Du Bois described and analyzed the role black people played in building the economy and in shaping social and political history. Du Bois argued that "despite our present Negro problem, the American Negro is, and has been, a distinct asset to this country and has brought a contribution without which America could not have been."[67]

For Du Bois, "the growth of democracy" was the central development in human progress. Within that development, "The emancipation of woman is ... but one phase." However, he continued, "It deserves perhaps separate treatment because it is an interesting example of the way in which the Negro has helped American democracy."[68] In the context of the black experience, Du Bois saw women's experience, in spite of the cruelty and exploitation, as a milestone in the emancipation of humanity. Just the title and abstract of his chapter on women pointed to the important social consequences of black women's experiences: "The Freedom of Womanhood: How the black woman from her low estate not only united two great human races but helped lift herself and all women to economic independence and self-expression." Du Bois characterized this experience as "not only a moral but an economic revolution."[69]

The principal area in which black women brought about emancipation was in the labor force, as "a group of workers, fighting for their daily bread like men; independent and approaching economic freedom."[70] Their economic role was a challenge to assumptions about women's place within the economy and the society. Du Bois noted that, although black women had not willingly entered the labor force, "economic independence is . . . the central fact in the struggle of women for equality."[71] Because the American industrial revolution had discovered the value of women workers and because "the usual sentimental arguments against women at work were not brought forward in the case of Negro womanhood,"[72] Du Bois concluded that black women had effectively challenged social custom. Du Bois recognized the significance of black women's work before later analyses also pointed to the challenge black women posed to traditional notions of women's place.[73]

In his analysis of race and American culture, Du Bois insisted that Americans were one people and that the imprint of Africa in America extended beyond the boundaries of black communities. Black women's sexual and domestic exploitation was the site of this contradiction. Concomitant with and facilitating black women's exploitation as concubines was their exploitation as nursemaids and houseservants. Du Bois argued that black women were to a certain degree responsible for the Africanization of the South. In spite or because of their coerced domestic roles, black women became agents of socialization and cultural diffusion within white families. Du Bois's observations subverted the assertions of E. Franklin Frazier and others that household service socialized or "civilized" black people. Du Bois wrote:

> Again and in more concrete ways the Negro woman has influenced America and that is by her personal contact with the [white] family—its men, women, and children. As housekeeper, maid and nurse—as confidante, adviser and friend, she was often an integral part of the white family life of the South, and transmitted her dialect, her mannerisms, her quaint philosophy and her boundless sympathy.[74]

Du Bois also argued that the consequences of the sexual exploitation of black women demolished any appeals to biology as an ideological defense of the color line and challenged any pretensions of white people to racial purity. This portion of the essay is difficult, however, because Du Bois has difficulty generating a rhetoric of outrage similar to that in "The Damnation of Women." Ostensibly his focus is on African American women's contributions to culture and society, and yet their sexual exploitation was often used against them to intensify their humiliation and degradation. Thus Du Bois chose to relativize their concubinage in spite of his earlier and clearly expressed anger. As a product of the nineteenth century, he was caught between the rock of

nineteenth-century white judgements labeling black women a "nation of pros-
titutes" and the hard place of extracting redeeming consequences from their
experience. Sensitive to the pain involved, Du Bois averred, "It [concubinage]
is a subject scarcely to be mentioned today with our conventional morals and
with the bitter racial memories swirling about this institution of slavery. Yet
the fact remains stark, ugly, painful, beautiful."[75]

Du Bois was sensitive to the moral damnation of black women, and his
analysis of this sexual history was an attempt to redeem it and wring meaning
out of it. If one considers that "Du Bois rejected explanations based on
biological differences or inherent inferiority,"[76] then perhaps it is not unreasonable to assume that part of Du Bois's strategy in stressing "the fact" "that
the colored slave women became the medium through which two great races
were united in America"[77] involved a challenge to white racial purity. Even
considering his consciousness of black women's sensitivity to the cultural
humiliation entailed in their sexual history, Du Bois's attempt seems clumsy in
light of contemporary critiques of sexual oppression.

In addition to the redeeming cultural challenge black women posed to
racism, they also presented a political challenge. Du Bois pointed to their
tradition of political rebellion, calling it "the work of Negro women in revolt
which cannot be forgotten."[78] This rebellious "work" was illustrated by the
lives of women such as Harriet Tubman and [Mary Ellen] Pleasants. One
exemplified military leadership and rebellion and the other economic leadership. Pleasants used her personal fortune to support John Brown and to
support the building of at least three black churches in California.[79]

These women were exemplars of a broader paradigm of activism, best
exemplified by the club movement for the work of racial uplift. Du Bois
argued that this work for racial uplift was a distinct contribution to social
change as well as a challenge to the elite image affluent white women attached
to community service. Pointing to this contrast, Du Bois wrote:

> [W]e have finally only to remember that to-day the women of America who are
> doing humble but on the whole the most effective work in the social uplift of the
> lowly, *not so much by money as by personal contact*, are the colored women. Little
> is said or known about it but in thousands of churches and social clubs, in mission-
> ary societies and fraternal organizations, in unions like the National Association of
> Colored Women, these workers are founding and sustaining orphanages and old
> folk homes; distributing personal charity and relief; visiting prisoners; helping
> hospitals; teaching children; and ministering to all sorts of needs.[80]

In sum, Du Bois described the historical role of black women as an emancipatory one for all women and for the entire black population: "We have noted

then the Negro woman in America as a worker tending to emancipate all women workers; as a mother nursing the white race and uniting the black and white race; as a conspirator urging forward emancipation in various sorts of ways...."[81] As people learned about the challenge to oppressive social customs and about the work for human improvement, Du Bois optimistically believed that the effect was a general improvement of "human sympathy" and "in minimizing racial difficulties." As part of his larger theory of history that envisioned an emergent democracy with a future of expanded social opportunity for all people, the historical role of black women was central to the realization of cultural and political change.

"AN EFFICIENT WOMANHOOD": BLACK WOMANHOOD AS CULTURE

Du Bois trusted black women politically and socially and he praised them as "the intellectual leadership of the race."[82] Du Bois described the way in which Black women's experience challenged cultural norms in a way that has come to be known as "the dialectics of black womanhood."[83] The historical consequences of the black female experience and the challenge of that experience to the dominant culture's prescriptions for women created a specially equipped community of women:

> The result of this history of insult and degradation has been both fearful and glorious. It has birthed the haunting prostitute, the brawler, and the beast of burden; but it has also given the world an efficient womanhood, whose strength lies in its freedom and whose chastity was won in the teeth of temptation and not in prison and swaddling clothes.[84]

This "efficient womanhood" was the central pillar in his argument for woman suffrage. Du Bois marshalled the full editorial power of the *Crisis* behind this cause. And because of his belief in black women, Du Bois passionately rejected every possible argument against women's suffrage.

In an editorial, published in November, 1915, to advocate "Woman Suffrage," Du Bois launched an impassioned argument concerning the effectiveness of black women's voting behavior.[85] This article was in opposition to an article by Kelly Miller "against woman suffrage" that he published in the same issue. Du Bois constructed a detailed and scathing refutation of Miller's arguments that childrearing, weakness, and the need for male protection made it impossible and unnecessary "for women to take any large part in general, industrial, and public affairs." He appealed inclusively to women's history to support his claims, saying "The sex of Judith, Candace, Queen Elizabeth, Sojourner Truth and Jane Addams was the merest incident of human function and not a mark of weakness and inferiority."[86]

In an editorial published in September, 1912, Du Bois described the compelling interest of black America in women's suffrage. He gave three reasons:

> First, it is a great human question. Nothing human must be foreign, uninteresting, or unimportant to colored citizens of the world.... Secondly, any agitation, discussion, or reopening of the problem of voting must inevitably be a discussion of the right of black folk to vote in America and Africa. Essentially the arguments for and against are the same in the case of all groups of human beings.... Finally votes for women mean votes for black women.[87]

This third reason, "votes for black women," was tied to Du Bois's observation of the black women's world. He noted that opportunities for black women in the urban labor force at that time were "larger ... than [for] their husbands and brothers." The suffrage argument took place when the black urban population was heavily female.[88] At that time, the urbanization of black women's work made collective action through the vote possible. Furthermore, rural black families were educating their daughters in order to provide occupational alternatives with less risk of sexual exploitation. Du Bois observed that urbanization and, later, northern migration were important strategies for black political empowerment. Black women as a group were "rapidly becoming better educated," and he saw this as a great political advantage to black America.

The fruits of this better education could be seen, he argued, in the "recent biennial convention of colored women's clubs with its 400 delegates."[89] This club movement was evidence that black women were moving quietly but forcibly toward the intellectual leadership of the race."[90] In Du Bois's view, black women's world view or standpoint was extremely valuable for the political fate of the black community:

> The enfranchisement of these women will not be a mere doubling of our vote and voice in the nation; it will tend to stronger and more normal political life, the rapid dethronement of the heeler and grafter, and the making of politics a method of broadest philanthropic race betterment, rather than a disreputable means of private gain.[91]

Du Bois advanced the same argument in another editorial, also titled "Votes for Women," published in November, 1917. He urged black male voters in the state of New York to "cast [their] ballot in favor of woman suffrage,"[92] insisting on black women's voters incorruptible perspective:

> Moreover, it is going to be more difficult to disfranchise colored women in the
> South than it was to disfranchise colored men. Even Southern "gentlemen," as
> used as they are to the mistreatment of colored women, cannot in the blaze of
> present publicity physically beat them away from the polls. [White men's]
> economic power over [black women] will be smaller than power over the men and
> while you can still bribe some pauperized Negro laborers with a few dollars at
> election time, you cannot bribe Negro women.[93]

Although Du Bois was overly optimistic about the public chivalry of white men, he sincerely believed that black women exercised a higher morality in their political behavior.

Du Bois's belief in "an efficient womanhood" was also based on his assessments of black women's religious orientation. Religious faith was not only the basis for the heroism of Sojourner Truth, Harriet Tubman, and others, but it was also at the foundations of their organizational efforts. All of the secular black women's organizations begun in the early twentieth century were started by church women. Prayer and church connections were part of black women's secular organizational life.

In "Damnation of Women," he cited religion, saying, "It was ... strong women that laid the foundations of the great Negro church of today, with its five million members and ninety millions of dollars in property."[94] He cited particularly the role of "early mothers of the church" such as Mary Still, and the founding of the African Methodist Episcopal Church.[95] He insisted that there was a connection between "such spiritual ancestry" and Tubman's efforts to free slaves, support John Brown, and serve the Union Army.[96] He cited Sojourner Truth's challenge to Frederick Douglass when he insisted that black people had "no hope of justice ... except in their own right arms." Sojourner Truth "spoke out in her deep, peculiar voice, heard all over the hall: 'Frederick, is God dead?'"[97] Du Bois also cited the work of Kate Ferguson, a nineteen-year-old widow who took in orphans and began the "first modern Sunday School in Manhattan."[98] He insisted that this foundation extended to "the sacrifice of Negro women for freedom and uplift" that was, he declared, "one of the finest chapters in their history."[99]

Du Bois's praise of black women was part of his criticism of his brothers. His own conflict with Booker T. Washington was symptomatic of a wide range of conflicts among black male clergy and other leaders that Du Bois felt hindered black progress. Du Bois called black women "efficient" because of their ability to work together across class and color lines in spite of their disagreements. He concluded his observations on black women's collective importance by saying:

As I look about me today in this veiled world of mine, despite the noisier and more spectacular advance of my brothers, I instinctively feel and know that it is the five million women of my race who really count. Black women (and women whose grandmothers were black) are today furnishing our teachers; they are the main pillars of those social settlements which we call churches; and they have with small doubt raised three-fourths of our church property. If we have today, as seems likely, over a billion dollars of accumulated goods, who shall say how much of it has been wrung from the hearts of servant girls and washerwomen and women toilers in the fields? As makers of two million homes these women are today seeking in marvelous ways to show forth our strength and beauty and our conception of truth.[100]

The organized world of urban black women was a center piece in the organizational integrity of black culture and a critical expression of its communal ethos. The "personal contact" Du Bois praised was a network of women that provided economic and social benefits to "the Race" as a whole, and provided a collective basis for a political challenge that offered an alternative morality and political philosophy to the racism and inhumanity of American society.

The serious questions about the "deep meaning" of black women's experience in the United States were important to Du Bois. He provided several answers to his questions. He argued, "One of the mightiest revolts of the century is against the devilish decree that no woman is a woman who is not by present standards a beautiful woman."[101] By present standards, Du Bois meant white standards. Black women simply by virtue of their physical beings challenged the oppression of appearance norms.[102] "Not being expected to be merely ornamental, they have girded themselves for work, instead of adorning their bodies only for play. Their sturdier minds have concluded that if a woman be clean, healthy, and educated, she is as pleasing as God wills and far more useful than most of her sisters."[103] Again he emphasized the consequences of the challenge posed by black women's experience:

Out of a sex freedom that today makes us shudder will come in time a day when we will no longer pay men for work they do not do, for the sake of their harem; we will pay women what they earn and insist on their working and earning it; we will allow those persons to vote who know enough to vote, whether they be black or female, white or male; and we will ward race suicide, not by further burdening the over-burdened, but by honoring motherhood, even when the sneaking father shirks his duty.... [O]ur women in black had freedom thrust contemptuously upon them. With that freedom they are buying an untrammeled independence and dear as is the price they pay for it, it will in the end be worth every taunt and groan.[104]

Du Bois's perspectives on African American women anticipated and influenced concepts and ideas we currently use to examine the intersection of gender, race, and class with reference to African American women.

CONCLUSION: IMPLICATIONS FOR A CRITICAL SOCIOLOGY

Gender, race, and movements for social change continue to be the crisis points for sociological thought.[105] Du Bois would not have been surprised at the emergence of multiple social movements from the struggle for civil rights, especially the women's movement and its impact on research and theory.[106] The political responses to these movements, especially the War on Poverty, provided a special stimulus for social research on inequality and on urban life and culture in black communities, something that Du Bois had insisted should be the priorities of sociology. However, Du Bois would have been outraged at the misplaced emphases on the family problems of black people and the gratuitous speculation on the role of black women. The condemnation of black women's work roles that emerged in the wake of the Moynihan report, its controversies, and the responses of black women to those controversies highlighted a society and social science that was still insisting upon counting bastards and ignoring the problems of inequities related to gender and race.[107] At the same time as social scientists discovered and defined as deviant black women, white upper-middle class women provided powerful insights into the overall problem of women's place in modern societies, focusing particularly on the trivialization and subordination of women and their work and on women's exclusion from the social spaces that make a public difference in society.[108] Their observations clearly paralleled those of Du Bois. The growth of the women's movement led to the growth of feminist theory. Feminist theorists, as had Du Bois, usually asked "What is life like for women?"[109] and sought to "create a new awareness of the situation of women in society and history."[110] These questions had a dramatic impact on sociology because of its traditional concerns with the family and sex roles.[111]

Yet these new movements and this new knowledge can be characterized by their failure to attend to the experience of black women. The continuing issues of racial and class inequality can be seen in the glaring tensions and sometimes conflicting concerns that erupt between black and white women. There are clear contradictions between black women's and white women's histories and their historical roles.[112] The results have been the perpetuation of racism within the feminist movement, misplaced and insensitive ideologies and practical strategies for social change, and an underdeveloped, unfinished, and inadequate feminist theory.[113]

Audre Lorde and bell hooks are heirs to the legacy of Du Bois and of the "efficient womanhood" he so much admired. They point out that one of the necessary revisions of feminist theory is the inclusion of the black experience in its theory of women's experience and an accounting for the tortured relationship between black and white experiences in the women's world. Audre Lorde identified manifestations of racial and class privilege that maintained barriers between women. One particularly telling incident pointed to the depths of race and class consciousness. She writes:

> I wheel my two-year-old daughter in a shopping cart through a supermarket in Eastchester in 1967, and a little white girl riding past in her mother's cart calls out excitedly, "Oh look, Mommy, a baby maid!" And your mother shushes you, but she does not correct you. And so fifteen years later, at a conference on racism, you can still find that story humorous. But I hear your laughter is full of terror and disease.[114]

These distortions of consciousness become the sources of operative myths that, according to bell hooks, allow ignorance to persist between women:

> Racist stereotypes of the strong, superhuman black woman are operative myths in the minds of many white women, allowing them to ignore the extent to which black women are likely to be victimized in this society and the role white women may play in the maintenance and perpetuation of that victimization.[115]

Du Bois's vision pointed to a society that could confront, respect, and embrace the gifts of all. Among women, the absence of black women and their experience cripples the prospects of justice for all women. Like Du Bois, hooks points to the gifts of unique experiences black women have to share:

> As a group, black women are in an unusual position in this society, for not only are we collectively at the bottom of the occupational ladder, but our overall social status is lower than that of any other group. Occupying such a position, we bear the brunt of sexist, racist, and classist oppression. At the same time, we are the group that has not been socialized to assume the role of exploiter/oppressor in that we are allowed no institutionalized "other" that we can exploit or oppress.[116]

Like Du Bois, hooks also points to the historical lessons in African American women's experience that should move us beyond defining liberation as "gaining social equality with ruling, class white men" and therefore maintaining "a vested interest in the continued exploitation and oppression of others."[117] Furthermore, like Du Bois, hooks points to black women's lack of privilege and extreme marginalization as the foundation of a unique view point and voice, which she sees as specially suited for the full articulation of a feminist theory and liberatory praxis. hooks concludes:

> It is essential for continued feminist struggle that black women recognize the special vantage point our marginality gives us and make use of this perspective to criticize the dominant racist, classist, sexist hegemony as well as to envision and create a counter-hegemony. I am suggesting that [black women] have a central role to play in the making of feminist theory and a contribution to offer that is unique and valuable.[118]

Sociological and feminist thought have just begun to confront the paradoxes and contradictions facing black women in the United States.[119] The genius of Du Bois's sociological perspective was his insistence that black women and men were at the nexus of international order or "the world system," and his articulation of their moral challenge to that order. Du Bois's sociology continues to be important because his theory of history and social change was grounded in systematic observation of the black experience and a detached but highly creative use of his own biography as a "a theory of my life ... with valuable testimony."[120] His cultural autobiography was shaped by his conscious observation of women's lives. As a result, his work is the earliest self-consciously sociological interpretation of the role of African American women as agents of social change. They were the marginal ones at the center of things.

For Du Bois, the African American women he knew and loved were role models for human emancipation. The prophetic insights he gleaned from their lives led him to prescribe political strategies such as women's suffrage and transformation of male leadership. While ahead of his time in his recognition of the challenge of African American women to a complexly unjust social order, Du Bois was a product and creature of his times—the last half of the nineteenth and the first half of the twentieth centuries—with many of its blindnesses and failures of perspective. Thus there are shortcomings in his perspective on sexuality and intimate relationships—a perspective that was shaped and motivated by his desire to be redemptive and to affirm the personhood of those who suffered. In spite of our current standards for assessing faults and failures, Du Bois was appropriately sensitive to the black women of his time. Finally, Du Bois's insights bear an ideological relationship to the perspective of prominent black women leaders of his day. He took their perspectives seriously in his analysis. Du Bois saw the empowerment of black women as central to establishing social justice. "[I]n all cases," he wrote, "the broader the basis of democracy the surer is the universal appeal for justice to win ultimate hearing and sympathy."[121] In light of the changes in perspective that were part of Du Bois's intellectual growth and his relationship with other intellectuals of that era, it is not unreasonable to assume that the feminism of the larger black women's club movement greatly influenced and nurtured the feminism and social analysis of W. E. B. Du Bois, and that W. E. B. Du Bois influenced these organized black women.[122] Du Bois's thinking indicates that in a cultural context of visible female leadership and intellectual debate across the boundaries of gender, sociological thought can account for the multiple realities and inequalities of human experience. Du Bois teaches us that the standpoints at the margins provide a center from which to challenge feminist and sociological thought in order to expand boundaries and account for the experiences of all women in the process of building theory and making a better world.

NOTES

1. Earlier versions of this paper were presented to the American Sociological Association's 1988 Annual Meeting in Atlanta, Georgia at a special session organized by Professor G. Franklin Edwards, "The Sociology of W. E. B. Du Bois," and to several colleges and universities. The author would like to acknowledge the suggestions and comments of Noel Cazenave, Emily Grosholz, Constantine Hriskos, Ronald Taylor, Cornel West, and Sarah Willie.

2. W. E. B. Du Bois, *Prayers for Dark People* (Amherst, Massachusetts: University of Massachusetts Press, 1980), 21.

3. I am very critical of the tendency to equate "American" with the United States, thus ignoring the fact that the Americas, north and south, incorporate many nations. Often I say "American" when I mean the "United States" because current literary conventions make it awkward to be consistent in using United States.

4. See Patricia Hill Collins, *Black Feminist Thought: Knowledge, Consciousness, and the Politics of Empowerment* (Cambridge, Mass.: Unwin Hyman, Inc., 1990), 26.

5. See Patricia Hill Collins, *Black Feminist Thought*; Deborah K. King, "Multiple Jeopardy, Multiple Consciousness: The Context of a Black Feminist Ideology," *Signs: Journal of Women in Culture and Society* 14, 1 (1990).

6. Anthony Giddens, *Sociology: A Brief but Critical Introduction*, 2nd ed. (San Diego: Harcourt Brace Jovanovich, 1987). See also C. Wright Mills, *The Sociological Imagination* (New York: Oxford University Press, 1961), for his criticisms of social theorists seeking to develop general or "grand theory." Mills is particularly critical of the trend to separate history from sociology, something Du Bois found inconceivable.

7. Manning Marable, *W. E. B. Du Bois: Black Radical Democrat* (Boston: Twayne Publishers, 1986), 17.

8. For chronologies of the lives and works of Durkheim and Weber, see Lewis A. Coser, *Masters of Sociological Thought: Ideas in Historical and Social Context* (New York: Harcourt Brace Jovanovich, 1971), 143–49, 234–43. See also Manning Marable's chronology of Du Bois's life and work in *Du Bois*, 219–22.

9. Marable, *Du Bois*, 63; W. E. B. Du Bois, "Die Negerfrage in den Vereiningten Staaten," *Archiv für Sozialwissenschaft und Sozialpolitik* (Tübingen) 22 (1906): 31–79.

10. Coser, *Masters of Sociological Thought*, 129, 217.

11. W. E. B. Du Bois, *The Gift of Black Folk: Negroes in the Making of America* (1924; reprint, New York: Simon and Schuster, 1970).

12. W. E. B. Du Bois, *Darkwater: Voices from Within the Veil* (1920; reprint, New York: Schocken Books, 1969), 154.

13. I tend to use the terms race, ethnicity, and race-ethnicity interchangeably. Whenever I use the term "race" I am referring to an historically derived experience and identity that has been socially constructed through external constraints and oppressions and through internal communal ideals and solidarities. Although race has some biological implications in terms of use of very rigid rules of biological descent and, quite often but not exclusively, physical appearance, the model and definition of race used in this paper and my reading of Du Bois's definitions of race, are purely social and historical. See K. Anthony Appiah's essay, "Illusions of Race," in his *In My Father's House: Africa in the Philosophy of Culture* (New York: Oxford University Press) 28–46, where the problematics of Du Bois's racial rhetoric are criticized and examined from an African political perspective.

14. For discussions of the status and problems of African American women in the nineteenth century, particularly from the perspective of African American women themselves, see Anna Julia Cooper, *A Voice From the South* (Ohio: Aldine, 1892); Paula Giddings, *When and Where I Enter: The Impact of Black Women on Race and Class in America* (New York: William Morrow and Company, 1984); Dorothy Sterling, *We Are Your Sisters: Black Women in the Nineteenth Century* (New York: W. W. Norton, 1985); Maria W. Stewart, *America's First Black Woman Political Writer: Essays and Speeches*, ed. Marilyn Richardson (Bloomington: Indiana University Press, 1987).

15. See Stanford Lyman, *The Negro American in Sociological Thought: A Failure in Perspective* (New York: Capricorn Books, 1972).

16. W. E. B. Du Bois, *The Souls of Black Folk* (Greenwich, Connecticut: Fawcett Publications, 1961), 23.

17. Du Bois, *Darkwater*, 134.

18. This connection was drawn most explicitly in Du Bois's preface to the fiftieth anniversary edition of *The Souls of Black Folk* (New York: Fawcett Publications, 1961), 14.

19. W. E. B. Du Bois, "Our Program," *Crisis* 37 (May 1930): 174.

20. Du Bois, "Our Program," 174.

21. Du Bois, "Our Program," 174.

22. Giddens, *Sociology*, 9.

23. Mills, *The Sociological Imagination*, 25–99.

24. Giddens, *Sociology*, 159. See also Irving M. Zeitlin, *Ideology and the Development of Sociological Theory* (Englewood Cliffs, New Jersey: Prentice-Hall, 1968), for an analysis of the Marxist foundations of sociological theory.

25. See Robert E. L. Faris, *Chicago Sociology: 1920–1932* (Chicago: University of Chicago Press, 1970), for a discussion of the "Chicago School." Rodney Stark, in his introductory text *Sociology* (Belmont, California: Wadsworth Publishing Company, 1994) 3, points out that Du Bois was, along with Albion Small, one of the two earliest founders of departments of sociology. Small founded the department at Chicago. Although Small is credited as the founder of academic sociology, Stark points out that Du Bois started the department at Atlanta around the same time, and that Small's "scholarly accomplishments are far overshadowed by Du Bois who poured out one major scholarly study after another. . . ."

26. Elliott Rudwick, "W. E. B. Du Bois as Sociologist," in *Black Sociologists: Historical and Contemporary Perspectives* ed. James E. Blackwell and Morris Janowitz (Chicago: University of Chicago Press, 1974), 27.

27.   W. E. B. Du Bois, "The Philosophy of Mr. Dole," *Crisis* 7 (February 1914): 24–26.

28.   Herbert Aptheker, *Annotated Bibliography of the Published Writings of W. E. B. Du Bois*, (Millwood, New York: Kraus-Thompson, 1973) 1–4.

29.   Aptheker, *Annotated Bibliography*, 5.

30.   Aptheker, *Annotated Bibliography*, 6.

31.   Aptheker, *Annotated Bibliography*, 8.

32.   Giddings, *When and Where*, 30, 83.

33.   See Elizabeth Lindsey Davis, *Lifting As They Climb: A History of the National Association of Colored Women* (Washington, D.C.: Howard University, Moorland Spingarn Library, 1933).

34.   W. E. B. Du Bois, *The Autobiography of W. E. B. Du Bois: A Soliloquy on Viewing My Life from the Last Decade of its First Century* (New York: International Publishers, 1968), 137.

35.   Aptheker, *Annotated Bibliography*, 6.

36.   Aptheker, *Annotated Bibliography*, 554.

37.   Du Bois, *Darkwater*, 134–60.

38.   Du Bois, *Darkwater*, 134–60.

39.   Du Bois, *Darkwater*, 134–60.

40.   Du Bois, *Darkwater*, 134–60.

41.   Du Bois, *Darkwater*, 134–60.

42.   Du Bois, *Darkwater*, 134–60.

43.   Du Bois, *Darkwater*, 134–60.

44.   Du Bois, *Darkwater*, 53.

45.   Du Bois, *Darkwater*, 53.

46.   Du Bois, *Darkwater*, 55.

47.   Du Bois, *Darkwater*, 105–108.

48.   Du Bois, *Darkwater*, 123–33.

49.   Du Bois, *Darkwater*, 161–62.

50.   Du Bois, *Darkwater*, 187–92.

51.   Du Bois, "The Woman" in *W. E. B. Du Bois: The Crisis Writings*, ed. Daniel Walden (Greenwich, Conn.: Fawcett Publications, 1972), 337–39. All of the quotations in this paragraph are taken from this version of the essay.

52.   Du Bois, "The Woman," 339.

53.   Du Bois, "The Damnation of Women," in *Darkwater*.

54.   Du Bois, *Darkwater*, 164.

55.   Du Bois, *Darkwater*, 165.

56.   Du Bois, *Darkwater*, 168.

57.   Du Bois, *Darkwater*, 171.

58.   Du Bois, *Darkwater*, 172.

59.   Anna Julia Cooper, *A Voice from the South by a Black Woman of the South* (Ohio: Aldine Publishing Company, 1892). Cited by Du Bois in *Darkwater*, 173.

60.   Du Bois, *Darkwater*, 174.

61.   Du Bois, *Darkwater*, 178.

62.   See Patricia Hill Collins, *Black Feminist Thought: Knowledge, Consciousness, and the Politics of Empowerment* (Cambridge, Mass.: Unwin Hyman, 1990).

63.   Du Bois, *Darkwater*, 179.

64.   Du Bois, *Darkwater*, 179.

65.   Du Bois, *Darkwater*, 179.

66. W. E. B. Du Bois, *The Gift of Black Folk: Negroes in the Making of America* (1924; reprint, New York: Simon and Schuster, 1970).

67. Du Bois, *The Gift*, viii.

68. Du Bois, *The Gift*, 141.

69. Du Bois, *The Gift*, 141.

70. Du Bois, *The Gift*, 141.

71. Du Bois, *The Gift*, 142.

72. Du Bois, *The Gift*, 142.

73. See Angela Y. Davis, *Women, Race and Class* (New York: Random House, 1981); Bonnie Thornton Dill, "The Dialectics of Black Womanhood: Towards a New Model of American Femininity," *Signs: Journal of Women and Culture in Society* 4 (1979): 543–55.

74. Du Bois, *The Gift*, 144.

75. Du Bois, *The Gift*, 145.

76. Rudwick, "Du Bois as Sociologist," 33

77. Du Bois, *The Gift*, 146.

78. Du Bois, *The Gift*, 147.

79. Du Bois, *The Gift*, 148; Giddings, *When and Where*, 73.

80. Du Bois *The Gift*, 149. Emphasis mine.

81. Du Bois *The Gift*, 149.

82. Walden, *The Crisis Writings*, 340.

83. Dill, "Dialectics."

84. Du Bois, *Darkwater*, 172–73. Emphasis mine.

85. Walden, *The Crisis Writings*, 347–49.

86. Walden, *The Crisis Writings*, 348.

87. Walden, *The Crisis Writings*, 339–40.

88. This is a constant and recurring theme in sociological analyses of the black family. See especially Kelly Miller, "Surplus Negro Women," in *Radicals and Conservatives and Other Essays on the Negro in America* (New York: Schocken Books, 1968); E. Franklin Frazier, *The Negro Family in the United States* (Chicago: University of Chicago Press, 1939).

89. Walden, *The Crisis Writings*, 340.

90. Walden, *The Crisis Writings*, 340.

91. Walden, *The Crisis Writings*, 340.

92. Walden, *The Crisis Writings*, 349–51.

93. Walden, *The Crisis Writings*, 351.

94. Du Bois, *Darkwater*, 174.

95. Du Bois, *Darkwater*, 174.

96. Du Bois, *Darkwater*, 174.

97. Du Bois, *Darkwater*, 177.

98. Du Bois, *Darkwater*, 177–78.

99. Du Bois, *Darkwater*, 178.

100. Du Bois, *Darkwater*, 179.

101. Du Bois, *Darkwater*, 183.

102. The phrase "appearance norms" is a term introduced by sociologist Edwin Schur. See Edwin Schur, *Labeling Women Deviant: Gender, Stigma and Social Control* (New York: Random House, 1984).

103. Du Bois, *Darkwater*, 183.

104. Du Bois, *Darkwater*, 185.

105. See Everett C. Hughes, "Race Relations and the Sociological Imagination," *American Sociological Review* 28, no. 6 (1963): 879–90; Stokeley Carmichael and Charles Hamilton, *Black Power: The Politics of Black Liberation in America* (New York: Random House, 1967); Joyce Ladner, ed., *The Death of White Sociology* (New York: Random House, 1973).

106. Sara Evans, *Personal Politics: The Roots of Women's Liberation in the Civil Rights Movement and the New Left* (New York: Random House, 1979); Mary King, *Freedom Song: A Personal Story of the 1960s Civil Rights Movement* (New York: William Morrow, 1987); Doug McAdam, *Freedom Summer* (New York: Oxford University Press, 1988).

107. See Lee Rainwater and William Yancey, *The Moynihan Report and the Politics of Controversy* (Cambridge, Mass.: M.I.T. Press, 1967); Tony Cade, *The Black Woman: An Anthology* (New York: New American Library, 1970); Pauli Murray, "The Liberation of Black Women," in *Voices of the New Feminism*, ed. Mary L. Thompson (Boston: Beacon Press, 1970); Pauli Murray, "Jim Crow and Jane Crow," in *Black Women in White America: A Documentary History*, ed. Gerda Lerner (New York: Random House, 1972), 592–99.

108. See Betty Friedan, *The Feminine Mystique* (New York: W. W. Norton, 1963).

109. Adrienne Rich, *Of Woman Born: Motherhood as Experience and Institution* (New York: W. W. Norton, 1976).

110. Margaret L. Andersen, *Thinking About Women: Sociological Perspectives on Sex and Gender* (New York: Macmillan, 1988).

111. Judith Stacy and Barrie Thorne, "The Missing Feminist Revolution in Sociology," *Social Problems* 32, no. 4 (1985): 301–16.

112. See Barbara Hilkert Andolsen, *"Daughters of Jefferson, Daughters of Bootblacks": Racism and American Feminism* (Macon, Georgia: Mercer University Press, 1986). See also Dill, "Dialectics," and King, "Multiple Jeopardy."

113. See bell hooks, *Feminist Theory: From Margin to Center* (Boston: South End Press, 1984); Cheryl Townsend Gilkes, "Roundtable Discussion: On Feminist Methodology," *Journal of Feminist Studies in Religion* 1, no. 2 (1985): 80–83; Audre Lorde, *Sister Outsider: Essays and Speeches* (Trumansburg, New York: The Crossing Press, 1984).

114. Lorde, *Sister Outsider*, 126.

115. hooks, *Margin*, 13.

116. hooks, *Margin*, 13.

117. hooks, *Margin*, 14.

118. hooks, *Margin*, 15.

119. See Andersen, *Thinking*.

120. W. E. B. Du Bois, *The Autobiography of W. E. B.Du Bois: A Soliloquy on Viewing My Life from the Last Decade of Its First Century* (New York: International Publishers, 1968), 12.

121. Walden, *The Crisis Writings*, 347.

122. See Aptheker, *Bibliography*; Paula Giddings, *In Search of Sisterhood: Delta Sigma Theta and the Challenge of the Black Sorority Movement* (New York: William Morrow, 1988).

The Profeminist Politics of W. E. B. Du Bois

6

with Respects to Anna Julia Cooper and Ida B. Wells Barnett

Joy James

The uplift of women is, next to the problem of the color line and the peace movement, our greatest modern cause. When, now, two of these movements—women and color—combine in one, the combination has deep meaning.

—W. E. B. Du Bois[1]

In the above quote from his 1920 essay, "The Damnation of Women," W. E. B.Du Bois designates the "great causes" as the struggles for racial justice, peace, and women's equality. His use of the phrase "next to" does not refer to a sequential order of descending importance. Concerns for racial equality, international peace, and women's emancipation combined to form the complex, integrative character of Du Bois's analysis. With politics remarkably progressive for his time, and ours, Du Bois confronted race, class, and gender oppression while maintaining conceptual and political linkages between the struggles to end racism, sexism, and war. He linked his primary concern, ending white supremacy—*Souls of Black Folk* (1903) defines the color-line as the twentieth century's central problem, to the attainment of international peace and justice. Du Bois wove together an analysis integrating the various components of African American liberation and world peace. Initially gender, and later economic, analysis were indispensable in developing his political thought.

I explore Du Bois's relationship to that "deep meaning" embodied in women and color by examining his representation of African American women and his selective memory of the agency of his contemporaries Anna Julia Cooper and Ida B. Wells-Barnett. I consider the contradictary aspects of Du Bois's gender politics, and their implications for black intellectualism and agency.

Du Bois's writings champion women's rights, denounce their exploitation, and extol women as heroic strugglers. While condemning the oppression of African American women, Du Bois "veiled" the achievements of women such as Cooper and Wells-Barnett from the political landscape. In his profeminist[2] politics, he obscured black women's radical agency in black women's intellectualism. In guaging Du Bois's profeminism, I consider both his political actions on behalf of women's rights and the place of women in his nonfictional essays and political autobiographies. I see that in theory and practice Du Bois opposed women's subjugation; yet his political representations reflect considerable ambivalence towards black women's political independence.

My premise in this discussion is that certain forms of profeminism, like certain forms of anti-racism, are deceptive. For instance, anti-racist stances that are contextualized within a larger eurocentric worldview present European American culture as normative; consequently, they inadvertently reinforce white dominance despite their democratic positions on racial politics. Likewise, profeminist or anti-sexist thinkers who articulate their political project within a larger paradigm in which the male is normative reinforce male dominance, despite their stances for gender equality.

I see that Du Bois's profeminist politics clearly mark his opposition to patriarchy and misogyny. Nevertheless, I consider his writings influenced by a masculinist worldview which de-radicalized his gender progressivism. Du Bois rejected patriarchal thought that posits the inferiority of women and the superiority of men. Yet his masculinist framework presents the male as normative. Since masculinist thought does not explicitly advocate the superiority of men or rigid gender social roles, it is not synonymous with patriarchal thought. Masculinism can share patriarchy's presupposition of the male as normative without its anti-female rhetoric. Men who support feminist politics, as profeminists, may advocate the equality or even "superiority" of women. For instance, Du Bois argued against sexism and occasionally for the superiority of women. However, even without patriarchal intent, their works may reinforce gender roles. Du Bois makes no chauvinistic pronouncements, like the aristocratic ones characterizing his early writings on the "Talented Tenth."[3] Still,

without misogynist dogma, his nonfictional writings minimize black female
agency. They consequently to naturalize as normative the dominance of black
males in African American political discourse.

PROSELYTIZING WOMEN'S NOBILITY
AND SUPPORTING WOMEN'S RIGHTS

A vocal supporter of women's equality and a tireless critic of patriarchy,
Du Bois provided important advocacy for ending women's oppression. He
consistently emphasized the equality of women with the least rights—African
American girls and women. A pioneering feminist scholar and interpreter of
Du Bois's pro-feminism, Bettina Aptheker notes that Du Bois began his scientific studies of Africans and African Americans "in an era when predominant
scientific and theological opinion held the Negro to be an inferior, if not
subhuman, form."[4] As "a pivotal figure in the struggle for human rights,"
writes Aptheker, Du Bois was also "strikingly advanced in his views on
women ... a conspicuous theme in much of his work is the subjugation of
women, especially Black women."[5]

That theme dominants in "The Damnation of Women." The essay argues
for the liberation of females from domestic exploitation: "Only at the sacrifice
of intelligence and the chance to do their best work can the majority of
modern women bear children. This is the damnation of women." Such declarations by Du Bois are often highlighted by those who note his profeminist
activism. Aptheker documents that through the *Crisis*, Du Bois celebrated
women in the "Men of the Month" column popularizing race leaders; and,
condemned lynching and violent attacks and sexual assaults against black
women as well as white men's violence against white women. An advocate of
women's enfranchisement, he was invited to address the predominantly white
National American Woman Suffrage Association.[6]

In January 1906, African American women in New York state formed a
women's Du Bois Circle. Charter members of this group, an auxiliary to the
male-dominated Niagara Movement, formed in 1905, organized to support
and popularize the work of Du Bois. They also organized around social issues
and sex education.[7] Despite opposition from some of the original all-male
membership, like Monroe Trotter who opposed women joining the Niagara
Movement, Du Bois successfully worked to ensure the inclusion of women.
He also unilaterally organized a Massachusetts Niagara women's Auxiliary.[8]

Holding exceptionally progressive positions on gender equality, sexual
violence, and the victimization of women and girls, Du Bois condemned
sexual assaults and endorsed initiatives waged by the women's movement. His
profeminist positions censured white society's denigration of African
American. In a strong denunciation of white males's sexual violence against

black females, he wrote: "I shall never forgive, neither in this world nor the world to come . . . [the white South's] wanton and continued and persistent insulting of the black womanhood which it sought and seeks to prostitute to its lust."[9] Du Bois eloquently condemns the hypocrisy of the prevailing sexual politics which legitimized violence against women: "All womanhood is hampered today because the world on which it is emerging is a world that tries to worship both virgins and mothers and in the end despises motherhood and despoils virgins."[10]

With references to Du Bois's essays on women's oppression, David Levering Lewis compares the familial patriarch with the public advocate of women's rights, describing Du Bois as a "theoretical feminist whose advocacy could erupt with the force of a volcano."[11] Indeed, Du Bois's condemnations of sexism and racial-sexual violence appear skewed by a "theoretical feminism" that simultaneously condemns social injustice and reproduces gender dominance. For Lewis, Du Bois's progressive sexual politics strongly emerge in his fiction, particularly Du Bois's first novel, *The Quest of the Silver Fleece* (1911):

> *The Quest* reflected the force and sincerity of Du Bois's feminism, his credo that the degree of society's enlightenment and of the empowerment of disadvantaged classes and races was ultimately to be measured by its willingness to emancipate women—, and, above all, black women. What he would later affirm with pistol-shot accuracy was found on virtually every page of the novel: that the race question is "at bottom simply a matter of the ownership of women; white men want the right to own and use all women, colored and white, and they resent any intrusion of colored men into this domain."[12]

Through his writings, we easily ascertain that Du Bois's response to the query "Should women be emancipated?" is an emphatic "Yes!" Answering the question "By whom?" is more difficult. Du Bois's fictional portraits of African American women differ from his nonfiction writing regarding individual African American women. His nonfiction presents vague and generalizing portraits of the agency of his female contemporaries. As Lewis notes, Du Bois largely reserves detailed depictions of specific black women leaders for fictive characters. In his nonfiction essays and autobiographies, Du Bois withholds from his female contemporaries the recognition given his invented women.[13]

BLACK FEMINIST ASSESSMENTS OF DU BOIS'S REPRESENTATIONS

Often the existing literature on Du Bois refrains from analyzing the ways in which his contributions paradoxically reproduced male elites or gendered black intellectualism. An uncritical acceptance of Du Bois's pro-feminist politics at their face value seems to be the norm. Generally, scholars who analyze gender relations examine Du Bois's sexual politics. For instance, Patricia Morton and Nagueyalti Warren demystify Du Bois's symbolic treatment of black women.

According to Morton, Du Bois "was a pioneer in the transformation" of anti-black woman stereotypes "into empowering symbols of worth."[14] Du Bois's literary representations of black women rewrote them into history. These same representations also obscured women's political agency with symbolic imagery that contradicted the pragmatic politics of his profeminist work. Morton argues that while challenging the demeaning racial-sexual stereotypes concerning black women, Du Bois failed to "reconstruct black women as full human beings in history."[15] Du Bois's writings were influenced by an Afro-American tradition presenting "both idealized and ambivalent images of black women."[16] Du Bois idealized the "black mother" as the responsible caretaker of the morals of black youth and communities, linking femininity to motherhood; Morton contends that his "emphasis on the primacy of women ... and his frequently feminized symbolization of the virtues he attributed to the Negro race" allowed him to employ the "all-mother" as "both the controlling metaphor of his vision of black womanhood ... [and] his mystique of race."[17] Du Bois's reading of history discerned a "legacy of survival and strength" rooted in the African American woman "epitomizing and nurturing the ability of her race to move ahead into the future."[18] Yet, his historical works praise women such as Sojourner Truth and Harriet Tubman but focus on male leaders.[19] For Morton, his writings venerated "a not more worthy, but a finer type of black woman" who embodied, in Du Bois's words, "that delicate sense of beauty and striving for self-realization which is as characteristic of the Negro soul as is its quaint strength and sweet laughter." Illustrating how gender idealization obscured political specificity and women's radical agency, Morton quotes Du Bois description of Mary Shadd in *Darkwater*: Shadd was, writes Du Bois, "a refined, mulatto woman of "ravishing dream-born beauty," whose "sympathy and sacrifice" were "characteristic of Negro womanhood." Morton elaborates on Du Bois's depiction, writing that Shadd also a confrontational abolition noted for being "strong-willed, independent, and highly intelligent."

Du Bois's "casting" black women as "types," contends Morton, transformed anti-black female stereotypes; for instance, he reworked the image of the stereotypical "mammy" into that of the black Christian martyr. However, the icon of black female martyr or noble sufferer, redeemed through crucifixion, can not accurately depict the defiant, militancy of race women such as Ida B. Wells-Barnett. Nagueyalti Warren examines how Du Bois's fiction depicts African American women as victims and survivors. Surmising that his representations mythologize female victimization as well as agency, Warren argues that Du Bois's *Darkwater* uses "the Black Madonna or messianic symbol" as a "literary archetype" to project "a covert image of powerlessness"; this "canonizing of virginity and immaculate conception" strips the woman of "the power and control of her body."[20] For Warren, the "strength of the positive, strong African American woman" paints her as "invincible" as this strength is "mythicized to the almost total exclusion of her victimization."[21]

Both profound strength and deep suffering exist in his fictive depictions of African American women. In general, Du Bois's fictional and nonfictional writings present varied and contradictory relationships with African American women. He evinces relationships of: symbiosis with his fictional female protagonists; admiration for the generic, composite symbol of womanhood in African American women's suffering and strength; reverence for his mother, familial women as well as personal friends and acquaintances; concern and committed activism to end the abuse and exploitation of African American women; censorious revisionism in obscuring the pioneering works of Cooper and Wells-Barnett. The multiplicity and contradictory nature of these relationships point to a "double consciousness" muddled with the contradictory gender politics.

Undoubtedly, the multiple oppressions and brutalities that women of African descent battled moved Du Bois to empathy and outrage. His 1914 poem, "The Burden of Black Women," pays tribute to the trials of African American women:

> Dark daughters of the lotus leaves that watch
> > the Southern sea,
> Wan spirit of a prisoned soul a-panting to
> > be free;
> The muttered music of thy streams, the
> > whispers of the deep
> Have kissed each other in God's name and
> > kissed a world to sleep[22]

This poetry echoes the sensibilities of "The Damnation of Women": "To no modern race does its women mean so much as to the Negro nor come so near to the fulfillment of its meaning."[23] Despite the moral sentiment and political commitment, those women, including the ones informing his politics, largely remain nameless in Du Bois's book(s). African American women were an essential cause to be championed for Du Bois. Still those black women leaders, whom Du Bois did not create as fictional characters, would have a difficult time finding themselves in his writings.

THE MARGINALIZATION
OF ANNA JULIA COOPER AND IDA B. WELLS-BARNETT

It is disingenuous to minimize Du Bois's significant contributions towards women's equality. It would also be deceptive to ignore his problematic literary representations of and political relationships with influential African American women activists.

The writings and political work of Cooper and Wells-Barnett are so significant in the life-struggles of their era that they compel juxtaposition with the work of Du Bois. Both Cooper and Wells-Barnett worked with, were influenced by, and influenced Du Bois. At times all three were members of the same organizations. Each struggled with and critiqued white supremacy and the conservative segments of African American leadership. Eventually each leader was isolated from mainstream African American leadership for his or her radical commitments. They were also alienated from one another. Cooper and Wells-Barnett independently made overtures to work with Du Bois which he rebuffed. Neither woman left a record of having sought the other out.

Hazel Carby observes that black American history commonly perceives the turn of the century "as the Age of Washington and Du Bois." Such a view, writes Carby, marginalizes black women's political contributions during "a period of intense intellectual activity and productivity" marked by their development of institutions and organizations. In the "Age of Washington and Du Bois," Cooper was a well-known figure among African American leaders. One of three African American women invited to speak at the World's Congress of Representative Women in 1893, she would later present a paper, "The Negro Problem in America," at the 1900 Pan African Congress Conference in London. Cooper had helped to organize that first Pan African conference and served as a member of its Executive Committee, working alongside another prominent conference organizer, Du Bois. She co-founded the Colored Women's YWCA in 1905, the same year that Du Bois founded the Niagara Movement. Widowed at as a young woman, and childless, she worked as a life-long activist in African American liberation. As principal of the prestigious M Street (later the Dunbar) High School in Washington, D.C., Cooper, who had a graduate degree from Oberlin, structured a curriculum enabling her students to be admitted to Harvard, Yale, and other prestigious universities. As a result of her successes, outraged European Americans and alarmed African Americans on the school board forced her out of the principalship. Racism and unsubstantiated rumors of sexual impropriety were the basis of the dismissal. Continuing her activism as an educator, she obtained her Ph.D. from the Sorbonne in 1930 at the age of sixty-six. As an elder, Cooper assumed the presidency of Frelinghuysen University, an independent school known as the "College Extension for Working People" for employed working class African Americans in Washington, D.C.

In advocating liberal arts higher education for African Americans and criticizing Booker T. Washington's ideology of vocational training for African Americans, Cooper became an important ally of Du Bois. Although Du Bois's *Black Reconstruction* was written as a response to Cooper's urging and her declaration of support for financing and distribution, he never acknowledged Cooper's request that the *Crisis* serialize her biographical sketch of Charlotte Grimke, the prominent activist-intellectual. He would nevertheless draw upon Cooper's intellectual resources more than once. Paula Giddings writes that in her 1892 political autobiography, *A Voice from the South*, she provides a "treatise on race and feminism ... anticipated much of the later work of W. E. B. Du Bois."[24] Du Bois's later democratic revisions of the "Talented Tenth" adapt Cooper's gender critique and expands upon the assertion that elite African Americans were neither the cure nor criteria for black liberation.

In *A Voice from the South*, Cooper calls for a mass, female standard for evaluating the effectiveness of African American praxis, ten years before Du Bois penned his concept of "The Talented Tenth." Cooper's standard to gauge the efficacy of African American praxis reflected the mass of people: "Is it not evident then that as individual workers for this race we must address ourselves with no half-hearted zeal to this feature of our mission [the lives of the masses and women]. The need is felt and must be recognized by all."[25] Rejecting the idealized "great leader" and the premise that the lives and (real and potential) contributions of elites were more consequential than those of laborers, she set new criteria for race leadership. Dispensing with black intellectual male elites as representative of Africana freedom, she reasserted the whole, starting with the bottom, as the measure for liberation. Emphasizing the conditions of working class and poor black women, Cooper writes:

> our present record of eminent men, when placed beside the actual status of the race in America today proves that no man can represent the race.... Only the black woman can say "when and where I enter, in the quiet, undisputed dignity of my womanhood, without violence and without suing or special patronage, then and there the whole *Negro race enter with me.*[26]

Quoting Cooper's now-famous "When and where I enter" sentence in "The Damnation of Women," Du Bois fails to mention her by name, prefacing his remarks with the proprietary phrase: "As one of our women writes."[27] Du Bois's selective quotations curtail Cooper's full argument; the passage preceding the quote more accurately reflects the critical mandate for black leadership echoing throughout *A Voice from the South*: "as individual workers for this race we must address ourselves with no half-hearted zeal to this feature of our mission"[28]—the uplift of the masses of African American women. Du Bois's failure to name this African American author independent of himself renders Cooper anonymous. With no attributed source, his citation allows Cooper to disappear as her words appear. In her absence, readers were unlikely to juxtapose Du Bois with Cooper. Nor would they fully benefit from her own gender analyses. Her anonymity allows Du Bois to appear as a transgender representative for the entire vilified and oppressed race. Washington contextualizes this erasure of Cooper's name within masculinist and patriarchal thought: "The intellectual discourse of black women of the 1890s, and particularly Cooper's embryonic black feminist analysis, was ignored because it was by and about women and therefore thought not to be as significantly about the race as writings by and about men."[29]

This "embryonic black feminism" maintained that the criterion for African American progress centers on the emancipation of black women, who labor the longest for the least wages under the most numbing and exploitive conditions. Du Bois himself suggests this position by using her quote. Sharing Cooper's advocacy for the struggles of impoverished black women, he detaches from her advocacy of leadership as the attribute of black female elites.

Cooper's gender politics centered poor black women's struggles and elite black women's agency. Du Bois's eventually more inclusive class politics theoretically allowed him to attribute greater agency to *poor* black women workers and laborers. Du Bois's increasingly nonclassist writings surpass Cooper's 1892 work in democratizing agency. Cooper repudiates masculine elites, or privileged black male intellectuals. However, her repudiations do not extend to feminine elites, or privileged black female intellectuals. Du Bois's criticisms were not self-referential regarding his male privilege. Cooper, who countered the dominance of male elites with that of female elites, was somewhat oblivious of the limitations of her caste.

The conservatism of A Voice From the South stems the double bounds by racism and sexism faced by black women elites such as Cooper who "had a great stake in the prestige, the respectability, and the gentility guaranteed by the politics of true womanhood."[30] The demanding conformism to standards of white, bourgeois "respectability" placed on middle-class African American women was partly self-imposed and self-policed. Du Bois had written critically of both this "cult of true womanhood" or bourgeois femininity and white society's hypocritical chasm imposed between black females and white "ladies." It would have been difficult but not impossible for Cooper to disengage from the mores of conventional feminine respectability to think about the radical agency of *non-elite* or non-bourgeois black women. Unlike Du Bois's later revisions of the "Talented Tenth" to include poor and working class back women and men, Cooper's writing failed to argue that the intellectual and leadership abilities of black women laborers equaled those of black women college graduates.

Not all middle-class race women were trapped by rigid social conventions. In the same year as the appearance of Cooper's *A Voice from the South*, Wells-Barnett's *Southern Horrors: Lynch Law in All Its Phases* was published. The anti-lynching crusader embodied the race militancy and intellectualism of a responsible womanhood that reflected and rejected the cult of womanhood. Her writing on the volatile racial-sexual politics of lynching focuses on issues of race, sex, and violence unmentioned in *A Voice From the South*'s pioneering discussions of sexual violence. As the lioness of the anti-lynching crusades, Wells-Barnett survived death threats, the destruction of her Memphis press by a lynch mob, and endured decades of exile from the south. Transgressing the notions of feminine gentility and masculine courage, armed, Wells-Barnett traveled extensively to organize against and document lynchings.

The university-educational campaigns of Du Bois and Cooper included and directly affected fewer blacks than the anti-lynching campaigns. Only a small percentage of African Americans were likely to attain a university education. Yet all were susceptible to the violence of a lynch mob (poorer Blacks were likely more vulnerable to racial violence). Du Bois and the former school teacher Ida B. Wells-Barnett participated in both the liberal arts educational campaigns and the anti-lynching crusades. Advocating liberal arts education for African Americans, Wells-Barnett in fact became a proponent of Du Bois's social thought. This stance placed her in the line of Booker T. Washington's fire. Wells-Barnett's memoir,*Crusade for Justice,* recounts how influential black and white leaders at a Chicago meeting debated the merits of *The Souls of Black Folk* were debated. Most of those present, writes Wells-Barnett, were "united in condemning Mr. Du Bois's views."[31] The Barnetts championed Du Bois's critique of Washington's promotion of industrial education as the racial panacea. Wells-Barnett's stands in the educational debates were consistent with her outspoken anti-lynching advocacy. The failure of Du Bois's memoirs to mention her work in the educational campaigns underscores his silence with respect to her extraordinary anti-lynching activism. Despite her prolific research and publications,[32] her political courage, and radical analysis of the sexual politics of lynching, Du Bois's autobiographical writings on anti-lynching mostly ignore Wells-Barnett.

As one of the most significant human rights campaigns in postbellum American, at the turn of the century, the anti-lynching crusades engendered a black liberation movement in which black women were prominent public leaders. African American women initiated the first major anti-lynching campaign in 1892. Without the backing of an influential, multi-racial organization such as the NAACP, which was later formed in 1909, early anti-lynching activism was extremely dangerous. With uncompromising demands for justice, women such as Florida Ruffin Ridley and Mary Church Terrell, and Wells-Barnett challenged the U.S. "red record" of African Americans disproportionately brutalized, imprisoned, and murdered at the whim of Whites. Skeptical that media, court, or mob prosecution was motivated by the desire to end sexual violence, they created a legacy of investigative reporting to ascertain facts distorted or denied by the media or legal institutions.

Just as Wells-Barnett had been transformed by the 1892 lynchings of her friends in Memphis and propelled into national leadership, lynchings had a tremendous impact on Du Bois, politicizing him into a militancy which left him ill-suited for academic society and liberal institutions. His *Darkwater* short story on lynching, "Jesus Christ in Texas," speaks to his profound pessimism concerning America's proclivity towards racist violence. Two decades later, *Dusk to Dawn* describes the young Du Bois being radicalized by American barbarity. The atrocities haunted and transformed his early adult life: "Lynching was a continuing and recurrent horror during my college days: from 1885 through 1894, seventeen hundred Negroes were lynched in America. Each death was a scar upon my soul, and led me on to conceive the plight of other minority groups. . . ."[33] *Dusk of Dawn* chronicles Du Bois's heightening consciousness about the need to actively oppose lynching. The pressing need to confront racist violence furthered his disaffection for and alienation in academic life:

> At the very time when my studies were most successful, there cut across this plan which I had as a scientist, a red ray which could not be ignored, I remember when it first, as it were, startled me to my feet; a poor Negro in central Georgia, Sam Hose, had killed his landlord's wife. I wrote out a careful and reasoned statement concerning the evident facts and started down to the Atlanta *Constitution* office. . . . I did not get there. On the way news met me: Sam Hose had been lynched, and they said that his knuckles were on exhibition at a grocery store farther down on Mitchell Street, along which I was walking. I turned back to the University. Two considerations thereafter broke in upon my work and eventually disrupted it; first, one could not be a calm, cool, and detached scientist while Negroes were lynched, murdered and starved; and secondly, there was no such demand for scientific work of the sort that I was doing, as I had confidently assumed would be easily forthcoming.[34]

Du Bois, who sat with a shotgun on the front steps of his home during the Atlanta race riots by whites, was both shaken and galvanized by his close proximity to a lynching victim.

Wells-Barnett critiqued the racial-sexual politics of interracial sex and the duplicity of the legal system's and its complicity in lynchings in language few male or female race leaders dared to use. Her writings discredited the apologias for lynchings noting that the rape charge was only used in a fraction of lynchings; and where employed, the accused black person was generally innocent of sexual assault. Her arguments paraphrase Frederick Douglass's critique of post-bellum rationalizations (like Du Bois, she did not always give credit her sources—*Crusade for Justice* does not fully acknowledge Douglass's influence on anti-lynching activism or the contributions of other activists). Wells-Barnett's unique contribution to the anti-lynching movement was her documentation and incendiary rhetoric on the hypocrisy of American sexual politics in which white men were the predominate assailants of white and black females, yet masked their violence (as well as their attempts to politically and economically dominate blacks) with racist terrorism.

Never fully acknowledging his debt, Du Bois built on and benefitted from the political and intellectual radicalism of Wells-Barnett. By refusing to name Wells-Barnett and her dynamic leadership, his writings erase her contribution much as he renders Cooper anonymous. Given their incendiary tone, Du Bois likely could not use Wells-Barnett's words, as he had Cooper's, without sharing her stigma and isolation as too combative in anti-racist activism. Failing to document Wells-Barnett's anti-lynching agency, Du Bois obscures both her individual contributions and the range of anti-racist militancy and radicalism. Consequently, Du Bois foregoes a critical examination of Wells-Barnett's political thought and so misses an opportunity to analyze the "deep meaning" of the lives of radical African American women activists.

Though not as prolific a writer nor as formally educated as Du Bois, Wells-Barnett's was widely influential during that era. With the decline in mob lynchings, her prominence wanned while Du Bois's prestige increased in the first part of the twentieth century. As Du Bois's writings were increasingly "mainstreamed" through the NAACP, her work was marginalized. In part, this occurred because of her uncompromising politics and opposition to Booker T. Washington. In retaliation to the Barnetts's political independence and vocal critiques, Washington used his influence over the Afro-American press to cripple the publishing and journalistic careers of the Barnetts.

Anti-lynching organizing unraveled rather than cemented the ties between Wells-Barnett and Du Bois. In August 1909, white race riots and the lynchings of African Americans in Springfield, Illinois led progressive European Americans and African Americans to form what would become the NAACP. As founding members, Du Bois and Wells-Barnett were active in the first meetings at New York City's Cooper Union. Outspoken from the floor, Wells-Barnett urged the assembly not to compromise its agenda with that of the

Tuskegee machine.[35] Seated on the dais, Du Bois wielded influence behind doors in closed meetings of the nominating committee for the organization's initial leadership. Unlike Wells-Barnett, Du Bois was not isolated by white and black NAACP liberals for his radicalism and opposition to Washington as accommodationist.

Du Bois's autobiographical record of the founding of the NAACP omits any reference to Wells-Barnett being ostracized at the NAACP founding conference. He writes: "the members of the Niagara Movement were invited into the new conference, but all save [William Monroe] Trotter and Ida Wells-Barnett came to form the backbone of the new organization."[36] *Dusk of Dawn* does not explain Wells-Barnett's absence from a key organization in a crusade she had initiated. Nor does Du Bois refer to maneuvers to bar her from NAACP organizational leadership. One of two African American women signing the conference "Call," Wells-Barnett's name was left off of the list of the Committee of Forty assigned to develop the NAACP. According to Wells-Barnett, Du Bois, in seeking a representative from the Niagara Movement Du Bois substituted for her name that of an absent Dr. Charles E. Bentley. Wells-Barnett also speculates that Mary White Ovington's friendship and influence with Du Bois led to "the deliberate intention of Dr. Du Bois to ignore me and my work."[37] Ovington, who later chaired the NAACP, was on less than cordial terms with Wells-Barnett. Lewis minimizes Wells-Barnett's account to argue that philanthropist Oswald Garrison Villard's aversion to radicalism and anti-Tuskegee activists bears the primary culpability for Wells Barnett's isolation. Yet Du Bois, also a radical and an outspoken critic of Washington, was not similarly censored. Lewis writes that Du Bois in attempting to achieve moderate representation, "was probably motivated far less by personal animus than by well-intentioned (though possibly sexist and perhaps mistaken) calculations."[38] Whatever its motivation, this slighting marginalized the era's most effective anti-lynching militant. After the restoration of her name to the Committee of Forty, following protests by herself and others, Wells-Barnett joined NAACP national leadership in name only. Holt notes that: "the singular irony of her career is that Wells-Barnett, the most prominent voice opposing lynching over the preceding decade and the most persistent advocate of a national organization to combat racial oppression, was not among the leaders of the NAACP. . . ."[39]

Wells-Barnett's bitterness must have been edged with a sense of betrayal. For years she had been an avid supporter of Du Bois and a critic of Washington and as a consequence she suffered the backlash from the Tuskegee machine.[40] Wells-Barnett consistently supported Du Bois until the 1907 break at the NAACP conference. This support was not reciprocated.

The most glaring omission by Du Bois regarding the significance Wells-

Barnett's anti-violence activism occurs in *Dusk of Dawn*. Here he erases her unparalleled contributions to the anti-lynching activism. Consider Du Bois's depiction of organizing around the Steve Green and Pink Franklin cases. In 1910, Steve Green arrived in Chicago, wounded from a shootout with a white Arkansas farmer who tried to indenture or enslave him on his farm. Green was extradited to Arkansas, ostensibly to be lynched. However, Ida B. Wells Barnett's Negro Fellowship League raised money and organized a defense committee that safely spirited Greene to Canada. Lewis comments on Du Bois's selective recollection: "Curiously Du Bois' coverage of the dramatic events behind Greene's removal from the clutches of his Arkansas warders, omitted any mention of Wells-Barnett and her Negro Fellowship League."[41] Several months earlier, in a similar case, the NAACP had struggled and failed to save Pink Franklin from a legal lynching or state execution. Franklin had shot and killed a white farmer breaking into his house in order to return Franklin to sharecropping. Such "curious omissions" concerning Wells-Barnett are not aberrational in Du Bois's autobiographies.

After military service in World War I, African American soldiers returned with raised expectations concerning equality and democracy. Instead, they encountered a white backlash. Lynchings increased, particularly in the south. *Dusk of Dawn* refers to the September 1917 military, legalized lynchings of African American soldiers in Texas where the Twenty-fourth colored infantry engaged in an armed rebellion against the local whites.[42] He does not mention Wells-Barnett's campaign to stop the executions and free imprisoned members of the 24th Infantry. Wells-Barnett describes these soldiers as "martyred." In 1917, while stationed in Houston, Texas, 100 armed black troops in response to racist assaults, marched on the town. The resulting confrontation left sixteen Whites and four black soldiers dead. Following the revolt, the U.S. Army executed nineteen soldiers and court-martialed and imprisoned fifty. Wells-Barnett's activism for the release of the 24th Infantry was so noteworthy that secret service agents threatened her with charges of war-time sedition if she continued agitating on behalf of the prisoners. Despite government threats to imprison her, she extended her organizing and remained free.

Dusk of Dawn forgoes relaying this information to detail the expansion of the NAACP's organizing to end lynching. According to Du Bois, in 1919 NAACP leadership was instrumental in two thousand anti-lynching public meetings and a government investigation of the Chicago riot; it also convened a national Conference on lynching in New York City which issued an address to the nation signed by prominent officials, including a former U.S. President and a current Chief Justice. Du Bois writes that the NAACP organized African American political power to "make it influential and we started a campaign against lynching and mob law which was the most effective ever organized and eventually brought the end of the evil in sight."[43] Reconstructing NAACP activity as *the* anti-lynching movement, he writes that "Mary Talbert started the anti-lynching crusade, raising a defense fund of $12,000," and that NAACP secretary James Weldon Johnson forcibly brought the Dyer Anti-Lynching Bill before Congress in 1921.[44] Du Bois's singular validation of NAACP anti-lynching activism deflects from the work of the Negro Women's Club Movement, Wells-Barnett, and other anti-lynching activists whose radicalism and analyses laid the foundations for later NAACP campaigns.

While describing, or embellishing upon, NAACP anti-lynching activism, Du Bois refers to internal contradictions and the organization's ineffectiveness and ideological liberalism. In "Revolution," the final chapter of *Dusk of Dawn*, he ends this memoir by expressing his disappointment over the increasing ineffectiveness of the NAACP, an organization to which he devoted decades of his life work. His regrets echo those of Ida B. Wells-Barnett.[45] Wells-Barnett reflects in her own autobiography that had she been more active in its national leadership, the NAACP would have been more responsive to the dire conditions of African Americans. Lacking allies for radicalizing organizational leadership, for instance allies with the tenacity and militancy of Wells-Barnett, Du Bois recalls that by 1930 he had increasing doubts about the viability of NAACP liberalism. For him the organization's ideology advocated: "a continued agitation which had for its object simply free entrance into the present economy of the world, that looked at political rights as an end in itself rather than as a method of reorganizing the state; and that expected through civil rights and legal judgments to re-establish freedom on a broader and firmer basis."[46] This ideology, wrote Du Bois, "was not so much wrong as short-sighted."[47] Du Bois maintained that liberalism, legalism, and inadequate economic program led the NAACP to miss an essential opportunity "to guard and better the chances of Negroes" to earn an adequate income. In the 1930s, he resigned as editor of the *Crisis* and from the NAACP national board. It is uncertain if a successful Du Bois-Wells-Barnett alliance might have influenced the NAACP national leadership towards civil rights radicalism with an economic program. In any case, such an alliance was apparently undesirable on Du Bois's part.

Du Bois's political distance from Cooper and Wells-Barnett persists in his autobiographies, despite his increasing radicalism. Du Bois, who lived into his nineties, developed a structural analysis of black oppression that addresses economic exploitation and state oppression, issues Cooper's and Wells-Barnett's analyses largely ignore.

REFLECTIONS ON GENDER ERASURE

The lack of specificity, or the detailed account of agency and subject identification, contextualizes Du Bois's profeminist and later pro-worker stances. This lack inadvertently highlights the black vanguardism which he eventually repudiates. Perhaps Du Bois's early, progressive views on women shielded him (and his own self-reflections) from criticism. This shield may blind us to the fact that his writings about African American women notably erase their political agency. Specificity and erasure inform Du Bois's gender politics. In their lack of documentation, his autobiographical records choose a generic rather than an empirical study regarding the achievements of his female and working class contemporaries. I do not suggest that Du Bois should have written his memoirs with the impressive detail found in *Black Reconstruction*. I only note that he reserves specificity in his memoirs and essays for fellow elites: his autobiographies privilege activists who were his personal friends or acquaintances—African American men such as Monroe Trotter and James Weldon Johnson, as well as European Americans Joel Spingarn and Mary White Ovington. In the process of democratizing African American leadership, Du Bois inadvertently reinscribed the primacy of elites through his representations of the agency. Non-elite blacks appear largely without specificity and names as he frequently withheld the attribute of political agency from them and black women intellectuals.

Following Du Bois's example, we may address black women as a generic topic without their specificity; yet we will obscure the radicalism of black politics and history. Portraying African American women in an aggregate as victims, icons, or the embodiement of a cause suggests that political change transpires without black female independence and leadership. Asserting black women's leadership in theory but minimizing the empirical record of African American women leaders, masculinizes black agency and implicitly relegates women to an inferior status as intellectuals.

Grappling with the strengths and limitations of Du Bois's legacy, we can see that non-specificity and erasure overlap to some degree. Non-specificity promotes the disappearance of the detailed historical or empirical record. In some respects, it erases the subjects, deeds and events, while simultaneously discussing them. With the solo appearance of the generic, the category becomes surrogate for the individual: the "black woman" replaces Ida B. Wells Barnett. The generic also supplants historical or empirical data in representation: black women's victimization stands in place for their political praxis in the suffragette movement or anti-lynching crusades. The documentary writer controls representation and memory in his or her use of the non-specificity of generic representations. Whereas with specificity, the historical subject appears to suggest her own ideas; at times, she interrupts the chronicler with her own voice. That intervention or corrective is no longer possible if her words are appropriated and her identity obscured, as happened with Du Bois's misuse of Cooper's intellectualism. If we understand "erasure" as the complete absence of representation, the refusal of agency and identity altogether, we routinely recognize that representations that refuse to reference marginalized groups manifest as forms of erasure. However, erasure or exclusionary bias also appears in reflections discussions about disenfranchised peoples that lack specificity.

Some may argue that the absence of specificity implies neither a male or elite bias nor an attempt to erase the significant contributions of black women leaders. To be consistent, we must also maintain that generalizing and vague discourse concerning the achievements of black males and elites is also acceptable. Whatever the intentions, non-specificity promotes erasure. The end result is that such works engaging in form of representation misrepresent agency and intellectual ability as the purview of elites. If we discuss marginalized groups largely as categories or characterize them in symbolic and abstract terms, we detract from the specificity of political analysis. In the distance between our attentiveness to black women as a category and our dismissal of their political praxis, non-specificity will disassemble our progressivism.

CONCLUSION

Given the racialized and sexualized constructions of intellectual ability, it is unsurprising that black male intellectuals intentionally or inadvertently reproduce sexist thought. African American women's intellectual and political productivity is not often mentioned in the writings of their male contemporaries. Du Bois's writings—his profeminism notwithstanding—prove no exception.

Contemporary thought on African American politics reflects both Du Bois's profeminist politics and his gendered oversights. Gender conservatives resist his profeminism. Gender progressives embrace and expand upon his profeminist politics. (Both groups may ignore his repudiation of an intellectual aristocracy of class-based elites.) Profeminism permitted Du Bois to include women in democratic struggles; paternalism allowed him to naturalize the male intellectual.

We may build upon the gift of sight which Du Bois shared and continues to share with many progressives to better comprehend the deep meaning that manifests when two movements for justice, "women and color," combine. Evaluating our inheritance from Du Bois, as well as our own gender and class relationships to oppressed peoples, we may envision strategies to further antiracist, feminist politics. Unpacking our legacy as the heirs of Du Bois might expand profeminist politics to serve democratic movements.

NOTES

1. Du Bois, 1920: 181.
2. I use the term "feminist" to denote women's gender progressive politics; "profeminist" refers to men whose politics advocate women's equality.
3. See "The Talented Tenth Recall," in Joy James, *Democratizing the Talented Tenth: Black Elites, Radical Women, and American Intellectualism*. New York: Routledge, 1996.
4. Aptheker, 1982: 78.
5. Aptheker, 1982: 78.
6. Aptheker, 1982: 77–88.
7. Hardnett, 1992: 66. Hardnett quotes from Jean F. Turpin's history of the Du Bois Circle.
8. Lewis, 1993: 328.
9. Du Bois, 172.
10. Du Bois, 164.
11. Lewis, 1993: 451.
12. Lewis, 1993: 449–50.
13. According to Lewis, after Du Bois's mother, Jessie Fauset and Mary Church Terrell figure peripherally in his political autobiographies.
14. Morton, 65.
15. Morton, 63.
16. Morton, 57.
17. Morton, 63.
18. Morton, 63.
19. Morton, 61.
20. Warren, 111. Warren uses Catherine Stark's definition of "archetype."
21. Warren, 111.
22. Du Bois, 1914: 105.
23. Du Bois, 173.
24. Giddings, 447.
25. Cooper, 31.
26. Cooper, 30–31.
27. Du Bois, 173. Mary Helen Washington also points this out in her introduction to Cooper's work.
28. Cooper, 31.
29. Washington, xxviii.
30. Washington, xlvii.
31. Wells, 1970: 280–81.
32. In 1889, revolutionizing journalism as an effective medium for anti-racist organizing, Wells-Barnett became the first woman secretary of the Afro-American Press Association. In addition to *Southern Horrors*, numerous newspaper articles, editorials, and the posthumously published memoir *Crusade for Justice: The Autobiography of Ida B. Wells*, Wells Barnett's written legacy includes: *A Red Record: Lynchings in the U.S., 1892, 1893, 1894* (1895) and *Mob Rule in New Orleans* (1900).
33. Du Bois, 1940: 29–30.
34. *Ibid.*, 67–68.
35. Lewis, 393–94.
36. Du Bois, 1940: 228.
37. Wells, 1970: 322–26.

38. Lewis, 397.

39. Holt, 50.

40. Holt observes that Wells-Barnett claimed to have elevated Du Bois to national leadership in 1899, by advocating that the Afro-American Council board of directors, whose anti-lynching bureau she headed, appoint him as director of their business bureau. This claim is likely overstated. Du Bois seemed destined for national prominence.

41. Lewis, 413.

42. Du Bois, 1940: 252.

43. *Ibid.*, 228.

44. *Ibid.*, 265.

45. *Ibid.*, 295–96.

46. *Ibid.*, 289.

47. *Ibid.*, 289.

REFERENCES

Bettina Aptheker (1982) "On 'The Damnation of Women': W. E. B. Du Bois and a Theory of Woman's Emancipation," in Aptheker, *Woman's Legacy: Essays on Race, Sex, and Class in American History*. Amherst: University of Massachusetts Press.

Joanne Braxton (1989) *Black Women Writing Autobiographies*. Philadelphia: Temple University Press.

Evelyn Brooks Higginbotham (1993) "The Female Talented Tenth," in Higginbotham, *Righteous Discontent: The Women's Movement in the Black Baptist Church, 1880–1920* . Cambridge, Mass: Harvard University Press.

John Brown Childs (1989) *Leadership, Conflict, and Cooperation in Afro-American Social Thought*. Philadelphia: Temple University Press.

Hazel Carby (1987) *Reconstructing Womanhood*. New York: Oxford University Press.

Anna Julia Cooper (1892) *A Voice From the South*, rprt, Schomburg Collection of 19th Century Black Women Writers. New York: Oxford University Press, 1988.

W. E. B. Du Bois (1914) "The Burden of Black Women," reprinted in *W. E. B. Du Bois: A Reader*, ed. Meyer Weinberg. New York: Harper and Row, 1970, 105.

——— (1920) "The Damnation of Women," *Darkwater: Voices from Within the Veil*, New York: Schocken books, 1969, reprint.

——— (1940) *Dusk of Dawn: An Essay Toward an Autobiography of a Race Concept*, New York: Harcourt, Brace & World, Inc, reprt, New York Schocken Books, 1968.

Leona C. Gabel (1982) *From Slavery to the Sorbonne and Beyond: The Life and Writings of Anna J. Cooper*. Northampton, Mass: Smith College Studies in History, Vol. XLIS.

Paula Giddings (1992) "The Last Taboo," in *Race-ing Justice, En-gendering Power: Essays on Anita Hill, Clarence Thomas, and the Construction of Social Reality*, ed. Toni Morrison, New York: Pantheon Books.

——— (1984) *When and Where I Enter: The Impact of Black women on Race and Sex in America*. New York: Bantam.

Carolyn J. Hardnett (1993) "The Unbroken Du Bois Circle: The Women Behind the Noted Historian," *Emerge* (October).

Thomas C. Holt (1982) "The Lonely Warrior: Ida B. Wells-Barnett and the Struggle for Black Leadership," in *Black Leaders of the Twentieth Century*. Urbana: University of Illinois Press, eds John Hope Franklin and August Meier.

David Levering Lewis (1993) *W. E. B. Du Bois: Biography of a Race, 1868–1919*. New York: Henry Holt Company.

Patricia Morton (1991) "The All-Mother Vision of W. E. B. Du Bois," in Morton, *Disfigured Images: the Historical Assault on Afro-American Women*. New York: Praeger.

Anne Frior Scott (February 1990) "Most Invisible of All: Black Women's Voluntary Associations" in *Journal of Southern History*. Vol. LVI., No.1.

Cheryl Townsend Gilkes (1996) "The Margin as the Center of a Theory of History: Afro-american Women, Social Change, and the Sociology of W. E. B. Du Bois" in *The Thought of W. E. B. Du Bois*, eds Bernard Bell, James Stewart, Emily Grosholz. New York: Routledge.

Nagueyalti Warren (1993) "Deconstructing, Reconstructing, and Focusing our Literary Image," *Spirit, Space and Survival: African American Women in (White) Academe*, eds Joy James and Ruth Farmer. New York: Routledge.

Mary Helen Washington (1988) "Introduction to *A Voice from the South*," by Anna Julia Cooper. rprt, Schomburg Collection of 19th Century Black Women Writers. New York: Oxford University Press.

Ida B. Wells Barnett (1991) *Selected Works of Ida B. Wells-Barnett*, compiled with introduction by Trudier Harris. New York: Oxford University Press, reprints of: *A Red Record: Lynchings in the U.S., 1892, 1893, 1894*. Chicago (1895); *Mob Rule in New Orleans* (1900); with Frederick Douglass and Ferdinand Barnett.*The Reason Why the Colored American in Not in the World's Colombian Exposition.* (1903); *Southern Horrors. Lynch Law in All Its Phases*. New York: New York Age Print (1892) .

—— (1970) *Crusade for Justice: The Autobiography of Ida B. Wells*. Chicago: University of Chicago Press.

Du Bois's Passage to India | 7

Dark Princess

Arnold Rampersad

In 1928, W. E. B. Du Bois published a novel, *Dark Princess*, that failed to make a lasting impression, much less a favorable one, on the American or the African American literary world. Du Bois's novel flopped even though the so-called Harlem Renaissance was then at its zenith and books by black Americans were being published and scrutinized as never before. In histories of the Harlem Renaissance, *Dark Princess* is seldom mentioned, and then usually dismissed as the reactionary attempt by one of the old guard to assert his authority over a cultural movement that properly belonged to the young.

This treatment of *Dark Princess* is unfortunate. Like all of Du Bois's fiction (he published five novels, including *Quest of the Silver Fleece* in 1911 and the *Black Flame* trilogy near the end of his life), *Dark Princess* is hardly flawless as a work of art. However, I would like to suggest that it deserves further scrutiny by anyone interested in taking a more exact measure of the range of Du Bois's interests and concerns, and of his extraordinary intellect and imagination. Few of his works tell us more about his ideas in the 1920s, and before and after that decade, concerning religion and philosophy. Few of his works give us a sharper sense of his vision of the fundamental ways in which the world community might change as the twentieth century moved toward its maturity. Few tell us more about Du Bois's fears and hopes, on a global scale, concerning the future of race relations.

In one sense at least, *Dark Princess* is very much a novel of the Harlem

Renaissance. Increasingly disturbed by some of the trends of the cultural movement he helped to start both as an independent writer and as founder and editor of the influential *Crisis* magazine, Du Bois clearly intended the novel, in part, as a corrective to the growing trend among the younger artists to assert their artistic independence at the expense of the radical political purposefulness that ruled his own life and career. The year he published this novel, 1928, he wrote scathingly of "the school of Van Vechten and McKay," by which he meant to chastise the white writer Carl Van Vechten for his sexually charged novel of Harlem, *Nigger Heaven* (1926), and Claude McKay for his *Home to Harlem* (1928), in which McKay dwelt unapologetically, even longingly, on the more sybaritic aspects of Harlem life.[1]

Du Bois's *Dark Princess* was intended, to some extent, to bring the younger writers to their senses by showing how a mature African-American artist should approach his craft. The novel surely was intended to exemplify the close and sympathetic relationship between art and propaganda that Du Bois had championed in organizing in 1926 in the *Crisis* a symposium on precisely this subject, and on the special political duty of the black American artist. "All art is propaganda, and ever will be," Du Bois had boldly declared when he finally had his say, "despite the wailing of the purists."[2] Other writers had disagreed, but Du Bois had held firm. *Dark Princess* was his definitive illustration of his main ideas about the duty of the black American artist.

However, *Dark Princess* is much more than a statement about aesthetics. Perhaps the most neglected of Du Bois's many neglected texts, the novel nevertheless offers a rich index to Du Bois's thinking on a variety of questions. Politically, it casts light on Du Bois's sense of the interplay between race and politics on a global scale; it also speaks, often in a startlingly prophetic way, to such diverse but related issues as European colonialism after World War I, the rise of Japanese militarism, the emergence of China and India from European domination, the role of black America in the modern world, the future of what only decades later would be called the Third World, and the role of radical socialism and socialists, including white socialists, in all of the above.

In the area of religion—a topic generally neglected in Du Bois studies (although Herbert Aptheker in this matter, as in other matters, has tried to establish its importance in Du Bois's thought)—*Dark Princess* is also important. The novel illuminates some of the gloomier recesses of Du Bois's spiritual beliefs, in particular those places where race and politics impinge on spiritual and religious consciousness, as race and politics impinged on every major aspect of Du Bois's thinking.

On the matter of philosophy, where the need for a more detailed assessment of Du Bois's thought is widely acknowledged but remains largely unfulfilled, *Dark Princess* is also significant. With this novel, Du Bois enters into a dialogue not only with classical non-Christian Eastern philosophies and religions but also with the elements of those philosophies and religions that have played an important role in American intellectual life, mainly through the transcendentalism of Du Bois's native New England and the philosophic successors to transcendentalism, especially pragmatism. For these reasons, and others, *Dark Princess* deserves closer scrutiny than it has been accorded over the decades since its publication.

What did India mean to Du Bois? To say that India played no important part in his formal education, or in the education of virtually all Americans of Du Bois's day, is an understatement. Indian philosophy and religion were not a part of the curriculum at Fisk or Harvard. The most complex notion of India he possessed as a young man probably came from the legacy of American transcendentalism—the famed gospel of Concord, Massachusetts—in the 1840s, a legacy richly augmented by Walt Whitman in successive editions of his *Leaves of Grass*, after the first edition in 1855. In writing about Du Bois's "passage to India" in my title, I deliberately allude not to E.M. Forster's celebrated novel but to the poem by Walt Whitman that inspired Forster's title. Whitman's poem "Passage to India," written in 1871, with its call to "Eclaircise the myths Asiatic, the primitive fables," is a token of the place of Indian religion, philosophy, and mythology in not only Whitman's work but also in the work and thought of Emerson, Thoreau, and other members of what has been called the American Renaissance.[3]

It is from the works and reputations of these writers, the brightest luminaries of the New England and American intellectual worlds, that Du Bois would have derived his initial understanding of, and respect for, India as a place of wisdom and enlightenment. Critics closer to our time, such as Perry Miller, have seen in the philosophic extravagances of transcendentalism not so much Indian religion and thought as an elaborate reworking of a Calvinist cosmos. Be that as it may, the evidence of a serious interest in and knowledge of Indian culture by Emerson, Thoreau, and Whitman is irrefutable, and Du Bois could not have become educated without some sense of the intellectual connections between his native land and the Indian subcontinent. The light of Transcendentalism was fading fast by the time Du Bois developed intellectually in Great Barrington, Massachusetts, at Fisk in Nashville, and at Harvard University. Still, it needs to be remembered that he was decidedly a contemporary—if only for a few years—of some of its major figures. If Thoreau had been dead six years when Du Bois was born, Du Bois was already fourteen when Emerson died. He was twenty-four, and well into his graduate study, when Walt Whitman died in 1892.

After the heyday of transcendentalism in the works of these figures, India would not again occupy a significant role in American intellectual life and consciousness until the 1960s, when an interest in Indian religion and culture, especially music, was a highlight of the cultural change that swept over America. Transcendental meditation became almost a household concept, and the sitar and ragas infiltrated western popular music. Between the 1840s and the 1950s, when certain of the Beat writers exhibited a definite interest in Indian culture, India virtually disappeared as an intellectual and spiritual force in America. Certain charismatic and itinerant Indian philosophers and spiritualists were always sure to appeal to some Americans, especially in California, but on the whole India was an unknown quantity. The one major exception in this history, or the in lack of it, is the prominent place accorded to India by T. S. Eliot in his poem *The Waste Land* (1922) and, much less so, in his *Four Quartets*. The former draws to a close with the climactic intonation "Datta. Dayadhvam. Damyata. / Shantih Shantih Shantih"; the latter offers its extended reference in the "Dry Salvages" section to "what Krishna said." In depicting the spiritual desolation of modern Europe and America, Eliot turned to ancient India, as well as to St. Augustine, among Christian ancients, as a contrast to the spiritual decline of the present day.

What has been true of America in general, in its lack of interest in India, has been even more true of black America. I make this point to emphasize the extent to which Du Bois was, once again, far ahead of others in his intellectual interests, the extent to which he was breaking new ground in *Dark Princess*. It is difficult to find any reference to India in the writings of African American intellectuals and artists before Du Bois. Why was this so? In the first place, African American culture, like American culture as a whole, and despite exceptions, has never been internationalist in outlook. From a pious black American point of view, Indian religion amounted not simply to paganism but to paganism of a particularly challenging sort, with its gods and goddesses, rituals and sacrifices, feasts and erotica. In the area of philosophy, Indian transcendentalism probably sat unhappily and unconvincingly with the necessary materialism that pervades black American intellectual culture, despite the undeniable appeal of religon to that culture. In addition, India was a royalist and aristocratic culture; African Americans, whatever their individual degrees of snobbery, historically have had a vested interest in the fortunes of radical democracy. Last but not least, the caste system of India, with its banishing of millions of people to a fate in some respects possibly worse than slavery, was an almost insuperable challenge to an African American vision of an ideal society.

In these and other ways, India decisively lacked prestige in African American eyes, as it lacked prestige in American eyes generally. The African American intellectual who would look to India as a legitimate source of guidance, or who would construct a complicated work of art based on an interest in and deep respect for India, would have to be highly unusual. Such a person was W. E. B. Du Bois, almost without doubt the most extraordinary of all black American intellectuals. Among his many firsts was probably this one, although it has perhaps never been recognized—that he was the first black American intellectual to look to India and the East as primary forms of inspiration in pursuing matters of fundamental importance to black America. Du Bois shared the general African American and American respect for the cultures of England and France, but he possessed the learning, wisdom, and foresight to see that light also came from the East.

How was Du Bois able to make this turn? The key to his almost singular respect for and knowledge of India among African Americans was ultimately his relentless interrogation, starting around 1900, of the category of race. In 1900, he told a Pan-African gathering in London "The problem of the twentieth century is the problem of the color line."[4] He would repeat this dictum to greater effect in his landmark collection of essays and sketches *The Souls of Black Folk* (1903). By this point, Du Bois seriously doubted the wisdom that held white nations to be the repository of all intellectual and cultural accomplishment, and the darker races as destined to be vassals of the whites in perpetuity. When he founded the *Crisis* in 1910, he subtitled it "A Record of the Darker Races"; and he had previously used that term elsewhere in his journalistic efforts. In 1911, when he attended the Universal Races Congress in London, organized by the English Ethical Culture movement, he not only heard powerful arguments against white racial supremacy but also heard these arguments delivered by both whites and gifted, educated intellectuals from among the darker races. Thereafter, India in particular would play a crucial role in his interrogation of the category of race.

According to his colleague and friend Mary White Ovington, who was present in London, Du Bois may also have met the woman on whom he later modeled the heroine of his novel. "I think I saw the dark Indian Princess in 1911," Ovington wrote,

> as she came down the steps of the ballroom at the last meeting of the First Universal Races Congress in London. I thought her the loveliest person there, except perhaps the darker daughter of the Haitian President, Legitime. And by the Princess's side was one of the the the most distinguished men of the Conference, Burghardt Du Bois. They were talking earnestly, of course of the race problem. Did this Indian Princess remain in the American Negro's memory to become the Titania of his Midsummer's Night's Dream?[5]

Such personal encounters, perhaps at least as much as scholarly articles and books of history, art, literature, sociology, and the like, helped Du Bois in his struggle with the notion of white racial supremacy. No one has written more powerfully about the hold on the black American mind of race as an intellectual construct and of racism and its intellectual consequences, or about the overpowering weight of Western scientific and pseudo- scientific evidence and opinion concerning the ability and character and inherent nature of blacks that formed, in effect, a cosmic solidity akin to the Great Chain of Being. Du Bois gave a vivid outline of his own formal miseducation in this subject. First, in geography classes in elementary and high school, the races of the world were pictured as if the category of race needed no discussion. Whites were exemplified by attractive individuals, but Indians, Negroes, and Chinese were marked "by their most uncivilized and bizarre representatives." As an undergraduate he had faced "scientific race dogma" spun out of theories of evolution and of the "Survival of the Fittest." In graduate school at Harvard and in Berlin, "race became a matter of culture and history," with the superior race "manifestly that which had a history, the white race. There was some mention of Asiatic culture, but no course in Chinese or Indian history or culture was offered at Harvard, and quite unanimously in America and Germany, Africa was left without culture and without history."[6]

In a real sense, Du Bois's entire career as a writer and an activist was aimed at contesting that cosmos of race. From books of history and empirical sociology to collections of essays, from a biography in 1909 to a first novel in 1911, he waged unceasing intellectual war on the notion of intrinsic and inevitable white racial superiority. In 1910, he left his tenured position at Atlanta University to found the *Crisis* and launch his career, on a national scale, as a crusading editor. From 1919 on into the 1920s he organized Pan-African Congresses that met mainly in Europe to try to influence the future of colonialism in Africa. During this time, he tried to work with the imperial nations and with the League of Nations, but was rebuffed not only by the League and the imperial powers but also by African leaders beholden to those powers. By 1927 or so, when he began *Dark Princess*, he had become largely disillusioned with these efforts. At that point he turned to fiction, and the imagining of a different world—but one fashioned, to be sure, out of the world in which Du Bois lived. Set between 1923 and 1927, Du Bois's *Dark Princess: A Romance* is a tale of passion, politics, and international intrigue. The hero is Matthew Towns, a brown-skinned black man whose hopes to become an obstetrician are dashed by racism in New York. Embittered—he was a man "whose heart was hate"—he flees to Europe.[7] One day he sees an exquisite, slightly colored woman at a cafe in Berlin. When a white American insults her, Matthew knocks him down with a blow to the jaw.

The woman is an Indian princess—Her Royal Highness Kautilya of Bwodpur. (Perhaps Du Bois took the name from Kautilya, the male author of the *Artha-sastra*, a treatise on politics and diplomacy dated uncertainly between 326 and 291 B.C.). At her invitation, Matthew attends a meeting of part of a grand council of the darker races who meet to plot the overthrow of white dominion around the world. Representatives of India, Japan, China, the Arab world, and Egypt are present. Matthew soon discovers that they scorn African Americans as a tribe of slaves. Matthew tries to convince them that a people can move from slavery to civilization in a few short generations, but only the princess—and perhaps the Chinese—are inclined to give him a hearing.

Matthew returns to the United States to prepare a report for the princess on the actual condition of black America. When members of her staff cut off his line of communications to her, he thinks she has abandoned him. The lynching of a coworker drives him to take part in a murderous and suicidal plot to destroy a train carrying a convention of the Ku Klux Klan. At the last moment, however, the princess appears. For his part in the plot, which is uncovered, Matthew is sentenced to prison. After serving some time in jail, he is released through the efforts of a corrupt black Chicago politician and his assistant, an attractive, bright woman who hopes that Matthew, now a hero to blacks because of his trial, can be of some use to her employer. After Matthew and the woman marry, she guides him to the brink of election to Congress from the South Side of Chicago. His path is through a sewer of graft and corruption to which he surrenders in despair.

However, just before his nomination, the princess reappears. The two fall into one another's arms. Since their last meeting, Kautilya has abandoned her royal prerogatives and identity and plunged anonymously into proletarian life, the better to understand it. In this seven-year passage, she has been befriended by Matthew's mother. Unnamed, and living in a cabin in rural Virginia Matthew's mother never speaks in the novel and is seldom present; but she is centrally important. Kautilya's hands are now rough with work— labor as a servant, a tobacco hand, a waitress. Her face, still exquisite, now bears the honorable lines of toil. From afar, she has been following Matthew's career and has come to save him.

Affronted and enraged, Matthew's wife throws him out of the house and their marriage. The lovers consummate their relationship in the sparsely furnished rooms he has kept elsewhere in the city as a token of his old, moral self. We learn of Kautilya's past, including her humiliations at the hands of the British both in India and in England, where she lived for a while. Those humiliations drove her to be a leader in the international plot. ("Hell!" she overhears her white fiancé telling his English true love, who cannot bear the thought of his 'mating with a nigger.' "I'm mating with a throne and a fortune. The darky's a mere makeweight" (239).

After living together for a while, Kautilya insists on leaving Matthew, at least for a while. Bwodpur needs a maharaja, and she must meet this need in some way. She returns to his mother in Virginia. Determined to purify himself, Matthew becomes a ditch digger in Chicago. Eventually he is summoned to Virginia to witness the crowning of the new Maharaja of Bwodpur. To his astonishment, he finds that the new maharaja is not only an infant but also his son, and Kautilya's. Their babe, Madhu Chandragupta Singh, is hailed as Maharaja of Bwodpur and Maharaja of Sindrabad, King of the Snows of Gaurisankar, Protector of Ganga the Holy, Incarnate Son of the Buddha, Grand Mughal of Utter India, and "Messenger and Messiah to all the Darker Worlds" (311).

Melodramatic and even operatic, Du Bois's novel amounts at the very least to an earnest meditation on a number of issues. *Dark Princess* is a commentary on black America, its achievement and its capacity; its place in the wide world; and on the relationship of black America to what would later to called the Third World. But the culture and heritage of India are specifically important to the novel. Kautilya's change, including her marriage, might be unspeakable to many Indians, but she is absolutely devoted to India. "You must know India," she implores Matthew late in the book. "India! India! Out of black India the world was born. Into the black womb of India the world shall creep to die. All that the world has done, India did, and that more marvelously, more magnificently. The loftiest of mountains, the mightiest of rivers, the widest of plains, the broadest of oceans—these are India" (227).

With these and other lines Du Bois effects a powerful shift. They contest the familar rhetoric about "purple mountained majesty" and "amber waves of grain" by which America is represented to Americans and the world as God's own country. One is similarly reminded of the extravagant claims by Emerson and Whitman about America as being itself the greatest poem in the world, because of its geographic endowment and because of its people. Kautilya and Du Bois make identical claims, but on behalf of dark India and Indians.

> Man is there of every shape and kind and hue. . . . The drama of life knows India as it knows no other land, from the tragedy of Almighty God to the laugh of the Bandar-log; from divine Gotama to the sons of Mahmoud and the stepsons of the Christ. . . . Loveliest and weirdest of lands; terrible with flame and ice, beautiful with palm and pine. . . . This is India—can you not understand?"

"No," Matthew replies, "I cannot understand; but I feel your meaning" (227).

Perhaps, however, he has been reading. When Kautilya at one point calls him "Krishna," Matthew knows enough to recognize that she is naming him after the popular manifestation of the god Vishnu. In turn, he calls her "Radha," the cowherdess who is Krishna's consort and creative essence (219).

As for the centrality of India in the modern clash of races, one should consider a passage in the introduction to a book by an Indian nationalist published the same year as *Dark Princess*:

> Whatever is really good and moral among the modern nations of the world is largely a gift of the East. . . . Europe's dominance over Asia is not more than two centuries old. It virtually began with the conquest of India, and, God willing, will end with her emancipation. . . . India is the crux of the problem of the clash of colour. India's freedom means the freedom of the whole coloured world.[8]

Matthew indeed appears to feel a connection between himself and India, loosely defined. Emerging from jail, he immerses himself in a regimen of purification that entails asceticism. He wants little, and what material goods he acquires speak of a possibly profound shift in his esthetic and cultural appreciations away from a slavish regard for white culture, or African American imitations of that culture, toward something more cosmopolitan, more sophisticated, and darker. He acquires a gloriously colored Chinese rug, which someone has given him; then he buys a Turkish rug, when he is better off; and he also buys a statue of "a deliciously ugly Chinese God" (143), to which he had found himself curiously drawn. He and Kautilya make love for the first time on the Chinese rug, and he jauntily wears a tarboosh on his head at breakfast the morning after.

By 1928, when he fashioned this narrative marriage of black America and India, Du Bois had not visited India. Nevertheless, his various magazines, notably the *Crisis*, had consistently noted the major stages of the *swaraj* or home-rule movement in India. Du Bois had met visiting Indian intellectuals in the United States, and later corresponded with some of them. In 1927, Du Bois sent passages from the manuscript of *Dark Princess* for commentary and correction to one of these acquaintances, the celebrated independence fighter Lajpat Rai of Calcutta. He received Rai's comments as he prepared the manuscript for the press, and incorporated small changes based on these comments.

Rai was the author of several books, including *Young India*, *The United States of America*, *The Political Future of India*, and *Unhappy India*, published in 1928, the same year as *Dark Princess*. Rai had lived for about five years in the United States and made "a special study of the Negro problem," as he wrote in *Unhappy India*.[9] He respected the work of Du Bois, whose writing is quoted extensively at one point in *Unhappy India*.

To read Lajpat Rai's books on India, especially *Unhappy India*, is to see fully illuminated, if in light refracted from a variety of angles, all the elements I enumerated earlier on as interposing themselves between India and black America. Almost all of elements, in and of themselves and quite apart from black America, were of profound concern to Indians as they wrestled with the array of problems engendered by the humiliating presence of the British in their land. A vast difference exists between Indian colonialism and the African American history of slavery and segregation. Nevertheless, Rai and Du Bois certainly saw the similarities, as well as the ties of a common subjugation to white power that united Indians to black Americans. In its own way, *Unhappy India* treats all of these elements, and more. The study worries such issues as the reputation and the efficacy of Indian religions, the justness of the caste system, the alleged excesses of Indian sexuality, or alleged hypersexuality, and the place of women in Indian culture. The book is written with some indignation, for it is from start to finish a response to another book, also a study of Indian life.

That book, called *Mother India*, was written by a white American woman, Katherine Mayo, who had recently visited India for about a year. This American connection further brought Rai's purposes and interests into closer alignment with Du Bois's. Mayo had concentrated on the role of women in Indian society, but ranged far enough, and in scathingly critical fashion, to earn the denunciation of many Indian intellectuals, including Gandhi himself. Du Bois, in the *Crisis* of November, 1927: "Katherine Mayo, white American, declares that brown India is sexually immoral. Thus the pot calls the kettle black."[10]

If there is one point in particular that links Mayo's effort to those of Lajpat Rai and Du Bois, in a triangle of signification, it is her suggestion that India is unfit for *swaraj*, or home rule, because of the existence of the untouchable caste. In rebuttal, in a chapter called "Less Than the Pariah," Rai identifies among Americans "a larger proportion of 'untouchables' and a severer form of untouchability than that in India. . . . Even today the untouchables in India are neither lynched nor treated so brutally as the Negroes in the United States are."[11] In an earlier book, *The United States of America*, he had already declared that "The Negro is the pariah of America."[12] (The term pariah, of course, is specifically Indian in origin, and refers to someone of extremely low caste. Members of pariah castes, according to one source, "are ordinarily so abhorred that physical contact with their members is considered ritually polluting.")[13]

This business of untouchability is crucial to *Dark Princess*. The novel may be grandly prophetic at one level, but it is also diplomatic in its negotiation of a relationship between India and black America. Du Bois is well aware of the pariah status of black Americans and blacks in the eyes of the rest of the world, including India. He knows, too, that the marriage of a pariah to a princess is unthinkable. Matthew is no pariah in Du Bois's eyes, nor in the princess's. The novel interrogates both India and black America on the questions of class and caste. Where Matthew and the black American world stand in Indian eyes is captured in a plea made to him by an Indian official near the end of the novel to leave Kautilya alone. Kautilya, he declares, was

> stooping to raise the dregs of mankind; laborers, scrubwomen, scavengers, and beggars, into some fancied democracy of the world! It is madness born of pity for you and your unfortunate people. . . . The Princess is mad—mad; and you are the center of her madness. Withdraw—for God's sake and your own—go! Leave us to our destiny. What have you to do with royalty and divinity? (300)

This Indian official's question is addressed to Matthew, but it is also addressed, insultingly, to black America. What could African Americans possibly know about royalty or about true religion?

Kautilya's eyes have been opened, so she is able to set aside notions of untouchability in viewing Matthew. In her seven years of labor she has atoned for her old ways and beliefs. Among these are her old belief in the absolute authority of an aristocracy of blood, her belief in the caste system that relegates millions to fixed and inferior stations in perpetuity and recognizes an entire caste of people who are perpetually untouchable, and her willingness to so treat people when the Lord Buddha has said, as she remembers near the end of the novel, that "humanity itself is royal" (248).

Nevertheless, her son by Matthew is crowned as maharaja. Du Bois is not about to renounce royalty, particularly when the member of royalty is brown-skinned. One bit of business in *Dark Princess* involves a bag containing the crown jewels of Bwodpur. Kautilya carelessly misplaces it, but in the end, the jewels are recovered. Finally, the author of *Dark Princess* is neither an ascetic not a Jacobite. A devotion to spiritual ideals does not mean the end of materialism. One is reminded how, between piously citing the Upanishads in *The Waste Land* and appealing to Krishna in his *Four Quartets*, T. S. Eliot nevertheless declared himself publicly to be a royalist in politics, as well as a believer in a religion, Anglicanism, whose official head is the secular monarch of Great Britain.

Matthew himself atones for the years of corruption when he served his Chicago politician employers and himself by graft and corruption. Also, perhaps, for a night spent at one point with a prostitute, an episode depicted by Du Bois about as casually as Claude McKay himself might have described it in *Home to Harlem*. Perhaps Matthew must atone for his first marriage, which had been caused by despair, by his lack of faith in his princess. And perhaps also for being too long a man "whose heart was hate," unable to differentiate between bad whites and those of good will. If so, race hatred is a force not unambiguously repudiated in *Dark Princess*. In this novel, progressive and radical whites, although approved of as allies of the darker peoples, are a seedy lot, especially next to the glory of Kautilya. Her last job is with the Box Makers trade union, but she remains untouched by their apparent dinginess. No whites appear to have received an invitation to the ceremony that closes the novel, when the birth of Matthew and Kautilya's son is celebrated.

In the ranks of the Grand Central Committee near the end of the book, "the strongest group among us believes only in Force," Kautilya reports. "Pound [the whites'] arrogance into submission, they cry; kill them; conquer them; humiliate them." Kautilya says only that "They may be right—that's the horror, the nightmare of it: they may be right. But surely, surely we may seek other and less costly ways" (297).

Almost disdainful of white "blood," Du Bois emphasizes a link between African blood and Indian blood. When one of the Indians and an Egyptian sneer at mixed blood (Matthew Towns is of mixed blood, with only one grandfather of "pure" blackness), Kautilya muses about her own mixed blood and about the essential mixed blood of India, "as our black and curly-haired Lord Buddha testifies in a hundred places" (19). When she calls Matthew "Krishna," surely Du Bois knows that Krishna in Sanskrit means black; and her identification of Matthew's mother as "Kali, the Black One" (Kali literally means the Black One in Hindi), completes her acknowledgement of her racial unity with Matthew and with despised black America.

For Kautilya, Matthew's mother presents a vision of the past of the world and of its future. Matthew loves his mother, who in his thoughts is "that poor but mighty, purposeful mother—tall, big, and brown. What hands she had—gnarled and knotted; what great, broad feet. How she worked!" (37) Out of jail he visits her for the first time in five years: "She was sitting in the door, straight, tall, big and brown. She was singing something low and strong. And her eyes were scanning the highway" (131). It is left to Kautilya to tell him who his mother is. No faith nor religion . . . ever dies," she tells him.

> I am of the clan and land that gave Gotama, the Buddha, to the world. I know that out of the soul of Brahma come little separations of his perfect and ineffable self and they appear again and again in higher and higher manifestations, as eternal life flows on. And when I saw that old mother of yours standing in the blue shadows of twilight with flowers, cotton, and corn about her, I knew that I was looking upon one of the ancient prophets of India and that she was to lead me out of the depth in which I found myself and up to the atonement for which I yearned. (221)

To Kautilya, Matthew's mother is "Kali, the Black One; wife of [Shiva], Mother of the World'" (220). Kali (the Indian deity after which Calcutta—the place of Kali—was named) is a complex figure, as indeed are all the major deities of India. Kali is often seen as the spirit of disorder and destruction essential to the life principle, with disorder and destruction accepted as part of the superfluid creative process of life itself. Du Bois's Kali is a tame version of such a force. Kali here seems to symbolize the patient, noble endurance of human suffering; his Kali is at once more Christian, more African American in her essence.

Perhaps it was in Lajpat Rai's *Unhappy India* that Du Bois found the clue for this formulation of Matthew's mother as Kali. Rai quotes the African American intellectual Kelly Miller on the black woman in America:

> The Negro woman has been made to bear the brunt of the evil passions of all the races of men living or sojourning in this country. Within the veins of the so-called Negro race there course traces of the blood of every known variety or sub-variety of the human family. Not only within the limits of the race itself, but even within the veins of the same individuals, the strains of blood are mingled and blended in inextricable confusion.[14]

Richard Wright has called the Negro "America's metaphor."[15] Here, in Du Bois, the black woman is the world's metaphor, born out of violation and shame, but then recuperated as the living symbol of the interrelationship of the races.

This is an expansive formulation on Du Bois's part, but in other important ways, as we have seen, *Dark Princess* stops short of a radical devotion to idealism. A shadowy, critical figure may be said to hover over the text of *Dark Princess*, although he is never mentioned there—the figure of Mohandas K. Gandhi, the Mahatma. In his weakness for royalty and wealth, in his unwillingness to repudiate even justifiable violence or to rise totally above racial antagonism, Du Bois (as the guiding spirit of *Dark Princess*) begs comparison and contrast with Gandhi. The Mahatma's life and career offer a practical critique of Du Bois's romance, although—ironically—Gandhi was in some ways a far more romantic personality than anyone imagined by Du Bois in *Dark Princess*.

Returning to India in 1915 from South Africa, and joining the struggle against the British, Gandhi had moved in seemingly naive, romantic ways against them. He had renounced Western ways, starting with Western dress and moving into the economic and technological spheres, until he was a half-naked brown man in a simple dhoti who squatted before his spinning wheel, which was as much a prop as a practical challenge to British industrial power. Arming himself for a protracted struggle, he had adopted nonviolence or *satyagraha* as offense and defense. In an avowedly sensual land he had embraced abstinence and spirituality. Where Indians were fanatical about caste, he had denounced the system and made his special cause the plight of the untouchables—he called them "harajin," or the children of God. In a predominantly Hindu world he had preached the power of Hindu, Moslem, and Christian ethics. Purging hate from his heart, he preached the unity of humanity under one god.

In *Mother India*, Katherine Mayo tersely recounts a visit to his house. Clearly she finds him theatrical, too theatrical by half. "His costume, being merely a loin-cloth," she wrote, "exposes his hairy body, his thin, wiry arms, and his bare, thin, interlaced legs, upon which he sits like Buddha." With barely concealed scorn, she asks Gandhi if he has a message to America. "What is my message to America?" Gandhi replies. "My message to America is the hum of this spinning wheel."[16]

Du Bois could not go as far into idealism as Gandhi could, no matter how deeply, from afar, he admired the Mahatma. In India, using romantic gestures, Gandhi could do something practical, or political, about his hatred of ugliness. He lived with the potentiality of a nation always before him, even if in 1928 his ways seemed the stuff of romances and his hopes still seemed chimerical. Gandhi had real politics; Du Bois had not even the realist novel; he had, in 1928, only the romance, as he called *Dark Princess* in its subtitle. Certainly he partook of the spirit of idealism that moved Gandhi, even though the novel never names Gandhi. *Dark Princess* insists, with a kind of mantra from Buddha, that "God is Love and Work is His Prophet." Near the end, Kautilya writes Matthew: "God lives forever—Brahma, Buddha, Mohammed, Christ—all His infinite incarnations. From God we came, to God we shall return. We are eternal because we are God" (295). But also near the end, Du Bois poses a threat.

Kautilya declares of her committee: "Ten years of preparation are set. Ten more years of final planning, and then five years of intensive struggle. In 1952, the Dark World goes free—whether in Peace and fostering Friendship with all men, or in Blood and Storm—it is for Them—the Pale Masters of today—to say" (297). If one takes the epochal Bandung Conference of non-aligned nations in 1955 as marking the emergence of the Third World, then Du Bois's schedule of liberation was off by only three years. The conference, sponsored by India, Pakistan, Indonesia, Ceylon, and Burma, had as its major goal the forging of African-Asian solidarity and neutrality in the cold war, as well as an end to colonialism. And Gandhi's life, of course, ended with his assassination in 1948. Before he died, he saw his dream of a harmonious Hindu and Moslem subcontinental nation shattered, and India partitioned. Lajpat Rai, incidentally, also met a violent end. Taking part in a nationalist demonstration, he was severely beaten and died of his injuries in 1928, the year *Dark Princess* appeared. Du Bois outlived them both.

In the critique of Gandhi implied in *Dark Princess*, Du Bois anticipated something essential about the major way in which India, and Gandhi specifically, was to serve black America in later years. That way was in the adaptation of *satyagraha* by a group of black American religious thinkers, notably Martin Luther King, Jr., and its implementation as the guiding principle of the civil rights movement in the 1950s and early 1960s. It needs to be noted, however, how this African American version of Gandhian nonviolence was almost clinically detached from its broader philosophical and religious contexts.

As one recent critic has said of King and his key African American advisers (learned, devout men such as Ben E. Mays, Mordecai Johnson, and even the mystic Howard Thurman): "They paid little or no attention to the communal Gandhi, the cloth-spinning Gandhi, the vegetarian Gandhi, the ascetic Gandhi, the celibate Gandhi, the Hindu Gandhi, and the fast-unto-death Gandhi. Instead they concentrated on the nonviolent Gandhi who orchestrated massive campaigns of civil disobedience."[17] However, nonviolence, learned from India, as well as from Thoreau (no doubt also out of India), proved to be the trumpet of Joshua that brought the outer walls of segregation down.

It might seem reasonable to infer that since *Dark Princess* does not endorse nonviolence, Du Bois had little use for Gandhi. In fact, this conclusion would not do justice to the novel. In it, not only Gandhi's nonviolence but also many other aspects of his philosophy are subsumed into Matthew and Kautilya's emerged philosophy of life. In spite of the threatening note on which the novel ends, the blow Matthew strikes at the start of the story is the last blow that he strikes. The story is about the imperatives of humility, duty, sacrifice, honor, labor, and love among people engaged in a just political struggle that might lead them away from these virtues and values. It clearly emphasizes the spiritual dimensions of the political struggle in which the dark heroes find themselves.

Whether Du Bois himself could actually live by these guidelines is another matter altogether, and irrelevant to his novel. With *Dark Princess* he opened a window onto a world largely undreamt of in African American philosophy, or what has passed for it historically. If no one followed him to the window, that was not his fault, but only typical of the response of others to the incomparable range of his vision.

NOTES
1. W. E. B. Du Bois, "The Browsing Reader," *Crisis* 35 (November 1928): 374.
2. See W. E. B. Du Bois, "Criteria of Negro Art," *Crisis* 32 (October 1926): 290–97.
3. Walt Whitman, *Complete Poetry and Selected Prose*, ed. James E. Miller (Boston: Houghton Mifflin, 1959), 288.

4.   W. E. B. Du Bois, "Address to the Nations of the World," in *W. E. B. Du Bois Speaks: Speeches and Addresses 1890–1919*, ed. Philip S. Foner (New York: Pathfinder Press), 125.

5.   Herbert Aptheker, Introduction to W. E. B. Du Bois, *Dark Princess: A Romance* (Millwood, N.Y.: Kraus-Thomson, 1974), 8.

6.   W. E. B. Du Bois, *Dusk of Dawn: An Essay Toward An Autobiography of A Race Concept* (New York: Schocken Books), 97–98.

7.   W. E. B. Du Bois, *Dark Princess,* 5. All subsequent parenthetical references are to this edition.

8.   Lajpat Rai, *Unhappy India,* 2nd. ed. (Calcutta: Banna Publishing Co., 1928), xvii–xviii.

9.   Rai, *Unhappy India,* 104.

10.   W. E. B. Du Bois, "As the Crow Flies," *Crisis* 34 (November 1927): 293.

11.   Rai, *Unhappy* India, 104.

12.   Lajpat Rai, *The United States of America: A Hindu's Impressions and a Study,* 2nd ed. (Calcutta, 1919), 88; cited in Rai, *Unhappy India,* 105n.

13.   "Pariah," in *The New Columbia Encyclopedia,* ed. William H. Harris and Judith S. Levey (New York: Columbia University Press, 1975), 2068.

14.   Rai, *Unhappy India,* 130–31.

15.   Richard Wright, "The Literature of the Negro in the United States," in Wright, *White Man, Listen!* (Garden City, N.Y.: Doubleday, 1964), 72.

16.   Katherine Mayo, *Mother India* (New York: Harcourt, Brace, 1927), 221–22.

17.   Keith D. Miller, *Voice of Deliverance: The Language of Martin Luther King Jr. and Its Sources* (New York: The Free Press, 1992), 98.

Nature and Culture in *The Souls of Black Folk* and *The Quest of the Silver Fleece*

8

Emily R. Grosholz

By giving his book *Dusk of Dawn* the subtitle, "autobiography of a race concept," W. E. B. Du Bois late in life reaffirmed that a theoretical and practical understanding of the race concept was his life work. Throughout his writings, he grapples time and time again with its definition, deploying all his powers as philosopher, scientist, and poet to fasten the elusive notion.

A venerable pair of metaphysical polar opposites, nature and culture, always loom in his thoughts as he struggles to give race its proper philosophical and political location. Given nineteenth-century discussions of race, this binary opposition was inescapable. Du Bois tells us that he encountered two particularly invidious, and incompatible, treatments of the race concept during his undergraduate and graduate education. At Harvard, he met with the biological reductionism of Agassiz, which invoked both the theory of evolution and the odd computations of craniology. At the University of Berlin, he was assailed by the cultural dogmatism of von Treitschke, which used philology to represent race as a transcendent entity, a kind of spriritual club to which one was elected or damned a priori.

Both accounts were, of course, used to reassert and legitimate the superiority of white European (and Yankee) culture, a rule which consciously and unself-consciously amassed and marshalled facts to support itself. One account made race a necessary effect of nature; the other made race a necessary effect of culture. Both made race an essence that dominated and constrained the individuals subsumed by it, and both invoked the prestige of science, biology or philology, to enforce their essentialism.

Metaphysical schemes that accord reality to development must display the structure of reality in terms of possible changes; change requires difference, and difference takes the form of binary oppositions in our language and thought. The venerable binary oppositions of metaphysics are a part of human wisdom; for all their indeterminacy, they stand for something fundamental and inescapable. Because he found the present state of human society in which he lived so intolerable, Du Bois had to create a metaphysics in which development (and therefore hope) was possible and real; so any student of Du Bois must pay close attention to the binary oppositions central to his way of thinking.

Binary oppositions can be considered internally and externally, though such considerations turn out to be complementary. A metaphysician can treat polar terms as utterly without relation or as utterly indistinguishable, positions that might be called dualism and monism. (No philosopher ever actually adopts a pure dualism or monism, because then there would be nothing to say.) But if the terms are treated as distinct and yet standing in intelligible relation to each other, that relation may be one of mediation, or of contradiction. Metaphysicians with a penchant for mediation elaborate stable systems (with an inherent instability that stems from the differentiation of the terms). Those with a penchant for contradiction develop dialectical processes (with an inherent stability that stems from the intelligible relatedness of the terms).

The external relations of binary oppositions in metaphysics are typically relations of analogy to other binary oppositions. A master opposition will organize other oppositions by aligning them under its own terms. This organization is bound to be imperfect (by the standards of a logician) because the analogy is not an equation; the terms shift and revise themselves as the alignment is carried out. But the attempt at organization is inevitable: how else can one investigate ratios except by examining them in proportions? And the analogies will be revealing both where they succeed and where they fail, if the thinker is reflective enough.

The internal and external positioning of binary oppositions is complementary, because a philosopher elaborates the mediations and explores the contradictions between a pair of terms by setting them in analogy with other pairs. For example, the philosophers of the seventeenth century who were interested in the relation of matter and spirit subordinated a whole series of other terms to that master opposition in their philosophical discourse: passion and action, multiplicity and unity, body and soul, science and religion, sensation and reason, corpuscles and animal spirits, and so forth. Broadly speaking, claims of systematicity succeed best when the alignments hold, whereas shifts of alignment signal the presence of useful contradiction.[1]

Whatever other reproaches one might direct at the ways the nineteenth-century biologists of Harvard and the philologists of Berlin handled the concept of race, one might well reproach them as metaphysicians for choosing monism, cutting loose nature on the one hand and culture on the other to function all alone as an explanatory category. The history of philosophy, and perhaps of human wisdom, suggests that this is an unpromising choice. Du Bois, by contrast, deploys the binary opposition of nature and culture as a master ratio in a particularly fruitful and reflective way to investigate the problematic concept of race. And his philosophical effort is especially rich because he writes as a man of action as well as a thinker, and as a singular voice that sometimes distances itself from its discourse, and sometimes reclaims that discourse as its own.

In his novel *The Quest of the Silver Fleece*[2], W. E. B. Du Bois consciously but unobtrusively allows the distinction between nature and culture to over-arch and organize the narrative, which traces the romance of a young Black man named Blessed Alwyn and a young Black woman identified (almost always) only as Zora.[3] At the novel's beginning, Zora is strongly associated with nature, and in particular with a wild patch of ground that figures centrally in the story's geography, the swamp. Blessed Alwyn, on his way to the school that will educate him and send him out into the great world, hears music: "It was human music, but with a wildness and a weirdness that startled the boy as it fluttered and danced across the dull red waters of the swamp ... sweet music, birdlike, abandoned."[4] The boy comes across Zora dancing in a cabin whose door has just been thrown open: "He heard her voice as before, fluttering like a bird's in the full sweetness of her utter music. It was no tune nor melody, it was just formless, boundless music."[5] Du Bois's Blessed sees her as an "elf-girl." Thus Du Bois aligns the female under nature, the male by implication under culture.

When the two children meet the next day (Blessed is fifteen, Zora twelve), their conversation bears out the alignment. Blessed communicates that he is on his way to school, the school founded by the white New England school marm, Miss Smith, and Zora responds with scorn. She inhabits a world of nature whose idiom is dreams, not the language of books. Characterized once again as a bird, brown and gleaming dull golden, she insists: "There ain't nothing but dreams—that is, nothing much."[6] Poetry and passion are thus drawn over to the side of nature; Blessed Alwyn and Miss Sarah Smith, the wise old lady he is soon to meet, are left with prose and reason, at least for the moment.

Yet Zora is not content to remain embedded in nature; Blessed exerts a powerful and permanent influence on her that draws her beyond her origins. And Du Bois lets us know from the very first that Zora's nature, female and severed by hostility from culture, is not just idyllic, an Eden where human music is as unforced and unformed as birdsong, but cruel and demonic. For Zora is after all not a bird, but a human child. We learn quickly by implication and later explicitly that Zora's witchlike mother Elspeth, one of two characters identified in the novel as evil, has delivered her own daughter into prostitution at the age of twelve. When Blessed first saw Zora dancing, she was dancing for the white customers who had raped her. That group included Harry Cresswell, debauched scion of the local landed gentry and the novel's other evil principal. The novel's action turns on this crime, which compounds blackness with femaleness and nature in the person of Elspeth, powerful and immoral.

Does the novel then immediately compound masculinity and culture with whiteness? No; for the figure of Blessed Alwyn, introduced on the first page (and indeed the figure of Du Bois himself, the voice and hand who creates the book) is so strongly associated with culture that the latter alignment is never quite allowed to dominate the novel's structure. Yet that configuration is introduced in a secondary and highly ironized context, for the person who lays claim to the three terms of whiteness, masculinity and culture, as Elspeth collects and demonizes blackness, femaleness and nature, is Harry Cresswell. Harry Cresswell, landowner, senator, financier, almost ambassador to Paris (the symbolic center of culture, the next best thing to paradise), lays claim to culture with the thoughtless assurance of an aristocrat. Not that we ever see him reading a book; but he often and vehemently affirms his entitlement to culture by denying it to the "niggers" who so lately belonged as slaves to his father and grandfather. Given the Dickensian precision of moral reckoning in the novel, his animus is directed most often towards the two students, Blessed and Zora.

For Zora rapidly places herself under the tutelage of her bookish new friend, though Du Bois is careful to show that both children have something to learn from their interaction. Zora knows the swamp with the insight of a sympathetic naturalist, who feels herself at home with the birds and other creatures she calls "people," honoring their sociability: "She had taken his hand and led him through the swamp, showing him all the beauty of her swamp-world—great shadowy oaks and limpid pools, lone, naked trees and sweet flowers; the whispering and flitting of wild things, and the winging of furtive birds."[7] Indeed, it is the "wistful, visionary tenderness" with which she shows Blessed these things that leads him to press book-learning upon her."Even if white folks don't know everything they know different things from us, and we ought to know what they know."[8] Her curiosity, sharp intelligence and affection for Blessed lead to her to begin, in the midst of the swamp, "that primal battle with the Word." Soon thereafter, she starts to earn money by picking cotton so that she can attend Miss Smith's school, and more and more stays away from her mother's house.

The novel's compelling narrative line is the romance between the two young people, as it flowers, is blighted, and opens up again after a long winter of grief and renunciation. Blessed and Zora are the free particulars that force a realignment of the binary oppositions that govern their world. But their development is far from the simple installing of blackness under the sign of culture; such a move would literally and figuratively denature Zora, whose power, wisdom and art stem from her sympathy with the natural world, whose origins lie after all in the swamp.[9] And Blessed's eclipse occurs when he rejects Zora because he is in the grip of a bloodless, spiritless, passionless Puritan morality. Rather, their true development is perhaps best captured by the word 'cultivation', an integrating of nature and culture that produces the silver fleece as a plant, a crop, a work of art, and a wedding gown, and that allows Zora to reclaim it from thieves in a series of ironic reversals. Grasping the silver fleece as material and immediate beauty, as transcendent meaning, and as her *own,* Zora places her blackness and femaleness under the sign of both nature and culture, in a novel combination neither her mother nor her despoiler could ever have foreseen.

The silver fleece starts as a common project between Blessed and Zora. Blessed wants Zora not only to attend Miss Smith's school, but also to board there, to stay away from the swamp which he can only associate with her mother. He wants to claim his friend for the party of culture. But Zora, wiser than he in this regard, knows that the swamp is also the locus of dreams and freedom, a home that she must not forsake. When he proposes that they raise their own crop of cotton together, she responds, "And I knows just the place! . . . Down in the heart of the swamp—where dreams and devils lives."[10] The two young people work long and hard to clear the swampland, in a secret place of the swamp that Zora had identified from the very first as "the place of dreams."

But strangely, it is Elspeth who must provide the seed, and indeed who must sow it. Appearing under her most terrifying aspect, she tells them: "Yes, . . . I'se got the seed—I'se got it—wonder seed, sowed wid the three spells of Obi in the old land ten tousand moons ago. But you couldn't plant it, . . . it would kill you."[11] The potent, dangerous seeds are from Africa and thus stand under the sign of nature, femaleness and blackness; Elspeth sows them with her own hand: "The form of the old woman suddenly loomed black above them, hovering a moment formless and vast, then fading again away, and the *'swish-swish'* of the falling seed alone rose in the silence of the night."[12]

Zora must face and absorb this moment, as she must later assimilate the terrifying moment of her mother's death. In a sense, the seed is her mother's sole wedding present for her, the germ of her own final redemption and escape from the tragedy of her childhood. But she must transform it by cultivation, at first in the company of the young man she loves and then alone. She must risk her life for it and renounce it, before it is finally restored to her. In the chapter which Du Bois entitles "The Flowering of the Fleece," Zora is gently invited by Miss Smith to stay in a little room at the school. It is like a nun's cell, just the opposite of Elspeth's cabin: "White curtains adorned it, and white hangings draped the plain bureau and wash-stand, and the little bed. There was a sturdy table, and a small book-shelf holding a few books, all simple and clean."[13] The essential element, of course, is the book-shelf, a token located under whiteness and culture, and because of the European tradition of convents, under womanhood as well. Miss Smith is the other wise woman in the story; her wedding gift to Zora is the book-shelf, real and imagined, that Zora will always thereafter carry with her. Miss Smith is not capable of passion, but she is capable of love.

On the day when the Fleece is fully in flower, the two children who are just about to become adults burst into song: "Not the wild light song of dancing feet, but a low, sweet melody of her fathers' fathers, whereunto Alwyn's own deep voice fell fitly in minor cadence."[14] The song is African, or perhaps an African American sorrow song, transformed into praise. But soon thereafter, unseasonable rain threatens to drown the cotton crop hidden in the swamp. Bles discovers Zora unconscious by the field, almost killed by the superhuman labor of digging a drainage canal to save her precious Fleece. On the day that she finally recovers from her subsequent illness, she and Bles meet again by the field where the cotton is now fully ripe, and confess their love. Du Bois describes their reunion in terms at once happily carnal and thoroughly spiritualized. The two lovers have brought the swamp under the sign of culture and through their cultivation made it beautiful and productive; Bles has schooled Zora, and Zora has made Bles visionary and passionate.

But the old alignments stand ready to reassert themselves and bring tragedy on the two anomalous particulars who disrupt the dominant order and its instrumental schisms. Harry Cresswell often expresses his intolerance in terms that relegate Blacks to the realm of nature, a bestial and immoral nature. His intolerance has two sources, which stand for slavery and rape: his expected inheritance of the Cresswell estate and his frequenting of Elspeth's cabin. Close to the novel's beginning, he initiates his courtship of Mary Taylor, a teacher in Miss Smith's school, by impugning Zora: "All these Negroes are, as you know, of wretchedly low morals; but there are a few so depraved that it would be suicidal to take them into this school. . . . There is a girl, Zora, who has just entered, who—I must speak candidly—who ought not to be here; I thought it right to let you know."[15]

The irony of Cresswell's self-righteous revelation must strike the reader on two levels. He is, of course, the man who raped Zora when she was only twelve years old. He is also a landowner implacably opposed to Miss Smith's school and all it strives and hopes for: education makes people much less tractable. "Do you think there's the slightest chance of cornering cotton and buying the Black Belt if the niggers are unwilling to work under present conditions? Do you know the man that stands ready to gobble up every inch of cotton land in this country at a price no trust can hope to rival? . . . The Black Man, whose woolly head is filled with ideas of rising."[16] Thus Harry Cresswell explains to Mary Taylor's brother why his sister's school must be stopped.

The disastrous disclosure of Zora's past comes from Cresswell's lips. Having just agreed that the Blacks of the surrounding countryside live "like animals" wherever they please, perhaps in the swamp, and breed without marriage, Cresswell and an entourage of rich Northerners comes across Zora and Blessed kissing by the roadside, just a few pages and by implication a few days after they have fallen in love. Cresswell tells them to stop; questioned by one of his companions he insists: "The girl is—notorious," while still within hearing of Blessed Alwyn. Alwyn insists on the truth behind this allegation, and learning it, leaves Zora and the school for good. Nature serves as his tragic chorus: "'It's a damned lie!' He shouted to the trees. 'Is it?—Is it?' chirped the birds. 'It's a cruel falsehood!' he moaned. 'Is it?—Is it?' whispered the devils within."[17] As he abandons Zora, he judges her by an appeal to biology; once deflowered, she can never be "pure" again.

Zora falls into a despair from which she emerges just at the moment when the Fleece is stolen from her. She harvests the cotton by herself, deep in the heart of the swamp, and then goes to the Cresswells, legal owners of the swampland, to settle with them. Harry carries out the reckoning in a way that typifies a system of economic peonage that annually bankrupts the tenant farmer. At the same time he threatens her once again with rape. Grabbing a rusty poker, Zora calls up the strength of her mother's side: "Somewhere way down in the depths of her nature the primal tiger awoke and snarled."[18] Truly afraid, Cresswell contents himself with taking the Fleece and paying nothing for it. "Your rent and rations with the five years' back debt . . . will be one hundred dollars. That leaves you twenty-five in our debt. Here's your receipt."[19] Having lost the most precious object and symbol in her possession, Zora realizes that she still maintains self-possession, all the more since she was able to defend herself against Cresswell's physical assault. Her swamp-self, by displaying its power and ferocity in self-defense, has acted in accord with the abstract precepts of Miss Smith; nature and culture have risen up together within her, and triumphed. "And yet, they should not kill her; they should not enslave her. A desperate resolve to find some way up toward the light, if not to it, formed itself within her."[20]

Zora then watches over her baled Fleece as it lies in the warehouse; grieves for it when it is taken away; reclaims it when it is returned to Harry Cresswell's sister as woven cloth for her wedding dress; embroiders it for that other woman and then snatches it up from fate, in the moment when the latter casts it aside for a Paris gown. For Zora it represents "not the great Happiness—that was gone forever—but illumination, atonement, and something of the power and the glory."[21] She takes it with her like a talisman to New York, where she goes as a lady's maid to the rich Mrs. Vanderpool, who opens doors for her and then betrays her. The over-civilized woman brings Zora to the cultural Mecca of the United States, and wishes to take her to Paris; she gives her time and place to read.

Zora's education, partly encountered through the tutelage of Miss Smith and Mrs. Vanderpool, partly driven by her own brilliance and curiosity, is Du Bois's ideal curriculum, and so worth quoting in detail. The dreamland of books is the Mediterranean of her Odyssey, the Vision Splendid of her pilgrimage, the ever-receding, ever-seductive grail-place of her quest. It is the Great World through which she must travel in order to come home, worldly and reconciled, to Miss Smith and the ghost of Elspeth, to the old school and the swamp. Where did she go?

> She gossiped with old Herodotus across the earth to the black and blameless Ethiopians; she saw the sculptured glories of Phidias marbled amid the splendor of the swamp; she listened to Demosthenes and walked the Appian Way with Cornelia—while all New York streamed beneath her window. She saw the drunken Goths reel upon Rome and heard the careless Negroes yodle as they galloped to Toomsville. Paris, she knew,—wonderful, haunting Paris: the Paris of Clovis, and St. Louis; of Louis the Great, and Napoleon III; of Balzac, and her own Dumas. She tasted the mud and comfort of thick old London, and the while wept with Jeremiah and sang with Deborah, Semiramis, and Atala. Mary of Scotland and Joan of Arc held her dark hands in theirs, and Kings lifted up their scepters. She walked on worlds, and worlds of worlds, and heard there in her little room the tread of armies, the paeans of victory, the breaking of hearts, and the music of the spheres.[22]

So, wed with Truth, she dwells above the Veil. This is just the language of that famous passage from *The Souls of Black Folk*:

I sit with Shakespeare and he winces not. Across the color line I move arm in arm
with Balzac and Dumas, where smiling men and welcoming women glide in gilded
halls. From out the caves of evening that swing between the strong-limbed earth
and the tracery of stars, I summon Aristotle and Aurelius and what soul I will, and
they come all graciously with no scorn or condescension."[23]

(This resonance suggests to me that the fiercest identification of narrator and
character in the novel is between Du Bois and Zora.)

Betrayed by Mrs. Vanderpool, as all pilgrims, wanderers and seekers must
finally be betrayed and enriched by the strangers they encounter far from
home, Zora returns to help Miss Smith run the school, to save other children
from ignorance, poverty, servitude, and vice. There at last she encounters
Blessed Alwyn again, who has been betrayed by the allegories of love and
power he encountered in his own version of the great world, Washington,
D.C., and so has come home for the serious business of living. Bles begins to
understand the transformation of his old friend when he sees the library she
has amassed in her living quarters: Plato's *Republic*, Gorky's "Comrades," a
Cyclopaedia of Agriculture, Balzac's novels, Spencer's "First Principles,"
Tennyson's poems.[24] Zora calls it her "university."

Their love, of course, reasserts itself. Zora has learned the virtues of renunciation and reflection; Blessed has overcome the curse of his puritan self-right-
eousness. New dangers arise at every turn, but the swamp has been
transformed, yet still remains "living, vibrant, tremulous," and the Silver
Fleece will serve as Zora's dowry and wedding dress. Zora in her history, her
reading, and her pilgrimage brings nature and culture, black and white into
stable relationship; Zora and Blessed Alwyn in their marriage share the integration of nature and culture equally between man and woman. At the end of
the novel, we see Du Bois's vision of the future when he was in the middle of
life's way and at the height of his powers.

I would now like to read this vision of realignment and integration back
into the great collection of essays published ten years earlier by Du Bois, *The
Souls of Black Folk*. For I believe it will shed light on his treatment of double
consciousness there, and the definition of race which he tries to articulate. *The
Souls of Black Folk* does not stand to *The Quest of the Silver Fleece* simply as
argument to narrative, or the discursive to the poetic. Indeed, it takes its
important place in the history of philosophical rhetoric because of the dense
interplay of genres and voices that structure it. To move his audience to understanding and action, Du Bois employs memoir, history, polemic, encomium,
elegy, treatise and narrative, and speaks as a social scientist, philosopher of
history, poet, man of action, journalist, educator, father, and son. His rhetorical strategies show how conscious he was of addressing a particular historical

audience (probably northern and educated, black and white) as well as a more universalized, future audience, and of speaking both in his own historical person and in a more universal mode, in a passionate reason that must take the long view in order to hope.

Thus, it is possible both to find narrative analogues of Zora and Blessed Alwyn in the stories, fictional and autobiographical, that Du Bois tells in *The Souls of Black Folk*; and to take Zora and Blessed as instances of the abstract arguments marshalled in the earlier and after all much more discursive work. The obvious analogue to Zora is the figure of Josie in the chapter entitled "Of the Meaning of Progress." While Du Bois was beginning his college education at Fisk in Nashville, he spent his summers teaching school in the surrounding countryside. Josie (like Zora never given a surname) was his first student; he comes across her as he is walking by, looking for employment. "Josie... told me anxiously that they wanted a school over the hill; that but once since the war had a teacher been there; that she herself longed to learn,—and thus she ran on, talking fast and loud, with much earnestness and energy."[25] Du Bois describes her in admiring terms: "She had about her a certain fineness, the shadow of an unconscious moral heroism that would willingly give all of life to make life broader, deeper, and fuller for her and hers."[26] That was just the New England ideal of striving and self-sacrifice that Du Bois held up for himself; he could see what this young woman might become.

But the ending of this story is not happy. Ten years later Du Bois returned to the region to see what had become of his students, only to discover that Josie had died of overwork and a broken heart. The longing to know had hovered like a star above this child-woman, Du Bois wrote, but she had not been allowed to follow her star. The chapter ends with this question: "How shall man measure Progress there where the dark-faced Josie lies?"[27] Josie's death indicts the system that denied her education; not by accident does the next chapter describe the student life at Atlanta University: "In a half-dozen class-rooms they gather then,—here to follow the love-song of Dido, here to listen to the tale of Troy divine; there to wander among the stars, there to wander among men and nations."[28] Surely the creation of Zora was Du Bois's way of mourning for and reviving Josie's star.

Likewise the figure of John Jones in the chapter, "Of the Coming of John" runs parallel to that of Blessed Alwyn, except that, like Josie, he represents another failure of education. In this case, he is a university student (at a fictional institution described as much like Du Bois's Atlanta University) whose classical education and prolonged excursion into the Great World leave him out of joint with the heartless apartheid he encounters on his return home to a country town in southeastern Georgia. He can no longer speak in the idiom of his own people, and the white world excludes him with these words:

"In this country the Negro must remain subordinate. . . . But when they want to reverse nature, and rule white men, and marry white women, and sit in my parlor, then, by God! we'll hold them under if we have to lynch every Nigger in the land."[29] At the story's end, having murdered a white man to save his sister from rape, John sits listening for the lynching mob and then chooses his own free death, walking over a cliff into the sea.

John is the archetype of a young man whom the "double consciousness" imposed by racist America on its Black population threatens to tear apart. In the familiar passage from the first chapter of *The Souls of Black Folk*, "Of Our Spiritual Strivings," where Du Bois introduces the notion of double consciousness, he observes, "The Negro is a sort of seventh son, born with a veil, and gifted with second sight in this American world,—a world which yields him no true self-consciousness, but only lets him see himself through the revelation of the other world." And the vision that hostile white spectators interpose as a ghostly *tertium quid* between the Black self and itself is a pitiable, contemptible figure, a creature less than human. The internal task for the African-American is then to examine and banish the third term that prevents the reconciliation of the soul with itself. The cure for this invidious double-consciousness, externally imposed, is not a unitary consciousness. Rather, it must be a double-consciousness that can relate itself to itself, that is all the richer for its gift of second-sight, that is all the more human for its duality.

The dualities that must be integrated stand first of all under the binary opposition of nature and culture. For all human beings are caught and defined at the boundary, shifting but permanent, between nature and culture: our culture elaborates the necessities of our nature, not the least of which is death; our nature requires us to be cultural, that is, linguistic, sociable creatures. One might say that the oldest human artifact is the corpse decorated for funerary rites, the three-million-year-old object that exhibits most clearly how our social and biological identities are linked and yet not isomorphic.[30] We have seen that the commonplace, divisive alignments criticized by Du Bois set Africa and womanhood, and with them poverty and ignorance, under nature; and America and manhood, and with them wealth and learning, under culture. Uncritical acceptance of those alignments by the people, real and fictional, about whom he writes can only lead to disintegration, for it sunders nature and culture without hope of mediation.

The suffering of hopeless division has a double aspect in Du Bois's essay. First, it is a duality of origins: "One ever feels his twoness,—an American, a Negro; two souls, two thoughts, two unreconciled strivings; two warring ideals in one dark body."[31] And second, it is "the contradiction of double aims," aims that arise from dual membership in Du Bois's "talented tenth" and the broader social group of African-Americans.

The would-be black *savant* was confronted by the paradox that the knowledge his people needed was a twice-told tale to his white neighbors, while the knowledge that would teach the white world was Greek to his own flesh and blood. The innate love of harmony and beauty that set the ruder souls of his people a-dancing and a-singing raised but confusion and doubt in the soul of the black artist; for the beauty revealed to him was the soul-beauty of a race which his larger audience despised, and he could not articulate the message of another people."[32]

The *tertium quid* is a figure for this disjunction; so, in a different sense, are Elspeth and Harry Cresswell.

But in the person of Zora, Du Bois invents a figure that embodies a new mediation between the master opposition of nature and culture, and a new alignment of the subordinate binary oppositions governed by it (which in turn rebounds upon its meaning). For Zora never denies her origins in the swamp, in her mother and the powerful magic of Africa, in the music of her father's fathers, in dream. She cultivates the African seeds, her mother's bride-price, into a crop that takes its place in the American economy and the European tradition under the appelation of Silver Fleece; and when it is returned to her as cloth (woven by white workers in northern mills) she converts it into a work of art by her embroidery, and into the emblem of her moral development and her ultimate marriage to a Black man. Zora also never backs away from her education: she takes her books with her everywhere, to the heart of white urban culture and back to the swamp. Once she has learned to read, nothing will stop her intellectual curiosity, or stop her from sharing it with the children, white and black, following in her footsteps.

In his numerous autobiographical writings, some of which punctuate and move *The Souls of Black Folk*, Du Bois describes his own acts of self-integration and indeed realizes some of them in the very act of writing. The tragic crux of the story of John Jones in "Of the Coming of John" is John's expulsion from a theatre where he has been watching Wagner's *Lohengrin*. Listening to the swan's song, he sits peacefully dreaming: "The infinite beauty of the wail lingered and swept through every muscle of his frame and put it all a-tune."[33] Great art, though it belongs to western Europe and was written by a vain anti-Semite, still has the power of harmonization. John's harmony is disrupted when he is asked to leave by an usher, at the instigation of his white childhood companion, another John, the John who will try to rape his sister and whom Du Bois's bitter irony has placed next to him in the theatre. John Jones is torn apart, suddenly seeing himself "through the revelation of the other world," and excluded from the art that gave him peace, albeit formal and momentary. But *The Souls of Black Folk* does not end here.

The chapter that follows John's tragic story is the final one of the book, entitled "The Sorrow Songs." There Du Bois shows the reader definitively, undeniably, that the folk music created by African-American slaves deserves a place beside Wagner and Schubert, beside Tennyson and King James's Solomon. Like the ballads recorded by Childe, the sorrow songs contain folk poetry of the first order, rooted in suffering and marked by the sublimity Longinus struggled to define. "I walk through the church-yard / To lay this body down; / I know moon-rise, I know star-rise; / I walk in the moonlight, I walk in the starlight; / I'll lie in the grave and stretch out my arms, / I'll go to judgment in the evening of the day, / And my soul and thy soul shall meet that day, / when I lay my body down."[34] By juxtaposing these two chapters, by placing his beloved Wagner in the company of his beloved sorrow songs, Du Bois enacts a harmonization of self denied to his younger and unluckier fictional counterpart.

This kind of self-integration, I believe, is the act that Du Bois hopes will produce the African American race. That race is not a fiction, and it could not be created negatively by white apartheid; but it is also not given by biology or history. It must be created to be affirmed. Zora's adult self, the marriage of Zora and Blessed Alwyn, the school they inherit and develop, and the new kind of community that grows up around that school, are created to banish the ghostly *tertium quid* and bring about a positive and novel double consciousness that flourished as well in the life and thought of W. E. B. Du Bois.

This essay is dedicated to the memory of my mother Frances Grosholz, and of my friend Marion Keys.

NOTES

1.   Much of the exposition in the preceding four paragraphs was inspired by thinking about James Redfield's reflections in his essay "Sex in Hesiod," forthcoming.

2.   W. E. B. Du Bois, *The Quest of the Silver Fleece*, reprinted in Northeastern Library of Black Literature, with a foreword by Arnold Rampersad. (Boston: Northeastern University Press, 1989). Originally published in 1911.

3.   Arlene A. Elder also discerns a dual symbolic structure in the novel; she uses two *places* as topoi in her analysis, "Swamp versus Plantation: Symbolic Structure in W. E. B. Du Bois' *The Quest of the Silver Fleece*," *Phylon* 34 (1973): 358–67, which reveals very clearly the moral and political issues of the book, as well as the centrality of the figure of Zora. Arnold Rampersad devotes the sixth chapter of his *The Art and Imagination of W. E. B. Du Bois* (New York: Schocken Books, 1990) to the novel, identifying the swamp and cotton as the two symbols that represent the book's dual structure. His account addresses Du Bois's economic theories and cultural ideals in a deep and interesting way. In general, he understands Du Bois as taking a more negative view of the swamp and what it symbolizes than I do, or indeed than Arlene Elder does.

4.   Du Bois, *Quest*, 14.

5. Du Bois, *Quest*, 15.

6. Du Bois, *Quest*, 19.

7. Du Bois, *Quest*, 45.

8. Du Bois, *Quest*, 46.

9. Arlene Elder observes, "There is, however, a beautiful, joyous, vibrant aspect to the swamp which is reflected in the souls of some of the black and white characters. Zora, 'black, and lithe, and tall, and willowy,' with her music, her poetry, and her dreams is Du Bois's most striking representative of good Swamp qualities." Elder, "Swamp versus Plantation," 360.

10. Du Bois, *Quest*, 52.

11. Du Bois, *Quest*, 75.

12. Du Bois, *Quest*, 100.

13. Du Bois, *Quest*, 120.

14. Du Bois, *Quest*, 128.

15. Du Bois, *Quest*, 85–86.

16. Du Bois, *Quest*, 159.

17. Du Bois, *Quest*, 168.

18. Du Bois, *Quest*, 187.

19. Du Bois, *Quest*, 188.

20. Du Bois, *Quest*, 188–9.

21. Du Bois, *Quest*, 215.

22. Du Bois, *Quest*, 251–52.

23. W. E. B. Du Bois, *The Souls of Black Folk* (1903; reprint, New York: Viking Penguin, 1989), 90.

24. Du Bois, *Quest*, 399.

25. Du Bois, *Souls*, 52.

26. Du Bois, *Souls*, 53.

27. Du Bois, *Souls*, 62.

28. Du Bois, *Souls*, 68.

29. Du Bois, *Souls*, 198.

30. This thought was also suggested by James Redfield's "Sex in Hesiod."

31. Du Bois, *Souls*, 5.

32. Du Bois, *Souls*, 6.

33. Du Bois, *Souls*, 192–93.

34. Du Bois, *Souls*, 204.

The

Question

of Pan-Africanism

The Pan-Africanism of | 9
W. E. B. Du Bois

Manning Marable

William Edward Burghardt Du Bois is generally accorded by black scholars and political leaders alike the title "Father of Pan-Africanism." Trinidadian historian and Marxist activist C.L.R. James writes that "more than any other citizen of Western civilization (or of Africa itself) [Du Bois] struggled over many years and succeeded in making the world aware that Africa and Africans had to be freed from the thralldom which Western civilization had imposed on them." Du Bois was "from start to finish . . . the moving spirit and active organizer" of five Pan-African congresses—in 1919, 1921, 1923, 1927, and 1945.[1] Kwame Nkrumah, leader of the Gold Coast independence movement in the late 1940s and 1950s, and subsequently Prime Minister of Ghana, referred to Du Bois as "a treasured part of Africa's history," and recounted his unique contributions to the evolution of Pan-Africanism in several works.[2]

Even social scientists who are openly hostile to Du Bois recognize, in a distorted manner, the rich Pan-Africanist legacy of the black scholar. Harold R. Isaacs criticized Du Bois as never having been "a successful leader or organizer or even a popular public figure." His Pan-Africanism was simply a type of "romantic racism" which "got nowhere." Nevertheless, Isaacs acknowledged grudgingly that modern black leaders recognize Du Bois as the "father of Pan-Africanism," and that his militant words on Africa now "ring in the air all around us."[3]

Du Bois's biographer, Francis S. Broderick, declared that none of his

subject's books "except *The Philadelphia Negro,* is first-class." Du Bois's voluminous studies on African culture, history, and politics, which include *The
Negro* and *The World and Africa,* "all possess some information, but nothing
which indicates the mind or hand of an original scholar." The Pan-African
congresses of the 1920s, Broderick adds, accomplished, if anything, less than
the failed Niagara Movement of 1905–1909. Yet even Broderick, blinded by
racism, must stand in awe of Du Bois's prophecy of African and Asian nationalism which swept the Third World in the 1950s and afterwards. "After the
Asian-African conference at Bandung in 1955," Broderick admits, "who had
the last laugh, Du Bois or his critics? Du Bois was a generation ahead of his
time. The leaders of at least two [African nations] have publicly made explicit
acknowledgment of their debt to Du Bois's inspiration."[4]

This essay is not a comprehensive analysis of Du Bois's Pan-Africanism, but
rather an examination of his role in the evolution of the Pan-Africanist political movement from 1900 to 1945. Special emphasis is given to the relationship between Du Bois's sponsorship and the development of political
programs at the Pan-African congresses during these years, and his overall
political life and activities within the United States.

Perhaps the clearest point of departure in the study of Du Bois's Pan-
Africanist thought is provided by his literary executor, Marxist historian
Herbert Aptheker. In a 1968 essay, Aptheker suggests two basic factors which
oriented Du Bois's intellectual endeavors. Aptheker rejects the nearly universal
thesis that Du Bois's central conception of black liberation varied from decade
to decade. Indeed, his philosophical orientation or method of analysis reveals
a startling consistency. "Du Bois's extraordinary career manifests a remarkable continuity," Aptheker states. First, "all his life Du Bois was a radical
democrat; this was true even with his 'Talented Tenth' concept which held that
mass advance depended upon leadership and service from a trained minority."
Certainly the black scholar's "political affiliations or affinities varied as times
changed, as programs altered." At various historical moments Du Bois was a
reform Republican, a Democrat, a Socialist, a Communist, and a supporter of
the Progressive Party of Henry Wallace. "These were, however, political
choices and not defining marks of philosophical approaches." At the root of
his politics was a commitment to a democracy defined by the realization of
racial equality and social justice for all social groups and classes within the
society.

Second, as Aptheker notes:

> [Du Bois's] penetrating observation, first offered in 1900 and twice repeated in a
> significant article published the next year—"The problem of the twentieth century
> is the problem of the color line"—was fundamental to his vision of the unity of all

African peoples (to grow, as Du Bois advanced in years, to the idea that this itself was preliminary, to the unity of all the darker peoples of the earth and *that* was part of the process of the worldwide unification of all who labor) and was, indeed, first enunciated as the Call of the original Pan-African Conference. This insight forms the inspiration for and thesis of his *The Negro* (London: Home Library, 1915), *Black Folk, Then and Now* (New York: Holt, 1939), *Color and Democracy: Colonies and Peace* (New York: Harcourt, Brace, 1945), [and] *The World and Africa* (New York: Viking, 1947).[5]

Throughout his adult life, Du Bois never identified racism as a purely American phenomenon. He understood that the resolution of the color line could occur only within the international political context, and that racism was tied directly to economic exploitation and the domination of the white West over peoples of color across the globe. Pan-Africanism then was merely the concrete political expression of Du Bois's intellectual commitment to eradicate racism, colonialism and all structures of exploitation.

DU BOIS AND THE PAN-AFRICAN VISION

What shaped Du Bois' evolving philosophy of Pan-Africanism? In *Dusk of Dawn*, he repeats Countee Cullen's memorable lines:

> What is Africa to me:
> Copper sun or scarlet sea,
> Jungle star or jungle track
> Strong bronzed men, or regal black
> Women from whose loins I sprang
> When the birds of Eden sang?
> One three centuries removed
> From the scenes his fathers loved,
> Spicy grove, cinnamon tree,
> What is Africa to me?[6]

"What is Africa to me?" Du Bois pondered. "Neither my father nor my father's father ever saw Africa or knew its meaning or cared overmuch for it. My mother's folk were closer and yet their direct connection, in culture and race, became tenuous; still, my tie to Africa is strong."[7] As a child, Du Bois heard an African melody that his great-grandmother Violet Du Bois had brought from the continent, which over generations had become a "tradition in his family."[8] There were no books on Africa in Great Barrington's modest library. Yet even as a child, he had become annoyed with the crude racial stereotypes depicted in his classroom textbooks. In his 1959 interview with

Isaacs, Du Bois reflected that he encountered pictures of the races of man in his earliest texts, "a white man, a Chinese mandarin, and a savage Negro. That was what the class got, and it made me especially sensitive. I did not recognize those pictures in the book as being my people."[9]

It was his undergraduate experience at Fisk University which first awakened Du Bois's lifelong identification with African culture. Fisk had the beginnings of an African museum, and young Will examined the small selection of African carvings and artifacts with fascination. Continuing his undergraduate studies at Harvard University, he encountered the pseudo-science of racial dogma, presented as if it were a consequence of the new theory of evolution. And no courses on African, Chinese, or Indian history were offered at Harvard. Returning from a period of study at the University of Berlin, Du Bois applied to the doctoral program in social science at Harvard in the spring of 1890. His topic was "the social and economic rise of the Negro people."[10]

For two years, Du Bois was preoccupied with thousands of hours of research in the *Congressional Record,* colonial and state documents, and secondary literature pertaining to the African slave trade. Simultaneously, he participated in the larger cultural and social life of Boston's black community, taking part in church plays and drafting a comprehensive program to improve and expand local black libraries, lectures, literary societies, and Chautauqua circles.[11] The final product of his labor was his thesis, *The Suppression of the African Slave-Trade to the United States of America, 1638–1870,* which was the initial volume published in the *Harvard Historical Studies* series in 1896. The importance of this pioneering study, published at a period of rising racial violence, political disfranchisement, and historiographical revision of the role of the Negro in American democracy, cannot be overemphasized. It provided the first serious examination of the impact of the Haitian revolution upon the domestic slave political economy. The chapter on the South's frenzied political attempts to rescind the 1808 ban on the trans-Atlantic slave trade, "The Final Crisis," was not equaled in historical research for decades.[12] The white academic establishment offered grudging praise: one review in the *American Historical Review* applauded the work as a "valuable review of an important subject," but added that Du Bois occasionally used phrases which "characterize the advocate rather than the historian."[13] For Du Bois, of course, that was the entire point: scholarship served to advance racial interests. Any anti-racist research which emphasized the humanity of African people and denounced the profit motive of white slaveholders contributed to the immediate struggle of destroying the color line and expanding democracy to include the Negro.

As Du Bois pursued an academic career, teaching briefly at Wilberforce University and the University of Pennsylvania before settling at Atlanta University from 1897 to 1910 as a professor of economics and history, other black intellectuals became more preoccupied with the cultural and political image of Africa. One of the most ambitious and visionary of this new generation was a young Trinidadian lawyer, Henry Sylvester Williams. Born in 1869, Williams traveled to the United States in 1891, and two years later went to Canada to attend law school. In 1896, Williams moved to London, and within a year he had organized a Pan-African Association. Gradually he established the basis for a political formation which would embrace blacks in the West Indies, the United States and Africa. Its unambiguous goals were "to secure to Africans throughout the world true civil and political rights" and "to ameliorate the conditions of our brothers on the continent of Africa, America and other parts of the world."[14] In this effort, assistance was provided by a curious benefactor, the conservative Afro-American educator Booker T. Washington. In one of history's little ironies, Washington in 1899 promoted the projected Pan-African conference as a "most effective and far-reaching" activity during a London visit. The president of Tuskegee Institute "beg[ged] and advise[d] as many of our people as can possibly do so" to take an active role in Williams's conference.[15]

Du Bois and approximately thirty other West Indian and Afro-American intellectuals attended the Pan-African Association's conference in July 1900. The meeting attracted minor attention in the press, and the delegates were welcomed by the Lord Bishop of London. Queen Victoria even forwarded a note through her minister Joseph Chamberlain, promising not to "overlook the interests of the natives." The conference drafted "An Address to the Nations of the World" which urged the democratic treatment of black people in majority white nations and the ultimate emancipation of Africa itself. Du Bois penned the most memorable statement of the assembly: "The problem of the Twentieth Century is the problem of the color line." The net results of this gathering, in the short run, were unfortunately minimal. In his *The World and Africa* (1947), Du Bois noted that "this meeting had no deep roots in Africa itself, and the movement and the idea died for a generation."[16] Williams soon returned to the Caribbean to establish branches of his Pan-African Association. In Jamaica he won the support of radical journalist Joseph Robert Love, while visiting the island in March, 1901.[17] But failing to build a viable organization, Williams returned to Trinidad in 1908, and died there in 1911.

The failure of this early attempt to forge an international forum for Pan-African opinion did not diminish Du Bois's interest in Africa. Throughout the first two decades of the twentieth century, he was one of the few American scholars who encouraged others to take an active interest in the cultural, economic, and political history of African people. In 1903, Du Bois wrote a review of Joseph A. Tillinghast's *The Negro in Africa and America* in the

Political Science Quarterly. The review is noteworthy in that Du Bois emphasized the centrality of African culture in the evolution of black American life
and history.[18] Several years later, writing for *The Nation*, Du Bois reviewed
seven books on African history, including the notable work of E. D. Morel,
The Black Man's Burden. Du Bois argued here that the recent history of Africa
was essentially that of European exploitation, characterized most clearly by
the atrocities committed by King Leopold of Belgium in the Congo Free
State.[19]

As editor of the *Crisis*, journal of the newly-founded NAACP, from 1910
until his resignation in 1934, Du Bois constantly provided his readers with
information on Africa and peoples of African descent outside the United
States. From 1903 through 1919, Du Bois's journalistic writings on Africa fall
into three distinct categories. First, Du Bois tried to popularize the idea of a
Pan-Africanist perspective, the then-utopian notion that the political demand
of "Africa for the Africans" inevitably would become a necessity.[20] Second, he
attempted to distinguish his version of Pan-Africanism from the nineteenth-
century African emigrationist views of black entrepreneur Paul Cuffe and
A. M. E. Bishop Henry M. Turner. As Harold R. Isaacs correctly notes,
Du Bois never

> chose the ultimate option of urging Negroes to migrate en masse to Africa. Neither
> in his greatest anger nor in his deepest despair was he driven to the notion that
> there was an answer for Negroes in recrossing the ocean to resettle in ... the
> homeland of their ancestors. Du Bois had the imagination and intelligence to see,
> long before anyone else, that the meaningful slogan for beleaguered American
> Negroes as far as Africa was concerned was not *Back to Africa*, but *Africa for the
> Africans.*[21]

In February, 1914, and again in January, 1916, Du Bois's editorials in the
Crisis attacked various plans by blacks to organize back-to-Africa efforts.
Criticizing the emigrationist movement led by Chief Alfred Sam, Du Bois
urged blacks not to become involved in speculative schemes destined for failure. To Oklahoma supporters of Chief Sam, Du Bois declared that there was
no need to travel across the Atlantic to combat racism: "Fight out the battle in
Oklahoma." He cautioned that there was "no steamship in New York building for the African trade and owned by Negroes."[22] Finally, Du Bois
attempted to advance a general thesis which linked the continued political
and economic exploitation of Africa with the expansion of European imperialism and war. Consistently, he used the *Crisis* to denounce both British and
German colonial policies in Africa.[23] More importantly, Du Bois drafted an
important essay in 1915, "The African Roots of the War," which in some

respects parallels the argument V. I. Lenin makes in his 1916 thesis, *Imperialism*. Both argued that the scramble to control raw materials, labor, and territories in Africa and Asia were the root causes of the world war. Du Bois also predicted that the conflict would bring forward new nationalist leaders in India, China, and Africa, and that black Americans would play a more central role in the "awakening" of Africa after the conflict in Europe ended.[24]

During World War I, Du Bois recognized that there was an opportunity to revive his Pan-African program in a more concrete form. In 1917, Du Bois advocated the creation of "a new African state formed from German possessions and from the Belgian Congo; the following year he wanted to include, if possible, Uganda, French Equatorial Africa, Angola, and Mozambique." As the conflict concluded, Du Bois received the NAACP's endorsement for the program of semi-autonomous governance for Africans living in former German colonies, and for the acceleration of educational, social and economic development on the continent generally.[25] Writing to President Woodrow Wilson on November 27, 1918, Du Bois proposed that the American government support his plans. J. P. Tumulty, the President's secretary, shared the memo with Wilson, but replied that it would be impossible for him to meet with Du Bois.[26] With the NAACP's approval, Du Bois immediately prepared to travel to Europe, hoping both to investigate "the treatment of Negro soldiers," and represent the interests of "the Negroes of the world . . . before the [Versailles] Peace Congress."[27] Securing passage abroad was a problem. But Du Bois learned that Wilson was sending Tuskegee Institute president Robert Russa Moton to France. Du Bois noted that Moton's duty was to speak to the returning Negro soldiers, pacify them, and forestall any attempt at agitation or open expression of resentment on their return to the United States. As Du Bois remarked much later, "Under those circumstances my request also to go could hardly be denied."[28]

Even before he arrived in Paris, Du Bois wrote back to the United States explaining his purposes to both white and black followers. He reiterated that his proposal for a new Pan-African conference was not a call for racial separatism. African emigration for the masses of American blacks was "absurd." However, Du Bois emphasized, "the African movement means to us what the Zionist movement must mean to the Jews, the centralization of race effort and the recognition of a racial fount."[29] Visiting members of the Peace Congress, Du Bois lobbied for his ambitious program without success. Colonel House, Wilson's chief aide, listened patiently to Du Bois but did not promise anything. Leaving nothing to chance, on January 1, 1919, Major F. P. Schoonmaker of the U.S. Army Ninety-second Division ordered intelligence officers to monitor "all of [Du Bois's] moves and actions while at station of

any unit."[30] Secretly watched by his own government, Du Bois spent six fruit-
less weeks in and around Paris, frustrated by his inability to obtain even
French permission to schedule his Pan-Africanist congress. The *Chicago
Tribune* correspondent, observing Du Bois's plight, cabled home:

> [Du Bois's] memorandum to President Wilson . . . is quite Utopian, and has less
> than a Chinaman's chance of getting anywhere in the Peace Conference, but it is
> nevertheless interesting. As self-determination is one of the words to conjure with
> in Paris nowadays, the Negro leaders are seeking to have it applied, if possible, in
> a measure to their race in Africa.[31]

As Du Bois later wrote, "My plan to have Africa in some way voice its
complaints to the world [was] . . . without political backing and indeed without widespread backing of any kind. Had it not been for one circumstance, it
would have utterly failed; and that circumstance was that black Africa had the
right to send from Senegal a member to the French Parliament."[32] This
deputy, Blaise Diagne, was "the most influential colonial politician in France
at the time," according to Pan-Africanist scholar, George Padmore, and "a
close friend" of then Prime Minister Georges Clemenceau.[33] Diagne had been
born on Gorée island, Senegal, in 1872. Despite his origins in poverty, he rose
through education to acquire a position as French colonial customs officer. In
1909 he confirmed his status within local white society by his marriage to a
Frenchwoman. Five years later, over the strenuous opposition of both the
coloured *métis* and local white entrepreneurs, the black man won election to
the Parisian Chamber of Deputies.

Despite his radical rhetoric, Diagne was always "a Frenchman before being
a Pan-African, and insisted upon praising French colonial rule, while attacking
the other European powers' operations in Africa."[34] When the French faced
"military disaster" in early 1911, Clemenceau named Diagne Commissaire-
Général for French West Africa, and he was charged "with the responsibility
of recruiting African troops for the Western front to help stem the German
offensive." Within twelve months, under Diagne's direction, 680,000 soldiers
and 238,000 laborers from French West Africa were in France.[35] Clemenceau
was "overjoyed," and offered Diagne the French Legion of Honor. Diagne
modestly refused, pleading that "he had only done his duty and that was
reward enough." Many African militants, suffering under the brutal heel of
French imperialism, denounced Diagne as "a traitor for having brought the
Africans to fight for France" and termed him "a tool of the rich white colonial
interests."[36]

However, when Du Bois approached Diagne for help in scheduling the Pan-
Africanist session, he quickly consented. Clemenceau could easily ignore the

unknown Afro-American petitioner; but when Diagne personally requested the Pan-African Congress, the French Prime Minister replied, "Don't advertise it, but go ahead."[37] Arrangements were made to reserve suites at the Grand Hotel in Paris. Madame Calmann-Lévy, the widow of an influential French publisher, "became enthusiastic over the idea of [Du Bois's] congress and brought together in her salon groups of interested persons" from the French and Belgian governments.[38] Frantically, American officials objected to the Pan-African Congress; one State Department official told the press that "no such conference would be held" and that, should the session take place, "no passports would be issued for American delegates desiring to attend the meeting."[39]

Despite belated American opposition, fifty-seven delegates from fifteen countries met on February 19, 1919 for the Pan-African Congress. Among them were twenty-one West Indians, sixteen delegates from the United States, and twelve from nine different African nations. The *New York Evening Globe* reported on February 22, 1919:

> [The Pan-African Congress is] the first assembly of its kind in history, and has for its object the drafting of an appeal to the Peace Conference to give the Negro race of Africa a chance to develop unhindered by other races. Seated at long green tables in the council room today, were Negroes in the trim uniform of American Army officers, other American colored men in frock coats or business suits, polished French Negroes who hold public office, Senegalese who sit in the French Chamber of Deputies . . .[40]

From the beginning of the assembly, Diagne, who was chosen as the President of the Congress, and Du Bois, its Secretary, were at odds. Diagne's chief concern was that French territorial interests in Africa should be preserved and expanded; the anticolonial polemics of Pan-Africanism should be levied against all other Europeans, but not the French.[41] Du Bois wrote the principal report of the Congress, which requested that the European and American powers turn over the former German colonies of Kamerun, Tanganyika, and Southwest Africa [Namibia] to an "international organization." The Allies were asked to "establish a code of law for the international protection of the natives of Africa, similar to the proposed international code of labor."

Nowhere in the Congress' demands were Europeans asked to grant Africans the right to complete self-determination. Rather, the Congress, speaking for "the Negroes of the world," resolved that "hereafter the natives of Africa and the peoples of African descent" should be governed according to more humane and democratic rules. Land and other natural resources "should be held in trust for the natives" while they acquired the means to "effective ownership of as much land as they can profitably develop." Capital should be "regulated as to prevent the exploitation of the natives and the exhaustion of the natural wealth of the country." All forms of "slavery and corporal punishment" must be abolished, the resolutions urged. The right of every black "child to learn to read and write his own language," and access to "higher technical and cultural training" must be guaranteed. In terms of political rights, all Africans should "participate in the government as fast as their development permits." Educated blacks must be given the "higher offices of State," culminating in the future to an "Africa ruled by consent of the Africans."[42]

At best, the resolutions had only a minor impact upon the deliberations of the Versailles Peace Conference. Despite the relative conservatism of these demands, for European leaders "the very idea of Pan-Africanism was so strange that it seemed unreal and yet at the same time perhaps potentially dangerous."[43] Optimistic, Du Bois returned to the United States, "from where he hoped to build a real organization capable of stimulating the national aspirations of the natives of Africa, and of securing wider support for the activities of the Congress."[44]

Over the next two years, Du Bois attempted to raise financial and political support for the Pan-Africanist movement. Throughout the rest of 1919, he and the NAACP were preoccupied with combatting the fierce upsurgence of postwar racist violence. But after "corresponding with Negroes in all parts of Africa and in other parts of the world," a second Congress was scheduled to be held in London, Brussels and Paris from August 28 to September 6, 1921.[45] One hundred and thirteen delegates attended the sessions—seven from the Caribbean, thirty-five American blacks, forty-one from Africa, and the remainder from Europe.

The London meetings were held facing Westminster Abbey in Central Hall, on August 28 and 29. Leading members of the British Labour Party and Fabian Socialists initiated a discussion on "the relation of white and colored labor." The London session unanimously adopted a statement which criticized Belgium's colonial rule in the Congo, which provoked "bitter opposition in Brussels" among government leaders. Once in Belgium, Diagne attempted "to substitute an innocuous cement concerning [the] goodwill" of both the Belgian and French colonialists, and in his capacity as chair, declared the resolution "adopted" despite "a clear majority in opposition." The final sessions in the Palais Mondial, located in Paris's Cinquantenaire Park, reversed Diagne's maneuver by upholding the basic London session drafts. The final document read, in part:

> To the World: The absolute equality of races, physical, political and social, is the founding stone of world and human advancements. No one denies great differences

of gift, capacity, and attainment among individuals of all races, but the voice of Science, religion, and practical Politics is one in denying the God-appointed existence of super-races, or of races naturally and inevitably and eternally inferior. . . . The habit of democracy must be made to encircle the earth. . . . Local self-government with a minimum of help and oversight can be established tomorrow in Asia, in Africa, America, and the Isles of the sea ... The Negro race, through their thinking intelligentsia, demand: l. The recognition of civilized men as civilized, despite their race or color. 2. Local self-government for backward groups, deliberately rising as experience and knowledge grow to complete self-government. . . . 3. Education in self-knowledge, in scientific truth, and in industrial technique, undivorced from the art of beauty. 4. Freedom in their own religion and social customs and with the right to be different and nonconformist. 5. Cooperation with the rest of the world in government, industry, and art on the bases of Justice, Freedom and Peace. 6. The return to Negroes of their land and its natural fruits, and defense against the unrestrained greed of invested capital. 7. The establishment under the League of Nations of an international institution for the study of African problems. 8. The establishment of an international section of the Labor Bureau of the League of Nations, charged with the protection of native labor.[46]

A small delegation of conference participants, led by Dantes Bellegarde, Haiti's Ambassador to France and representative to the League of Nations, traveled to the Geneva headquarters of the League of Nations and presented the Congress's petition. The League's Mandates Commission studied the Congress's proposals, and soon published them with favorable commentary: "Consciously or subconsciously there is in the world today a widespread and growing feeling that it is permissible to treat civilized men as uncivilized if they are colored and more especially of Negro descent. . . . [We] urge that the League of Nations take a firm stand on the absolute equality of races and that it form an International Institute for the study of the Negro problem, and for the evolution and protection of the Negro race."[47] The second Pan-African Congress's success in attracting a level of international support also generated, for the first time, criticism from the European press. British Africanist Sir Harry Johnston chided the Pan-Africanist intellectuals, noting curtly that American "colored people . . . know so *little about real* Africa." The British humor magazine *Punch* parodied the "Pan-African Manifesto."[48]

More seriously, the *Neptune,* a major Brussels newspaper, levied the accusation that the Pan-Africanist Congress was "an agency of Moscow and the cause of native unrest in the Congo." It asserted that the Congress's leaders had "received remuneration" from the Bolsheviks, and predicted darkly that Pan-Africanist propaganda would "some day [cause] grave difficulties in the Negro village of Kinshasa."[49] Other European leaders and colonial officials confused Du Bois's Pan-Africanist movement with the alarming growth of the militant Black nationalist organization, the Universal Negro Improvement Association [UNIA], led by the charismatic Jamaican Marcus Mosiah Garvey. Du Bois later complained, "News of [Garvey's] astonishing plans reached Europe and the various colonial offices, even before my much more modest proposals. Often the Pan-African Congress was confounded with the Garvey movement with consequent suspicion and attack."[50] Even as the 1919 Pan-African Congress was meeting in Paris, the UNIA newspaper *Negro World* was banned by the acting governor in British Honduras [Belize] and by the Trinidadian governor "on grounds that it [was] seditious." In May, 1919, the British Guianan government seized and destroyed the *Negro World;* on August 6, 1919, the acting governor of Jamaica ordered postal agents to seize copies of the newspaper; on August 19, "legislation to ban the *Negro World* in the Windward Islands [was] advocated by the governor, G. B. Haddon-Smith."[51] Thus from Du Bois's perspective, any perceived connection with the threat of Garvey's militant black nationalism compromised his Pan-Africanist objectives.

On the other side of the color line, Garvey and his followers denounced the Pan-Africanism of Du Bois as early as 1918. Always the polemicist, Garvey himself was not above distorting the facts to suit his immediate political objectives. Speaking before the Baltimore UNIA branch on December 18, 1918, for example, Garvey stated erroneously that Du Bois and Moton were sent jointly "to France to prevent Negroes from getting the fruits of their sacrifices on the battlefields." Negroes should enjoy democracy, Garvey declared, but whites had "sent for men like Du Bois and Moton to prevent us from getting it."[52] In retrospect, the famous Du Bois-Garvey debate which characterized so much of the politics of the black world during the 1920s began in the circumstances surrounding the first Pan-African Congress.

On November 10–11, 1918, the UNIA proposed a series of "Peace Aims" to the Allies. Learning of the pending Versailles Peace Conference, the UNIA appointed three members to go to Paris. Only one, a nineteen-year-old Haitian named Eliézer Cadet, was able to secure a passport for the trip.[53] In Cadet's possession were two addresses, to the "People of England and France" respectively, urging them to grant "fair play and justice on the continents of Africa, America and on the West Indies." Europeans were asked to "help us to abolish the lynching institutions and burning at the stake of men, women, and children of our race in the United States of America, to abolish industrial serfdom, robbery, and exploitation in the West Indies and the new slavery and outrages inflicted on our race in Africa."[54] Unfortunately, Cadet did not arrive in Paris until March 1, several days after the Pan-African Congress had ended, and he did not deliver the UNIA's documents to Clemenceau's offices until March 9.

His failure to attract the attention of the French authorities or the press was attributed to the intervention of "adversaries." Garvey incorrectly assumed that Du Bois was somehow responsible for Cadet's problems. At a mass assembly of three thousand UNIA supporters, which included A. Philip Randolph and socialist editor Chandler Owen, Garvey declared that the NAACP leader had placed "obstacles in the way of the elected representative efficiently discharging his already difficult duties on behalf of the Negro race." A resolution which "denounced the reactionary leader, W. E. B. Du Bois, and upheld Eliézer Cadet," passed unanimously "with acclamation."[55] On April 5, 1919, the *Negro World* repeated the charges that the U.S. government had asked "Dr. Du Bois to go to France," and that he had sabotaged the UNIA's initiatives. To say that Garvey deliberately libeled Du Bois would be too generous, for the UNIA leader cynically distorted the facts: "Cadet presented these [UNIA] aims to the French people and to the Peace Conference, [but] Du Bois . . . who was never elected by any one except by the capitalist class . . . has come out to attack [our aims] in the French papers."[56]

Other black American activists repeated Garvey's charges. Chandler Owen asserted that only "good niggers" like Du Bois could get passports to attend the Pan-African Congress. Only "men who positively would not discuss lynching, peonage, disfranchisement and discrimination" were allowed to go to Paris.[57] Du Bois at first ignored the slanders, but as he prepared for the Second Pan-African Congress, he responded to Garvey's attacks. Throughout his visit to France, he "never saw or heard of [Cadet], never denied his nor anyone's statements of the wretched American conditions, did everything possible to arouse rather than quiet the French press, and would have been delighted to welcome and cooperate with any colored fellow-worker." The entire affair had convinced Du Bois that Garvey had "very serious defects of temperament and training: he is dictatorial, domineering, inordinately vain, and very suspicious."[58]

This minor conflict shortly grew into an ideological war, as the two men who Pan-Africanist George Padmore identified as "the two outstanding Negro leaders in the Western Hemisphere" debated their respective Pan-African programs.[59] A full critique of the Du Bois-Garvey debate transcends the scope of this essay. However, as Padmore notes, "Where Du Bois differed from Garvey was in his conception of the Pan-African movement as an aid to the promotion of national self-determination among Africans under African leadership, for the benefit of Africans themselves. Garvey, on the other hand, looked upon Africa as a place for colonizing Western Negroes under his personal domination."[60] More generous is the assessment of Garvey scholar Theodore G. Vincent, who viewed the most important contrast between Du Bois and Garvey as their radically different social positions. The "famous feud pitted an introspective scholar" against a "gregarious, virtually self-educated, mass leader. As a social analyst, Du Bois made critical evaluations of all leading blacks; most could accept it in good spirit; Garvey could not."[61] Historian John Henrik Clarke, surveying the debate, notes that "Du Bois often addressed advice to Marcus Garvey as if . . . [he] were a misguided child, and Garvey spoke of Du Bois as if he were a fraud, and a traitor to his people. At a critical period, this kind of conduct was a negation of the cause that had been the life work of both men."[62]

The 1921 Pan-African Congress was in many respects the high point of the Pan-African movement in the 1920s. An international secretariat established in Paris to facilitate correspondence soon closed for lack of funds. Diagne postponed the scheduled 1923 Congress, and "finally without proper notice or preparation" the sessions were held in London and Lisbon.[63] British author H. G. Wells and socialist Harold Laski attended the London sessions; Labour Party leader Ramsay MacDonald wrote to the Congress affirming his support. The Lisbon sessions were more productive, with delegates from eleven nations in attendance. Two former colonial administrators of Portugal "promised to use their influence in getting their Government to abolish conscript labour and other much overdue reforms in the African colonies." In their manifesto, the delegates repeated their demands of two years before, concluding, "In fine, we ask in all the world, that black folk be treated as men. We can see no other road to peace and progress."[64] Nkrumah would later write that the 1923 Congress "lacked funds and membership was limited. The delegates were idealists rather than men of action. However, a certain amount of publicity was achieved, and Africans and men of African descent for the first time gained valuable experience in working together."[65] After the Congress, Du Bois visited Africa for the first time, seeing four African islands and five countries. In Liberia, he represented the U.S. government at the inaugural of President C. D. B. King.[66]

In the mid-twenties, Du Bois recognized that "the Pan-African idea was still American rather than African, but it was growing, and it expressed a real demand for examination of the African situation and a plan of treatment from the native African point of view." His plans for a fourth conference, which was to be held in "Jamaica, Haiti, Cuba, and the French islands" in 1925 failed to materialize. Efforts to charter a ship to carry participants across the region were unsuccessful, and one French firm demanded "the prohibitive price of fifty thousand dollars" to transport the black delegates.[67] One year later, Addie W. Hunton, an NAACP field organizer and leader of a black women's association, the Circle of Peace and Foreign Relations, largely initiated the plans for another Pan-African Congress, which was held in New York City in August, 1927.[68] The sessions attracted five thousand people, far more than the number of participants at all previous Congresses combined. There were 208 paid delegates from twenty-two states and the District of Columbia. Others came from India, China, Egypt, Liberia, Nigeria, Sierra Leone, the Gold Coast, and other nations. Despite the presence of Chief Amoah III of the Gold Coast, Du Bois was disappointed with the small number of African delegates. Nevertheless, largely due to the spirited presence of Afro-American women leaders, the Congress was productive. As Padmore writes, "while these Negro women had no intention of voluntarily going back to Africa, they, like so many of their menfolk, took a lively interest in the land of their ancestors."[69] The delegates emphasized "six points" in their resolutions:

Negroes everywhere need:

1. A voice in their own government.
2. Native rights to the land and its natural resources.
3. Modern education for all children.
4. The development of Africa for the Africans and not merely for the profit of Europeans.
5. The reorganization of commerce and industry so as to make the main object of capital and labor the welfare of the many rather than the enriching of the few.
6. The treatment of civilized men as civilized despite difference of birth, race or color.[70]

The delegates also ratified other resolutions which widened the scope of Pan-Africanism. The Soviet Union was applauded "for its liberal attitude toward the colored races and for the help which it has extended to them from time to time." Echoing Marx's famous observation in *Capital*, the Congress told the white working class "to realize that no program of labor uplift can be successfully carried through in Europe or America so long as colored labor is exploited and enslaved and deprived of all political power."[71]

The Great Depression and the rise of fascism contributed decisively to the temporary collapse of Pan-Africanism. In 1929, Du Bois attempted to hold a fifth Pan-African Congress in Tunisia. "Elaborate preparations were begun," Du Bois noted in *The World and Africa*. "It looked as though at last the movement was going to be geographically in Africa. But two insuperable difficulties intervened: first, the French government very politely, but firmly, informed us that the Congress could take place at Marseilles or any French city, but not in Africa; and second, there came the Great Depression."[72] Six weeks after the stock market crash of October, 1929, Du Bois admitted to his *Crisis* readers that "the importance of these [Pan-African] meetings is not yet realized by educated and thinking Negroes" in the United States. He attributed much of the problem to "the unfortunate words and career of Marcus Garvey," who had dampened the interest of many Afro-Americans in African issues. "Nevertheless, the idea back of the Pan-African Congress is sound, and in less than a hundred years, it is going to be realized."[73] Most of the leadership of the NAACP had never been interested in Du Bois's Pan-Africanist vision, and with the failure of the 1929 Tunis Congress to occur, the organization silently retreated from involvement in African affairs. Du Bois's departure from the editorial and political leadership of the NAACP in the summer of 1934, and the elevation of the staunch integrationist and anti-Communist Walter White as NAACP Secretary, ended a distinct phase of Pan-Africanist history.

PAN-AFRICANISM: PADMORE, NKRUMAH, AND THE LEGACY OF DU BOIS

The focus of the Pan-Africanist movement returned to London during the 1930s, largely due to the dynamic personality of George Padmore, the nephew of Henry Sylvester Williams.[74] Born Malcolm Nurse, the young Trinidadian came to the United States in 1924 to pursue a career in law. Joining the Communist Party in 1927, he helped to direct the party's Harlem newspaper for a time. Padmore advanced quickly: by the early 1930s he had become "the foremost black figure in the Communist International—the Comintern— culminating in his receiving appointment as a colonel in the Red Army." Padmore traveled across colonial Africa, recruiting African militants to revolutionary Marxism, and later "as head of the African Bureau of the Comintern in Germany he organized an International Conference of black workers in Hamburg."[75]

But in 1934, Padmore abruptly severed his association with the Communists. In his judgment, the Communists had been incorrect to condemn Garvey's UNIA and Du Bois's Pan-African Congresses "as manifestations of petit bourgeois nationalism, to be fought and destroyed before Communism could ever hope to make inroads in Africa or win the allegiance of the Negro masses in America to the cause of the 'Proletarian Revolution'. . . . The attitude of most white Communists towards Negro organizations has been one of contempt," he wrote. "If they cannot control them, they seek their destruction by infiltration."[76] Relocated in London during the Depression, Padmore's home became an informal headquarters for African and West Indian students and activists. A young Kenyan studying anthropology, Jomo Kenyatta, was a visitor and close disciple of Padmore's. Two other associates consulted frequently with Padmore: C. L. R. James and Paul Robeson. Born in Trinidad in 1901, James was the leading black Trotskyite in Europe and, within Padmore's circle of associates, the most articulate theoretician of Pan-Africanism. Writing in the tradition of Du Bois, he produced during these years several classic texts: *The Case for West Indian Self-Government* (1933), *The Black Jacobins: Toussaint L'Ouverture and the Haitian Revolution* (1938), and *A History of Negro Revolt* (1939).[77] Robeson, the great black Shakespearean actor and vocalist, was profoundly interested in African culture and politics. The Afro-American artist appeared in the title role as *Toussaint L'Ouverture,* a 1936 play written and staged by James. These men represented a new generation of black scholarship and political action, which would create the nucleus of the Pan-Africanist upsurge after World War II.

With the Italian invasion of Ethiopia, this new leadership helped to create the International African Friends of Abyssinia (IAFA). Their immediate goal was "to arouse the sympathy and support of the British public for the victims of Fascist aggression and to assist by all means in their power in the maintenance of the territorial integrity and political independence of Abyssinia."[78] Participants in the IAFA included Amy Ashwood Garvey, the first wife of the leader of the UNIA, who served as honorary treasurer; T. Albert Marryshaw of Grenada; Gold Coast leader J. B. Danquah; Mohammed Said of Somaliland; Jomo Kenyatta, the organization's honorary secretary; and James, who was IAFA chairman. Several years later, the International African Service Bureau was founded upon the initiation of T. R. Makonnen. Padmore chaired the Bureau, writing much of the correspondence in his kitchen. James edited the Bureau's *International African Opinion;* Kenyatta served as assistant secretary, and Makonnen, the treasurer, successfully raised funds for the group's activities. Robeson and Max Yergan, a black YMCA secretary who had worked in South Africa, initiated plans during a 1939 London meeting to establish the Council on African Affairs in the United States. Based in New York City, the new Council attracted the energies of Alphaeus Hunton, a Howard University professor of literature and husband of Addie W. Hunton, the chief planner of the Fourth Pan-African Congress of 1927. Robeson, Yergan, and Hunton started a regular monthly which was devoted to developments in the continent. The Council invited African intellectuals and political leaders to speak at public forums.[79]

Despite these hopeful signs, few outside of this circle of intellectuals and radicals perceived the Pan-Africanist cause as anything but a visionary and quite abstract discourse. Having returned to Atlanta University from 1934 to 1944, Du Bois was, however, still optimistic about the possibility of reviving the Pan-African Congress movement. In a June, 1940 column in the *Amsterdam News,* he suggested holding a "Fifth Pan-African Congress" in Haiti in 1942. In the wake of A. Philip Randolph's March on Washington Movement of 1941, the two leaders suggested the preparation of a "Congress of Black people" to coincide with the end of World War II.[80] In his personal correspondence, Du Bois admitted in February, 1941 that Pan- Africanism "is only an idea on paper and in the memory of a considerable number of former [Congress] participants in America, the West Indies and Africa." But he also predicted, "if the world ever settles down to peace again, there will be another meeting of the Congress."[81] In 1944 Du Bois discussed the idea of developing "an African Freedom Charter and the scheduling of another Pan-African Congress with Amy Jacques Garvey, the recent widow of the UNIA leader, Robeson, Yergan, and Harold Moody, chairman of the London Missionary Society."[82]

In the summer of 1944, Du Bois returned to the NAACP as Director of Special Research. One of his immediate objectives was to "revive the Pan-African movement and give general attention to the foreign aspects of the race problem."[83] However, the actual planning of the October, 1945 Pan-African Congress was accomplished by Padmore and a young, idealistic Gold Coast student, Francis (later Kwame) Nkrumah. James had traveled during the war to North America, first conducting a series of discussions with exiled Marxist Leon Trotsky in Coyoacan, Mexico, then organizing dissident black and white rural workers.[84] In 1943, quite by accident, James met the young African, who was attending Lincoln University. From 1943 to early 1945 Nkrumah "would come up to New York to spend a day or two" with James and his associates. James comments, "Even in those years, Nkrumah was noted for his acute intelligence, his intellectual energy, the elegance of his person, the charm of his manners, and his ability to establish easy relations with any company in which he found himself." When Nkrumah left for England to study law, James scribbled a note of introduction to Padmore. Within weeks, Nkrumah joined Kenyatta as a regular "student" in the Padmore household.[85]

Padmore's opportunity to revive the Pan-African Congress concept came with the February, 1945 establishment in London of the World Federation of Trade Unions, which brought dozens of "representatives of black labour from Nigeria, Gold Coast, Sierra Leone, Gambia, Jamaica, Trinidad, Barbados, British Guiana, and other colonial lands." A second World Federation of Trade Unions had been scheduled in Paris from September 25 to October 9, 1945. Padmore successfully persuaded these black trade unionists and other political leaders to come to Manchester following the Paris meeting. In March, 1945, a "provisional programme and agenda" was set and a working committee formed, which included Padmore and Nkrumah as "joint political secretaries"; South African writer Peter Abrahams as "publicity secretary"; Kenyatta as "assistant secretary"; Peter Milliard of British Guiana as chairman; and Makonnen working once more as treasurer.[86] In the United States, Du Bois had established correspondence with Danquah, who was then the general secretary of the Gold Coast Youth Conference, and with Jamaican attorney Norman W. Manley, who would later serve as his country's Prime

Minister.[87] It is clear that Padmore had issued the call for a Pan-African Congress without Du Bois's prior knowledge. On March 22, 1945, he wrote to Padmore insisting that the meeting "ought to be held in Africa," and that the "meeting should not be set for a definite date as yet" since the war had not ended.[88] Within several weeks, however, Du Bois wrote to Padmore that he was "in complete sympathy" with his plans, and had "changed my mind as to the time" of the Congress as well. During the next six months the two men worked closely in coordinating the Congress.[89]

The Manchester Pan-African Congress attracted the political and intellectual vanguard of the black world. Participants came from across the black diaspora: Wallace Johnson, secretary of the Sierra Leone Youth League; Magnus Williams of the National Council of Nigeria and the Cameroons; Raphael Armattoe of Togoland; J. S. Annan, secretary of the Gold Coast Railway Civil Servants' and Technical Workers' Union; G. Ashie Nikoi, a leader of the Gold Coast Farmers; Marko Hlubi, Zulu representative of the African National Congress; Jamaica's Norman Manley, and Alma LaBardie of the Jamaica Women's Movement; P. M. Harper of the British Guiana Trade Union Congress; E. de Lisle Yearwood of the Barbados Labour Party; Claude Lushington and John Rojas of the West Indian Nationalist Party. Certain individuals stood out at the Congress. Kenyatta was the leading spokesperson for East African affairs. Heretofore unknown, Nkrumah quickly emerged as a dominant personality among West African delegates. Padmore and Milliard were the essential organizers of the forums. Amy Jacques Garvey received warm applause from all participants. Yet the guiding spirit of the Congress, all recognized, was Du Bois. As Padmore wrote:

> These discussions were conducted under the direction of Dr. Du Bois, who, at the age of seventy-three, had flown across the Atlantic from New York to preside over the coming of age of his political child. This 'Grand Old Man,' politically ahead of many much younger in years, was given an enthusiastic welcome by the delegates. For he had done more than any other to inspire and influence by his writings and political philosophy all the young men who had foregathered from far distant corners of the earth. Even among the older delegates there were many who were meeting the 'Father' of Pan-Africanism in the flesh for the first time. Dr. Du Bois was by no means a silent spectator at the Fifth Pan-African Congress. He entered into all the discussions and brought to the deliberations a freshness of outlook that greatly influenced the final decisions; the implementations of which are already shaping the future of the African continent.[90]

The Fifth Pan-African Congress differed from the earlier sessions in several important respects. Most of the Manchester participants were elected leaders of various mass constituency organizations, or had direct contacts with nascent independence movements. Thus their programs had an immediacy and a comprehensive character that drew strength from actual workers' struggles. Most of the two hundred delegates and observers were proposing "a mass movement intimately identified with the underprivileged sections of the coloured colonial populations."[91] The sessions on West Africa focused on the immediate tasks of the independence movements in that region, especially in Nigeria and the Gold Coast. Resolutions in this area included demands for the creation of "independent trade unions and cooperative movements without official interference." British rule was denounced for tolerating "mass illiteracy, ill-health, malnutrition, prostitution, and many other social evils"; and organized Christianity was described as a tool which facilitated "the political and economic exploitation of the West African peoples by alien powers." Significantly, delegates also criticized "the artificial divisions and territorial boundaries created by the imperialist powers" which were viewed as "deliberate steps to obstruct the political unity of the West African peoples."

Congress participants were already proposing the cardinal principle of what would afterwards be referred to as Nkrumahism: that only by the political and economic unity of all Africa could the legacy of European colonial rule be uprooted:

> The delegates believe in peace. How could it be otherwise, when for centuries the African peoples have been the victims of violence and slavery? Yet if the western world is still determined to rule mankind by force, then Africans, as a last resort, may have to appeal to force in the effort to achieve freedom, even if force destroys them and the world. We are determined to be free. We want education. We want the right to earn a decent living; the right to express our thoughts and emotions, to adopt and create forms of beauty. We demand for Black Africa autonomy and independence, so far and no further then it is possible in this One World for groups and peoples to rules themselves subject to inevitable world unity and federation.... We condemn the monopoly of capital and rule of private wealth and industry for private profit alone. We welcome economic democracy as the only real democracy.[92]

The aftermath of the Manchester Congress is, of course, well known. Nkrumah formed the West African National Secretariat to implement the Pan-African Congress's resolutions. Returning to the Gold Coast in 1947, he built the powerful Convention People's Party, and under his leadership the independent nation of Ghana was born in 1957. Kenyatta became the leader of Kenya's independence movement, and emerged as that nation's President. Du Bois's subsequent intellectual activities on African affairs continued to increase. His two major books after the war focused specifically on the pressing necessity of African liberation. After his dismissal from the NAACP in 1948, he became Vice-Chairman of the Council on African Affairs. From March, 1947 through February, 1948, Du Bois wrote a total of fifty-three essays on African politics, economic development and history for the Harlem weekly *People's Voice,* owned by Congressman Adam Clayton Powell.

Du Bois's voluminous early works on Africa and race relations became more widely distributed across the Caribbean and Africa during the 1950s, as another new generation of black activists and intellectuals looked for proper theoretical groundings to their national liberation struggles. They recognized, in Padmore's words, that Du Bois "was the first American Negro leader to realize the significance of the colonial liberation movements as part of the struggle of the darker races of Asia and Africa and the importance of fostering closer cooperation between native-born Americans and peoples of African descent in the Western Hemisphere.[93] For Du Bois himself, the pursuit of the Pan-Africanist ideal was linked directly to his vision of radical democracy, or perhaps more accurately, multicultural democracy. Africa and peoples of the African diaspora could not be truly free so long as democracy existed only for the few:

> The iron curtain was not invented by Russia; it hung between Europe and Africa half a thousand years. When the producer is so separated from the consumer in time and space that a mutual knowledge and understanding is impossible, then to regard the industrial process as 'individual enterprise' or the result as 'private enterprise' is stupid. It is a social process, and if not socially controlled sinks to anarchy with every possible crime of irresponsible greed. Such was the African slave trade, and such is the capitalist system it brought to full flower. Men made cotton cloth and sold sugar; but between the two they stole, killed, and raped human beings....If a world of ultimate democracy, reaching across the color line and abolishing race discrimination, can only be accomplished by the method laid down by Karl Marx, then that method deserves to be triumphant no matter what we think or do.[94]

NOTES

1. C.L.R. James, *The Future in the Present: Selected Writings* (Westport, Conn.: Lawrence Hill, 1980), 202, 208.

2. Kwame Nkrumah, *Revolutionary Path* (New York: International Publishers, 1973), 42–43; Nkrumah, *Africa Must Unite* (New York: International Publishers, 1970), 132–33, 135.

3. Harold R. Isaacs, "Pan-Africanism as 'Romantic Racism'," in *W. E. B. Du Bois: A Profile,* ed. Rayford W. Logan (New York: Hill and Wang, 1971), 213, 240, 242.

4. Francis L. Broderick, *W. E. B. Du Bois: Negro Leader in a Time of Crisis* (Stanford: Stanford University Press, 1959), 130, 135–36, 228.

5. Herbert Aptheker, "The Historian," in *W. E. B. Du Bois: A Profile*, ed. Logan, 258–60.

6. W. E. B. Du Bois, *Dusk of Dawn: An Essay Toward An Autobiography of a Race Concept* (New York: Schocken Books, 1968), 115–16.

7. Du Bois, *Dusk of Dawn*, 116.

8. Du Bois, *Dusk of Dawn*, 111.

9. Harold R. Isaacs, "Pan-Africanism as 'Romantic Racism'," 223.

10. Broderick, *W. E. B. Du Bois: Negro Leader in a Time of Crisis*, 16.

11. Broderick, *W. E. B. Du Bois: Negro Leader in a Time of Crisis*, 20.

12. Not until the publication of Ron T. Takaki's book, *A Pro-Slavery Crusade: The Agitation to Reopen the African Slave Trade* (New York: Free Press, 1970), was there another examination of this issue in any substantial manner.

13. Stephen B. Weeks, *American Historical Review*, 2 (April, 1897): 555–59.

14. William Claypole and John Robottom, *Caribbean Story, Book Two: The Inheritors* (London: Longman, 1981), 79–80.

15. Manning Marable, "Booker T. Washington and African Nationalism," *Phylon*, 35 (December, 1974), 398. Also see Louis R. Harlan, "Booker T. Washington and the White Man's Burden," *American Historical Review*, 71 (January, 1966): 441–67.

16. Claypole and Robottom, *Caribbean Story*, 80; and W. E. B. Du Bois, *The World and Africa: An Inquiry into the Part which Africa Has Played in World History* (New York: International Publishers, 1965), 7–8.

17. Robert A. Hill, ed., *The Marcus Garvey and Universal Negro Improvement Association Papers*, vol. 1 (Berkeley: University of California Press, 1983), 534.

18. W. E. B. Du Bois, review in *Political Science Quarterly*, 18 (December 1903): 695–97.

19. W. E. B. Du Bois, review in *The Nation*, 111 (September 25, 1920): 350–52.

20. W. E. B. Du Bois, "The Black Soldier," *Crisis*, 16 (June 1918), 2.

21. Isaacs, "Pan-Africanism as 'Romantic Racism'," 238.

22. W. E. B. Du Bois, "Migration," *Crisis*, 7 (February 1914): 190; Du Bois, "The Latest Craze," *Crisis* (January 1916): 133–34. On Chief Alfred Sam, see William E. Bittle and Gilbert Geis, *The Longest Way Home: Chief Alfred C. Sam's Back-to-Africa Movement* (Detroit: Wayne State University Press, 1964); J. Ayo Langley, "Chief Sam's African Movement and Race Consciousness in West Africa," *Phylon*, 32 (Summer 1971): 164–78; and "Chief Alfred Sam," in Hill, ed., vol. 1, 536–47.

23. For example, "Germany," *Crisis*, Vol. 11 (February 1916), 184; and "The World Last Month," *Crisis*, 13 (March 1917).

24. W. E. B. Du Bois, "The African Roots of the War," *Atlantic Monthly*, 115 (May 1915): 707–14. Also see Manning Marable, "Peace and Black Liberation: The Contributions of W. E. B. Du Bois," *Science and Society*, 47 (Winter 1983–1984) 390–91.

25. Broderick, *W. E. B. Du Bois: Negro Leader in a Time of Crisis*, 129.

26. J.P. Tumulty to W. E. B. Du Bois, November 29, 1918, in Aptheker, ed., *The Correspondence of W. E. B. Du Bois*, vol. 1, (Amherst: University of Massachusetts Press, 1973), 231–32.

27. Du Bois, *Dusk of Dawn*, 260.

28. Du Bois, *Dusk of Dawn*, 261. Moton was probably distressed to learn that the preminent opponent of the "Tuskegee philosophy" was to be his roommate aboard the Orizaba.

29. W. E. B. Du Bois, "The Future of Africa," *Advocate of Peace*, 81 (January 1919):

12–13; and "Letters from Dr. Du Bois," December 8 and 14, 1918, *Crisis,* 17 (February 1919).

30. F. Schoonmaker, Major, General Staff, to Intelligence Officers, Secret Memo, January 1, 1919, in Aptheker, ed., *The Correspondence of W. E. B. Du Bois,* vol. 1, 232. Du Bois soon obtained a copy of the secret order, which was stamped by division headquarters.

31. W. E. B. Du Bois, "The Pan–African Movement," in Philip S. Foner, ed., *W. E. B. Du Bois Speaks: Speeches and Addresses, 1920–1963* (New York: Pathfinder Press, 1972), 163.

32. Du Bois, *Dusk of Dawn,* 261.

33. George Padmore, *Pan-Africanism or Communism* (Garden City, New York: Anchor Books, 1972), 98.

34. James, *The Future in the Present,* 207.

35. Of the heroic conduct of French West African troops during the war, Du Bois wrote: "Against the banked artillery of the magnificent German Army were sent untrained and poorly armed Senegalese. They marched at command in unwavering ranks, raising the war cry in a dozen different Sudanese tongues. When the artillery belched they shivered, but never faltered. They marched straight into death; the war cries became fainter and fainter and dropped into silence as not a single black man was left living on that field." Du Bois, *The World and Africa,* 7.

36. Padmore, *Pan-Africanism or Communism,* 98–99.

37. Du Bois, *The World and Africa,* 10.

38. Du Bois, *Dusk of Dawn,* 262.

39. Du Bois, *The World and Africa,* 10. Padmore notes that "the American officials in President Wilson's entourage were afraid that the Congress might discuss, among other things, the lynching of Negroes in the United States and the treatment of Afro-American troops in France. The American statesmen had good reason to be alarmed, for apart from maintaining racial segregation between black and white troops serving under the Stars and Stripes, the U.S. Army authorities in France tried to impose their racial prejudices on the French people." Padmore, *Pan-Africanism or Communism,* 99–100. Also see "The Denial of Passports," *Crisis,* 17 (March 1919): 237–38; and "Negro Passports Refused," *Messenger,* 2 (March 1919): 4.

40. Du Bois, *The World and* Africa, 10.

41. James, *The Future in the Present,* 207.

42. Du Bois, *The World and Africa,* 11–12.

43. Nkrumah, *Africa Must Unite,* 133.

44. Padmore, *Pan-Africanism or Communism,* 103.

45. Padmore, *Pan-Africanism or Communism,* 104–105. In his capacity as Pan-African Congress secretary, Du Bois also notified U.S. Secretary of State Charles Evans Hughes and Sir Auckland Geddes, British Ambassador to the United States, that a second Congress would be held. He emphasized to Hughes that the meeting "has nothing to do with the so-called Garvey movement and contemplates neither force nor revolution in its program." See Du Bois to Hughes, June 23, 1921, and Hughes to Du Bois, July 8, 1921, in Aptheker, ed., *The Correspondence of W. E. B. Du Bois,* vol. 1, 250–51.

46. Du Bois, "The Pan-African Movement," in Foner, ed., *W. E. B. Du Bois Speaks,* 169–71.

47. Du Bois, *The World and Africa,* 240–41; Padmore, *Pan-Africanism or Communism,* 112.

48. Du Bois, *The World and Africa,* 240.

49. Padmore, *Pan-Africanism or Communism,* 110–11.

50. Du Bois, *Dusk of Dawn,* 277–78.

51. Hill, ed., *Garvey Papers,* vol. 1, cxv–cxvii.

52. Extracts from Garvey speech, Baltimore, December 18, 1918, in Hill, ed., *Garvey Papers,* vol. 1, 332.

53. The other delegates selected were the black socialist journalist Asa Philip Randolph and antilynching activist Ida B. Wells Barnett. D. Davidson, "Bureau of Investigation Reports," December 5, 1918, in Hill, ed., *Garvey Papers,* vol. 1, 305, 308.

54. Garvey scholar Robert A. Hill suggests that Garvey himself wrote these speeches. Garvey, Editorial, *Negro World* (March 1, 1919), in Hill, ed., *Garvey Papers,* vol. 1, 377–81.

55. Cadet's charges against Du Bois had been sent on either March 22 or 23, 1919, but Du Bois had left France on March 22. Cadet quickly tired of pursuing the UNIA 's agenda at the Peace Conference, and for most of the remainder of the year worked in Paris as an auto mechanic. He returned to Haiti in late 1919, and eventually "became a vodun high priest of the cult of Damballah (the serpent god)." Hill, ed., *Garvey Papers,* vol. 1, 308, 393.

56. "Addresses Denouncing W. E. B. Du Bois," *Negro World* (April 5, 1919), in Hill, ed., *Garvey Papers,* vol. 1, 395–96.

57. Hill, ed., *Garvey Papers,* vol. 1, 399.

58. W. E. B. Du Bois, "Marcus Garvey," *Crisis,* 21 (December 1920): 58–60, and (January 1921): 112–15.

59. Padmore, *Pan-Africanism or Communism,* 106.

60. Padmore, *Pan-Africanism or Communism,* 106–07.

61. Theodore G. Vincent, *Black Power and the Garvey Movement* (San Francisco: Ramparts Press, 1972), 58.

62. John Henrik Clarke, ed., *Marcus Garvey and the Vision of Africa* (New York: Vintage Books, 1974), 97. As Clarke writes, Garvey and Du Bois were both "Pan-Africanists and both of them had as their objectives the freedom and redemption of African people everywhere. Yet there was no meeting of minds on the methods of reaching these desirable goals" (97).

63. Du Bois, *The World and Africa,* 241.

64. Du Bois, *The World and Africa,* 242; Padmore, *Pan-Africanism or Communism,* 117–20.

65. Nkrumah, *Africa Must Unite,* 133. Also see W. E. B. Du Bois, "Pan-Africa in Portugal," *Crisis,* 27 (February 1924): 170.

66. W. E. B. Du Bois, "Opinion," *Crisis,* Vol. 27 (March 1924): 202; Du Bois, "Sketches From Abroad: Le Grand Voyage," *Crisis,* Vol. 27 (March 1924): 203–205; Du Bois, "Opinion," *Crisis,* 27 (April 1924): 247–51.

67. W. E. B. Du Bois, *The World and Africa,* 242.

68. W. E. B. Du Bois, "Opinion," *Crisis,* Vol. 32 (October 1926): 283.

69. Padmore, *Pan-Africanism or Communism,* 121.

70. Du Bois, *The World and Africa,* 243.

71. "The Pan-African Congresses," *Crisis,* 34 (October 1927): 263–64. Marx's statement on race and class oppression is: "Labor with a white skin cannot emancipate itself where labor with a black skin is branded." In 1914 Du Bois stated the same concept: "So long as black laborers are slaves, white laborers cannot be free." See Manning Marable, "Why Black Americans are Not Socialists," in Phyllis and Julius Jacobson, eds., *Socialist Perspectives* (New York: Karz-Cohl, 1983), 63–95.

72. Du Bois, *The World and Africa,* 243.

73. W. E. B. Du Bois, "Postscript," *Crisis*, 36 (December 1929): 423–24.

74. W. E. B. Du Bois, "The Winds of Time," *Chicago Defender* (September 29, 1945). Historians disagree as to the actual relationship between Williams and Padmore. Padmore himself claimed kinship in a personal letter to Du Bois. But Padmore biographer James R. Hooker states that he "was not related to the lawyer." See Hooker, *Black Revolutionary: George Padmore's Path from Communism to Pan-Africanism* (New York: Praeger, 1967).

75. Azinna Nwafor, "The Revolutionary as Historian: Padmore and Pan-Africanism," in Padmore, *Pan-Africanism or Communism*, xxv.

76. Padmore, *Pan-Africanism or Communism*, 111, 117.

77. Robert A. Hill, "C. L. R. James in England, 1932–1938," in *Urgent Tasks*, 7 (Summer 1981): 19–27.

78. Padmore, *Pan-Africanism or Communism*, 123.

79. W. E. B. Du Bois, *The Autobiography of W. E. B. Du Bois: A Soliloquy on Viewing My Life from the Last Decade of Its First Century* (New York: International Publishers, 1968), 344–45.

80. W. E. B. Du Bois, "As the Crow Flies," *Amsterdam News* (June 22, 1940); W. E. B. Du Bois, "As the Crow Flies," *Amsterdam News* (December 26, 1942).

81. W. E. B. Du Bois to George A. Finch, February 11, 1941 in Aptheker, ed., *The Correspondence of W. E. B. Du Bois*, vol. 2 (Amherst: University of Massachusetts Press, 1976), 277

82. W. E. B. Du Bois to Amy Jacques Garvey, February 9, 1944; Garvey to Du Bois, April 4, 1944; Garvey to Du Bois, April 5, 1944; Du Bois to Paul Robeson, April 7, 1944; Du Bois to Harold Moody, April 7, 1944; Du Bois to Garvey, April 8, 1944; Garvey to Du Bois, April 24, 1944; Garvey to Du Bois, April 26, 1944, in Aptheker, ed., *The Correspondence of W. E. B. Du Bois*, vol. 2: 375–83.

83. Du Bois, *The Autobiography of W. E. B. Du Bois*, 326.

84. James became the leading black theoretician of the Workers Party during the early l940s. But he and his faction, called the "Johnson-Forest tendency," feuded with the orthodox Trotskyists over the nature of the Soviet Union and other issues related to race, class, and social change in the Third World and in advanced capitalist societies. James's other associates of the period who became Marxist theorists of note include Grace Lee (now Grace Lee Boggs) and Raya Dunayevskaya. See Stuart Hall, "C.L.R. James: A Portrait," 3–16; see Paget Henry and Paul Buhle, *C.L.R. James's Caribbean* (Durham: Duke University Press, 1992); C.L.R. James, *Modern Politics: Selected Writings* (Westport, Conn.: Lawrence Hill, 1980); and C. L. R. James, *Nkrumah and the Ghana Revolution* (Westport, Conn.: Lawrence Hill, 1977).

85. C.L.R. James, "Kwame Nkrumah: Founder of African Emancipation," *Black World*, Vol. 21 (July 1972): 4–10.

86. Padmore, *Pan-Africanism or Communism*, 132–33.

87. W. E. B. Du Bois to J. B. Danquah, September 12, 1944; Du Bois to Norman W. Manley, October 10, 1944, in Aptheker, ed., *The Correspondence of W. E. B. Du Bois*, vol. 3 (Amherst: University of Massachusetts Press, 1978): 1–3.

88. Du Bois had learned about the proposed meeting from a press release published in the March 17, 1945 issue of the *Chicago Defender*. It is curious that Padmore chose not to inform Du Bois directly. Aptheker suggests that "while Du Bois and Padmore knew each other before, during the work that led to this congress they became friends, though significant disagreements marked their relationship." Du Bois to Padmore, March 22, 1945, in Aphtheker, ed. *The Correspondence of W. E. B. Du Bois*, 56–57.

89. Du Bois to Padmore, April 11, 1945; Padmore to Du Bois, April 12, 1945; Du Bois to

Padmore, July 9, 1945; Du Bois to Padmore, July 20, 1945; Padmore to Du Bois, August 17, 1945, in Aptheker, ed., *The Correspondence of W. E. B. Du Bois*, 60–61, 62–65, 67–68, 75–81.

90. Padmore, *Pan-Africanism or Communism*, 139–48.

91. Padmore, *Pan-Africanism or Communism*, 139.

92. Padmore, *Pan-Africanism or Communism*, 141–42.

93. Padmore, *Pan-Africanism or Communism*, 115.

94. Du Bois, *The World and Africa*, 258–59.

Kinship of the Dispossessed | **10**

Du Bois, Nkrumah, and the Foundations of Pan-Africanism

Segun Gbadegesin

INTRODUCTION

Pan-Africanism is both an idea and a movement. A propos its status as an idea, it probably cannot be dated; though it should be clear that the idea is older than the movement. The sentiments that developed into the Pan-African idea and movement were inspired by the racist doctrines and actions that people of African descent were forced to succumb to in the New World. The experience of racist prejudice and injustice forced Africans in the diaspora to start giving serious thought to the idea of a return to the fatherland. For instance, as early as 1787, a petition was addressed to the Legislative Assembly of Massachusetts by a committee of the African Lodge, urging help toward the voluntary emigration to Africa by people of African descent.[1] This interest in emigration grew stronger over the next several years, with various individuals, including Prince Hall, Paul Cuffe, and Reverend Lott Cary, leading the struggle. The American Colonization Society (ACS) was also deeply involved. But there was also a strong principled opposition, especially from African Americans who perceived a sinister motive behind the idea. In 1830, Peter Williams argued that the real objective of the ACS was to remove colored population from the country, that it was illogical to suggest that the conditions of African Americans would be improved in Africa while at the same time acknowledging that conditions of life there were worse than in America, and that if African Americans were considered "vile and degraded," it was illogical and hypocritical to expect them to build a "virtuous and progressive Africa."[2]

In spite of this sound objection, interest in the "Back to Africa" idea continued to grow and it reached its climax in the founding of the Universal Negro Improvement Association (UNIA) by Marcus Garvey, otherwise known as "Black Moses." Garvey launched the campaign in 1920 and by 1923 the UNIA had over six million members. Garvey's objective was to build the greatest black nation, on the principles of capitalist democracy. He emphasized racial purity and insisted that Africa could only be developed by Africans. By all accounts, Garvey's UNIA was the best-organized Negro mass-movement in the United States during its time.[3] Garvey thought that people of African descent could only achieve genuine political freedom and economic emancipation in Africa, and that for this to be realized, there had to be unity. He organized conventions, established a black national church, and founded a newspaper. In 1920, he founded a "Negro Empire" in New York with subjects "scattered throughout the world."[4] Due to a variety of factors, Garvey's empire ultimately collapsed, but not before he made an undeniable contribution to the heightening of African consciousness. Therefore, his ideas, and the movement he founded, must be counted among those various influences, which include the experience of the humiliation of enslavement and the infinite confidence in the future glory of Africa, that led to the development of Pan-Africanism as a movement.

Though Garveyism is usually contrasted with Pan-Africanism as a rival political ideology,[5] it is clear that both derived from similar experiences, and aimed at similar achievements—primarily, the emancipation of Africans at home and abroad. The difference between them was in methods of approach. For while Garvey advocated the emigration of Africans to Africa, Du Bois argued that such a strategy was unrealistic and that the improvement in the conditions of people of African descent in America must be sought and achieved in America. And though Garvey succeeded in building a mass movement of people of African descent while Du Bois's movement was mostly an elite affair, both of them had the cooperation of white folks in different ways. Garvey was able to secure the cooperation of white supremacists whose interest in ethnic cleansing coincided with his Back to Africa movement, while Du Bois relied on the support of the white-dominated National Association for the Advancement of Colored People (NAACP).

It appears to me that Garveyism, as a group of ideas and as a movement, should be regarded as a significant landmark in the development of Pan-Africanism rather than as its rival. Garvey was inspired by the works of

Mojola Agbebi, the African theologian whose inaugural sermon at the African Church in Lagos in December 1902 defended the African way of life and initiated serious discussions on the need for strengthening the African personality against attack from Christian missionary prejudice. Edward W. Blyden further developed this idea in series of articles on "African Life and Customs," which provided further inspiration for Garvey.[6] All this work was subsequent to the first Pan-African Congress of 1900 and the formation of the Pan-African Association.[7] These were the beginnings of the African resentment of, and reaction to, racial injustice.

Garvey contributed to these endeavors with his unique approach and the popularization of the ideas and the movement among the masses. However, it cannot be doubted that W. E. B. Du Bois remains the most famous intellectual defender of the Pan-African idea and movement. As he understood it, the aim of the movement was to facilitate "the industrial and spiritual emancipation of the Negro people."[8] It started as an organized reaction against perceived injustice against black people on the basis of their color. Enslavement was clearly a color-based wickedness as was colonial exploitation of the human and natural resources of Africa. The holocaust of the enslavement of Africans started in 1444 when the Portuguese raided the coast of Africa and went back with slaves and gold dust. This was sanctioned by the Pope and, for long, the Portuguese had the monopoly of the "trade" by the Papal Bull of 1493. In 1562, the English joined in the violence against Africa. John Hawkins took three hundred slaves back to England and was knighted by Queen Elizabeth I. Over 40 million able-bodied young men and women were forcibly taken to English and Spanish plantations in America and the West Indies from West Africa alone. Many more died in the raids. The "trade" continued for more than four hundred years and so did the brutalization and dehumanization of Black Africa. Apologists for the slave "trade" usually refer to the existence of domestic slavery in Africa prior to the time of the Atlantic trade. But what is referred to as domestic slavery in Africa was totally different from the chattel slavery that was introduced by Europe. The latter involved the forceful stripping from a person of all their rights and property. In the case of "domestic slavery," the slave was more like a serf. The basis for the relationship, usually the result of a war, did not allow for the stripping of all rights. The domestic slave in Africa was not regarded as a property. He/she could regain his/her freedom, become a full citizen, and marry and take titles. As Basil Davidson rightly noted,

> the "slave peoples" of the coastal regions, like those of the Sudanese grassland were in truth serfs and vassals, often with valued individual rights. Their status was altogether different from the human cattle of the slave ships and the American plantations.[9]

Between 1760 and 1840, Britain's industrial revolution spread to other parts of Europe and to America, and a new crop of wealthy-class—the capitalists—emerged. This class did not rely on land and agriculture and certainly had no use for slave labor. Its need was for raw materials to feed industries and as a market to sell products. For labor, it relied on the excess hands of serfs and peasants who were now forced out of the rural areas into the urban centers for wage labor. Africa was seen as a fertile source for both raw materials for industries and as a market for goods. This was the beginning of colonial exploitation. Africa was again savagely brutalized, her economy devastated and her institutions destroyed, From 1837 to 1884, the trade in goods was one-sided. Europe was in full control, dictating the terms of trade. As Obafemi Awolowo observed, "the economy of Africa and its direction were perverted and the African themselves were harshly exploited without their being aware of it."[10] The rivalry between Europeans for parcels of land to control in Africa soon came to an end with the recognition of their common interest. In 1884, the Berlin conference was convened to settle scores. Africa was partitioned among European countries without consultation with or the consent of its people. The economy and politics of the various lands became the exclusive domain of the colonial powers. This went on till the end of the nineteenth century, when a new generation of Africans and African Americans began to emerge. It was this group that recognized and resented the undignified treatment of Africans by Europe and America.[11]

As a political movement, Pan-Africanism developed in reaction against these racist and unjust practices. The first Pan-African conference was organized in London in 1900 by Henry Sylvester-Williams, a West Indian lawyer based in London. Its aims were to serve as a forum for protest against the aggressiveness of white colonizers, to bring people of African descent into touch with one another, and to start a movement which would secure to all African peoples their full rights and promote their interests.[12] After the death of Sylvester-Williams, the mantle of leadership for the movement was voluntarily assumed by Du Bois, and between 1919 and 1945 he had organized five international congresses.

The 1919 Conference, the first to be organized by Du Bois, adopted a resolution which, among other things, emphasized the need for international legal protection of the natives of Africa and called for the prevention of exploitation of natives, for respect of their social needs, and for the abolition of slavery and corporal punishment. The 1921 Conference, held in London and Brussels, also adopted some moderate resolutions. For instance, it called for local self-government for "backward" peoples, democratic institutions tied to experience; recognition of civilized men as civilized, despite race or color, and return of Negroes to their land and its natural fruits. The third and fourth Congresses were held in London (1923) and New York (1927) respectively. I will argue later that the resolutions adopted by the various conferences offer a legitimate basis for a Pan-Negroid interpretation of Pan-Africanism. Of course, there are also legitimate grounds for a pan-humanist and a pan-continental interpretation. The idea that pan-Africanism is not only a recognition of injustice to black peoples, but of any form of injustice, makes it a pan-humanist movement. On the other hand, the emphasis on the unity of post-colonial continental Africa, especially as advocated by Kwame Nkrumah, makes it susceptible to a pan-continental interpretation.[13]

As a movement, Pan-Africanism was based on a foundation of ideas. First, there was an idea of moral value that recognized the morally unjustifiable conditions to which Africans and people of African descent were subjected. A belief in the dignity of human persons, in their equality before God, and the realization of the fact that Africans had been brutalized and humiliated without justification fueled the flame of indignation and resentment, and led to the development of the Pan-African idea and movement.

Second, once this undignified treatment had been recognized and resented by the young generation of Africans and African Americans mentioned above (see note 11), they recognized that the evil had to be fought. The strategic importance of a united front led to their resolve to work together and, therefore, to the development of the Pan-African political movement. Third, the combination of the moral foundation and political movement helped in raising the consciousness of the people regarding their common suffering and humiliation. This further increased their awareness of belonging to a common racial stock and this, in turn, fueled their struggle. At this point, by 1900, Pan-Africanism had become a serious political force resting on the complex of ideas that

1. Africa has been unjustly subjugated, devalued and humiliated;
2. Africans at home and abroad share a common destiny and are a common unit, and there is an African personality worth preserving in the face of oppression and brutalization by Europe;
3. Africans should be free to govern themselves and to seek a continental political union as a defense against imperialist exploitation.

In the remainder of this paper, I will be concerned with the philosophical foundation of Pan-Africanism as elaborated by W. E. B. Du Bois and Kwame Nkrumah, focusing on the set of ideas listed in the preceding lines.

The claim that Africa has been unjustly subjugated, devalued and humiliated is hardly disputable. From the holocaust of enslavement to the genocide of colonial exploitation, Africa has been treated like a pawn in the chessboard of Europe. The issue is whether this fact and its recognition by Africans at home and abroad is sufficient to ground a Pan-African movement, in the absence of any other facts. Historically, this question, if posed at all, would be answered in the affirmative. Africans abroad have especially considered the plight of mother Africa as essentially tied to theirs and have always felt a need to rally to its cause. Du Bois states this point of view very clearly:

> As I face Africa I ask myself: what is it between us that constitutes a tie that I can feel better than I can explain? Africa is of course my fatherland. Yet neither my father nor father's father ever saw Africa or knew its meaning or cared overmuch for it. . . . But the physical bond is least and the badge of color relatively unimportant save as badge; the real essence of this kinship is its social heritage of slavery; the discrimination and insult; and this heritage binds together not simply the children of Africa, but extends through yellow Asia and into the South Seas. It is this unity that draws me to Africa.[14]

In recent times, however, the basis for this feeling has been questioned by scholars. Is there a common destiny shared by Africans at home and abroad? Indeed, is there even a commonality among Africans at home to warrant this consideration and this feeling? Du Bois, as we know, struggled very hard to come to grips with this question and his resolution, which affirms the claim that Africans at home and abroad share a common destiny, has been under attack in recent African scholarship.[15]

This claim is connected with one other which I also consider to be straightforward—that Africans should be free to govern themselves. It goes without saying that if the allegation of unjust subjugation, devaluation and humiliation is confirmed, then the right to freedom must be recognized and respected. There is hardly any argument about this, for the argument of the enslaver and colonizer regarding the inferiority of the enslaved and colonized amounts to no more than an attempt at self-justification. Of the three claims, then, the two most fundamental to Pan-Africanism are the second and the third. It is with regard to the explanation and defense of these claims that Du Bois' contribution takes on a unique character.

The claim that Africans at home and abroad share a common destiny and constitute a common unit is the variant of Pan-Africanism that sees itself as a concept and a movement looming larger than the geographical boundaries of Africa. This has two parts. First there is the perception of race as the basis of the African degradation and thus the most important basis for Pan-Africanism. Here, then, Pan-Africanism becomes Pan-Negroism. Du Bois has been identified as an exponent of this view. To a large extent, this is correct. However, it ought to be noted that race, as a foundation of Pan-Negroism, also has a dual meaning, and it is here that one has to be careful to identify the meaning that Du Bois used: is race physical or socio-cultural? It is, for instance, misleading to identify Du Bois as a "race-man" or to condemn him as someone who introduced race as a defining feature of Pan-Africanism. In any case, it is also important to note that Du Bois did not create the concept, and that he simply took over a concept that had been in use and sought to clarify it and reject the ways it had been used, especially regarding people of African descent.

The second part of this first claim is that the commonality of degradation, subjugation and humiliation is the basis for the Pan-African idea. In this case, then, it is not so much the unity of race as the unity of suffering. Here, Pan-Africanism means Pan-Humanism. Of course, the observation that Africans have been the most degraded humans in history may be made to justify the applicability of Pan-Africanism even to this apparently more universal idea; yet it remains true that once it is recognized that the emphasis is on a union of the humiliated and not one of blood, we are dealing a different idea. In this case, there will be no justification for limiting membership of the movement to people of African descent. The question to be addressed is whether this is the meaning that Du Bois attached to the concept.

The third meaning of Pan-Africanism is Pan-Continentalism. According to this, the geo-political features of Africa constitute the foundations of Pan-Africanism. Here the emphasis is on the unity of Africa in the face of colonial and neo-colonial exploitation. While this was not original to the idea, it clearly played an important role in its development, especially in the hands of African statesmen, whose concern was to adopt a united stance against colonialism and racism. It became an important aspect of the movement during the struggle for decolonization and in the years following flag independence. As we will see below, Kwame Nkrumah was in the forefront of this development. This was not designed to block out African descendants in the New World from African affairs. Rather, it was a method of rallying continental Africans of diverse origins and ideological persuasions to the task of total liberation and development of the continent.

From the foregoing, it is clear that Pan-Africanism does not have one clear meaning. Indeed, it has at least three:

1. Pan-Negroism—an idea that Africans at home and abroad share a common destiny in virtue of being a common race. And race here refers to either (a) physical traits or (b) socio-historical traits
2. Pan-Humanism—an idea that Pan-Africanism refers to the kinship of the dispossessed and the degraded and that this includes but goes beyond people of African descent.

3. Pan-Continentalism—a view that Pan-Africanism is limited to the idea and movement of African unity and restricted to the continent of Africa in its struggle for emancipation against colonial exploitation.

These three are, indeed, elements in the complex idea of Pan-Africanism, and each has played a significant role at one point or another in the evolution of the concept. Therefore, rather than eliminate all but one, it seems to me reasonable to take them all as significant strands in the development of the idea. My concern is to identify which of them is central to Du Bois's thought and action.

W. E. B. DU BOIS AND THE MEANING OF PAN-AFRICANISM: PAN-AFRICANISM AS PAN-NEGROISM

Du Bois's conception of Pan-Africanism shifts between identifying it by its foundation and rationale with race, and therefore as Pan-Negroism, and identifying it with a broader foundation of humanism, and therefore as Pan-Humanism. Doubtless, he was historically attracted to the Pan-African movement by his own experience of racial discrimination in the New World, as his various autobiographical writings confirm. It was this experience that directed his intellectual attention toward Africa and motivated him to learn more about the motherland concerning which he had little or no knowledge as a boy.

According to Du Bois, the Pan-African idea, as it developed in the New World, was to facilitate "the industrial and spiritual emancipation of the Negro people."[16] As seen above, the movement started as an organized reaction against perceived injustice against black people on the basis of their skin color. From this standpoint, Pan-Africanism was an anti-racist, pro-justice movement of ideas and emotions. If we look carefully at the content of the resolutions adopted at the end of the various conferences, as indicated above, it should also be clear that Du Bois's conception of Pan-Africanism was clearly Pan-Negroism, and that therefore Pan-Africanism was, for him, a racial solidarity of people of African descent at home and abroad.

In fact, however, there is a more substantial evidence for this claim. Writing in "The Conservation of Races" in 1897, Du Bois defended the concept of race as coherent and argued for the need to conserve the races. After surveying the history and significance of race distinctions, Du Bois noted that the Negro race may not as yet have "given to civilization the full spiritual message which they are capable of giving."[17] He then raised the question regarding how this message shall be delivered. His answer: "By the development of these race groups, not as individuals, but as races.... For the development of Negro genius, of Negro literature and art, of Negro spirit, only Negroes bound and

welded together, Negroes inspired by one vast ideal, can work out in its fullness the great message we have for humanity."[18] In short, according to this
view, Negroes have a mission as a group—wherever they are—to develop
their genius and give their full spiritual message to civilization. This is the
foundation of the Pan-African idea for Du Bois. It is, as can be seen, also a
Pan-Negro idea and this is why Du Bois could call on the people of Negro
blood in America to "take their just place in the van of Pan-Negroism" and to
realize that if they are to do this, "their destiny is not absorption by the white
Americans."[19] It is clear, then, that Du Bois's involvement with the Pan-
African movement stems from his understanding of the common destiny of
Africans at home and abroad and his conviction that Pan-Africanism as Pan-
Negroism is the conduit for the spiritual message that Negroes are capable of
giving. The question remains, though—what is the basis of this common
destiny? What is Du Bois's conception of the Negro? The answer, Du Bois
believes, is that the Negro constitutes a race. Ultimately, then, the race concept
plays a dominant role in Du Bois's conception of Pan-Africanism. Is he right?
To answer this important question, we need a clear account of Du Bois's
conception of race and of what led him to this conception.

Du Bois's definition of race and his conception of the importance of race in
human history are indicative of his acceptance of the intellectual and political
developments of his time. He did not create the race concept; he took it over
from common usage and made an effort to refine it and to define the role of
the Negro by reference to this refined definition. Thus in "The Conservation
of Races," he acknowledges the "scientific" criteria of race—such as color,
hair and cranial measurement—but finds them problematic and inadequate
for classificatory purposes because they are "most exasperatingly intermingled." Yet science arrives at a conclusion that "we have at least two, perhaps
three great families of human beings—the whites, Negroes and possibly the
yellow race"[20] (239). This seems to be a concession that science has no clear
criteria for race, and that physical differences between human beings do not
explain all the differences in their history. In other words, whereas race seems
to have no scientific foundation—no objective classificatory basis—scientists
still recognize certain groups as constituting races. Moreover, though certain
physical differences can be identified, the configurations do not explain the
use to which such classifications have been put historically.

Recognizing all this, one would expect Du Bois to abandon the concept of
race. It seems, however, that he recognizes some other route to an adequate
definition. Physical differences, he observes, "go but a short way toward
explaining the different roles which groups of men have played in Human
Progress" because as we have seen, they also go only a short way towards an
adequate classification of human beings into groups. Yet Du Bois believes that

there are differences—subtle, delicate and elusive, though they may be—which
have silently but definitely separated men into groups. While these subtle forces
have generally followed the natural cleavage of common blood, descent and physical peculiarities, they have at other times swept across and ignored these. At all
times, however, they have divided human beings into races, which, while they
perhaps transcend scientific definition nevertheless, are clearly defined to the eye of
the Historian and Sociologist.[21]

The question is what these subtle forces are and what accounts for the different routes they follow at different times. What it amounts to is that race is not
a scientific concept; it is rather a socio-historical concept. Du Bois' definition
clearly identifies it as such: "What then is a race? It is a vast family of human
beings, generally of common blood and language, always of common history,
tradition and impulses, who are both voluntarily and involuntarily striving
together for the accomplishment of certain more or less vividly conceived
ideals of life."[22] And in "The Concept of Race," Du Bois goes on to suggest,
"Race is a cultural, sometimes a historical fact. . . . [T]he black man is a
person who must ride 'Jim Crow' in Georgia."[23] This is after he has recognized the fact that a "scientific definition of race is impossible . . . [and] that
physical characteristics are not so inherited as to divide the world into
races. . . ."[24] If, then, Du Bois recognizes the impossibility of a scientific definition of race, why does he still believe that there are races? And why does he
use race as a basis for his Pan-Africanist idea?

The answer to the first question is provided by Du Bois himself. Apparently
for him, a scientific definition does not exhaust the set of available definitions
and has no privileged status. Recognizing the futility of adopting a scientific
definition, and unwilling to give up the concept of race, Du Bois opted for a
socio-historical definition. Race differences "have followed mainly physical
race lines," he observes. But he goes on to suggest that there are "deeper
differences" which physical distinctions cannot explain. These deeper differences, which include "spiritual and psychical difference," make for the "cohe-
siveness and continuity of the groups" and transcend physical distinctions.[25]

There appears to be a confusion here, and we should attempt a clarifica-
tion. On the same page of "The Conservation of Races," Du Bois moves from
"race" to "nation" as if he is using the terms interchangeably. Thus, he notes
that we "find upon the world's stage today eight distinctly differentiated races,
in the sense in which History tells the word must be used." And after identifying them by name, he raises a question in the following paragraph: "What is
the real distinction between these nations?" His answer is that physical differences play a great part, but not the whole part. Then, as if this apparent confusion is not enough, he goes on: "The forces that bind together the Teuton

nations are, then, first their race identity and common blood; second, and more important, a common history, common laws and religion, similar habits of thought and a conscious striving together for certain ideals of life."[26] Notice here that "race identity and common blood" is brought in as a defining feature of the Teutonic nations. But if "nation" is used interchangeably with "race"—as it appears Du Bois uses it here—then what we have is a circular definition of race in terms of race identity.

There must be a different reading! It seems that Du Bois's point is that nations are historically constituted by race groups; and nations have, historically, through their spiritual, psychical and mental characteristics, transcended the physical differences of race. Thus while physical race identity was a first basic feature of the Teutonic nation, this identity has been transcended by common history, habits of thought, laws and religion. The point is that growth in human groups does not allow for physical race distinctions to endure and therefore to serve as a valid basis for group classification. This is the point that Du Bois emphasizes when he observes, "The whole process which has brought about these race differentiations has been a growth, and the great characteristic of this growth has been the differentiation of spiritual and mental differences between great races of mankind and the integration of physical differences."[27] In other words, as growth occurs, physical differences between groups dissipate and may become trivial, while spiritual differences continue to be sharpened. The maximum physical differences occurred at a point in the history of the humanity when there was little intermingling of groups. This is Du Bois's historical perspective.

> As the families came together to form cities, the physical differences lessened, purity of blood was replaced by the requirement of domicile, and all who lived within the city bounds became gradually to be regarded as members of the group; i.e. there was a slight and slow breaking down of physical barriers. This, however, was accompanied by an increase of the spiritual and social differences between cities.[28]

This explains what Du Bois calls "the sociological and historical races of men" as opposed to the physical races. It is for the former that he seems to reserve the word "nation." For in this view, nations are constituted by race groups which are originally identified physically and later socio-historically and spiritually. Thus the English nation (originally identified by color, hair and physical proportions) now stands for "constitutional liberty" while the German nation stands for "science and philosophy." Physical differences are thereby transcended by spiritual differences as a result of the historical growth of human groups.

Though Du Bois does not totally accept the idea of a physical definition of race, he notes its influence and historical warrant while arguing for its transcendence, again on the basis of history. This is why Du Bois still believes that there are races even when he concedes the impossibility of a scientific definition. And this is why he appeals to race in his Pan-Africanism as Pan-Negroism, implying that whatever physical differences there are among peoples of African descent cannot approximate the sharpness of the physical differences between them and non-Africans; and the spiritual and psychical identitications among Africans are great and make up well for those apparent physical differences. While a hostile reading will see Du Bois as contradicting himself and not using the evidence available to him to reject the concept of race, a sympathetic reading may interpret him as offering a cultural definition of race; or, indeed, as offering culture as an alternative way to looking at race. Thus, Molefi Asante has observed, "What Du Bois intended, when one examines the perspective of his work, was a statement about culture, not about race."[29]

If he intended a statement about the concept of culture, then it is understandable why he would emphasize spiritual and psychical identities and why he would identify "nation" (a cultural idea) with race. Where others see physical race identity, Du Bois sees socio-cultural identity. If physical race is an impossible idea, socio-cultural identity is a real one, because physical integration does not eliminate social-cultural differentiation. Indeed, Du Bois's identification with Africa is a matter of feeling which was real: "I felt myself African by 'race' and by that token was African and an integral part of the group of dark Americans who were called Negroes."[30] And while he still traces his ancestral line to Africa and acknowledges the mark of his ancestors' heritage upon him in color and hair, he also recognizes that these "objective factors" are "only important as they stand for real and more subtle differences from other men."[31] In other words, the fact of physical difference becomes significant only as an indicator of socio-historical and cultural differences. Common physical characteristics do not have any normative significance except as they stand for some unique historical features. Common Negro ancestry, common blackness and common cephalic index stand for something in Du Bois's history; and in recognizing this fact, he identifies with those who share that history with him. This is why he insists that "the black man is a person who must ride 'Jim Crow' in Georgia."[32]

PAN-AFRICANISM AS PAN-HUMANISM:
THE SOCIAL HERITAGE OF SUFFERING

There are then two parts to Du Bois's account of race: the commonality of ancestry and the commonality of historical experience. While he tries to do away with the former by bringing up the difficulties with scientific definition, he cannot really expunge it. For it still identifies the group which shares the common historical experience. The mark of the ancestors' heritage in color and hair is important because it is the foundation of the common experience to which people who share the heritage are exposed. It is this common experience, however, that underscores the distinctiveness of the group—it is the social heritage of suffering that identifies those who share this common ancestry as a group. Du Bois puts it clearly and he deserves to be quoted at length:

> But one thing is sure and that is the fact that since the fifteenth century these ancestors of mine and their other descendants have had a common history; have suffered a common disaster and have one long memory. The actual ties of heritage between the individuals of this group vary with the ancestors that they have in common and many others: Europeans and Semites, perhaps Mongolians, certainly American Indians. But the physical bond is least and the badge of color relatively unimportant save as a badge; the real essence of this kinship is its social heritage of slavery; the discrimination and insult; and this heritage binds together not simply the children of Africa, but extends through yellow Asia and into the South Seas. It is this unity that draws me to Africa."[33]

The Pan-African idea is inspired, then, by this social heritage of suffering. It is the solidarity of the oppressed, the kinship of the dispossessed. The significance of race does not lie in the physical identity of its members; it is rather a matter of sociology and history. Du Bois's point is simply that the White world created the problem of race by the history of its dealings with other people, and by its assumption of its superiority over others and its denial of their humanity. Pan-Africanism is the clarion call of one portion of this dispossessed humanity to rise up to the challenge and demonstrate the wealth of its heritage and its ability to contribute to the "civilization of the universal," in Leopold Senghor's elegant phrase. Thus, even when Du Bois insists that the chief fact of his life has been Race, he makes it clear that it is not "scientific race" (the possibility of which he denies) but its "spiritual provincialism" according to which it is believed that there are congenital differences among men which condition their individual destinies.

Racists probably know that no scientific definition of race is possible; that does not prevent them from engaging in racial discrimination anyway. For Du Bois, it is the reality of the race problem—the problem of the color line— that inspires him to embrace the race concept and to mobilize people of African descent to unite to uplift the motherland. After all, the mark of its heritage is on them and the burden of its denial they cannot escape. The impossibility of a scientific definition does not lighten the burden:

[I]t is easy to see that scientific definition of race is impossible; it is easy to prove
that physical characteristics are not so inherited as to make it possible to divide the
world into races; that ability is the monopoly of no known aristocracy; that the
possibilities of human development cannot be circumscribed by color, nationality,
or any conceivable definition of race; all this has nothing to do with the plain fact
that throughout the world today organized groups of men by monopoly of
economic and physical power, legal enactment and intellectual training are limiting
with determination and unflagging zeal the development of other groups, and that
the concentration particularly of economic power today puts the majority of
mankind into slavery to the rest.[34]

The point here is that even when the race problem is "rationalized in every
way"—that poverty is cause of race prejudice, ignorance is the cause of
poverty etc.—we still must admit the fact of a white world which dominates
human culture and subordinates the colored races. To deny the reality of race
does not remove the fact of race prejudice.

Two issues must now be raised. First, in Du Bois's socio-historical conception of race, it appears that the fact of the social heritage of indignity,
contempt and violence draws together not only people of African descent but
also people of yellow Asia and others who have suffered similar fates. How
then can this concept of race be a foundation for a Pan-African solidarity?
Second, is this heritage of indignity, contempt and violence commonly and
equally shared by all peoples of African descent to warrant its being a valid
basis for a Pan-African solidarity? These are two of the issues raised by
Kwame Anthony Appiah against Du Bois' Pan-Africanism.[35]

On the first issue, Du Bois seems to have anticipated the objection. In "The
Concept of Race," he refers us to "the fact of a white world dominating
human culture and working for the continued domination of the colored
races." And when Du Bois talks of the problem of the twentieth century as the
problem of the color line, he explains it as the problem of the relations
between lighter and darker races. In short, for him, the significance of race
distinction is that it divides people on the basis of their skin color. The lighter
race assumes superiority and dominance over the darker race. What is
required is for the darker race to get together to give their complete message to
the world. However, they are to do this as a group, not as individuals, because
they have been brutalized as a group. Not only this, the individual member of
the darker race is seen and usually judged as a member of his race and not as
an individual. The meaning of this then is that the liberation of the individual
member of the group is tied up with the liberation of the race: "For the development of Negro genius, of Negro literature and art, of Negro spirit, only
Negroes bound and welded together, Negroes inspired by one vast ideal, can

work out in its fullness the great message we have for humanity."[36] It seems then that, for Du Bois, even when a common heritage of insult and suffering is acknowledged as joining people of African descent with people of "yellow Asia," the differences in the "ideals of life" for which these peoples struggled and the differences in their motivations must be a basis for smaller groupings. Therefore, this common heritage of insult plus the specific genius and spirit of the Negro must be a basis for Pan-Africanism. Du Bois does not fully explain the features of this specific genius, but he gives us some hint. It lies in the cultural realities of the African milieu, realities which resist the devaluation of the white world. Though common heritage of insult is shared by black Africans and yellow Asians, the specific genius of the African cultural heritage is different enough to ground a Pan-African solidarity as a basis for giving the full message of the Negro race. It is the recognition of these realities that informed Du Bois's Pan-Africanism.

The second issue is whether there is any experience of indignity, contempt and violence shared by Africans on the continent and those in the African diaspora on which Pan-African solidarity might be grounded. Appiah has argued that the experiences are not the same; that the insult of race discrimination in the streets of New York or Chicago cannot quite compare with the experience of African continental elites in the hands of white racists.[37] It is true that African elites who pop in and out of New York or London cannot have the same experience as African Americans. But it is also true that these continental Africans have the awareness that they would be treated the same way for the same reasons were they to find themselves in Europe or the U.S. In any case, they know quite well that enslavement, colonial exploitation and imperial domination derive from the same mind-set that fosters race prejudice. The continental African elite raises the same questions to himself as the diaspora African raises: "Why should I be treated in this way?" While the experience cannot be identical, it is certainly similar, and so can be, and indeed has been an effective basis for grounding the African agenda—first as a Pan-Negro movement, and later as a Pan-Continental movement. The move from Pan-Negroism to Pan-Continentalism does not indicate a weakening of the appeal of common Negritude.[38] It is not a severance of the ties that bind; rather it is the shift of agenda from the struggle against colonial exploitation to the post-colonial struggle for unity and development. The first three Pan-African congresses focused on the political liberation of the continent. Subsequent ones, led by African leaders, focused on development, unity and the elimination of racism from Africa. They all derived their rationale from the same ground: the social heritage of insult in slavery and colonial exploitation. Du Bois's Pan-Africanism, based on his understanding of the agony of African's experience as a racial group, struggling under the burden of a social heritage of prejudice, insult and humiliation, was therefore a Pan-Negro movement.

But it was also a Pan-Humanist movement. The fact that it was derived from the experience of a people identified as a "race" does not preclude the active involvement of others. Indeed, as the socio-cultural definition of race which we have attributed to Du Bois makes clear, people who share this social heritage of indignity, contempt and violence cut across racial boundaries. In any case, those who do not share that heritage, but are moved by the undeserved fate of those who do, could belong. The movement for the abolition of the holocaust of enslavement was a coalition of forces. The Pan-African movement also included people from other racial groups, though, as the saying goes, only the wearer knows best where the shoes pinch. Pan-Africanism as Pan-Humanism appeals to the sensibilities of all groups who know what it means to experience indignity, contempt and injustice. It emphasizes the significance of the common experience of subjugation and identifies those who suffer as a family. It capitalizes on the social kinship of humiliation to appeal to the sentiment of the marginalized and to their sympathizers, who included notable European politicians like H. G. Wells, Harold Laski, Lord Olivier and Ramsay MacDonald.[39]

PAN-AFRICANISM AS PAN-CONTINENTALISM:
KWAME NKRUMAH AND THE STRUGGLE FOR AFRICAN UNITY

Though Du Bois was not fully involved in the Pan-African movement on the continent, there is reason to believe that he worked actively towards it and that it was his ultimate objective to see the seed of the movement germinate on the continent. In a 1919 article, he observed, "It is the question of the reapportionment of this vast number of human beings (in Africa) which has started the Pan-African movement."[40] The vision of Du Bois inspired the subsequent activities of Kwame Nkrumah who, together with George Padmore, organized the Manchester Pan-African Congress of 1945. It was the sixth in the series and the one which drew the most participants from the continent. The congress demanded "for Black Africa, autonomy and independence, so far, and no further than it is possible in this one world for groups and peoples to rule themselves subject to inevitable world unity and freedom."[41] Expressing their determination to be free, they resolved that "if the Western world is still determined to rule mankind by force, then Africans, as a last resort, may have to appeal to force in the effort to achieve freedom, even if force destroys them and the world."[42]

On the occasion of Ghana's independence in 1957, Du Bois sent a message of solidarity to Kwame Nkrumah, who had successfully led the country's struggle for independence. The message was to encourage Nkrumah to work for the unity and development of Africa. It was to have a lasting impact on Nkrumah and it focused the Pan-African idea on the continent. In the message, Du Bois urged that

> Ghana must ... be the representative of Africa, and not only that, but of Black Africa below the Sahara desert. As such, her first duty should be to come into close acquaintanceship and cooperation with her fellow areas of British West Africa and Liberia with the great areas of black folk in French West and Equatorial Africa, with the Sudan, Ethiopia and Somaliland ... and with all other parts of Africa.[43]

More significantly, Du Bois pleaded, "All the former barriers of language, culture, religion and political control should bow before the essential unity of race and descent, the common suffering of slavery and the slave trade and the modern color bar."[44] He challenged Ghana to ignore "the old sources of division and lack of knowledge of and sympathy for each other" and to "lead a movement of black men for Pan-Africanism, including periodic conferences and personal contacts of black men from the Sahara to the Indian ocean."[45] Du Bois's wish was that the

> consequent Pan-Africa, working together through its independent units, should seek to develop a new African economy and cultural center standing between Europe and Asia, taking from and contributing to both. It should stress peace and join no military alliance and refuse to fight for settling European quarrels. It should avoid subjection to and ownership by foreign capitalists who seek to get rich on African labor and raw materials and should try to build a socialism founded on old African communal life.[46]

Finally, Du Bois urged Nkrumah to use all his power "to put a Pan-Africa along these lines into working order at the earliest possible date," and enjoined him to

> seek to save the great cultural past of the Ashanti and Fanti peoples, not by inner division but by outer cultural and economic expansion toward the outmost bounds of the great African peoples, so that they may be free to live, grow and expand; and to teach mankind what non-violence and courtesy, literature and art, music and dancing can do for this greedy, selfish and war-stricken world.[47]

Those were the admonitions of the Grand Old Man of Pan-Africanism to the youthful and energetic Nkrumah. There is reason to believe that the youth took the words of the old man seriously, going with the tradition of African

social life. Nkrumah insisted that the independence of Ghana would be mean-
ingless unless it was tied to the independence of the whole of Africa. He used
the resources of Ghana to strengthen the liberation movements, and he spear-
headed the movement for unity. Even when it was considered premature for
Africa to have a continental political union, Nkrumah pressed for a United
States of Africa. He gave loans to African states as they became independent.
He moved with Sekou Touré of Guinea to form the Ghana-Guinea union in
1958 and saw it as a basis for a continental union. Two years later, Mali
joined them to form the Union of African States, which was intended to be a
step to the United States of Africa.[48] Despite the many odds against this move-
ment, Nkrumah's initiatives led to the formation of the Organization of
African Unity (OAU) in 1963. And though this was short of his vision for a
United States of Africa, it was the culmination of his unswerving efforts.

The idea of African unity became something of an article of faith for
Nkrumah, fired by Du Bois's inspiration and vision. Like Du Bois, he recognizes the ideological roots of division: "There are those who maintain that
Africa cannot unite because we lack the three ingredients for unity, a common
race, culture and language."[49] He acknowledges the historical fact of division,
aggravated by the imposition of arbitrary boundaries. "Yet in spite of this," he
insists

> I am convinced that the forces making for unity far outweigh those which divide
> us. In meeting fellow Africans from all parts of the continent I am constantly
> impressed by how much we have in common. It is not just our colonial past, or the
> fact that we have aims in common, it is something which goes far deeper. I can best
> describe it as a sense of oneness in that we are Africans.[50]

But what could be responsible for this sense of oneness despite the acknowledgement of differences in race, culture and language? Nkrumah does not
address this question. But what could it be if culture, race and language are
discounted along with the common experience of colonialism? What is left
seems to be territorial unity, but this cannot be what Nkrumah regards as a
deep-seated sense of unity. For it is from this deep-seated unity that Pan-
Africanism and African Personality emerge. It does not appear that oneness of
territory alone is the basis for the development of African Personality, which is
also believed to be shared by people of color in the New World. When the
commonality of colonial experience is discounted along with common aims
for the future as a basis for this sense of unity, then it is hard to see what could
ground it. It becomes a feeling that has no explanation. Obviously, there are
problems with this approach.

Nkrumah argues for the economic and political integration of Africa on the ground of its potential benefits to all. He criticizes those who think only of their narrow political interests which make them resist the idea of political unity. He derides those states of Africa which seek to align with European associations in the "mistaken belief that they will profit sufficiently to prosper their economies."[51] He argues that it is naive to suppose that the European Common Market "should consciously promote industrialization in the raw-material-producing countries of Africa."[52] President Leopold Senghor of Senegal, one of Nkrumah's targets, had argued that the English-speaking countries of Africa should join the European Common Market so they might be able to harmonize their technical and economic cooperation between Africans. But Nkrumah rejects this as "a special plea for collective colonialism of a new order," since the Common Market is a European organization promoted to further European interests. Instead, he argues for "an African Common Market, devoted uniquely to African interests" which "would more efficaciously promote the true requirements of the African states."[53]

Nkrumah insists that the idea of an African union is not sentimental, but an indispensable "precondition for the speediest and fullest development, not only of the totality of the continent but of the individual countries linked together in the union."[54] This is the only weapon against continued political and economic colonization. Balkanization is the major instrument of neo-colonialism, which is Africa's greatest enemy, and the only weapon against it is political and economic integration. Nkrumah's Pan-Africanism is a continuation of Du Bois's vision for the continent. Thus he insists that "in all relations with the world overseas, the key consideration must be not merely the superficial or even intrinsic advantage of such relationships for the given African country but the obligation to the African continent as a whole."[55] Pan-Africa and not EurAfrica, he argues, should be the watchword of African leaders and the guide to their policies. Finally, for Nkrumah, a Union of African States "will raise the dignity of Africa" and "will make possible the full expression of the African personality."[56]

It should be noticed that Nkrumah's vision of a Union of African States goes beyond Du Bois's prescription. While Du Bois urged him to work through the independent units to fashion out a new African economy and cultural center, Nkrumah struggled for a United States of Africa which would be economically integrated and in which the idea of independent units would be superseded. There are, no doubt, advantages to be derived from such a unity; the question is its feasibility. As Nkrumah himself recognized, the colonial experience intensified old divisions and created new ones. That aspect of Africa's history cannot be wished away, and it continues to haunt the continent. This is why, more than thirty years after the wind of independence first blew across most of Africa, the vestige of colonialism is still notoriously visible, and at the level of individual states, the forces of separation continue to operate to the embarrassment of the agents of unity.

Nkrumah argues for strong unitary governments and considers the idea of regional federations dangerous because of the possible development of regional loyalties and of consequent resistance to African unity. He insists that the forces that have separated Africa must be eradicated and that "the best means of doing so is to begin to create a larger and all-embracing loyalty which will hold Africa together as a united people with one government and one destiny."[57] Sovereignty of individual states may be lost, but Nkrumah argues, in a Rousseauian idiom, that as long as the loss is equal and legal equality is protected "under a constitution to which all have laid their hands," this should not be of concern to such states.[58] Furthermore, "We do not intend a relationship of unequal partners. We envisage the African Union as a free merging together of people with a common history and a common destiny."[59] And he thinks that "it is only when full political unity has been achieved that we will be able to declare the triumphant end of the Pan-African struggle and the African liberation movement."[60] From which it follows that, since the political unity envisaged by Nkrumah has not been fully realized, we cannot yet proclaim the end of the Pan-African struggle.

In any case, political unity is not an end in itself, and it is clear that Nkrumah did not see it as such. Unity is a means to the total liberation of the productive forces of a continent that has been brutalized. Therefore, even if political unity is fully achieved, there must still be the struggle for the full development and utilization of all productive forces. And now that political unity is still far from being achieved, and economic development is fast becoming an illusion, the Pan-African struggle is very much alive. Perhaps Nkrumah aimed too high; perhaps his idea of a continental government was overly ambitious for a continent that hardly experienced the kind of political unity that could ground such a government even before the era of colonial exploitation. He probably should have settled for a progressive integration of regional economies, since the benefits for individual states could be more easily quantified and recognized by the states. The idea of a continental government was perceived as a threat to the sovereignty of the newly independent states, whose leaders were not prepared to relinquish the power and privileges that they had acquired in the new scheme of things. Yet Nkrumah's position must be appreciated. He saw, as Du Bois before him, that there is strength in unity and that Africa has adequate resources to take care of its own if those resources can be pulled together. He understood well the mechanics of neo-colonial exploitation; he saw independent states of Africa entering into suicidal alliances with their erstwhile colonial rulers, and he saw the danger in that trend. He saw beyond the narrow confines of statism and made an effort to correct the trend by prescribing an African unity that transcends states.

I have been concerned with Nkrumah's vision as a Pan-Africanist in the tradition of Du Bois. I do not think there is any basis for denying this. However, it is true that Nkrumah, like every statesman, had his problems. At his graveside, Colonel Acheampong observed that "like all of us, Dr. Nkrumah had his shortcomings. Perhaps the problem of Africa and the world loomed so large in his horizon that he overlooked certain serious difficulties and irregularities at home."[61] To some, this may be an understatement, in view of the serious allegations of dictatorial abuses of power in Nkrumah's Ghana, including the establishment of the notorious Preventive Detention Act which silenced opposition members.[62] Of course, Nkrumah also had his own defenders.[63] This only goes to confirm the age-old truth that perfection is not a human trait. The mistakes he made at home should certainly be put at his doorstep, and if, as some have argued, Nkrumah did not do anything that the Constitution did not allow, it must be remembered that a Constitution that validates authoritarianism in the name of freedom and development undermines the achievement of both. However, without underplaying the seriousness of the mistakes he made as a statesman on the domestic arena, it appears to me that Nkrumah's contributions to the development of an African consciousness and to the sense of accomplishment by Africans throughout the world should earn him the title of the Crown Prince of Pan-Africanism. For, as Basil Davidson has observed, "as Nkrumah's Ghana led the way for black men and women to speak as equals in the councils of the world, and the world began to listen as they spoke, the dignity of Africans began to have a new and modern meaning."[64]

CONCLUSION

That the African world is greatly indebted to the intellectual output and political struggles of W. E. B. Du Bois is, no doubt, an understatement. His analysis and understanding of the struggle that Africa must engage in, and his vision of the future that it must embrace, remain valid even today. Du Bois's message to Nkrumah on the occasion of Ghana's independence remains as powerful and relevant today as it was thirty-eight years ago. Unfortunately, Du Bois's hopes are yet to be totally fulfilled, and victory is yet to be fully assured in the struggle that he so ably initiated and to which he committed his mature life. African leaders have yet to absorb the significance of his message because it appears that they have taken flag independence as genuine independence, and the economic and political development of Africa now appears to be a shattered dream. On the bright side, however, there is increasing cooperation between continental Africans and the African diaspora. Indeed, the task of

"erasing from literature the lines of distortions about black folk," which
Du Bois assigned to Nkrumah, has been effectively taken up by African scholars in the diaspora, and this has succeeded in heightening the consciousness of
people of African descent concerning their identity.[65] Of course, this is just one
aspect of the problem that confronts contemporary Africa. Economic development and political stability are equally pressing problems. And in the context
of political struggle, it is also heartening to witness the involvement of African
Americans in the efforts to terminate the indignity of apartheid in South
Africa. There is hardly any doubt that, without the economic sanctions
imposed by the United States, largely as a result of the effective campaign
mounted by the Congressional Black Caucus and its allies, it would have been
more difficult to achieve any measure of success in the struggle for a democratic South Africa. In all this, it seems legitimate to say that the dream of Dr.
W. E. B. Du Bois is being realized. But much remains to be achieved, especially
in the area of effective political leadership on the continent. The present
economic and political predicament of Africa is due to a combination of internal and external factors. But it seems to me that, in the spirit of his message to
Nkrumah, Du Bois would, even today, place the bulk of the responsibility for
the full realization of the Pan-African idea on the political class on the continent. I think he would be right.

Notes

1. P. O. Esedebe, *Pan-Africanism: The Idea and Movement, 1776–1963* (Washington,
    D.C.: Howard University Press, 1982), 8. For further critical studies on Pan
    Africanism, the following are useful sources: George Padmore, *Pan-Africanism or
    Communism* (New York: Doubleday, 1971); Adekunle Ajala, *Pan-Africanism:
    Evolution, Progress and Prospects*, (New York: St. Martin's Press, 1974); Colin
    Legun, *Pan-Africanism: A Short Political Guide* (Westport, Conn.: Greenwood Press,
    1962); W. Ofuatey-Kodjoe, ed., *Pan-Africanism: New Directions in Strategy*
    (Lanham: University Press of America, 1986).

2. Esedebe, *New Directions*, 11.

3. Ajala, *Evolution, Progress and Prospects*, 5.

4. Padmore, *Pan-Africanism or Communism*, 70.

5. Padmore, *Pan-Africanism or Communism*, 67.

6. Mojola Agbebi, *Inaugural Sermon Delivered at the Celebration of the First
    Anniversary of the "African Church,"* African Church Reports of Proceedings of the
    African Church for Lagos and Yoruba Land 1901–1908 (Liverpool: The African
    Church, 1910); Edward W. Blyden, *African Life and Customs* (London: African
    Publication Society, 1908).

7. See Esedebe, *Pan-Africanism: The Idea and the Movement, 1776–1963*, ch. 2.

8. Du Bois, "Pan-Africanism and Radical Philosophy," *Crisis*, (November 1933), 247.

9. Basil Davidson, *The African Slave Trade: Pre-colonial History, 1450–1850* (Boston:
    Little, Brown, 1961), 19.

10. Obafemi Awolowo, *The Problems of Africa: The Need for Ideological Reappraisal* (London and Basingstoke: Macmillan, 1977), 27.

11. A complete list of those who belong to this group will be difficult to provide. However, it must include those already mentioned above and some others: Mojola Agbebi, Edward W. Blyden, James Africanus Horton, Duse Mohammed, Paul Cuffee, Peter Williams, Fredrick Douglass, Olaudah Equiano, John Chilembwe, Simon Kinbangu, James Johnson, Alexander Crummell, Booker T. Washington, Casely Hayford, Henry Sylvester-Williams, Marcus Garvey, W. E. B. Du Bois, Kwame Nkrumah, Obafemi Awolowo, Nnamdi Azikwe, Julius Nyerere, Leopold Sedar Senghor and Sekou Touré.

12. See Ajala, *Evolution, Progress, and Prospects,* 4; P. O. Esedebe, *Idea and Movement,* 49.

13. See Kwame Nkrumah, *Africa Must Unite* (New York: International Publishers, 1970).

14. W. E. B. Du Bois, *Dusk of Dawn: An Essay Toward an Autobiography of a Race Concept* (New York: Schocken Books, 1968).

15. See Kwame Anthony Appiah's *In My Father's House: Africa in the Philosophy of Culture* (New York: Oxford, 1992).

16. Du Bois, "Pan-Africanism and Radical Philosophy," *Crisis,* (November 1933): 247.

17. W. E. B. Du Bois, "The Conservation of Races," in W. E. B. Du Bois, *On Sociology and the Black Community,* ed. Dan S. Green and Edwin D. Driver (Chicago and London: University of Chicago Press, 1978), 243.

18. Du Bois, "The Conservation of Races," 243.

19. Du Bois, "The Conservation of Races," 243.

20. Du Bois, "The Conservation of Races," 239.

21. Du Bois, "The Conservation of Races," 240.

22. Du Bois, "The Conservation of Races," 240.

23. Du Bois, "The Concept of Race," in *Dusk of Dawn,* 153.

24. Du Bois, "The Conservation of Races," 137.

25. Du Bois, "The Conservation of Races," 241.

26. Du Bois, "The Conservation of Races," 242.

27. Du Bois, "The Conservation of Races," 242.

28. Du Bois, "The Conservation of Races," 242.

29. Molefi K. Asante, *The Afrocentric Idea* (Philadelphia: Temple University Press, 1987), 122.

30. Du Bois, "The Concept of Race," 115.

31. Du Bois, "The Concept of Race," 117.

32. Du Bois, "The Concept of Race," 153.

33. Du Bois, "The Concept of Race," 117.

34. Du Bois, "The Concept of Race," 137–38.

35. See Appiah, *In My Father's House,* ch. 2

36. Du Bois, "The Conservation of Races," 130, 243.

37. See Appiah, *In My Father's House,* 6.

38. Negritude is the doctrine popularized by Leopold Sedar Senghor, former President of Senegal and a great poet and scholar. For him, Negritude is the affirmation of the distinctiveness of African cultural values and the confirmation of the African being in reaction to the European denigration of African civilization. See Leopold Senghor, "The Spirit of Civilization or the Laws of African Negro Culture," *Présence Africaine,* nos. 8–10 (June–Dec. 1956); 51–64; "Negritude: A Humanism of the Twentieth Century," *The African Reader: Independent Africa,* ed. Cartey and Kilson,

(New York: Random House 179–99). See also Segun Gbadedgesin, "Negritude and Its Contribution to the Civilization of the Universal: Leopold Senghor and the Question of Ultimate Reality and Meaning" *Ultimate Reality and Meaning: Interdisciplinary Studies in the Philosophy of Understanding* 14, no. 1 (1991): 30–45.

39. Colin Legum, *Pan-Africanism: A Short Political Guide* (Westport, Conn: Greenwood Press, 1962), 29.

40. *Crisis*, 17 (1919), reprinted in W. E. B. Du Bois, *An ABC of Color*, (New York: International Publishers, 1963), 102.

41. Legum, *A Short Political Guide*, 137.

42. Legum, *A Short Political Guide*, 137.

43. W. E. B. Du Bois, *The World and Africa* (New York: International Publishers, 1981), 295–96.

44. Du Bois, *The World and Africa*, 296.

45. Du Bois, *The World and Africa*, 296.

46. Du Bois, *The World and Africa*, 296.

47. Du Bois, *The World and Africa*, 297.

48. Nkrumah, *Africa Must Unite*, 142.

49. Nkrumah, *Africa Must Unite*, 142.

50. Nkrumah, *Africa Must Unite*, 132.

51. Nkrumah, *Africa Must Unite*, 159.

52. Nkrumah, *Africa Must Unite*, 159.

53. Nkrumah, *Africa Must Unite*, 162.

54. Nkrumah, *Africa Must Unite*, 163–64.

55. Nkrumah, *Africa Must Unite*, 185.

56. Nkrumah, *Africa Must Unite*, 193.

57. Nkrumah, *Africa Must Unite*, 215.

58. Nkrumah, *Africa Must Unite*, 148.

59. Nkrumah, *Africa Must Unite*, 188.

60. Nkrumah, *Africa Must Unite*, 140.

61. See Basil Davison, *Black Star: A View of the Life and Times of Kwame Nkrumah* (New York: Praeger Publishers, 1974), 206.

62. See Peter Omari, *Kwame Nkrumah: The Anatomy of a Dictatorship* (New York: Africana Publishing Co., 1970).

63. Omari, *The Anatomy of a Dictatorship*, 209–10.

64. Omari, *The Anatomy of a Dictatorship*, 158–59.

65. See, in this regard, the following: Molefi Kete Asante, *Afrocentricity: The Theory of Social Change* (Buffalo: Amulefi, 1980); Molefi Asante and Kariamu Asante, *African Culture: The Rhythms of Unity* (Trenton: African World Press, 1990); Mulefi Kefe Asante, *Kemet, Afrocentricity and Knowledge* (Trenton: African World Press, 1990); Martin Bernal, *Black Athena* (Trenton: Rutgers University Press, 1990); Maulana Karenga, *Introduction to Black Studies*, (Inglewood, Cal.: Kawaida, 1982).

Culture, Civilization, and Decline of the West

The Afrocentrism of W. E. B. Du Bois

Wilson J. Moses

There is a passage in *The Souls of Black Folk* that has been quoted with stupe-fying frequency, in which W. E. B. Du Bois confesses to struggling with double consciousness, the conflicts of being "an American, a Negro; two souls, two thoughts, two unreconciled strivings; two warring ideals in one dark body."[1] This was almost certainly an instance of rhetorical oversimplification, because, like all persons of intellectual depth, the Doctor experienced numerous conflicts within his complex identity. Much additional turmoil, equally evident, and at least equally as important, stormed constantly within his soul. There was a warfare between his loyalties as social democrat and racial romantic, another battle between his impulses as traditionalist and iconoclast. There was a tension between his austerity and his enthusiasm, another between his elitism and his folkishness, and yet another between his blatant Prussianism and his latent Bohemianism.

Lerone Bennett accurately observed Du Bois's liberal strain by focusing on his noted role as a founder and officer of the National Association for the Advancement of Colored People (NAACP).[2] And Bennett correctly appreciated Du Bois's importance as editor of the NAACP journal, *Crisis*, where he championed racial integration and ethnic tolerance. On the other hand, Charles T. Davis was equally correct when he observed the less regarded counter-tendencies towards black nationalism and romantic racialism, so evident in Du Bois's poetry and fiction.[3] As a Pan-Africanist, Du Bois had more in common with Marcus Garvey than he cared to admit. Like Garvey, he was a Pan-African chauvinist with a penchant for the theatrical, and, like Garvey, he was faced with the problem of controlling his authoritarian emotions in observance of egalitarian niceties and democratic protocols.

Du Bois was a trained social scientist, with a Ph. D. from Harvard, and two years of advanced studies at the University of Berlin, but he also displayed excellent polemical gifts and the skills of a poet. He wrote with convincing sincerity on the "midnight beauty" that he saw in the faces of peasants in rural Tennessee, and he wrote with conviction on the color and the fantasy that he discovered in the African American consciousness. His rhapsodies on black mass culture were always more sympathetic, however, when they focused on small farmers in the South, than when directed at the behavior of the urban proletariat. In his youth, he worked as a country school teacher in Tennessee, and years later he wrote:

> I bent with tears and pitying hands
> Above those dusky star-eyed children,
> Crinkly haired, with sweet-sad baby voices
> Pleading low for light and love and living
> And I crooned:
> Little children weeping there,
> God shall find thy faces fair;
> Guerdon for thy deep distress,
> He shall send His tenderness.[4]

But Du Bois's tenderness was often hidden behind the dark veil of a stern, partriarchal formalism that manifested itself in his earliest writings. Dogmatic, prickly, fastidious, and impatient, Du Bois sought to impose universal discipline on black Americans in order to lead them into an era of political and economic power. "Bismarck was my hero," he admitted in his autobiography, remembering how he had chosen the German chancellor as the subject of his Fisk University commencement oration in 1888. "He had made a nation out of a mass of bickering peoples. He had dominated the whole development with his strength until he crowned an emperor at Versailles." Du Bois's fascination with the strong man, the political or military leader who could bend nations to his will and force a squabbling *Pöbel* into a national entity, was to be a recurrent theme in his work. Thus, one witnesses his youthful homage to the "unbending righteousness" of Alexander Crummell, and his admiration in later years for Joseph Stalin, the dictator, and for Kwame Nkrumah, the Leninist Tsar.[5]

In 1897, at the age of twenty-nine, Du Bois appeared before the American Negro Academy to deliver a paper "On the Conservation of Races." He insisted that the individual must be subordinated to the race, and that the African race must work as one union of "200,000,000 black hearts beating in one glad song of jubilee." He called on black Americans "to take their just place in the van of Pan-Negroism," and embrace a collectivist racial ideal, rather than "the individualistic philosophy of the Declaration of Independence and the laissez faire philosophy of Adam Smith." The goal of racial leadership was to be realized within an American Negro Academy, a group of "unselfish men and pure and noble women," who would be "firm in leadership."[6]

In another early work, *The Negro Church* (1903), Du Bois had more to say about leadership and authority, when he descanted on the power of religion embodied in the African priest or medicine man. Unfortunately, the power of the priest had never fully realized its potential in Africa, and that was a partial explanation for the failure of the Negro race to deliver its full message to the world. Africa had never been able to fashion an enduring political authority. This failure had led to questions about the Africans' capacity for self-government and made them vulnerable to outside domination through colonialization and the slave trade. "The central fact of African life [was] its failure to integrate—to unite and systematize itself in some conquering whole which should dominate the wayward parts." The "central problem of civilization" was embodied in this need for conquest and domination, "and some consolidation of power in religion."[7]

The Africans who were transported into the New World were sometimes Muslims, sometimes Christians, but were, for the most part, tied to the traditional religions of their respective ancestral clans. Some of the transported Africans were priests, Du Bois posited, and along with them "a degraded form of African religion and witchcraft appeared." The Negro church in the United States represented the survival, however faint, of the "vast power of the priest." It therefore seemed legitimate to assert that the Negro chuch in America was essentially an African institution. The Obeah sorcery of the West Indies was a survival of an ancient African religion that was perhaps traceable even to Egypt.[8] He proclaimed that the religious expression of the black peasants of the South represented "the sole surviving social institution of the African fatherland," and it was from this fact that it derived its "extraordinary growth and vitality."

If Du Bois was influenced by Alexander Crummell and the American Negro Academy to stress the idea of a civilizing mission to be carried out by a strong-minded elite, he was equally attracted by a more Germanic conception of *Kultur,* which implied the idea of a folk spirit rising up out of the souls of the masses. Influenced by the nationalist traditions in German scholarship that had dominated lectures while he was at the University of Berlin, Du Bois began to adapt the concept of *Volksgeist* (folk soul or people's spirit) to the black American and the Pan-African condition. Like Johann Gottfried von Herder, Du Bois was attached to a conception of the people as a mystical or metaphysical entity, a communal consciousness that would manifest itself in the form of folk art, folk tales, myths and legends.[9]

The title of his best known series of essays, *The Souls of Black Folk*, could be loosely translated as *Der Schwarze Volksgeist*. In this work Du Bois looked to the roots of black culture as preserved in the rural South as the source of that power that he hoped would eventually transform the world. The African American people were portrayed as the "sole repository of simple faith and virtue in a dusty desert of dollars."

But, as always, Du Bois found himself caught up in an internal dialectic, uncomfortable with the idea of elite "civilization" while calling for a talented tenth; emotionally uncomfortable with popular "culture," and yet intellectly committed to the idea of *Volksgeist*. Therefore he made no systematic attempt to distinguish between the concepts of culture and civilization in his essay "What is Civilization? Africa's Answer."[10] Some scholars were making this distinction—notably Robert E. Park and Oswald Spengler. Both had used "culture" to denote the sacred intimacy of vigorous local ethnic groups, and "civilization" to denote the secular impersonal life of disjointed cosmopolitan societies.[11] In this essay, however, Du Bois used the terms interchangeably. His search for a core set of African values was in the tradition of Willhelm and Jakob Grimm, who attempted to valorize a core ethnic personality and mythology, but wedded this adulation of racial singularities to a curious spirit of cosmopolitanism.[12]

Du Bois identified three distinctively black currents running through world civilization, to the enduring benefit of all humanity. These three things, "the essential elements of African culture," were "Beginnings; the village unit; and Art in sculpture and in music." Within the tradition of racial vindicationism, it had always been important to demonstrate that black Africans had made a special contribution to the general history of mankind. Du Bois was still cautious in making such claims, however, and the mind grows restless at the task of deciphering the following nicely constructed sequence of ideas:

> Wherever one finds the first faint steps of human culture, the first successful fight against wild beasts, the striving against weather and disease, there one sees black men. To be sure they were not the only beginners, but they seem to have been the successful and persistent ones. Thus Africa appears as the Father of mankind, and the people who eventually settled there, wherever they may have wandered before

and since—along the Ganges, the Euphrates, and the Nile, in Cyprus and about
the Mediterranean shores—form the largest and often the only group of human
beings successfully advancing from animal savagery toward primitive civilization.

He did not actually assert that Africans had initiated human progress by
forging the primal civilization, but then, on the other hand, he did not deny
the idea either. He did not say they were the only group to achieve such
progress; he said they were "often the only group." He did state that while
"probably the properties of iron have been discovered in the world many
times," it seemed "likely" that Africans were making use of iron technology
while Europe was still in its stone age. This was a task that neither Egypt, not
Western Asia, not ancient China had achieved, and it was "a moment big with
promise for the uplift of the human race." Without iron, modern industrial
progress would have been impossible, "and this marvelous discovery was
made by African Negroes."

With respect to the idea of "Progress," Du Bois wanted to have his cake
and eat it, too. Like many intellectuals of his generation, he was skeptical
regarding Victorian notions of progress. He was not beyond the influences of
a new cultural relativism, that rejected the idea that some societies were better
or more advanced than others. Nonetheless, in "What is Civilization," he
clung to the idea of progress, and was determined to show that black folk had
contributed to the evolution of civilization. His theory of history was
"progressive" and evolutionary. He did not challenge the view that various
stages of human advancement can be identified with such terms as "animal
savagery," "primitive civilization," and "modern civilization." Therefore, on
the one hand, he seemed to question the commonly accepted definitions of
progress and civilization, while, on the other, he asserted that Africa was the
source of progress and civilization.

However, in defining the second of Africa's gifts to the world, Du Bois
revealed that the ideas of modernity and progress were not essential to his
theory of African contributionism. Africans, he stated, had given the world
the village unit. He presented an idealistic vision of the West African village as
"a perfect human thing."[13] The genius of the African village was its ability to
reconcile oppositions, in that it "socialized the individual completely, and yet
because the village was small this socialization did not submerge and kill indi-
vuality." This was an implicit critique of modernism, and of urban society.
"When the city socializes the modern man he becomes mechanical, and cities
tend to be all alike. When the nation attempts to socialize the modern man the
result is often a soulless Leviathan." Unlike modern theorists of Afrocentricity, Du Bois did not view individualism as a European invention. He
saw individualism as an essential feature of the village culture, and accused

Africa of producing a society that was individualistic to a fault. "Africa paid for her individualistic village culture by the slave trade."[14]

The description of modern urbanized civilization as a Leviathan that swallowed up the individual was reminiscent of ideas developed by such of Du Bois's contemporaries as Robert E. Park, Oswald Spengler, and Ferdinand Tönnies.[15] In pointing out the differences between the African village and the modern city, Du Bois was making the same sort of distinction that Tönnies had made in differentiating *Gemeinschaft* and *Gesellschaft*. It was this difference that was at the root of Park's culture-civilization distinction. A similar idea was at the root of Spengler's distinction between living culture and dead civilization. In each case the author recognized the importance of a society's bringing the individual into some sort of harmony with society. Park and Tönnies were particularly attracted by the idea of the small town as an institution that performed such functions effectively. Their theories were a critique of modern societies that, because of their cosmopolitanism, produced disorientation and anomie. In a similar vein, Spengler saw the socializing functions of healthy organic cultures as distinct from the mechanical groupings of "civilizations." Eventually Spengler defined civilization as "dead culture," meaning that the elements of society were no longer integral and organically interrelated. Du Bois never specifically endorsed Spengler's pejorative definition of civilization, but he did critique modern civilization as disintegrated, and he idealized the small village as a place where "religion, industry, government, education, and art . . . were bred as integral, interrelated things."

The third gift "out of Africa and out of the souls of black folk was music and rhythm." Du Bois, wrote with breathless enthusiasm of "the terrible beautiful music" that he had heard forty years earlier in a rustic church in backwoods Tennessee. "It was the demoniac possession of infinite music. . . . I stood and wept, and when in a flash of silence, a woman leapt into the air and shrieked as the dying shriek, I sat down cold with terror and hot with new ecstasy."[16] He personalized his sense of a tie to the music of Africa by referring to a "heathen melody" that had been passed down in his family by his grandfather's grandmother. "The child sang it to his children and they to their children's children, and so 200 years it has traveled down to us and we sing it to our children, knowing as little as our fathers what its words may mean, but knowing well the meaning of its music."[17]

> Do ba-no co-ba, ge-ne me, ge-ne me!
> Do ba-no co-ba, ge-ne me, ge-ne me!
> Ben d'nuli, nuli, ben d'le!

He alluded to "the tom-tom in O'Neill's *Emperor Jones*, and he praised the audience of a church in New York for listening spellbound to the music of Henry Burleigh sung by a white choir. By now he was able even to celebrate the sound of "a Negro orchestra playing Jazz." Du Bois was trying hard to understand folk and popular culture, and perhaps he was succeeding; but he simply did not seem to have much natural affinity to the spirit of jazz.

> Your head may revolt, your ancient conventions scream in protest, but your heart and body leap to rhythm. It is a new and mighty art which Africa gave America and America is giving the world. It has circled the world, it has set hundreds of millions of feet a-dancing—it is a new and American art which has already influenced all music and is destined to do more.[18]

He was much more convincing when he spoke of black music in terms of what he called "The Sorrow Songs." But he was not insensitive to the fact that composers who made use of Negro themes were gaining acceptance by white theatre and concert goers. He was capable of making a passing allusion to W. C. Handy,[19] but Du Bois's best known treatments of black music are his essay on the "Sorrow Songs," in *The Souls of Black Folk*, and his treatment of the British mulatto composer, Samuel Coleridge-Taylor, who wrote "classical" music on African themes. Coleridge-Taylor was something of a cultural hero to the black bourgeoisie in the earlier years of the twentieth century. Despite the assimilation that he represented in body and in mind, Coleridge-Taylor also represented a variety of cultural Pan-Africanism that they found acceptable.

If Du Bois was fascinated by the musical Pan-Africanism of Coleridge-Taylor, he was influenced by the socio-political Pan-Africanism of Joseph Ephraim Casely Hayford. Hayford, a barrister in the British colony of the Gold Coast in West Africa, had organized a Pan-African Conference in 1905, which Du Bois had not attended.[20] In 1911, Hayford had written a book called *Ethiopia Unbound*, in which he mocked some of Du Bois's ideas in *The Souls of Black Folk*, especially that of "double consciousness." In that same book, he made an obvious allusion to an image that Du Bois had employed at the end of his second chapter of "a figure veiled and bowed," who sits in the king's highway. Hayford criticized Du Bois as a prodigal son, who instead of hastening to his father's house "sits sulkily by the wayside over Jordan apples." Hayford had described Du Bois's attitude toward the race question as "pathetic" referring especially to the passage in which Du Bois had described his sense of "twoness" as an American and an African. Hayford dismissed this as the pathetic cry of a man who had foolishly elected to remain in a limbo of unreconcilable strivings:

> To be a puzzle to others is not to be a puzzle unto one's self. The sphinx in the

Temple of the Sphinx in ancient Egypt is a recumbent figure with the head of a lion, but the features of King Chephron, the Master of Egypt, somewhere about 3960 B.C. Now, fancy Candace, Queen of Ethiopia, or Chephron, the Master of Egypt, being troubled with a double consciousness. Watch that symbolic, reposeful figure yonder, and you can but see one soul, one ideal, one striving, one line of natural, rational progress. Look again, and you must agree that the idea of a double consciousness is absurd with these representative types.[21]

Ironically, the ambimorphous symbolism of the Sphinx seemed to mock the absolutist ideal that Hayford sought to advance. Double consciousness and the timeless problems of mixed identity were not unfamiliar to the ancient Egyptians. In fact, the pharaohs themselves wore a double crown, symbolic of the mixed cultural identity of Egypt, where the ethnic heritages of the black upper and the brown lower Nile were combined.

For his part, Du Bois developed an admiration for Hayford, and cited his works in subsequent publications.[22] He also paid tribute to the work of other black scholars, even William H. Ferris, a black graduate of Yale University, and a member of the American Negro Academy, who had challenged some of Du Bois's ideas in "The Conservation of Races."[23] Ferris was the author of a massive collection of essays, which he called *The African Abroad*, published in 1911. This two-volume work constituted an operational definition of Pan-Africanism, with its disquisitions on Africa and Egypt and its impressive discussions of leading black men and ideas of the day.[24]

In "The Conservation of Races," Du Bois had balked at an unequivocal declaration of any ties between Egypt and Central Africa, but when he published *The Negro*, eighteen-years later, he seemed more convinced. He buttressed his work with social scientific references and quotations from the works of Leo Frobenius and Franz Boas. He cited A. F. Chamberlain's "The Contribution of the Negro to Human Civilization" as "one of the special works on which the author has relied for his statements or which amplify his point of view." One of the views expressed by Chamberlain that particularly pleased him was a statement that

the Egyptian race ... had a considerable amount of Negro blood, and one of the reasons why no civilization of the type of that of the Nile arose in other parts of the continent, if such a thing were possible, was that Egypt acted as a sort of channel by which the genius of Negroland was drafted off into the service of Mediterranean and Asiatic culture."[25]

Du Bois was now convinced of the upper Nilotic origins of Egyptian high culture. The Egyptians, he wrote, certainly were not white in any sense of the modern use of that word—neither in color nor physical measurement, in hair nor countenance, in language nor social customs. They stood in relationship nearest the Negro race in earliest times, and then gradually through the infiltration of Mediterranean and Semitic elements became what can be described in America as a light mulatto stock of Octoroons or Quadroons."[26]

Europeans boasted that they were the sole inventors of human progress, but Africa, true mother of civilization had only been sleeping. "Who raised the fools to their glory?" asked Du Bois in a poem entitled, "The Riddle of the Sphinx." It was "black men of Egypt and Ind, Ethiopia's sons of the evening, Indians and yellow Chinese, Arabian children of morning, And mongrels of Rome and Greece? Ah, well!" In the coming world revolution, "they who raised the boasters [would] drag them down again."[27]

Du Bois was fifty-six years old when he first set foot on African soil. He travelled in 1924 as minister plenipotentiary and envoy extraordinary, representing President Calvin Coolidge at the inauguration of Liberia's President Charles King. Once again, Du Bois waxed poetic:

> Africa is the spiritual Frontier of human kind—oh the wild and beautiful adventures of its taming! But oh! the cost thereof—the endless, endless cost! Then will come a day—an old and ever, ever young day when there will spring in Africa a civilization without coal, without noise, where machinery will sing and never rush and roar, and where men will sleep and think and dance and lie prone before the rising sons, and women will be happy.
>
> The objects of life will be revolutionized. Our duty will not consist in getting up at seven, working furiously for six, ten and twelve hours, eating in sullen ravenousness or extraordinary repletion. No— we shall dream the day away and in cool dawns, in little swift hours, do all our work.[28]

During the five years preceding his first trip to Africa, Du Bois had been involved in organizing a series of Pan-African Congresses. He was not the first to engage in such activities, as there had been previous attempts to organize a world-wide union of black peoples. One of these was the London Conference of 1900, organized by the Trinidadian barrister Henry Sylvester-Williams, and the Methodist Bishop Alexander Walters. It was at this conference that Du Bois made his famous statement, "The problem of the twentieth century is the problem of the color line."[29] Nineteen years later Du Bois began the series of Pan-African Congresses which met in Paris, 1919; London, Brussels and Paris, 1921; London, Paris, and Lisbon 1923, and New York, 1927.[30] The proceedings of these conferences were of varied significance. Du Bois believed that the conference of 1919 had at least planted the idea that the former German colonies ought to be administered by an international organization "instead of being handled by various colonial powers. Out of this idea came the Mandates Commission."[31] Du Bois made no grandiose claims for the Pan-African movement; it represented simply "the centralization of race effort and the recognition of a racial fount." The slogan "Africa for the Africans" did not mean "any lessening of effort in our own problem at home." Pan-Africanism, as he defined it was "not a separatist movement." and was not intended to encourage the deportation of "any large number of colored Americans."[32] Within a month of this disclaimer, Du Bois was denounced by Marcus Garvey, who was pushing his own variety of Pan-Africanism.[33]

The feud between Du Bois and Garvey was largely, but not entirely, a clash of egos. The two men shared a fascination with nineteenth-century imperialist conceptions of power and authority. Du Bois was less inclined than was Garvey to take his theater into the street, but the pages of the *Crisis*, like those of *Negro World*, were filled with Afrocentric rhetoric and racial romanticism. Both men claimed to represent the true interests of the masses of poor black Americans. Du Bois constantly presented sentimentalized portraits of Southern peasants, while Garvey rubbed elbows with the urban workers. Both men were, no doubt, sincere in their commitments to uplifting the race, but neither was completely convincing as an advocate of popular culture. Both were reminiscent of the nineteenth-century prophets of African Civilizationism, an ideal that was to be imposed from the top down, rather than growing organically from the bottom up. Both Garvey and Du Bois betrayed more attachment to the symbols of cosmopolitan civilization than to the homely folkways of the American Negro. Neither of them supported the cabaret culture or the new sexual freedom that thrived in the cities of the Jazz Age. They were in competition for control of high-culture symbolism and monumental imagery, and they were of one mind in their disparagement of the raunchy folksiness of gut-bucket blues.

Du Bois, like Garvey, became involved in the culture wars of Harlem in the 1920s. His early involvement in the German rhetoric of *Volksgeist* had prepared Du Bois intellectually for a promotion of cultural nationalism based on the folk culture of the rural South. He was ill-prepared to sympathize with the blues culture that had arisen in the South and was flourishing in the North. His roots in classical "civilizationist" black nationalism did not prepare him to embrace the proletarian-Bohemian culture celebrated by Carl Van Vechten and his circle, which included individuals of unconventional sexual orientations. Aside from his professed disbelief in the existence of homosexuals, Du Bois was not entirely unfamiliar with alternative lifestyles. He had first encountered "loose sexual customs" when he went South to college, and had committed adultery while teaching during a summer in rural Tennessee.[34] During his years in Berlin he had practically lived with a young German "shop girl." Still, his reviews of the novels of Claude McKay and Carl Van Vechten, with their mild, non-explicit allusions to ribaldry, were immoderately hostile. As if fearing the charge of prudishness, Du Bois produced his *Dark Princess* in 1928—a representative Harlem Renaissance novel, although he chose to locate much of the action in Chicago. The hero's extramarital affair is central to the development of *Dark Princess,* and the passage in which the hero and heroine make love on an Oriental rug, although leaving much to the imagination, is arguably more erotic than the sketchy sexual encounters in McKay's *Home to Harlem.* Du Bois's objection to McKay's creations was not that McKay's characters deviated from bourgeois ideals of Victorian chastity, but that their sexual encouters were casual and untouched by romantic love. There was no room in Du Bois's cultural nationalism for the tom-cat sexual adventurism that he, correctly or incorrectly, associated with blues culture.

Du Bois had become a complete Afrocentrist by 1939, when he published *Black Folk Then and Now.* In this book he provided a broad survey of Egyptian history, written from secondary sources. Much of the material was incorporated into Du Bois's third major work on Africa, *The World and Africa*, published seven years later. In these works, he insisted that Egyptian culture had originated among the blacks of inner Africa, and then flowed down the Nile to the Mediterranean. He also demonstrated considerable interest in the cultures of western and southern Africa, which he continued to depict as admirable in their own right, aside from any ties that may have developed between them and Egypt or the Islamic world. He continued to speak of the gifts of black folk to America and to the world. Anticipating by several decades Oswald Spengler's assertion that the soil of Europe had become culturally impoverished, Du Bois often spoke of the modern European ethos as dry, dull, and money grubbing. He idealistically presented the Negro as the world-saving remnant of cultural health.

The First World War provided Du Bois, and many other intellectuals, with ample opportunity to reflect on the ruined claims of European cultural supremacy. At the time of America's entry into the Great War, Du Bois still conceded that European culture was superior to that of the rest of the world; and at least up to this time, he had never doubted this. But European cultural supremacy was not due to Europeans being "better, nobler, greater and more gifted than other folk." Europe was great "because of the foundations which the mighty past had furnished her to build upon: The iron trade of black Africa; the religion and empire building of yellow Asia; the art and science of the dago Mediterranean shore, east south and west as well as north." Europe had risen only when she had built securely on her non-European past, but when she had departed from the wisdom of Africa and the Orient, she had "shown the cloven hoof of poor crucified humanity." Similar observations were made by modernist intellectuals who adopted a cultural relativism that viewed all cultures as fundamentally equal, and who came to see the very concept of "civilization" as an ethnocentric mythology that had been undermined by the Great War.[35]

Unlike the modernists, Du Bois, showed little interest in the problem of cultural relativism.[36] In fact, his views seemed to resemble those of Sigmund Freud, who said in 1927, "I scorn to distinguish between culture and civilization."[37] History for Du Bois, as for most progressives, was the struggle of humanity to triumph over animal savagery. He viewed civilization as the process whereby human beings developed progressively higher forms of culture, not only in the material but in the moral realm. The War demonstrated a failure of Europe to realize the highest ideals of civilization; it did not lead Du Bois to question the validity of the concept of civilization.

If Du Bois believed that black folk had much to gain from racial integration as a means of discovering the higher cultural ideals of Europe and America, he never fully accepted the idea of integration as a panacea for America's racial problems. In his 1897 addresss on "The Conservation of Races" he had asserted that voluntary separatism and racial solidarity were often desirable: "if the Negro is going to develop his own power and gifts... [and] also to unite for ideals higher than the world has realized in art and industry and social life, then he must unite and work with Negroes and build a new and great Negro ethos." He did not desire to see the black race drowned in a sea of white culture, because he felt that black folk had much to teach the world. Indeed, in his 1924 publication, *The Gift of Black Folk,* he provided evidence and arguments that black folk had already given much to America. Thus while, on the one hand, he was committed to continuing the fight for integration, he recognized a need for continuing to build racial institutions.

The idea of separate institutions was fundamantally unacceptable to the board of directors of the NAACP, and Du Bois's advocacy of them led to his being forced out of the editorship of the *Crisis* at the age of sixty-six. Leading the opposition to Du Bois was Walter White, a man of undoubted courage and intelligence, but a bitter foe of all institutional separatism, whether voluntary or involuntary. In the course of his battles with the board and with Walter White, Du Bois attempted to have the NAACP pass a resolution in support of black churches, colleges, businesses, and industrial enterprises. He asserted that the NAACP should support them "not with the idea of perpetuating artificial **separations of mankind but rather with the distinct object of proving Negro efficiency, showing Negro ability and discipline and demonstrating how useless and wasteful race segregation is."** The board responded by passing a much abbreviated resolution that made no mention of the need for institutional development. The resolution correctly opposed "both the principle and the practice of enforced segregation," but ignored the issue of black institutions as bases for the development of an ethnic power base.[38]

Du Bois's position closely resembled the "nation within a nation" position that Alexander Crummell had stated in his "The Social Principle Among a People." Crummell had spoken against "the dogma . . . that the colored people of this country should forget as soon as possible, that they are colored people." Crummell had denounced the doctrine not only as dogmatic folly, but had gone on to describe it as "disintegrating and socially destructive." Black folk were "shut out from the cultivated social life of the superior classes," and were thus forced to depend upon themselves for higher forms of social-intellectual discourse. Du Bois had practically rewritten these sentences in his essay on "Jim Crow," published in the *Crisis* of January 1919. Like Crummell, he recognized that "much of the objection to segregation and Jim Crowism was in other days the fact that compelling Negroes to associate only with Negroes meant to exclude them from contact with the best culture of the day." With the passage of time, conditions had changed and "culture [was] no longer the monopoly of the white, nor [was] poverty and ignorance the sole heritage of the black. Crummell had rejected "the demand that colored men should give up all distinctive effort, as colored men, in schools, churches, associations and friendly societies." Resurrecting Crummell's ideas Du Bois said, "The real battle is a matter of study and thought; of the building of loyalties; of the long training of men; of the growth of institutions; of the inculcation of racial and national ideals."[39]

In 1934, Du Bois left the NAACP and the city of New York to return to Atlanta University, where he was able to act on his principles of dedication to black institution building. He travelled frequently in the rural South, carrying his own lunch to avoid having to eat in segregated restaurants, and bringing along coveralls and mechanic's tools so that he could service his own automobile in the event of break-down. He returned to Fisk University in 1938 as a commencement speaker, delivering an oration, "The Revelation of St. Orgne the Damned." It was, as its title indicated, a mystical and visionary address, in which he called on the graduating class to dedicate itself to "racial unity and loyalty." At the end of the decade, he published his autobiography, *Dusk of Dawn,* in which he advocated the development of black cooperatives and community-controlled institutions, saying:

> In the African communal group, ties of family and blood, of mother and child of group relationship, made the group leadership strong, even if not always toward the highest culture. In the case of the more artificial group among American

Negroes, there are sources of strength in common memories of suffering in the
past; in present threats of degradation and extinction; in common ambitions and
ideals; in emulation and the determination to prove ability and desert. Here in
subtle but real ways the communalism of the African clan can be transferred to the
Negro American group.[40]

This statement was clearly both nationalistic and Afrocentric; it demonstrated a continuing committment to the "nation within a nation" model of
Alexander Crummell; but Du Bois added an element that Crummell had never
envisioned. He presupposed an African heritage as the basis for building
national strength within a regenerated African-American community. Black
America would eventually pass on to the world a blend of its African and its
American heritages. Black Americans, by "achieving new social institutions,"
would "teach industrial and cultural democracy to a world that bitterly needs
it," and "move pari passu with the modern world into a new heaven and a
new earth."[41]

In later years, Du Bois repudiated what he had once said about the essentially individualistic nature of African culture. Du Bois had once theorized that
the cause of Africa's historic weakness before the onslaught of slavery, colonialism, and racism was that no African Bismarck had arisen, no king or
priest, sufficiently strong, to forcefully merge his interests with the destiny of
the tribe. His communalism, socialism and Afrocentrism were now blended
into one holistic doctrine of Pan-African socialism. Whereas in 1919 he had
attributed the fall of Africa before the slave trade to an excess of individualism, in 1958 he denied that an African individualism, or even an African freedom, had existed within traditional societies. He insisted that Africa had never
harbored more than a trace of "private enterprise or individual initiative. It
was the tribe which carried on trade through individuals, and the chief was
mouthpiece of the common will."[42]

In 1958, Du Bois was too ill to attend the All-Africa Conference that
Kwame Nkrumah convened in Accra, Ghana, but from a hospital bed in
Moscow, he sent a message. His wife, Shirley Graham, read his address before
the assembly—the only American allowed such an honor. In the address, Du
Bois once again turned to the writings of the now deceased Casely Hayford as
a source for his Pan-Africanist ideas. From Casely Hayford, he borrowed his
conception of the African patriarch, who became a key figure in his theories.
In the coming unified Africa, the individual would have to give up his or her
individual interests for the good of the whole, and so, too, must each African
tribe "give up a part of its heritage for the good of the whole." He called on
Africans to achieve a new unity, based on their common heritage of oppression, saying, "Your bond is no mere color of skin but the deeper experience of

wage slavery and contempt." He described traditional African life as a world in which "No tribesman was free. All were servants of the tribe of whom the chief was father and voice."[43]

In Kwame Nkrumah, Du Bois hoped to have found his African Bismarck, his Stalinist Czar, the "father and voice" of sufficient strength to bring unity to a continent of squabbling tribes. He hoped Nkrumah would create a new variety of socialism, based on the hereditary communalism of West African institutions. As Stalin had forged "one nation out of [Russia's] 140 groups without destroying their individuality," so would Nkrumah overcome the divisive tribalism, encouraged by British imperialists. If brutal methods were required, Du Bois could accept the necessity, just as he had accepted the repressive methods of Stalin. Scarred and embittered by his own experiences with caste and class humiliation, Du Bois sympathized with men like Stalin and Nkrumah, who had risen from humble beginnings and were often snubbed by persons of more aristocratic background. Du Bois's sympathy for Nkrumah was reinforced when Nkrumah was opposed by Joseph Appiah, an Oxford-educated Ashanti prince, married to the daughter of Sir Richard Stafford Cripps.[44] And Du Bois made no apologies when Nkrumah sent his political enemies to prison.

One should not readily accept the idea that Du Bois joined the Communist party and applied for Ghanaian citizenship because he was "disillusioned and disheartened."[45] His commitment to an Afrocentric brand of socialism under strong leadership was the natural culmination of remarkably consistent theorizing over seventy years. Du Bois believed that the tide of history was on the side of communism, and in his final days he accepted the invitation extended to him by Casely Hayford a half-century earlier, and returned to the Fatherland when another Gold Coast leader, Kwame Nkrumah, renewed the invitation. He turned his face

> From reeking West whose day is done
> Who stink and stagger in their dung[46]

In summary then, Du Bois's theory of history from beginning to end was tied up with the problem of power and authority. He developed a theory in which individuals must always be subordinated to collective goals and racial destiny. Egypt, the African culture that had most successfully achieved power and authority, had become a cosmopolitan center, but it channelled the essence of African genius into the Mediterranean, where other civilizations had built their glory on Africa's gifts. The tragedy of Africa was that conquering kingdoms below the Sahara were constantly overthrown before they could integrate their political, social, and religious powers. Du Bois idolized

Bismarck in his youth and Stalin in his old age. Kwame Nkrumah, an increasingly ruthless dictator, married to an Egyptian wife, represented the sort of Pan-African leadership for which Du Bois had longed. In the end, Du Bois was able to synthesize his Pan-Africanism with his socialism by making use of an Afrocentric model. But the model that he developed has become increasingly unacceptable to the power brokers of the American Negro intellectual establishment.

NOTES

1. W. E. B. Du Bois, *The Souls of Black Folk* (Chicago: McClurg, 1903), 3.

2. Lerone Bennett, *Pioneers in Protest* (New York: Penguin, 1969), 241–56.

3. Charles T. Davis, *Black is the Color of the Cosmos*, ed., Henry Louis Gates, Jr., (New York: Garland Publishers, 1982), pp. 219-20. In a similar vein see, Harold Isaacs, "Pan Africanism as Romantic Racialism," in *The New World of Negro Americans*, Harold R. Isaacs (New York: The John Day Company, 1963), and Vincent Harding, "W. E. B. Du Bois and the Black Messianic Vision," in *Freedomways* (1st Quarter, 1969), 44–58. Also see Eric Sundquist, *To Wake the Nations: Race in the Making of American Literature* (Cambridge, Mass.: The Belknap Press of Harvard University Press, 1993).

4. W. E. B. Du Bois, "Easter Emancipation, 1863–1913," in Herbert Aptheker, ed., *Creative Writings by W. E. B. Du Bois* (New York: Kraus Thomson, 1985), 28–32. Reprinted as "Children of the Moon," in W. E. B. Du Bois, *Darkwater: Voices From Within the Veil*, (New York: Harcourt, Brace and Howe, 1919), 187–92.

5. Du Bois's tribute to the "unbending righteousness" of Crummell is in *The Souls of Black Folk*, 226. Du Bois's homage to Stalin is in "He Knew the Common Man . . . Followed his Fate," *National Guardian* (March 16, 1953), reprinted in Julius Lester, ed., *The Seventh Son: The Thought and Writings of W. E. B. Du Bois* (New York: Vintage, 1971), 617–19. Du Bois's opinions on Nkrumah are conveniently indexed in Lester, *The Seventh Son*. For more on Nkrumah see Ali Mazrui, "Kwame Nkrumah: The Leninist Czar," in S. Okechukwu Mezu, *Black Leaders of the Centuries* (Buffalo: Black Academy Press, 1970), 249.

6. W. E. B. Du Bois, *The Conservation of Races, American Negro Academy Papers*, no. 2 (Washington, D.C.: American Negro Academy, 1897).

7. W. E. B. Du Bois, ed., *The Negro Church* (Atlanta: Atlanta University, 1903), repr. in Lester, ed., *The Seventh Son*, vol. 1; 253–54.

8. Lester, ed., *The Seventh Son*, vol. 1; 256.

9. Du Bois, *The World and Africa*, (New York: International Publishers, 1965), 258–59. On Herder, see K. R. Minogue, *Nationalism* (New York: Penguin, 1970), 58. Also see Hans Kohn's article "Nationalism," in Philip K. Weiner, ed., *Dictionary of the History of Ideas* (New York: Charles Scribner's Sons, 1973), cf. "Conservation of Races."

10. W. E. B. Du Bois, "What is Civilization? Africa's Answer," *Forum*, vol. 73 (February 1925), 178–88. Reprinted in Meyer Weinberg, ed., *W. E. B. Du Bois: A Reader*, (New York: Harper and Row, 1970), 378.

11. Oswald Spengler, *The Decline of the West*, trans. Charles Francis Atkinson (New York: Knopf, 1926). Originally published as *Der Untergang des Abendlandes, Gestalt und Wirklichkeit*, (München: C. H. Beck'sche Verlagsbuchhandlung, 1918), 31. My references are to the twenty-seventh printing of March 1988. Robert E. Park,

"Culture and Civilization," was first published in Robert E. Park, *Race and Culture*, ed. Everett Cherrington Hughes et. al. (New York: The Free Press, 1950), 15–23.

12. Hans Kohn speaks of the wedding of German nationalism and cosmopolitanism. See his "Nationalism," in Philip P. Wiener, ed., *Dictionary of the History of Ideas* (New York: Scribner, 1973), vol. 3, 324–39. K. R. Minogue, *Nationalism* (New York: Pelican Books, 1968), 26–27, remarks the importance of the Brothers Grimm to German nationalism.

13. W. E. B. Du Bois, "What is Civilization? Africa's Answer," *Forum* (February, 1925). Reprinted in Weinberg, ed., *W. E. B. Du Bois: A Reader*, 376–81.

14. Du Bois, "What is Civilization," 378.

15. Park himself made the analogy between Du Bois's concepts and those of Tönnies in "Culture and Civilization." See Park, *Race and Culture*, 12.

16. Du Bois dated the experience in 1886, "at the time I was a youth of eighteen." See "What is Civilization?" 380–81. For a similar sequence of images and theme of demoniac possession cf. Percy Shelley's "I shrieked and clapped my hands with ecstasy," in his "Hymn to Intellectual Beauty," in *The Complete Political Works of Percy Bysshe Shelley*, Thomas Hutchinson, ed., (London: Oxford University Press, 1961), 531.

17. W. E. B. Du Bois, "Africa and the American Negro Ingelligentsia," *Présence Africaine* (December, 1954–January, 1955), 34–51.

18. Du Bois, "What is Civilization," 381.

19. W. E. B. Du Bois, "Mencken," *Crisis* (October, 1927), in Weinberg, ed., *W. E. B. Du Bois: A Reader*, 262.

20. The conference was perhaps nothing more than a literary invention, although Hayford may have been recollecting any of several meetings treating on the problem of African interests held in Gold Coast during the first decade of the twentieth century. Du Bois organized his conference in 1919.

21. J[oseph] E[phraim] Casely Hayford, *Ethiopia Unbound: Studies in Race Emancipation*, (London: Phillips, 1911), 181.

22. See for example the quotation in *Darkwater*, 167, which is taken from J. E. Casely Hayford, *Gold Coast Native Institutions* (London: Sweet and Maxwell, Ltd., 1903), 77. The the same work in is quoted in W. E. B. Du Bois, *The Negro* (1915; repr., New York: Oxford, 1970), 71.

23. See Wilson J. Moses, "The Conservation of Races and the American Negro Academy: Nationalism, Materialism, and Hero Worship," *The Massachusetts Review* (Summer, 1993) 275–95.

24. The present author concurs with the judgement of the late Professor Rayford Logan, editor of *Dictionary of American Negro Biography*, who says: "Despite its verbiage and erudite digressions, *The African Abroad* (New Haven: Tuttle and Morehouse, 1911) has been a valuable source for later historians."

25. Du Bois, "What is Civilization," 378.

26. Du Bois, *The Negro*, 17

27. This poem by Du Bois was originally published in the *Horizon* 2 (November, 1907) as "The Burden of Black Women," and reprinted in the *Crisis* 9 (November, 1914). It was published again, with some interesting alterations, as "The Riddle of the Sphinx," in *Darkwater*, 53–55. For publication histories of this and other poems, I am indebted to the very useful notes of Herbert Aptheker, ed. *Creative Writings by W. E. B. Du Bois*, 12.

28. W. E. B. Du Bois, "Little Portraits of Africa," *Crisis*, (April, 1924): 273–74; Reprinted under the title, "The Place, The People," in Lester, ed., *The Seventh Son*, vol. 2, 350–51.

29. There is some disagreement as to the numbering of the Pan-African Congresses. Richard B. Moore credits Walters and Williams with the organization of the first Pan-African Congress in London 1900, and views Du Bois's Paris Congress of 1919 as the Second Pan-African Congress. See Richard B. Moore, "Du Bois and Pan-Africa," in John Henrik Clarke, et. al., *Black Titan: W. E. B. Du Bois* (Boston: Beacon, 1970), 187–212.

30. In W. E. B. Du Bois, *Dusk of Dawn* (New York: Harcourt, Brace and World, 1940), 278, Du Bois says that the 1923 meetings were held in London, Paris, and Lisbon. He is unclear as to whether a Paris meeting actually took place in another article, W. E. B. Du Bois, "The Pan-African Movement," in George Padmore, ed., *Colonial and Coloured Unity* (Manchester, n.d.), 13–26; reprinted in Elie Kedourie, ed., *Nationalism in Asia and Africa* (New York: Meridian Books, 1970), 372–87.

31. W. E. B. Du Bois, "The Pan-African Movement," in Kedourie, ed., *Nationalism in Asia and Africa*, 375.

32. W. E. B. Du Bois, "Reconstruction and Africa," *Crisis* (February 1919). Reprinted in Weinberg, ed., *W. E. B. Du Bois: A Reader*, 373.

33. An article in *Negro World* (April 5, 1919), reported "An Address Denouncing W. E. B. Du Bois" was announced by Garvey at an "enthusiastic convention" meeting of March 25, 1919.

34. W. E. B. Du Bois, *The Autobiography of W. E. B. Du Bois*, Herbert Aptheker, ed., (New York: International, 1968), 280

35. Du Bois, *Darkwater*, 39.

36. Numerous references in the index to George W. Stocking, Jr. *Race, Culture, and Evolution: Essays in the History of Anthropology* (New York: The Free Press, 1968), offer a discussion of the discourse on cultural relativism, especially as it relates to Franz Boas. The putative culture/civilization dichotomy is posited in Robert E. Park, *Race and Culture* (London: The Free Press, 1950), 15–23.

37. Sigmund Freud, *The Future of an Illusion*, ed. and trans. James Strachey (New York: W.W. Norton, 1961), 6. Originally published as *Die Zukunft Einer Illusion* (Leipzig, Vienna, & Zurich: Internationaler Psychoanalytischer Verlag, 1927).

38. W. E. B. Du Bois, "The Board of Directors on Segregation," *Crisis* (May 1934). Reprinted in Nathan Huggins, ed., *W. E. B. Du Bois: Writings*, (New York: The Library of America, 1986), 1252.

39. Alexander Crummell's address, "The Social Principle Among a People," was delivered in 1875 and reprinted in his collection, *The Greatness of Christ and Other Sermons* (New York: Thomas Whittaker, 1882): 285–312. Du Bois's recapitulation of Crummell's theme is in W. E. B. Du Bois, "Counsels of Despair," *Crisis*, (June 1934). Reprinted in Huggins, ed., *Du Bois*, 1258.

40. Du Bois, *Dusk of Dawn*, 219.

41. The allusion to Revelation 21:1, "a new heaven and a new Earth," with which Du Bois ended this chapter of *Dusk of Dawn* (220), is interesting because the same words were used by Booker T. Washington at the conclusion of his "Atlanta Exposition Address."

42. Du Bois, *Autobiography*, 403.

43. Citation of Hayford and other quotations from Du Bois, *Autobiography*, 403–404.

44. Lester, ed., *The Seventh Son*, Vol. 2, 638.

45. Bennett, *Pioneers in Protest*, 243.

46. W. E. B. Du Bois, "Ghana Calls," *Freedomways* (Winter 1962). Reprinted in Aptheker, ed., *Creative Writings by W. E. B. Du Bois*, 52–55.

In Search of a Theory of Human History

12

W. E. B. Du Bois's Theory of Social and Cultural Dynamics

James B. Stewart

I. INTRODUCTION

This analysis explores W. E. B. Du Bois's contributions to the collective under-standing of broad patterns of social and cultural change. Much of the existing literature examining Du Bois's scholarship treats individual areas of interest or specific writings in isolation. I argue here, however, that much of his research focuses on two major themes: (a) how different components of social systems are linked, and (b) how changes in societal subsystems aggregate into transformation of total systems. In fact, many of the specialized investigations that Du Bois undertook were designed to generate basic data to inform this larger inquiry.

More specifically, Du Bois initially subscribed to a one-cycle, four-stage model that hypothesizes monotonically increasing levels of "development." The model uses "race" and "culture" as critical constructs. Later in his career, Du Bois endorsed a three-stage, one-cycle model of the rise and fall of civiliza-tions. In this second model, "culture" and "civilization" are the primary constructs and "race" is subordinated. There is, however, an organic connection between the two models, despite the fact that they were developed and articu-lated some forty years apart. This study examines these linkages in the context of the evolution of Du Bois's thinking regarding race, culture, and civilization.

Du Bois's original model of development, articulated in an essay entitled

"The Development of a People" (1904), is examined in the second section.[1]
The refined model, articulated in a co-authored review essay entitled "Mr.
Sorokin's Systems" (1942), is explored in the third section.[2] The fourth section
analyzes the similarities and differences between the models and suggests
further extensions. The differences reflect, in part, Du Bois's gradual alteration
of his view of social and cultural dynamics as he incorporated elements of the
Marxist critique of monopoly capitalism and concurrently observed the
declining isolation of African Americans from the forces shaping global
economic transformation.

In presenting Du Bois as a major theorist of social change, this study locates
him in the tradition of scholars like Spengler and Toynbee.[3] The many previous
studies of Du Bois's scholarship have generally overlooked this important
dimension of his work, and have focused attention instead on his more specialized writings and endeavors. In contrast, this essay attempts to lay the foundations for a broader appreciation of Du Bois's intellectual contributions.

II. DU BOIS ON THE DEVELOPMENT OF A PEOPLE

As noted previously, in "The Development of a People" (1904) Du Bois
proposed a four-stage theoretical model of social development describing the
process "which groups of men have usually taken in their forward struggling.[4]
He "tests" the theory using the experience of Africans and African Americans
as a case study. For present purposes it is critical to note that the case study is
ensconced in a broader "test" of the theory, which entails the use of the model
to characterize stages of development of Western civilization. The model was
designed as a mechanism to answer the question:

> But what is good and better and best in the measure of human advance? and how
> shall we compare the present with the past, nation with nation, and group with
> group, so as to gain real intelligent insight into conditions and needs, and enlight-
> ened guidance?[6]

Du Bois maintained that answering this question was "extremely difficult in
matters of human development, because we are so ignorant of the ordinary
facts relating to conditions of life, and because, above all, criteria of life and
the objects of living are so diverse."[6] He further insisted that

> if we are to judge intelligently or clearly of the development of a people, we must
> allow ourselves neither to be dazzled by figures nor misled by inapt comparisons,
> but we must seek to know what human advancement historically considered has
> meant and what it means to-day, and from such criteria we may then judge the
> condition, development and needs of the group before us.[7]

Du Bois then introduced the four stages of development:

> First, there is the struggle for sheer physical existence.... Above this comes the
> accumulation for future subsistence—the saving and striving and transmuting of
> goods for use in days to come.... Then in every community there goes on ...
> some essay to train the young into the tradition of the fathers—their religion,
> thought and tricks of doing. And, finally, as the group meets other groups and
> comes into larger spiritual contact with nations, there is that transference and sift-
> ing and accumulation of the elements of human culture which makes for wider
> civilization and higher development.[8]

The assumptions of social continuity across stages and comparable levels of development at the time of intercultural contact are especially critical if Du Bois's predicted positive outcomes of cross-cultural interaction are to occur. Guidance in progressing through the four stages of development is provided, in Du Bois's view, from four sources: the precepts of parents, the sight of peers, the opinion of the majority, and the traditions of the past. Du Bois emphasized that these four stages are neither disconnected nor discrete, suggesting that "in every stage of a nation's growing all these efforts are present," even though a particular label may be applied to characterize what is seen as a distinct stage of development.[9] More specifically, he asserted, "The growth of society is an ever-living, many-sided bundle of activities, some of which are emphasized at different ages, none of which can be neglected without peril, all of which demand guidance and direction."[10]

It is important here to note Du Bois's use of the construct "a nation grow-ing."[11] There is substantial overlap in his use of the constructs "people," "society" and "nation." What he seems to imply is (1) that nationhood can be used to describe a society at different stages of development, and (2) that intergenerational transfers of knowledge are the principal source of social cohesion and a deepening sense of nationhood. Du Bois's failure to articulate any constraints on the effectiveness of these transmission mechanisms across different types of social organization suggests that he viewed the process as universal and relatively invariant across cultures. Moreover, the lack of a well-organized socialization mechanism and/or forms of social organization does not invalidate a people's claim to nationhood.

The methodology that Du Bois used to "test" the model flowed directly from his concurrent work on the Atlanta Studies and *The Philadelphia Negro*. Du Bois took the reader through a tour of the lives and living conditions of representative families. As an example, he wrote:

> Let me take you journeying across mountains and meadows, threading the hills of

Maryland, gliding over the broad fields of Virginia, climbing the blue ridge of
Carolina and seating ourselves in the cotton kingdom. I would not like you to
spend a day or a month in this little town; I should much rather you would spend
ten years, if you are really studying the problem; for casual visitors get casual
ideas, and the problems here are the growth of centuries.[12]

Du Bois's reference to a ten-year examination of the setting was not acciden-
tal. He consistently advocated the repeated examination of a specific aspect of
the development of African Americans once every decade. Du Bois proposed a
research design in which ten topics would be studied in succession during each
decade as part of a century-long project.[13] He believed that this approach
would produce "a continuous record on the condition and development of a
group of 10 to 20 millions of men—a body of sociological material unsur-
passed in human annals.[14]

His application of this development model to the record of Black advancement led Du Bois to the following conclusion:

Here, then, is a group of people in which every one of these great sources of inspiration is partially crippled: the family group is struggling to recover from the
debauchery of slavery; the number of enlightened leaders must necessarily be
small; the surrounding and *more civilized* [emphasis added] white majority is cut
off from its natural influence by the color line; and the traditions of the past are
either lost, or largely traditions of evil and wrong.[15]

This evaluation is consistent with his summary assessment of the insights
gained from the tour of the hypothetical town: "Upon the town we have
visited, upon the state, upon this section, the awful incubus of the past broods
like a writhing sorrow, and when we turn our faces from that past, we turn it
not to forget but to remember, viewing degradation with fear and not
contempt, with awe and not criticism."[16]

It is critical to take note of the fact that Du Bois characterized European as
"more civilized" than Africans in the Americas, at least *after* the onslaught of
enslavement. There is no question that he attributed the disruption of the
normal process of group development in Africa to what he termed the
"African slave trade." Du Bois argued that the slave trade provided the foundations of European development over a five-hundred-year period:

The African Slave trade was the child of the Renaissance. We do not realize this;
we think of the slave trade as a thing apart, the incident of a decade or a century,
and yet let us never forget that from the year 1442 ... until 1807 ... for three
hundred and sixty-five years Africa was surrendered wholly to the cruelty and

rapacity of the Christian man-dealer, and for full five hundred years and more this frightful heart disease of the Dark Continent destroyed the beginnings of Negro civilization, overturned governments, murdered men, disrupted families and poisoned the civilized world.[17]

At another point in the essay, Du Bois summarized the relationship between the distortion of African development patterns and Western "development" in a more succinct fashion; "from 1442 to 1860, nearly half a millennium, the Christian world fattened on the stealing of human souls."[18]

At this point in his career Du Bois believed that Africa had been less "civilized" than the West prior to the advent of the trans-Atlantic slave trade. His subsequent modification of this view will be considered later in this essay. As in the overall examination of the status of African Americans, he used the case study approach to emphasize his point. His description of the destruction of a particular collective—the Wa-Nkonde, which, according to Du Bois, had been one of the most prosperous tribes in East and central Africa—illustrates both the method and the bias associated with the notion of Africa as "uncivilized." Du Bois described the Wa-Nkonde prior to contact with the West as a people who "by their own inherent ability and the natural resources of their country, *were on the high road to civilization* [emphasis added]."[19] He suggested that

> No one pretends that the family life of African tribes had reached modern standards—barbarous nations have barbarous ideals. But this does not mean that they have no ideals at all. The patriarchal clan-life of the Africans, with its polygamy protected by custom, tradition and legal penalty, was infinitely superior to the shameless promiscuity of the West Indian Plantations, the unhallowed concubinage of Virginia or the prostitution of Louisiana.[20]

The comparisons invoked by Du Bois reflected his view that "the dark damnation of slavery in America was the destruction of the African family and of all just ideals of family life.[21]

In his "empirical" assessment Du Bois made distinctions among patterns of social organization during different stages of development. As an example, he clearly differentiated among social institutions associated with the pre-slavery, slavery and post-slavery periods. This raises the question of whether the effects of the slave trade and slavery were so perverse as to render his model inapplicable for examining post-slavery development among African Americans.

Du Bois argued that the nature of the slavery experience was such that it

> must of necessity send into the world of work a mass of unskilled laborers who have no idea of what thrift means; who have been a part of a great economic

organization but had nothing to do with its organizing; and so when they are suddenly called to take a place in a greater organization, in which free individual initiative is a potent factor, they cannot, for they do not know how; they lack skill and, more than that, they lack ideals.[22]

He went on to discuss the source of the "ideals" of African Americans in detail, emphasizing the role of local leaders who

set the tone to that all-powerful spiritual world that surrounds and envelopes the souls of men; their standards of living, their interpretation of sunshine and rain and human hearts, their thoughts of love and labor, their aspirations and dim imaginings—all that makes life life.[23]

The required qualifications of these group leaders were described in the following terms:

The leader of the masses must discriminate between the good and bad in the past ... he must ... stand ... to this group in the light of the interpreter of the civilization of the twentieth century to the minds and hearts of people who, from sheer necessity, can but dimly comprehend it. And this man—I care not what his vocation may be—preacher, teacher, physician, or artisan, this person is going to solve the Negro problem for that problem is at bottom the clash of two different standards of culture, and this priest it is who interprets the one to the other.[24]

The prominent role assigned by Du Bois to the highly educated is, of course, consistent with his emphasis on the "Talented Tenth" as a leadership cadre at this stage of his career. Du Bois had argued earlier "The Talented Tenth of the Negro race must be made leaders of thought and missionaries of culture among their people. No others can do this work and Negro colleges must train men for it. The Negro race, like all other races, is going to be saved by its exceptional men."[25] Du Bois's view of both the "Talented Tenth" per se, and of the leadership described in the model reflected the sexist biases of the time. In other writings, however, Du Bois expressed a view of the role of women that was much more progressive than those of most of his counterparts.[26]

Despite Du Bois's negative assessment of the baseline position of African Americans, he remained optimistic about future prospects. "What the figures of Negro advancement mean is, that the development has been distinctly and markedly in the right direction," he wrote, "and that given justice and help, no honest man can doubt the outcome."[27] As noted previously, this assessment rested, to a large extent, on his faith in the ability of educated leadership.

Thus he argued, "If the meaning of modern life cannot be taught at Negro hearthsides because the parents themselves are untaught, then its ideals can be forced into the centres of Negro life only by the teachings of higher institutions of learning and the agency of thoroughly educated men."[28]

III. DU BOIS AND "MR. SOROKIN'S SYSTEMS"

Du Bois's second theory of social and cultural dynamics is embedded in an obscure co-authored review essay of Pitrim Sorokin's monumental four-volume treatise, *Social and Cultural Dynamics*.[29] Du Bois's review of Sorokin's work is of special interest to the present volume because it was co-authored with a credentialed philosopher, Rushton Coulburn, while both were members of the faculty of Atlanta University during the early 1940's. The obscurity of the review is evidenced by its inadvertent exclusion from Herbert Aptheker's comprehensive annotated bibliography of Du Bois's writings.[30]

The model is developed deductively via a systematic critique of Sorokin's formulations. This contrasts with the deductive approach used in articulating the model in "The Development of a People." There are other important differences as well. First, the original model was largely designed to describe the ideal developmental trajectory for African Americans. It provided a standard by which to judge the distortions in the experiences of African Americans that had occurred as a result of the oppression experienced from contact with the West. The second model was used to examine social and cultural development on a global scale. In fact, the experiences of neither Africans nor African Americans are explicitly mentioned! I maintain, however, that the modifications Du Bois and Coulburn proposed to Sorokin's framework, in fact, were designed to provide a vehicle for allowing the contributions of Africans and African Americans to be appropriately reflected in a general record of human civilization.

A second differentiating characteristic between the first and second models is the much more sophisticated theory of knowledge embedded in the latter. It will be recalled that Du Bois limited his discussion of these issues in "The Development of a People" to a fairly general consideration of the process of inter-generational knowledge transmission and the role of educated leadership. In the second model he adapts Sorokin's theory of inquiry in ways that create what might be called "cultural production space" for groups situated in ways similar to African Americans. Again, however, Du Bois himself does not acknowledge that this is a goal of his proposed modifications.

Third, the second model posits a synergistic relationship between the articulation of ideal models of system organization and operation and the actual functioning of so-called "empirical systems." The disjunction between the ideal and the empirical is seen as the engine of change. The use of the ideal model proposed by Du Bois in "The Development of a People" to assess the actual patterns of inter-cultural interaction is largely an intellectual exercise and not assumed to serve as a direct initiator of corrective actions.

In many respects Du Bois's attraction to the work of Pitrim Sorokin is curious because Sorokin attempts to interpret the history of modern civilization exclusively in terms of intellectual developments. The type of materialist interpretation found in the writings of Marx is wholly absent. Yet we know that by the time that "Mr. Sorokin's Systems" was authored, the writings of Marx had significantly influenced Du Bois's thinking. To illustrate, in 1948 Du Bois observed; "Very gradually as the philosophy of Karl Marx and many of his successors seeped into my understanding, I tried to apply this doctrine to Negroes."[31]

Pitrim Sorokin attempted to differentiate his interpretation of the history of humanity from those of Spengler and Toynbee.[32] He rejected their view that great civilizations had been distinguished in only one creative area. More importantly, he rejected the concept of a "civilization" as an appropriate unit of analysis. For Sorokin, the appropriate unit of analysis was what he termed a "cultural system." The concepts of "systems" and "congeries" play a special role in Sorokin's formulation. Systems are comprised of persons and things, referred to respectively as agents and vehicles. Congeries are persons or things juxtaposed in time but without any connection to the systems.

Systems have meanings attached to them and exist first in a pure state in the mind of agents. They enter the empirical world by acquiring vehicles. For Sorokin, the growth and decline of these systems constituted the functioning of society and the unfolding of the historical process. Sorokin drew a further distinction between social and cultural systems. As Coulburn and Du Bois observed,

> A social system is to him any real system, such as the family or the state. A cultural system is, on the other hand, discrete: language, science, religion, fine arts, and ethics are his five main cultural systems, and all other cultural systems and subsystems are mixtures of these or derivatives of them. Thus the system of politics is a derivative of the system of ethics.[33]

The state, according to Du Bois and Coulburn, is a distinct type of social system "which 'bears' the cultural system politics; thus, the state is a 'specialized' social system, while there are other social systems such as the family, the university . . . which are encyclopaedic, bearing many cultural systems."[34] Sorokin argued that "the five main cultural systems are integrated into what is, in effect, an attitude of mind; that the prevailing attitude of mind is not stable but passes through a threefold rhythm corresponding with one of the three basic ways of knowing."[35]

Sorokin disaggregated the general concept of creativity into three epistemological approaches, or attitudes of mind, that, he argued, could be used to classify phases in the search for meaning of different cultures: "the ideational, corresponding with intuition; the idealistic corresponding with reason; and the sensate, corresponding with sense perception."[36]

Coulburn and Du Bois maintained that Sorokin "sees the functioning of society and the making of history as man's struggle to know himself and to know the cosmos, passing eternally through a threefold rhythm of epistemological phases. The process may be described briefly as 'intuition over sensation, reason, and matter; reason over intuition, sensation, and matter; sensation over reason, intuition, and matter'."[37]

Friction in the socio-historical process produces the social and cultural congeries defined previously. The more integrated the network of systems, the fewer congeries exist. Over time system disintegration proceeds and the system declines. In Sorokin's view individuals are acting "in system" when they behave in ways that further the existing stability of the society. Acting "in congeries" entails antisocial and/or antihistorical behavior.[38]

The most curious and criticized dimension of Sorokin's work was the attempt to test his theory via an elaborate statistical scheme and to classify all of the so-called "major" civilizations. He attempts this by characterizing and weighting the importance of the work of selected individuals identified as important intellectual figures. For present purposes it is useful to note that Africa, including Egypt, is given short shrift in Sorokin's assessment.

Du Bois and Coulburn endorsed Sorokin's basic framework with the caveat that "it be kept in mind that the causation of all systems is supplied by their human agents."[39] They also accepted his classification of systems: "A priori there appears to be nothing wrong with the theoretical concept of cultural systems existing of themselves or with the idea of social systems bearing certain aspects of the culture, either in a specialized or an encyclopedic manner."[40]

And they not only concurred with, but extended Sorokin's view of the socio-historical process by hypothesizing that the sequential dominance of each mode of knowing "is universal for all civilizations."[41]

Behind Du Bois's and Coulburn's basic acceptance of Sorokin's scheme, however, were several fundamental disagreements. First, they charged that Sorokin failed to retain human agency in the model, with the result constituting a theory of social and cultural statics rather than a theory of social and cultural dynamics.[42] For Du Bois and Coulburn it is always human agents who create, operate and change systems. They further observe that this change process sometimes requires degeneration in order for transition to a new stage to proceed.[43]

The importance of this corrective for establishing the potential agency of

African Americans is self-evident. If systems operate and have meaning that is external to the actions of some potential agents who are disenfranchised, then these potential agents are non-entities vis-à-vis the major forces shaping human history. The recourse of agents who are so positioned is to seek change in the system rather than to accept the status quo.

This reformulation is related to the attack on Sorokin's assertion that the dominant culture is the sole source of meaning for a society during each period in its development. Du Bois and Coulburn asserted instead that

> the "dominant culture" ... [does] not ... make ... ontological and ethical truth for a given cultural period.... It is man in his historical evolution who makes, prescribes, and does these many things; and Sorokin has not grasped the realities of this evolution—the dynamics of society and culture—by the childish device of inverting his 'dominant culture' and painting the mighty and serene countenance of a deity on its backside.[44]

Again, the need to reject Sorokin's position from the standpoint of preserving the role of groups situated in a manner similar to Africans and African Americans is clear. The notion of a dominant culture presumes the existence of a subordinate culture. If the meaning assigned to a particular historical era is determined solely by the dominant culture, then members of a subordinate culture become passive vehicles manipulated by "superior" interests.

Sorokin's efforts to decouple cultural and social systems was also assailed by Du Bois and Coulburn. They asserted; "We think ... that always where there is a social system there tends to be a cultural system, and vice versa. Even such a small social system as the family does tend to create its specific culture, different in a few small, perhaps minuscule, ways from any expressions of the culture to be found elsewhere in the society."[45]

> The various detailed cultural systems, main and subsidiary, are if you like, "borne" by the various detailed social systems in an illogical, unsystematic sort of way, in spite of what we have called (modestly we think) the "tendency for social and cultural systems to correspond." But where the total culture and the total society are concerned, the correspondence must be complete and exact."[46]

Du Bois and Coulburn counterposed this formulation to Sorokin's view that an integrating supersystem exists for the five main systems of culture, but not for social systems.[47]

This critique provided the foundation for Du Bois's and Coulburn's most spirited attack, lodged against Sorokin's concept of "congeries." They argued that the concept of congeries made it impossible for Sorokin to admit any total society is a system.[48] To illustrate the error in Sorokin's reasoning, they maintained:

> It is not true that, for example, at a moment when the culture is predominantly ideational, minor systems of an idealistic and of a sensate character exist in congeries to—that is, in total scission from—the predominant ideational supersystem. Surely no human mind can think in terms of ideation, which is to say, intuition or belief, alone; to attain, develop, and defend the belief there must be some sense-perception and some reasoning. In other words, the mind must employ—in systematic relation with one another—all three methods of cognition.[49]

Du Bois's and Coulburn's attack can be seen, as noted previously, as a vehicle for establishing the non-congerial status of groups situated like African Americans, i.e., outside of the institutional network of the dominant culture. The cumulative effect of their reformulations is to assert a reversal of the relationship between culture and society asserted by Sorokin. In their view, "The three attitudes of mind bear, perhaps, a relationship to the culture similar to the relationship that the culture bears to the society. If the culture is an attribute of the society, then the prevailing attitude of mind is an attribute of the culture."[50] The significance of this reformulation is, as Du Bois and Coulburn maintained, that "these three attitudes of mind do not themselves constitute systems; they are qualities of the culture—of its supersystem, its main systems, its subsystems, all its systems."[51]

In the comprehensiveness and detail of their critique, Du Bois and Coulburn, in effect, fashioned their own theory of social and cultural dynamics that was largely distinct from that of Sorokin but built upon his superstructure. This expanded theory incorporates the following important elements: (a) a systems model of society, (b) a tripartite model of knowledge production, with one mode dominating during any single period, (c) a model of comprehensive and inclusive human agency, (d) a close correspondence between cultural and social systems, (e) a one-cycle model of the accession and decline of civilization, and (f) a periodization scheme characterizing major historical epochs.

The specific linkages between the elements of this expanded model and those articulated in "The Development of a People" are examined in the next section. The goal of the discussion is to support the claim that issues of race are not wholly invisible in the second model and that the reformulations of Du Bois and Coulburn are in fact designed to elevate the visibility of the contributions of peoples of African descent to the forward flow of human history.

IV. RECONCILING "THE DEVELOPMENT OF A PEOPLE" AND
"MR. SOROKIN'S SYSTEMS"

Understanding the linkages between Du Bois's earlier and later approaches to the issue of social and cultural change requires a resolution of several issues associated with the framework presented in "The Development of a People." First, there is the question of the nature of Du Bois's "people" construct. In particular, what are the correlates of "peoplehood"—race, nationality, ethnicity and/or culture? Moreover, can the nature of a people shift over time as progression across stages proceeds? As an example, could a people initially organize itself around shared phenotypical characteristics and later modify its basis for solidarity to a more "cultural" position, as broadened awareness emerges via formal education and cross-cultural contacts?

A second critical issue is the extent to which Du Bois is suggesting that African Americans remained at a different stage of development than European Americans following the end of slavery. Did Jim Crow segregation following slavery systematically restrict inter-cultural contacts such that African Americans remained in Stage 3 while American society at large progressed to Stage 4?

A third query is the extent to which progression through stages is unidirectional. Can a "people" retreat to a previous stage? Is the development process limited to one cycle or can all or part of the cycle repeat? As an example, once the stage of culture contacts is attained, can a people voluntarily retreat to a more isolationist mode? If so, does this represent a retrogression in level of development or is this a pattern that can actually produce a higher level of development?

Another issue that requires explication is the nature of the impact of economic organization on the development process. It is clear that economic considerations dominate the first two stages. However, Du Bois seemed to relegate these considerations to a minor role in the third and fourth stages. At the same time, his discussion of the constraints facing African Americans entering the world of work associated with the industrial order would suggest that economic issues are indeed important in later stages.

Fifth, Du Bois implicitly suggested that knowledge generated via rational inquiry is superior to folk wisdom. He does not appear to allow for the possibility that cultural differences in preferred modes of information-seeking may produce styles of inquiry of explanatory power and social utility comparable to Western science. This issue is related to the question of how Du Bois's notion of psychic duality or double-consciousness is related to the model. His often quoted specification of double-consciousness is that

> It is a peculiar sensation, this double-consciousness, this sense of always looking at

one's self through the eyes of others, of measuring one's soul by the tape of a
world that looks on in amused contempt and pity. One ever feels his two-ness—an
American, a Negro; two souls, two thoughts; two unreconciled strivings; two
warring ideals in one dark body, whose dogged strength alone keeps it from being
torn asunder.[52]

Does Du Bois's model imply that it is necessary to resolve this double-
consciousness via higher education in ways that subordinate the African-
centered dimension of the psyche in order for development to proceed? If so,
is this approach consistent with his own critique of the theory and praxis of
traditional disciplines that are integral components of the educational
process? Du Bois's efforts to grapple with these questions took various directions prior to and concurrent with the publication of the Sorokin review.

On the question of the meaning of the term "people," it is clear that
Du Bois originally intended the term to apply primarily to a largely phenotypical conception of race. In "The Conservation of Races" (1897), he argued that

> the history of the world is the history, not of nations, but of races, and he who
> would ignore or seeks to override the race idea in human history ignores and over-
> rides the central thought of all history. What, then, is a race? It is a vast family of
> human beings, generally of common blood and language, always of common
> history, traditions and impulses, who are both voluntarily and involuntarily striv-
> ing together for the accomplishment of certain more or less vividly conceived
> ideals of life.
>
> Turning to real history, there can be no doubt, first, as to the widespread, nay,
> universal, prevalence of the race idea, the race spirit, the race ideal, and as to its
> efficiency as the vastest and most ingenious invention for human progress. We,
> who have been reared and trained under the individualistic philosophy of the
> Declaration of Independence and the Laissez-faire philosophy of Adam Smith, are
> loath to acknowledge this patent fact of human history?[53]

At this point in time, then, Du Bois saw racial differentiation as crucial to the
development of mankind's full potential. In his mind, the function of each race
was "to develop for civilization its particular ideal, which shall help to guide
the world nearer and nearer that perfection of human life for which we all
long, that 'one far off Divine event.'"[54] Du Bois asserted that the African race
was the only one "which has held at bay the life destroying forces of the trop-
ics, [and] has gained there from in some slight compensation a sense of beauty,
particularly for sound and color, which characterizes the race."[55]

Although the conception of race advanced in "The Conservation of Races"
is dominated by phenotype, Du Bois does indicate a growing affinity for a

cultural definition in discussing the nature and source of differences among races:

> While race differences have followed mainly physical race lines, yet no mere physical distinctions would really define or explain the deeper differences—the cohesiveness and continuity of these groups. The deeper differences are spiritual, psychical, differences—undoubtedly based on the physical, but infinitely transcending them. The forces that bind together the Teuton nations are, then, first, their race identity and common blood; secondly, and more important, a common history, common laws and religion, similar habits of thought and a conscious striving together for certain ideals of life. The whole process which has brought about these race differentiations has been a growth, and the great characteristic of this growth has been the differentiation of spiritual and mental differences between great races of mankind and the integration of physical differences?[56]

The extent to which phenotype defines the conception of race in "The Conservation of Races" has been hotly debated (see the essays by Boxill, Gooding-Williams and Outlaw in this volume). Du Bois's later writings make it clear, however, that he gravitated toward a cultural definition. This shift culminates in "The Talented Tenth Memorial Address," delivered after publication of the Sorokin review (1948), in which he asserted that African Americans were "not simply a physical entity: a black people, or a people descended from black folk but, what all races really are, a cultural group."[57]

Decrying the fact that the term "cultural" has so many meanings, Du Bois advanced the claim that the term

> means in modern scientific thought . . . that 15,000,000 men and women who for three centuries have shared common experiences and common suffering, and have worked all those days and nights together for their own survival and progress, that this complex of habits and manners could not and must not be lost. That persons sharing this experience formed a race no matter what their blood may be . . . [that] this race must be conserved for the benefit of the Negro people and for mankind.[58]

Du Bois's application of his original model to African Americans then, reflected a conception of African Americans as a distinct racial collective that possesses unique characteristics of various types including physical characteristics, mental attributes, social institutions and shared historical experiences. Those familiar with Du Bois's educational background will recognize the influence of his association with William James in the use of the concept of a "complex of habits and manners."[59] In addition, the preceding quotation clearly indicates Du Bois's continuing commitment to the preservation of a distinct African American culture during the same period in which the review of Sorokin's work was authored. Thus it is inconceivable that the formulation in the Sorokin review totally ignores the construct of race, although it is not explicitly discussed.

Another key aspect of Du Bois's application of the early model to the situation of African Americans was his insistence that, despite the oppression experienced at the hands of the West, the basic orientation of African Americans as agents attempting to shape their own destiny had conditioned the entire period of inter-cultural contact. To illustrate, in 1911, Du Bois endorsed the then controversial view that African Americans had transformed the nature of the U.S. Civil War into a war of liberation through their own actions:

> So far as the great mass of people in the United States were concerned, the war had begun with no thought of emancipation. It was the Negro himself who forced the issue in two ways. As black men had gained freedom before the war by running away to the North and Canada, now in larger and larger hordes they escaped to the nearer refuge of the invading armies. . . . From this rose the second reason for emancipation, the use of Negroes as soldiers.[60]

As conscious agents, African Americans, therefore, always retained the matter of choice in setting distinct developmental objectives for each stage of the process. The essential choice was the mix between Eurocentric and Afrocentric development patterns.

In response to social transformation over time and exigencies, Du Bois oscillates over the course of his career regarding what constitutes the ideal mix, but he never vacillated on the criticality of the Afrocentric foundation for development efforts. As an example, in 1907 Du Bois asserted:

> The Negroes of the United States who are really thinking of their situation are not wholly foolish or blind concerning the future. They know very well how acceptable it would be to many people in this country if they should equip themselves so that they would be merely workmen and make larger dividends. They are not satisfied, however, to be looked upon merely as producers of wealth or to sacrifice themselves simply for that. They mean to enter modern civilization—they mean to achieve in this country a place where every single right that belongs to an American citizen shall be theirs; they believe just as strongly as they believe that they are living that the great historic race which they represent is one of the world's great races which in time is going to play a part in the theatre of the world, side by side with other races and not one whit behind them in accomplishment or in desert.[61]

In "The Conservation of Races" (1897), Du Bois maintained in a similar vein:

> For the development of Negro genius, of Negro literature and art, of Negro spirit,
> only Negroes bound and welded together, Negroes inspired by one vast ideal, can
> work out in its fullness the great message we have for humanity ... if the Negro is
> ever to be a factor in the world's history—if among the gaily-colored banners that
> deck the broad ramparts of civilization is to hang one uncompromising black, then it
> must be placed there by black hands, fashioned by black heads and hallowed by the
> travail of two hundred million black hearts beating in one glad song of jubilee.[62]

The language used in the preceding two quotations is extremely important. In
particular the use of five specific constructs clearly connects Du Bois's early
focus to that found in "Mr. Sorokin's Systems." First, there is the idea of
"entering modern civilization." The second is the characterization of African
Americans as representatives of a "great historic race" and "one of the world's
great races which *in time* [emphasis added] is going to play a part in the theatre
of the world, side by side with other races." The third construction of interest is
the vision of working out a "great message ... for humanity," and the fourth is
the idea of peoples of African descent being "a factor in the world's history."
The fifth and final construct is the hanging a Black banner "among the gaily-
colored banners that deck the broad ramparts of civilization."

The upshot of the preceding discussion is that even if the levels of development resulting from the initial interaction of Africans and Europeans were
comparable, in some empirical sense, significant qualitative differences in the
character of social institutions and values would still be expected to persist.
These differences would result from conscious choices by African descended
people to retain their cultural distinctiveness even if the option of total assimilation to Eurocentric patterns existed. The concern with the "agency" of
African Americans is directly linked to the thrust of the critique of Sorokin's
dominant culture model of social and cultural change. Because Du Bois interpreted the history of African Americans as one of struggle to determine their
own destiny, Sorokin's notion of congeries was all too facile a device for justi-
fying the historical record of oppression.

One of Du Bois's last explicit declarations of the self-contained development
strategy for African Americans is found in "A Negro Nation Within A Nation"
(1935). Here he argues, "There exists today a chance for the Negroes to organize a co-operative state within their own group. By letting Negro farmers feed
Negro artisans, and Negro technicians guide Negro home industries, and
Negro thinkers plan this integration of cooperation, while Negro artists drama-
tize and beautify the struggle, economic independence can be achieved."[63]
There are at least two significant aspects of the preceding quotation that

require explication. First, implicit in the presentation is the belief that African Americans can attain a higher level of development via self-contained networking than through greater intercourse with white Americans. This addresses the question raised earlier regarding whether the retreat to greater isolation increases or decreases development; i.e., Du Bois saw this self-contained development process as promoting rather than retarding development. Second, there is a decidedly greater emphasis on the specification of economic institutions and other social structures required for development than appears in "The Development of a People." This reflects, in part Du Bois's greater awareness of, and commitment to, elements of Marxist analysis during later periods of his career. The question is, however, to what extent the commitment to self-contained development was inconsistent with the class focus of Marxism. There are at least three dimensions of Du Bois's exploration of Marxism that warrant discussion. First is his examination of the feasibility of collaboration between black and white workers. In "The Economic Aspects of Race Prejudice" (1910) Du Bois offered this view:

> We are seeing arise in the South two great groups of laborers: one white and one black, one with the power of the ballot and one disfranchised. . . . These two groups of workingmen are coming more and more into economic competition and the industrial education of the Negro is bound to increase this competition. The result is a situation which is being taken advantage of by two different kinds of selfish interests. . . It]he politician in the South [and] the exploiting capitalist.[64]

Du Bois saw the litmus test of the utility of Marxism to be adoption of a stance by white workers rejecting racism in favor of a cooperative attack on capitalist exploitation. To illustrate, he argued in 1936: "The real problem . . . is this concert of the workers. The real emphasis today is not on revolution but on class consciousness and this is the job of socialism and the first proof of conversion is the abolition of race prejudice."[65]

A second impact of Marxist thought on Du Bois's constructions was his re-evaluation of the role of educated elites in the struggle for black liberation. In 1948 he observed:

> Very gradually as the philosophy of Karl Marx and many of his successors seeped into my understanding, I tried to apply this doctrine to Negroes. My Talented Tenth must be more than talented, and work not simply as individuals. Its passport to leadership was not alone learning, but expert knowledge of modern economics as it affected American Negroes; and in addition to this and fundamental, would be its willingness to sacrifice and plan for such economic revolution in industry and just distribution of wealth, as would make the rise of our group possible.[66]

It is important to note that, in the preceding quotation, Du Bois's expression of interest in applying Marxist ideas is geared toward the elevation of African Americans as a distinct collective, and does not suggest establishing and emulating some alternative reference group. Du Bois viewed class divisions among African Americans prior to World War II as a relatively minor problem because of the operation of a racial caste system whereby "the Negro leaders are bound to their own group."[67] In the post-World War II period he saw the potential for a widening class division among African Americans, such that "When the whole caste structure finally does fall, Negroes will be divided into classes even more sharply than now, and the main mass will become a part of the working class of the nation and the world."[68] Thus Du Bois argued in 1948 that "Negroes are in a quasi-colonial status. They belong to the lower classes of the world. These classes are, have been, and are going to be for a long time exploited by the more powerful groups and nations in the world for the benefit of those groups."[69]

Concurrent with the "proletarianization" of the masses of African Americans, Du Bois believed that the development of socialist organizations would proceed more rapidly among African Americans than among other segments of the American working class. Thus even though the long term trajectory would be toward a deemphasis on race, in the transition even socialist initiatives would retain specific group characteristics. This perspective was advanced in a 1953 essay in which Du Bois maintained,

> The United States, with its existing social structure, cannot today abolish the color line despite its promises. It cannot stop injustice in the courts based on color and race. Above all, it cannot stop the exploitation of black workers by white capital, especially in the newest South. White North America beyond the urge of sound economics is persistently driving black folk toward socialism.[70]

In the context of Du Bois's model of development, African Americans would be able to establish socialist economic institutions as part of a quasi-separate development pattern because of the limited cross-cultural contact with white Americans. At the same time, the manner in which America and African Americans are linked to the global economic order restricted the overall potential level of development achievable by Blacks. From this vantage point Du Bois saw the establishment of socialist economic structures as being wholly consistent with the traditional functioning of black institutions:

> the Negro group is continually pushed toward socialistic experiment; the churches try it in recreation and relief; the fraternal orders experiment in insurance; the fraternities give scholarships; there have been trials of consumers' cooperation. In

time, this group, with any increase in pressure, might become a veritable school of socialism.[71]

The third impact of Marxism on Du Bois's thinking was the reassessment of his previous scholarship and the conscious integration of Marxist ideas into his subsequent analyses. To illustrate, in an "Apologia" to the 1954 edition of *Suppression of the African Slave Trade*, Du Bois proclaims that "if the influence of economic motives on the action of mankind ever had clearer illustration it was in the modern history of the African race, and particularly in America. No real conception of this appears in my book."[72] He further indicates that *Black Reconstruction* (1935) is the first major piece that reflects the synthesis of his earlier and Marxist-influenced approaches to historical investigation.[73]

Du Bois, in fact, incorporated elements of Marxist analysis in the essay "Mr. Sorokin's Systems." In making the case for the agency of human beings, Du Bois and Coulburn used the following example:

> Consider the mercantile system of economics. In the minds of its great protagonists, such as J. B. Colbert, a pure system, within Sorokin's meaning of the term undoubtedly existed. But, when the empirical system developed, it approximated only roughly the pure system. The vehicles, that is the commodities of trade, the ships in the trade, the presence or absence of precious metals in various places, the suitability of various climates for agriculture or for manufacture—these did not fit at all easily into the scheme of the pure system. Hence, the agents, the myriad human beings operating the system, modified it, and the empirical system differed from the pure system. The part played here by the vehicles was entirely passive: they offered inertia to the process theoretically conceived in the pure system. But the agents played an active part; indeed, they created something new—new links or details to take the place of those of the pure system which were incapable of empiricization.[74]

It is clear that the preceding passage was informed both by Du Bois's critique of capitalist expansion and by the reconsideration of the slave trade. Moreover, there are three additional features of Du Bois's understanding of Marxist analysis that were consistent with the argumentation advanced in the review of Sorokin's work.

Du Bois identified what might be termed the "leveling effect of capitalism on cultural diversity" as one of the major threats associated with the progressive expansion of monopoly capitalism. As he argued in 1954,

> The result of worldwide class strife has been to lead civilization in America and Western Europe toward conformity to certain standards which became predominant in the 19th century. We have refused continually to admit the right of

difference. The type of education, the standards and ideals of literature and art, the methods of government must be brought very largely to one single white European standard?[75]

Du Bois's concern with the homogenization of cultures under capitalism helps to explain why the specific mention of race is absent in the essay, "Mr. Sorokin's Systems." The threat to the cultural integrity of African Americans was seen as part and parcel of the broader threat to general cultural diversity. To attack this problem Du Bois and Coulburn focused on Sorokin's homage to the idea that dominant groups define social meaning. While Du Bois focused on the aggregate construct of monopoly capitalism, others like Karl Polanyi have identified the infectious nature of the market mechanism per se as a major source of the alteration of traditional patterns of societal inter-course.[76]

A second influence of Marxist analysis reflected in "Mr. Sorokin's Systems" is the insistence by Du Bois and Coulburn on comparable status for social and cultural systems. This constitutes a rejection of the premise that material real-ity is secondary to the world of ideas. This move provides space for potential agents who lack access to the means of "cultural production" to be recognized as contributing to the advance of human history via their creation of func-tional modes of social organization, or vehicles, using Sorokin's terminology.

The third characteristic of Sorokin's scheme that is compatible with Marxist analysis is the idea of a one-cycle pattern of growth and decline of the macro-system. Of course, in Marxist analysis the notion of periodic busi-ness cycles is important, but the macro-system is seen as inherently degenera-tive. Similarly, Sorokin held to the view that great civilizations go through one three-phase period of rise and decline. It is important to note, however, that the one-cycle assumption has been questioned as it relates to both Marxist analysis and Sorokin's work. In the first case, economists, including Nikolai Kondratieff, have proposed the existence of long cycles in capitalist economies that are inconsistent with the basic degenerative assumption."[77] With respect to Sorokin's formulation, Du Bois and Coulburn discussed the difficulties encountered by Sorokin in his efforts to avoid the conclusion that "the Greco-Roman and Western cultures have passed through the processus [rhythm] 'at least' twice."[78]

Special problems obtain when efforts are made to apply a one-cycle model to the experiences of African Americans. Du Bois was well aware that the progression of society was not necessarily linear as implied in the model presented in "The Development of A People." In "The Evolution of the Race Problem" (1909) he insisted that the problem facing African Americans had "passed through a great evolutionary circle," repeating a cycle in the past that "began with caste—a definite place preordained in custom, law and religion where all men of black blood must be thrust."[79] He further asserted that

> Today in larger cycle and more intricate detail we are passing through certain phases of a similar evolution. Today we have the caste idea—again not a sudden full-grown conception but one being insidiously but consciously and persistently pressed upon the nation. The steps toward it which are being taken are: first, political disfranchisement, then vocational education with the distinct idea of narrowing to the uttermost of the vocations in view, and finally a curtailment of civil freedom of travel, association and entertainment in systematic effort to instill contempt and kill self-respect.[80]

Acknowledging Du Bois's recognition of the cyclical character of the status of African Americans does not, however, directly answer the question as to whether the basic model has a linearity assumption. The cyclicality that Du Bois describes derives from the subordinate status of African Americans. It is safe to assume, however, that he viewed the general process of the advance and decline of civilizations as being as intimately tied to the rape of Africa at the time that he wrote "Mr. Sorokin's Systems" as he did when he authored "The Development of a People." To illustrate, in 1944 he argued that "the immigration of African blacks to America in the 15th, 16th, 17th, 18th, and 19th centuries was the greatest social event of modern history," leading not only to the foundation of modern capitalism and the evolution of democracy but also constituting "the greatest controlled laboratory test of the science of human action in the world."[81]

Sorokin discussed "less advanced" stages of societal organization in ways that are compatible with Du Bois's original model. To illustrate, Du Bois and Coulburn related that Sorokin

> offers an interesting passage of a broad, general character contrasting closely knit and loosely knit societies, characterizing the former as the totalitarian and the latter as the laissez-faire societies. In so far as the passage describes the two types of society, it is one of the best pieces of historical synthesis in Sorokin's work. It sums up and correlates a foregoing analysis of society, in the manner of the sociologists, into familistic, contractual, and compulsory systems of relationship.[82]

However, Sorokin's analysis is not wholly satisfactory, as noted previously, because he denies that Africa contributed anything of significance to global civilization. This view is inconsistent with Du Bois's growing belief in the contributions of ancient Africans to global civilization. For Du Bois, Africans were active contributors to world civilization until they were forced into a dysfunctional form of sustained cross-cultural interaction with Europeans via the slave trade. Even here, however, the trade provided a second African-based impetus for global development to the detriment of the well-being of African descended peoples.

Du Bois's interest in Pan-Africanism, examined extensively in the other chapters in this section, constituted an effort to disengage temporarily from exploitative international structures in search of economies of scale through collective efforts. Presumably this collective action would reduce the time required for people of African descent to re-emerge as major actors on the global stage.

Du Bois and Coulburn, in fact, proposed such a scenario. They asserted that it was possible for a collective to withdraw from the dominant systems and pass

> into the next, or even the third, phase of the processus; on return it will be drawn
> back into the dominant phase of the moment. We are disposed to think that with-
> drawal and return is both a much more frequent and at the same time a much
> more partial and particular phenomenon than it is described by Toynbee. That is
> to say, that it is really concerned, not with the major aspects of the society's life,
> but with minor and partial aspects; and that in this sense it occurs constantly and
> so explains the constant local and temporary appearance of idealism in the
> ideational phase of a civilization, sensation in the idealistic phase, and so on.[83]

One especially critical aspect of this passage is its failure to speak directly to the character of the social organizations that would be established by a withdrawing collective. Instead, it focuses on the existence of epistemological distinctiveness within the disengaging collective. Recalling that Sorokin's model relies heavily on the role of individual elites as cultural innovators, the question arises as to whether Du Bois provides any clues as to how a distinctive epistemology might emerge within an oppressed collective.

It will be recalled that Du Bois's conception of the "Talented Tenth" was an important construct that undergirded his notion of group leadership in advanced stages of development. Further, in the critique of Sorokin's formulations, Du Bois and Coulburn rejected the sharp distinction between theory and praxis. As noted previously, in "The Talented Tenth Memorial Address" (1948) Du Bois offers a revision of his original conception that reflects the influence of Marxist analysis but also preserves a special role for the intelligentsia in creating a distinct epistemology that can enable a group to realize its potential to contribute to the advance of global civilization.[84]

Du Bois used fiction as a vehicle to explore some of the ramifications of pursuing such an internally-focused development strategy. Through this medium he was able to articulate a continuing ambivalence about the relative merits of a self-contained versus integrationist developmental strategy without doing a disservice to his long-established political positions. This ambivalence was most cogently expressed through a pseudo-autobiographical character in his fictional trilogy, *The Black Flame* (1957, 1959, 1961).[85] The protagonist, Manuel Mansart, exhibits the very characteristics that Du Bois identified as critical for effective leadership in "The Talented Tenth Memorial Address" in his struggles to promote the education of African Americans in the post-Civil War period. He dies shortly after the U.S. Supreme Court decision in the *Brown v. Topeka Board of Education* is announced in 1954. On his death bed Mansart offers the following prognostication:

> [I]f for another century, we Negroes taught our children—in our own bettering schools, with our own trained teachers—we would never be Americans but another nation with a new culture. But if beginning now, gradually, all American children, black and white, European, Slavic and Asiatic are increasingly taught as one—in one tradition and one ideal—there will emerge one race, one nation, one world.... Am I glad? I should be, but I am not. I dreamed too long of a great Negro race. Now I can only see a great Human Race. It may be best, I should indeed rejoice—[86]

After years of protracted study and struggle Manuel Mansart, like Du Bois, came to the final realization that the relationships among race, culture, humanity and civilization are complex and dynamic. As a consequence, simplistic formulas for creating forms of social organization that can promote collective progress are impossible.

V. CONCLUDING COMMENTS

If Du Bois could observe the world some forty years after the *Brown* decision, he would likely revise Manuel Mansart's assessment of the emergence of a unified global culture. We have witnessed the resurgence of ethnic nationalism in Europe and elsewhere and the growing attraction of a younger generation of African Americans to an internally focused development strategy. At the same time the collapse of the Eastern bloc has accelerated the leveling of culture patterns under capitalism about which Du Bois warned. Finally, we are observing the resurgence of biological theories of race that claim that there are genetic differences between peoples of African descent and Europeans that render the former intellectually inferior. Such views are rife in the journal *The Mankind Quarterly*, and in books like *The Bell Curve* and *Race, Evolution and Behavior*.[87]

These are but some of the important reasons to pursue the line of research that Du Bois began. However, in extending Du Bois's approach, it is impor-

tant to keep in mind his use of a two-pronged assault on traditional notions
of civilization and progress. First, he sought to correct what was perceived as
the misreading of the history of civilization by articulating the contributions
of ancient Africans. A growing body of scholarship, including that of Bernal,
Karenga and Van Sertima, supports Du Bois's views regarding the African
origins of Egyptian civilization and his claims that subsequent major civilizations were built substantially on its foundation.[88]

The second thrust of Du Bois's efforts to reconceptualize civilization and
culture entailed documentation of contemporary dysfunctional patterns that
could be ameliorated potentially through the efforts of peoples of African
descent. As noted, Du Bois was particularly concerned with what he
described as the "leveling of culture patterns" resulting from the operation of
monopoly capitalism. This process was seen as destructive to global civilization because of its corrosive effect on the very sources of cultural innovation,
i.e., cultural differences. Thus, he argued:

> If this [leveling of culture patterns] is going to continue to be the attitude of the
> modern world, then we face a serious difficulty in so-called race problems. They
> will become less and less matters of race, so far as we regard race as biological
> difference. But what is even more important, they will even become less and less
> matters of conflicting cultures.[89]

To take up the challenge posed by Du Bois would also require an in-depth
exploration of the sources of the cultural advances identified by Sorokin. As
an example, many scholars writing from an Afrocentric perspective argue
that much of the knowledge upon which Western civilization is built had its
origin in Africa. There have obviously been complex patterns of cultural
exchange that have produced widespread dissemination of this knowledge
with subsequent adaptations that have produced cultural variations. In many
respects, such a "knowledge-mapping" project is the logical extension of the
hundred-year research project that Du Bois advocated. The results of such a
project would more than likely reinforce the cogency of Du Bois's assessment
that:

> what we can look forward to, and what the racial strife in the United States ought
> to teach us to look forward to is that it is possible to have in this world a variety
> of cultural patterns; that men can live and work together in tolerance and mutual
> appreciation; that by vast and spiritual natural selection out of those different
> cultures may arise in the future, a more and more unified culture, but never
> completely unified, which would express and carry out the cultural possibilities of
> the mass of men.[90]

The evolution of Du Bois's theories about the relationships among race, culture and civilization point to one possible approach to reconciling the ongoing tension between Afrocentric and Eurocentric models of the dynamics of social and cultural change. It is both ironic and unfortunate that neither school of thought has recognized Du Bois as a major theorist of social change, given his solid contributions to both intellectual traditions. This essay will hopefully provide a basis for correcting the neglect of this dimension of Du Bois's scholarship.

NOTES

1. W. E. B. Du Bois, "The Development of a People," *International Journal of Ethics* 14 (1904): 292–311.

2. Rushton Coulburn and W. E. B. Du Bois, "Mr. Sorokin's Systems," *Journal of Modern History*, 14 (1942): 500–21.

3. See Oswald Spengler, *The Decline of the West*, 2 vols., *Form and Actuality*, and *Perspective of World History* (New York: A. A. Knopf, 1926, 1928), and Arnold Toynbee, *The Study of History*, 6 vols. (London: Oxford University Press, 1934–1939).

4. Du Bois, "The Development of a People," 295.

5. Du Bois, "The Development of a People," 293.

6. Du Bois, "The Development of a People," 293.

7. Du Bois, "The Development of a People," 294–95.

8. Du Bois, "The Development of a People," 295.

9. Du Bois, "The Development of a People," 295.

10. Du Bois, "The Development of a People," 296.

11. Du Bois, "The Development of a People," 295.

12. Du Bois, "The Development of a People," 297.

13. W. E. B. Du Bois, "The Atlanta Conferences," *Voice of the Negro*, 1 (March 1904): 85–90.

14. Du Bois, "The Atlanta Conferences," 85.

15. Du Bois, "The Development of a People," 308.

16. Du Bois, "The Development of a People," 305.

17. Du Bois, "The Development of a People," 299.

18. Du Bois, "The Development of a People," 303.

19. Du Bois, "The Development of a People," 300.

20. Du Bois, "The Development of a People," 304–05.

21. Du Bois, "The Development of a People," 304.

22. Du Bois, "The Development of a People," 306.

23. Du Bois, "The Development of a People," 306–07.

24. Du Bois, "The Development of a People," 307–08.

25. W. E. B. Du Bois, "The Talented Tenth," in *The Negro Problem: A Series of Articles by Representative Negroes of Today*, contributions by Booker T. Washington, W. E. B. Du Bois, et al. (New York, 1903), 75.

26. As an example Du Bois writes in *The Gift of Black Folk: The Negro in the Making of America* (1924; reprint, New York: Washington Square Press, 1970), 142: "the Negro woman more than the women of any other group in America is the protagonist in the fight for an economically independent womanhood in modern countries."

27. Du Bois, "The Development of a People," 309.

28. Du Bois, "The Development of a People," 311.

29. Pitrim A. Sorokin, *Social and Cultural Dynamics*, vols. 1–4, (New York: American Sociology Series, 1937–41).

30. See Herbert Aptheker, *Annotated Bibliography of the Published Writings of W. E. B. Bois* (Millwood, N.Y.: Kraus-Thomson, 1973).

31. W. E. B. Du Bois, "The Talented Tenth Memorial Address," *The Boule Journal* (October 1948): 5.

32. See note 3.

33. Coulburn and Du Bois, "Mr. Sorokin's Systems," 513.

34. Coulburn and Du Bois, "Mr. Sorokin's Systems," 513.

35. Coulburn and Du Bois, "Mr. Sorokin's Systems," 514.

36. Coulburn and Du Bois, "Mr. Sorokin's Systems," 514.

37. Coulburn and Du Bois, "Mr. Sorokin's Systems," 500.

38. Coulburn and Du Bois, "Mr. Sorokin's Systems," 501.

39. Coulburn and Du Bois, "Mr. Sorokin's Systems," 506.

40. Coulburn and Du Bois, "Mr. Sorokin's Systems," 513.

41. Coulburn and Du Bois, "Mr. Sorokin's Systems," 520.

42. Coulburn and Du Bois, "Mr. Sorokin's Systems," 503.

43. Coulburn and Du Bois, "Mr. Sorokin's Systems," 513.

44. Coulburn and Du Bois, "Mr. Sorokin's Systems," 509.

45. Coulburn and Du Bois, "Mr. Sorokin's Systems," 513–14.

46. Coulburn and Du Bois, "Mr. Sorokin's Systems," 515.

47. Coulburn and Du Bois, "Mr. Sorokin's Systems," 514.

48. Coulburn and Du Bois, "Mr. Sorokin's Systems," 516.

49. Coulburn and Du Bois, "Mr. Sorokin's Systems," 519.

50. Coulburn and Du Bois, "Mr. Sorokin's Systems," 519.

51. Coulburn and Du Bois, "Mr. Sorokin's Systems," 515.

52. W. E. B. Du Bois, "Strivings of the Negro People," *Atlantic Monthly* 70 (August 1897), 194–95; reprinted in *The Souls of Black Folk* (1903). For a detailed analysis of the construct see James B. Stewart, "Psychic Duality of Afro-Americans in the Novels of Du Bois," *Phylon* 44 (1983): 93–107.

53. W. E. B. Du Bois, "The Conservation of Races," *American Negro Academy Occasional Papers*, no. 2 (1897); reprinted in Philip Foner, ed., *W. E. B. Du Bois Speaks: Speeches and Addresses 1890–1919* (New York: Pathfinder Press, 1970), 75–76.

54. W. E. B. Du Bois, "The Conservation of Races," 78.

55. W. E. B. Du Bois, "The Negro in Literature and Arts," *The Annals of the American Academy* (September 1913): 233.

56. Du Bois, "The Conservation of Races," 77.

57. Du Bois, "The Talented Tenth Memorial Address," 5.

58. Du Bois, "The Talented Tenth Memorial Address," 5–6.

59. James's model was based in part on the idea that neural stimuli following certain pathways with repetition create predispositions toward certain behaviors and interpretations of stimuli, i.e., habits and manners. See William James, *Psychology: The Briefer Course* (New York, 1961), or his longer work *The Principles of Psychology* (New York, 1950). In his second autobiography, *Dusk of Dawn*, Du Bois indicated that he was a frequent guest in James's house and that James was his guide to clear thinking. Du Bois also observed that his knowledge of James's psychological models prepared him for the Freudian revolution.

60. W. E. B. Du Bois, "The Economics of Negro Emancipation in the United States," *The Sociological Review* 4(1911): 310–11.

61. W. E. B. Du Bois, "Sociology and Industry in Southern Education," *Voice of the Negro* 4 (1907): 174.

62. Du Bois, "The Conservation of Races," 79.

63. W. E. B. Du Bois, "A Negro Nation Within A Nation," *Current History* 42 (1935): 270.

64. W. E. B. Du Bois, "The Economic Aspects of Race Prejudice," *Editorial Review* 2 (1910): 489.

65. W. E. B. Du Bois, "Social Planning for the Negro: Past and Present," *The Journal of Negro Education* 5 (1936): 125.

66. Du Bois, "The Talented Tenth Memorial Address," 5.

67. W. E. B. Du Bois, "Negroes and the Crisis of Capitalism," *Monthly Review* 4 (1953), 483.

68. Du Bois, "Negroes and the Crisis of Capitalism," 482–83.

69. W. E. B. Du Bois, "Race Relations: 1917–1947," *Phylon* 9 (1948): 245.

70. Du Bois, "Negroes and the Crisis of Capitalism," 484–85.

71. Du Bois, "Negroes and the Crisis of Capitalism," 483.

72. W. E. B. Du Bois, "Apologia," in Du Bois, *The Suppression of the African Slave Trade to the United States of America, 1638–1870* (New York: Schocken Books, 1969), xxxii.

73. Du Bois, "Apologia," xxxii.

74. Coulburn and Du Bois, "Mr. Sorokin's Systems," 504.

75. Du Bois, "Race Relations: 1917–1947," 245.

76. Karl Polanyi, *The Great Transformation* (New York: Rinehart, 1944).

77. See Nathan Mager, *The Kondratieff Waves* (New York: Praeger, 1987). For an analysis of the implications of Kondratieff waves on the circumstances of African Americans see James B. Stewart, "Long Cycles and the Political Economic Status of Black Americans," (mimeo, 1990).

78. Coulburn and Du Bois, "Mr. Sorokin's Systems," 518, note 19.

79. W. E. B. Du Bois, The Evolution of the Race Problem," *Proceedings of the National Negro Conference* (New York, 1909); reprinted in Philip Foner, ed., *W. E. B. Du Bois Speaks, Speeches and Addresses 1890–1919*, 196.

80. Du Bois, "The Evolution of the Race Problem," 197–98.

81. W. E. B. Du Bois, "Phylon: Science or Propaganda," *Phylon* 5, no. 1 (1944): 8.

82. Coulburn and Du Bois, "Mr. Sorokin's Systems," 507.

83. Coulburn and Du Bois, "Mr. Sorokin's Systems," 518–19, note 19.

84. Du Bois, "The Talented Tenth Memorial Address," 5.

85. W. E. B. Du Bois, *The Black Flame: A Trilogy.* 3 vols (New York: Mainstream Publishers, 1957, 1959, 1961).

86. Du Bois, *Worlds of Color*, Vol. 3 of *The Black Flame: A Trilogy,* 290.

87. *Mankind Quarterly* has published studies in the fields of ethnology and human heredity since 1960; C. Murray and R. J. Herrnstein, *The Bell Curve: Intelligence and Class Structure in American Life* (New York: Free Press, 1994); J. Philippe Rushton, *Race, Evolution, and Behavior* (New Brunswick, N.J.: Transaction Publishers, 1995).

88. See for example, Molefi Asante and Kemet, *Afrocentricity and Knowledge* (Trenton: Africa World Press, 1990); Martin Bernal, *Black Athena: The Afroasiatic Roots of Classical Civilization*, 2 vols. (New Brunswick, N.J.: Rutgers University Press, 1987, 1991); Maulana Karenga, *Reconstructing Kemetic Culture. Proceedings of the Third*

*and Fourth ASCAC Conferences. (*Los Angeles: The University of Sankora Press, 1989); Ivan Van Sertima, ed., *Egypt Revisited*, 2nd ed. (New Brunswick, N.J.: Transaction Publishers, 1989). For a general assessment of Du Bois's relationship to the modern African Studies movement see James B. Stewart, "The Legacy of W. E. B. Du Bois for Contemporary Black Studies," *The Journal of Negro Education* 53, no. 3 (1984): 296–311.

89.   Du Bois, "Race Relations: 1917–1947," 247.

90.   Du Bois, "Race Relations: 1917–1947," 247.

Afterword

W. E. B. Du Bois and the Making of American Studies

Arnold Rampersad

The appearance of the first volume of David Levering Lewis's projected two-volume biography of W. E. B. Du Bois (New York: Henry Holt, 1993) promises to inaugurate a new age in Du Bois scholarship. Until now, the record of such scholarship has been uneven at best and poor by almost any standard when one considers the importance of Du Bois. I refer not to the quality of the books published on Du Bois by skilled scholars such as Francis Broderick and Elliott Rudwick, but to the quantity of such work, which has never matched or even approached the conspicuous importance of Du Bois as an American writer on the subjects of race and African American history, sociology, and culture. The notable exception in scholarship has been, of course, the excellent editions of Du Bois's work produced over the past generation by Professor Herbert Aptheker. Nevertheless, scarcely half a dozen scholarly books have been published on Du Bois's life and work.

"The Thought of W. E. B. Du Bois," the March 1992 conference at the Pennsylvania State University out of which this volume comes, was therefore of particular timeliness and even urgency. Indeed, the neglect of Du Bois had become so critical that one had to face the possibility that his reputation might become completely eclipsed. Once, during the darkest days of Senator Joseph McCarthy's anticommunist campaign in the early 1950s, Du Bois himself had mourned the fact that, because of a combination of intimidation by the right wing and cowardice on the part of many people, "the colored children ceased to hear my name."[1]

Certainly it is clear now that few young people are hearing Du Bois's name. Far too many of the latest generation of students, perhaps impatient with archaic aspects of his style in certain passages of *The Souls of Black Folk* (1903) and beset by other distractions, have begun to turn their backs on that book, arguably his most impressive single work. If *The Souls of Black Folk* goes, can the rest of Du Bois be far behind? And where would we be, especially as students and scholars, critics and professors in the academy, without the guidance and authority of W. E. B. Du Bois?

There are other reasons that this conference was so important and timely. I would like to suggest that Du Bois bears a special relationship to some of the more perplexing trends and currents in contemporary American intellectual life, and especially where the university is concerned. I refer here not to all of the intellectual ferment of this generation but to certain of its salient aspects. The most obvious, perhaps, is the rise of "Black Studies" in the last twenty years or so. Also germane is the rise of scholarly work emphasizing the diasporic aspect of African culture; with his publication of *The Negro* in 1915, Du Bois virtually inaugurated that aspect of African Studies. His career relates, in addition, to the general rise in the United States of what is called cultural studies; and to the general assertion of the importance of the troika of Race, Class, and Gender as the major tool in critical discourse across a wide range of disciplines in American universities.

If it would be difficult to relate Du Bois directly, in addition, to those intricacies of deconstruction and poststructuralism that have seized the attention of large sections of the American academy in the past dozen years or so, his life and career are connected nevertheless both to certain direct aspects of these intellectual forces and to certain germane trends and tensions. I refer both to the rise of relatively new and discrete disciplines and departments and to our vastly increased sense of the benefits of the interdisciplinary approach. I am thinking also about the growing tension between traditional humanistic discourse and the new antihumanist and posthumanist emphasis that has surfaced so strongly among the latest generation of scholars, and definitely among many of the brightest and most politically engaged among them. In Du Bois, I would suggest, one sees elements of this antihumanism and posthumanism peering out in spite of the deep commitment to humanism that Du Bois long cherished.

I have referred to disciplinarity and interdisciplinarity; but I am also thinking of the increasing tendency of the cultural studies movement toward an antidisciplinarity that is distinct from interdisciplinarity. In other words, I refer to important elements in the volatile dynamic of American intellectual life today, which is itself but a token of the volatile and sometimes ominous quality of contemporary American culture in general; and I see Du Bois, born almost 125 years ago and dead now almost 30 years, as having been intimately involved, in one way or another, in many of these questions I have mentioned.

Fifteen years ago or so, when I published my own modest book on Du Bois, *The Art and Imagination of W. E. B. Du Bois*, I referred (as I was able to do in those critically less sophisticated days) to his "prophetic" quality. I meant then not so much his ability to see ahead—indeed, I meant that virtually not at all—as I meant his idealistically expansive sense of self and sometimes almost volcanic style of utterance, his sense of grand moral connection and responsibility. But Du Bois was of course prophetic in the other sense of seeing ahead, and in few places more so, I think, than in the way he anticipated our intellectual turmoil in the United States, our gropings and intuitions, especially those having to do with race. However, I would also suggest that he was prophetic in the way most prophets are prophetic: in spite of themselves, uncannily so, often erratically, and often at a terrible cost to themselves. Du Bois both intellectually understood the major national and international problems he addressed, such as race and the African American character, and to some extent "only" intuited their complexities, and responded to them with a similar mixture of wisdom and improvisation. Why was Du Bois's apprehension of these questions so inspired and yet so unstable? The answer surely has to do with various factors: who Du Bois was in terms of his birth and upbringing, and endowed ability, and the other particulars of his experience; but it also has to do with the way, cherishing the (Victorian) concept of the individual's "life work" and of general duty, he pushed himself forward as close to the center of the intellectual and cultural action of his age as he could go. The answer must also have something to do with the ways of the university—the American academy—which he longed to inhabit as a full citizen, but was never allowed to inhabit in such a way.

Above all, I would argue, the answer must take into account Du Bois's lifelong wrestling with the hydra-headed, hallucinatory, and devious power of racism, as well as (separately and yet tightly connected to that force) the inexorable power of race as an idea. The answer must deal simultaneously with his determination to be a scholar and an intellectual—to know, to delve into, to explicate the central mysteries of American life, and even of life itself. For Du Bois sometimes had an almost Promethean view of himself as a link between the gods and humanity—at least, between the gods and black humanity—and yet knew, too, that he was painfully human, little more than a reasoning man and a searching scholar, and thus inevitably at some distance from the Truth.

W. E. B. Du Bois, on the one hand, and a determination to understand American racism, on the other, are virtually synonymous. No major American intellectual has shown a more determined grasp of the slippery and treacherous nature of the discourse surrounding this subject and how it has affected American life. No one has searched more diligently to plumb the mysteries of American racism, or written more vigorously over a longer period about more aspects of the American experience where race and racism are most concerned. In 1940, at the age of seventy-two, in a foreword to his autobiography *Dusk of Dawn*, which he subtitled *An Essay Toward an Autobiography of a Race Concept*, Du Bois wrote about the urgent need for humanity to chart a course not only through "the resistances of physical force" but also through "the vaster and far more intricate jungle of ideas conditioned on unconscious and subconscious reflexes of living things; on blind unreason and often irresistible urges of sensitive matter." Of these ideas, he warned, "the concept of race is today the most unyielding and threatening."[2] Du Bois understood clearly what immense power he was up against in his probing of the role of race in our lives.

In some ways, his remarks above were only a more complicated way of saying what he had declared for the first time in 1900: "The problem of the twentieth century is the problem of the color line."[3] Where did the wisdom at the core of that prediction come from? Seldom noted is the fact that, around 1900, Du Bois was hardly alone in taking such a view of race and the future. Others had used almost the same language, although usually with a different intent—mainly, to warn about the dangers to white people of race-mixing. Du Bois struck a different note, but he was playing on the same instrument of race that was used—indeed, invented—by those who professed to be frightened and appalled most of all by the very "race" to which he himself belonged.

Du Bois was first drawn into race as an idea "naturally," by his experience of racism; then as part of his formal education. In the tension between these two factors—between the hurt and outrage of racism and the prestige of a racial science that endorsed first biology, then culture as the great measure of humanity and scorned blacks at the same time, his sensibility and intelligence were ground fine.

Du Bois's education was fairly orthodox in its beginnings in western Massachusetts, where he was born, and where he attended elementary and high schools. It continued in more or less orthodox fashion at Fisk University in Nashville, Tennessee. Race was not an important part of the curriculum of such schools. Race became more important in this respect at Harvard University, where Du Bois earned a second bachelor's degree and also his doctorate, and at the University of Berlin, where he virtually completed a second doctorate. By Du Bois's time, race had acquired immense respectability and prestige as a branch of science. To be educated was to believe in race as a category, as a science. Committed as he was to the idea of race, however (as he was obliged to be), Du Bois did not make himself comfortable in that commitment. Instead, he strove mightily for the rest of his life to understand the structure of race, its myths and its truths, its dangers and its opportunities, and—above all—what it portended for the peoples of African descent in America and around the world. Looking back in 1940, he had no illusions about what his life finally had amounted to, despite his honors, awards, and volumes. "My life had its significance and its only deep significance," he declared, "because it was part of a Problem." That problem, however, was "the central problem of the greatest of the world's democracies and so the Problem of the future world."[4]

Understanding race was one thing; feeling the raw power of racism was another. Such experiences could be educational. They could also be destructive of education, and of moral and psychological balance and judgment. The sensitive, intelligent individual had to tread carefully to find the true meanings of these episodes. In this regard, one may identify at least four crucial moments in Du Bois's early life—that is, between 1868 (the year of his birth) and 1910, when he left Atlanta University and the academic world for New York, the NAACP, and the life of what he himself called "propaganda." As he recounts movingly early in *The Souls of Black Folk*, the shadow of race fell one day across him, never to be removed, as a child at school in Great Barrington. A little white schoolmate, a girl, refused to accept a gift from him—"refused it peremptorily, with a glance." That glance transformed Du Bois's life: "Then it dawned upon me with a certain suddenness that I was different from the others; or like, mayhap, in heart and life and longing, but shut out from their world by a vast veil." For a while he held the white world "in common contempt, and lived above it in a region of blue sky and great wandering shadows." But cold contempt was not enough: "Alas, with the years all this fine contempt began to fade; for the worlds I longed for, and all their dazzling opportunities, were theirs, not mine."[5]

Almost as decisive was his encounter with a white woman on a sidewalk in Nashville in 1885, when Du Bois was seventeen and newly arrived in the South. "No one but a Negro," he recalled, "going into the South without previous experience of color caste can have any conception of its barbarism."[6] Without thinking, he had dared to raise his hat and apologize to the white woman for having "quite accidentally jostled" her on a sidewalk. "The woman was furious," he recalled near the end of his life, when he seemed still baffled by her reaction; "why I never knew; somehow, I cannot say how, I had transgressed the interracial mores of the South. Was it because I showed no submissiveness? Did I fail to abase myself utterly and eat spiritual dirt? Did I act as equal among equals? . . . I do not know. I only sensed scorn and hate; the kind of despising which a dog might incur."

A part of him died that day on the Nashville sidewalk. "Thereafter for at least half a century," he would write, "I avoided the necessity of showing them courtesy of any sort." But who exactly did Du Bois mean in writing of "them"? White women? Southern white women? Whites in general? Southern whites? "If I did them any courtesy which sometimes I must in sheer deference to my own standards of decency, I contrived to act as if totally unaware that I saw them or had them in mind."[7] Thus, it might be argued, Du Bois committed himself to a systematic practicing of ways of being at sharp variance with his preferred standards of behavior. Could he act in these variant, inherently deviant and transgressive ways, however much they were forced on him, and still think (understand, analyze) clearly? And yet I would suggest that no one would be more aware of this tension, in Du Bois's case, than Du Bois himself.

The third occasion was a bittersweet combination of personal triumph and the American racial carnival. It was also a moment that perhaps more accurately than the first two episodes captured the inherent pathos of Du Bois as an educated intellectual seeking to teach America about race and racism. It happened on a sunny day in June 1890, in Cambridge, Massachusetts, when Du Bois delivered one of the student addresses at the annual commencement exercises of Harvard University. His appearance created a sensation. To the whites—the overwhelming majority of the audience, needless to say—his crisp hair and brown skin indicated that he was of African descent, and hence a "Negro," although he "doubtless has some white blood in his veins," as a Harvard professor attending the ceremony reported to a leading magazine. These facts—the youth's color and the texture of his hair—stirred the audience even before he had uttered a word. Before he could begin to speak, the distinguished gathering, which included the president of the university, the Governor of the State of Massachusetts, and the Bishop of New York, broke into spontaneous applause. "The applause burst out heartily," one reporter noted about the youth and the moment, "as if in recognition of the strange significance of his appearance there."[8]

Du Bois had come to Harvard two years previously, after earning a bachelor's degree at Fisk University in Nashville, Tennessee. There, his appearance on a similar occasion two years before had been unremarkable in this way. At Fisk, virtually all of his classmates had been black. At Harvard, virtually all had been white. In both places, obscure Fisk and renowned Harvard, all of his professors had been white. Certainly Du Bois had not been the first black to attend Harvard. However, so few persons of his color had been admitted previously that his simple presence at the commencement ceremony, and his place on the platform, constituted an event. He stood on the platform as a symbol of many things. To some of the applauding whites, he doubtless symbolized the future of his "race," which other people believed had no future, just as it had nothing that might accurately be called a past. He symbolized, too, the heroic and sacrificial effort of the North—that is, whites in the North—to end slavery through the Civil War; the power of education as represented by the greatest of American universities, Harvard; the power of the moral force of Truth and Right, which had triumphed in the Civil War. In applauding the brown young man, the assembly also applauded itself on its choices, its decisions, its heritage, and its deeds.

To his audience, Du Bois's chosen topic that day was an important but by no means essential part of the drama; he might have been, in Dr. Johnson's famous antifeminist jibe, a dog walking on its hind legs. But in electing to speak on "Jefferson Davis as a Representative of Civilization," the young black man stood in judgment not only of a white man, the president of the defeated confederacy, but also in judgment of civilization itself. Evidently he rose to the occasion; he played his part in the racial carnival with skill. The *Nation* declared: "Du Bois handled his difficult and hazardous subject with absolute good taste, great moderation, and almost contemptuous fairness." Another observer reported "a ten-strike," and general agreement that he had been "the star of the occasion."[9]

With this speech, in a real sense, Du Bois began his life's work, a kind of interposing of his life—his intelligence, his reading, his opinions, his writings—into the American academy and before the mainly white American world. It seems fair to say that the carnivalesque elements of his interposing would never disappear or even seriously be diminished. Du Bois would say and do nothing of a public nature that would not be subject to at least something of the same gaudy public theatricality, the same ultimately demoralizing mixture of amusement, bemusement, good will, understanding, and contempt that characterizes the general American view of racial "inferiors."

The fourth of the major moments, as I see Du Bois's early life, came in April 1899, while Du Bois lived in Atlanta. As Du Bois himself later reported it, Sam Hose, a poor Negro in central Georgia, had killed his landlord's wife. A threat of massive white retaliation hung in the air. "I wrote out a careful and reasoned statement concerning the evident facts and started down to the Atlanta *Constitution* office, carrying in my pocket a letter of introduction to Joel Chandler Harris [author of the Uncle Remus stories and an editor at the *Constitution*]. I did not get there. On the way news met me: Sam Hose had been lynched, and they said that his knuckles were on exhibition at a grocery store father down on Mitchell Street, along which I was walking. I turned back to the university. I began to turn aside from my work. I did not meet Joel Chandler Harris nor the editor of the *Constitution*."[10] Racism took him away from his "work," which is to say that it took him away from what he had conceived to be his ideal life, his ideal habits of thought and action. Now, finally, racism had succeeded in breaking him in two, or in opening a fissure that could not be repaired. Which was the true, the better half?

Racism was one thing. As brutal and terrible as it could be, Du Bois could ascribe it to ignorance, or lack of breeding, or irrationality, and move on—as far as racism allowed him to move. Racial science was another matter altogether, especially to a young black boy who delivered himself to his teachers in Sunday School and in every other school with an almost lyrical faith in the power of knowledge: "Ye shall know the Truth and the Truth shall set ye free!"[11] "In the elementary and high school," he recalled about race, "the matter was touched on only incidentally." Only in geography was it touched on, when the races of the world were pictured, with Indians, Negroes, and Chinese marked "by their most uncivilized and bizarre representatives; the whites by some kindly and distinguished-looking philanthropist." At Fisk University, race was faced openly, and racial equality stressed. At Harvard, however, "I began to face scientific race dogma: first of all, evolution and the 'Survival of the Fittest'." Always stressed was the idea of "a vast difference in the development of the whites and the 'lower' races; that this could be seen in the physical development of the Negro. I remember once in a museum, coming face to face with a demonstration: a series of skeletons arranged from a little monkey to a tall well-developed white man, with a Negro barely outranking a chimpanzee. Eventually in my classes stress was quietly transferred to brain weight and brain capacity, and at last to the 'cephalic index.'"[12]

In graduate school at Harvard and Berlin, Du Bois went on, "the emphasis again was altered, and race became a matter of culture and history. . . . Which was the superior race? Manifestly that which had a history, the white race." Although Asiatic culture was sometimes mentioned, there was no course in Chinese or Indian history or culture offered at Harvard, "and quite unanimously in America and Germany, Africa was left without culture and without history. Even when the matter of mixed races was touched upon their evident and conscious inferiority was mentioned."[13]

To guide Du Bois through this dark wood, as it were, he could rely on only a few allies and forces. What degree of help and comfort and guidance did his teachers and their disciplines provide? How did the American academy help Du Bois hold his mind and his heart and his life together? The record is, again, mixed. In psychology at Harvard he encountered William James, who was also something of a friend; in philosophy, Josiah Royce and George Santayana; in history, Albert Bushnell Hart; in geology, Nathaniel Southgate Shaler; in English, Barrett Wendell; in economics, Frank Taussig. In Berlin, Du Bois was exposed to Heinrich von Treitschke, Gustav Schmoller, and Adolph Wagner. Most of these professors were liberals, and yet racist by any plausible definition of the term; others were not liberal at all (Barrett Wendell certainly was not).

Shaler tossed out of his classroom a Southern student who objected to Du Bois's presence there; but von Treitschke declaimed from the lectern, with Du Bois present, that mulattos were naturally, irrevocably, inferior.

To put into perspective Du Bois's intellectual growth as well as the question of the extent to which he was helped and guided, or confused and hindered, by his professors and their disciplines, one must also move to consider the norms of racial thought in the United States in his lifetime, and especially in his youth. As Thomas Gossett pointed out in his landmark *Race: The History of an Idea in America* in the long aftermath of the end of Reconstruction, "the virulent racism of southern politicians was reflected in a torrent of racist books and articles. . . . A compendium of popular knowledge published in 1887 had a page of drawings entitled 'The Levels of Intelligence,' with a Negro resembling an ape representing the lowest level. Books pretending to have the last word of science concerning the importance of race and the nature of Negroes multiplied."[14]

For the statistically minded Du Bois, a crucial text was that by the Prudential Life Insurance Company statistician Frederick L. Hoffman, whose *Race Traits and Tendencies of the American Negro* (American Economic Association, 1896), predicted that exposure to diseases, especially syphilis and tuberculosis, would wipe out the American Negro. But Du Bois also had to take into account works such as Charles Carroll, *The Negro a Beast; or In the Image of God* (1900); William Calhoun, *The Caucasian and the Negro in the United States* (1902); William B. Smith, *The Color Line: A Brief in Behalf of the Unborn* (1905); and Robert Shufeldt, *The Negro, A Menace to Civilization* (1907). Before 1907, outside of so-called science had come the no less powerful and influential novel *The Clansman* (1905), by Thomas Dixon, Jr. (This novel would be the basis of D.W. Griffith's landmark film *Birth of a Nation* in 1915). Du Bois would also have to contend with the historical work of Houston Stewart Chamberlain, whose two-volume *Foundations of the Nineteenth Century* (published originally in 1899 in German by this English-born son-in-law of the composer Richard Wagner, and first translated in abridged form in the U.S. in 1911) powerfully emphasized the idea of Aryan supremacy. Then, in 1912, came an abbreviated translation of a work that had long dominated "scientific" racial discourse—Count Arthur de Gobineau's *Essay on the Inequality of Human Races*, with its identification of blacks as "inherently gluttonous, sensual, and stupid, with superior sensory development to compensate for inferior intelligence."[15]

Hard on the heels of and in response to Chamberlain and Gobineau would come American works such as Madison Grant's 1916 bestselling *The Passing of the Great Race*, which warned desperately that unchecked immigration would dilute the "Nordic" purity of white America. In 1921, William

MacDougall's Lowell Lectures, *Is America Safe for Democracy?* (1921), on the perils of race inter-mingling, were published. Then there was the work of probably the most influential of the racist scientists—Theodore Lothrop Stoddard, author of twenty-two books, including *The Revolt Against Civilization*, in which Stoddard warned his country—that is, its whites—that it was about to be overrun by inferior peoples. To such books may be added Charles W. Gould's *America a Family Matter* (1922), about the danger of degenerate racial stock; Clinton Stoddard Burr's *America's Race Heritage* (1922), which warned against "races impregnated with radicalism, Bolshevism and anarchy"; Charles Conant Josey's *Race and National Solidarity* (1923), which railed against the menace of colored races at home and abroad; and Kenneth L. Roberts: *Why Europe Leaves Home* (1922), with its thesis that with the immigration of more "Alpine, Mediterranean and Semitic races" into America, "the result must inevitably be a hybrid race of people as worthless and futile as the good-for-nothing mongrels of Central America and Southeastern Europe."[16]

Du Bois's first major statement on race—the Harvard address of 1890 on "Jefferson Davis as a Representative of Civilization"— is, in hindsight, an embarrassment. His essay "The Conservation of Races," delivered in March 1897 to the American Negro Academy, is more refined, more laudatory of blacks—but may be no less problematic than his 1890 Harvard address. The American Negro, Du Bois declared, "has always felt an intense personal interest in discussion as to the origins and destinies of races: primarily because back of most discussions of race . . . have lurked certain assumptions as to his natural abilities, as to his political, intellectual and moral status, which he felt were wrong." Some people had been led, therefore, to minimize race distinctions. "Nevertheless," he went on, "in our calmer moments we must acknowledge that human beings are divided into races." The last word of science, "so far," is of three great "families" of humans—"the whites and Negroes, possibly the yellow race." Out of these had emerged eight races, including "the Negroes of Africa and America."

Physical differences were not the main factor: "The deeper differences are spiritual, psychical, differences, undoubtedly based on the physical, but infinitely transcending them." How will the Negro "message" be transmitted? "For the development of Negro genius, of Negro literature and art, of Negro spirit, only Negroes bound and welded together, Negroes inspired by one vast ideal, can work out in its fullness the great message we have for humanity." Negroes are members of "a vast historic race." "We are that people whose subtle sense of song has given America its only American music, its only American fairy tales, its only touch of pathos and humor amid its mad money-getting plutocracy."[17]

Three years later, in 1900, came his celebrated statement at the so-called "first" Pan-African Congress (Du Bois would renumber the congresses starting with his own congress in 1919): "The problem of the twentieth century is the problem of the color line, the question as to how far differences of race—which show themselves chiefly in the color of skin and the texture of hair—will hereafter be made the basis of denying to colored peoples their rights."[18] Despite its portentous element, restraint and an attempt at judiciousness characterized this statement about race. The same might be said of the place of race three years later in *The Souls of Black Folk*, where Du Bois might easily have given in to the liberties of the essay format and let his passion displace his reason in the area of race. He did not.

Between 1900 and 1909, however, Du Bois was exposed to many ideas and experiences that affected his understanding of race. Not least of these was his exposure to the ideas of Franz Boas, notably about the historicity and cultural complexity of Africa, and about the relativity of cultures and cultural values. Here, around 1906 (when Boas spoke at Atlanta University), began the most serious phase of Du Bois's struggle to come to terms with and substantially revise his beliefs in race-science. This attempt, in many respects, was doomed, with Du Bois's record illustrating my belief that it is probably as difficult to divest oneself completely of race myths as it is to divest oneself of religious myths when one has been brought up within a religion.

One can note an obvious shift in Du Bois's race thinking in his essay "The Evolution of the Race Problem" (adapted from a section of his biography *John Brown*, published in 1909). Du Bois noted that the scientific racists say: "You cannot legislate against nature, and philanthropy is powerless against deficient cerebral development." Nevertheless, he attacked the major proponents of the doctrine of social Darwinism: "The splendid scientific work[s] of Darwin, Weissman, Galton and others have been widely and popularly interpreted" to mean that change is impossible. In reply, Du Bois asserts: "When a social policy based on a supposed scientific sanction leads to such a moral anomaly it is time to examine rather carefully the logical foundations of the argument." He invited his readers to see through the specious and calculated manipulation of words and images around a small core of scientific fact. "The present hegemony of the white races" has "a whole vocabulary of its own: the strong races, superior peoples, race preservation, the struggle for survival and a peculiar use of the word 'white'." This theory "makes the possession of Krupp guns the main criterion of mental stamina and moral fitness."[19]

Paradoxically, turning against racial science did not mean that Du Bois had become immune to the power of racialist thought—that is, to racialist thought that exalted blacks and devalued whites. This kind of thinking began to invade his writing after *The Souls of Black Folk*, as his difficulties with

Booker T. Washington increased and his place in the university became more tenuous. This thinking surfaced first in quite surreptitious fashion, as might be expected—in Du Bois's attempts at verse, as in poems such as "The Smoke King" ("the blacker the mantle / The mightier the man").[20] It broke into the open, again as might be expected, when Du Bois became a full-fledged polemical journalist, as editor of the *Crisis*, after 1910.

However, the struggle by Du Bois to resist such thinking, as well as to resist anti-black racial thought, is written into his work from the start. Two powerful anti-race-science forces existed in Du Bois's life and education before he was exposed to Franz Boas in 1906. One was socialism, to which he was introduced in Germany between 1892 and 1894 (although socialists can, of course, be racist). The other force was represented best perhaps by the scrupulous historiographic methods insisted on by scholars such as Albert Bushnell Hart, who oversaw Du Bois's doctoral dissertation on the suppression of the African slave trade to the United States, as well as by the empirical sociology taught to Du Bois, especially in Berlin, as represented in his own work by *The Philadelphia Negro* (1899).

In his *The Suppression of the African Slave-Trade to the United States*, Du Bois himself sought to stand at the farthest remove from racial feeling, or indeed from any "subjective" feeling altogether. He concluded:

> It behooves the United States ... in the interest both of scientific truth and of future social reform, carefully to study such chapters of her history as that of the suppression of the slave-trade. The most obvious question which this study suggests is: How far in a State can a recognized moral wrong safely be compromised? And although this chapter of history can give us no definite answer suited to the ever-varyinging aspects of political life, yet it would seem to warn any nation from allowing, through carelessness and moral cowardice, any social evil to grow.... We may conclude that it behooves nations as well as men to do things at the very moment when they ought to be done."[21]

By the time *The Philadelphia Negro* appeared, Du Bois was clearly less of a believer in scientific objectivity, but still warned about the dangers of subjectivity. He wrote about the lack of certitude in even the most rigorously empirical sociology:

> The best available methods of sociological research are at present so liable to inaccuracies that the careful student discloses the results of individual research with diffidence; he knows that they are liable to error from the seemingly ineradicable faults of the statistical method, to even greater error from the methods of general observations, and, above all, he must ever tremble lest some personal bias, some

moral conviction or some unconscious trend of thought due to previous training, has to a degree distorted the picture in his view. Convictions on all great matters of human interest one must have to a greater or less degree, and they will enter to some extent into the most cold-blooded scientific research as a disturbing factor."

(Nevertheless, "We must study, we must investigate, we must attempt to solve.")[22]

The essays, short story, and elegy (for his son) in *The Souls of Black Folk* gave him even greater possible latitude for an exploration of racial meanings not only in the areas of history and sociology but also in art, religion, and psychology. Still, Du Bois distrusted the role of racial feeling in his overall enterprise, which paradoxically was the illumination of racial character, the character of black Americans. In a brief essay in the *Independent* of November 17, 1904, he declared apologetically of his book, which was already a decided success, that its "style and workmanship" did not make its meaning "altogether clear." The collection of pieces conveyed "a clear central message," but around this center floated "a penumbra of vagueness" and veiled allusions. "In its larger aspects the style is tropical—African."[23]

Du Bois's apology was surely half-hearted. He must have known that "Africa" had taken over his prose and empowered it in ways essential to its success. If he regretted anything about the book, it probably was that its Africanness had been as involunatry as it had been irresistible; he himself had not deliberately seized the occasion to be "African." The word "African" here refers surely not simply to Du Bois's connection by descent to Africa but to his surrender to feeling, above all his surrender to the conflicted feelings that arose when ideas about race and feelings about racism came together in turbulent ebbs and flow. Du Bois was in control, and not in control.

Already his search for Truth had taken him a great distance from the frosty spirit that informed his doctoral dissertation. In the next few years, before he left Atlanta, it would take him even further afield. Thomas Gossett has included Du Bois among his examples of individuals who responded to race "science" not by arguing against such pseudo-science but by—at least at one point—indulging in it by writing about the racial superiority of blacks to whites. Although this accusation does not do justice to the range of Du Bois's writings, those writings may indeed, among other things, offer testimony to the corrosive nature of racial theory and racism itself.

In *The Art and Imagination of W. E. B. Du Bois*, I suggested a triangulation in Du Bois's intellect and psychology between "a soulful, impassioned liberalism, the discipline of Marxism, and the power of racial partisanship."[24] All of Du Bois's books in the main period I am investigating (until around 1910) testify to his fear of the destabilizing power of racial feeling even as the texts themselves centrally involved one or another aspect of black American culture. The patterns of his writing generally illustrate this fear by showing his vigorous, inspired response to it. That response took him as a writer from one field to another, from one mode of inquiry and expression to another, as he sought the most efficacious instruments to triumph over that fundamental fear.

Between 1905 and 1910 he edited two publications, both of which became vehicles for the expression of racial partisanship: *The Moon: Illustrated Weekly* (1905–1906), then *Horizon: A Journal of the Color Line* (1907–1910). In the midst of this journalistic effort he also wrote and published in the genre of biography—that often curious and often intellectually disreputable amalgam of scholarship, psychologizing, narrative art, and pure invention. Du Bois's effort was *John Brown*, published in 1909, the fiftieth anniversary of Brown's suicidal raid on Harpers Ferry. In defense of this book he was apologetic:

> The only excuse for another life of John Brown is an opportunity to lay new emphasis upon the material which they have so carefully collected, and to treat these facts from a different point of view. The view-point adopted in this book is that of the little known but vastly important inner development of the Negro American. John Brown worked not simply for Black Men—he worked with them; ... The story of John Brown, then, cannot be complete unless due emphasis is given this phase of his activity."[25]

Guiding Du Bois's sense of composition here were the race-inflected theories of the French historian Taine, with his famous troika of Race, Milieu, and Moment as the determining factors in historiography. Gone was the methodological puritanism or asceticism of his doctoral thesis and his Philadelphia book. Such restraint was, indeed, gone forever from Du Bois's work.

Lastly, Du Bois broke with science altogether, or almost altogether. He ventured into full-fledged art, if a novel based on a close reading of the economics of cotton farming in the United States may accurately be called full-fledged art. Du Bois's offering was *The Quest of the Silver Fleece* (1911), which he called not a novel but a romance (as he would also identify his next novel, *Dark Princess*, published in 1928).

How far Du Bois had come from an obsessive avoidance of the subjective and the racial might be judged from his essay, "The Souls of White Folks," first published in 1910, then expanded and updated for his collection *Darkwater: Voices from Beyond the Veil* (1920). There he wrote of whites: "I know their thoughts and they know that I know. This knowledge makes them now embarrassed, now furious! They deny my right to live and be and call me misbirth! My word is to them mere bitterness and my soul, pessimism." What was the main lesson of the world war just ended? "This is not Europe gone mad; this seeming Terrible is the real soul of white culture—back of all culture—stripped and visible today." Du Bois debates the crucial issue of the relationship between race and culture. Is European culture not "better than any culture that arose in Africa or Asia?" "It is." Of this there has never been doubt. But why? Not because Europeans are "better, nobler, greater, and more gifted" than others. No: "The greatness of Europe has lain in the width of the stage on which she has played her part, the strength of the foundations on which she has builded, and a natural, human ability no whit greater (if as great) than that of other days and races. In other words, the deeper reasons for the triumph of European civilization lie quite outside and beyond Europe—back in the universal struggles of all mankind." Europe's greatest sin, like Africa's and Asia's, lies "in human hatred." However, America is in "the van of human hatred." To the white world, "this modern Prometheus," Du Bois cries out: "Divine thief!" "Is not the world wide enough for two colors, for many little shinings of the sun? Why, then, devour your own vitals if I answer even as proudly, 'I am Black.'"[26]

From one point of view, Du Bois's career between his first publication and his departure for the NAACP and New York in 1910 (and the appearance of his first novel in 1911) may be seen as an unstable, even erratic thing. His career in this period may be seen as a spasmodic darting from one intellectual approach to another, from one field to another: from history to sociology to essays, then to journalism, poetry, and biography, and finally to fiction. Normally, for an academic, especially for a trained historian or sociologist, this kind of progression is tantamount to professional suicide, and the overall pattern is one of failure, resulting usually in the loss of tenure. In a sense, Du Bois did indeed fail, and he certainly (albeit voluntarily) lost his tenured position within the academy.

A more penetrating reading, however, might insist on two other conclusions besides which the questions of failure and of Du Bois's loss of tenure may dwindle in significance. The first is the uncanny extent to which Du Bois's career in the period described amounts to an anticipation by one remarkable Protean individual of what might be called the American Studies project, or the American Studies area, with its acknowledgement, embodied in the variety of fields in which Du Bois worked, that only a multidisciplinary and interdisciplinary approach to America has any chance of bringing us reasonably close to the most intimate truths of the American experience.

The second conclusion speaks to a quality inherent both in Du Bois as a practicing intellectual and in American Studies itself, and perhaps even in the phenomenon of the United States as a subject of serious inquiry. Above all, I would argue, race is the factor that made—and still makes—the complications that demand interdisciplinariness and mutidisciplinariness as a necessary scholarly response. In grappling with race, with its overt but also covert power to complicate, subvert, and compromise virtually every important aspect of American life, Du Bois almost instinctively resorted to the unstable but highly creative patterns of investigation and adaptations of investigations that characterized his career as an intellectual and scholar.

I do not mean to suggest at all that Du Bois finally solved anything, that he unraveled the mystery of the role of race in American culture. It might be argued, in fact, that Du Bois was as much a prisoner of race as he was a liberator on the question of race. He who wrote, in *Dusk of Dawn*, of "anarchy of consciousness" being the ideal goal of human thought often achieved anarchical effects in certain respects without intending to do so—while intending, indeed, to make settled statements about race and culture in the United States and the modern world.[27]

His mixture of success and failure alerts us above all, however, to the indefatigable, irresistible power of race and racism as forces in our American lives. His record also points to the complex heroism, humanity, and intelligence of W. E. B. Du Bois. As the most gifted American to attempt to plumb the depths of racial meaning in modern times, he deserves our serious attention. The conference that gave rise to this volume, and this volume itself, are tokens of that attention.

NOTES

1. Du Bois, *The Autobiography of W. E. B. Du Bois: A Soliloquy on Viewing My Life from the Last Decade of Its First Century* (New York: International Publishers, 1968), 395.

2. Du Bois, *Dusk of Dawn: An Essay Toward an Autobiography of a Race Concept* (New York: Harcourt, Brace, 1940), xxx.

3. Du Bois, "Address to the Nations of the World," in Philip S. Foner, ed. *Speeches and Addresses of W. E. B. Du Bois 1890–1919* (New York: Pathfinder, 1970), 125.

4. Du Bois, *Dusk of Dawn*, vii–viii.

5. Du Bois, *The Souls of Black Folk* (Chicago: A.C. McClurg, 1903), 2.

6. Du Bois, *Autobiography*, 121.

7. Du Bois, *Autobiography*, 121–22.

8. Du Bois, *Autobiography*, 147.

9. Du Bois, *Autobiography*, 147.

10. Du Bois, *Autobiography*, 222.

11. Du Bois, *Autobiography*, 89.

12. Du Bois, *Dusk of Dawn*, 97.

13. Du Bois, *Dusk of Dawn*, 98.

14. Thomas Gossett, *Race: The History of an Idea in America*, (Dallas: Southern Methodist University Press, 1963), 280.

15. Gossett, *Race*, 343.

16. Gossett, *Race*, 402.

17. Du Bois, "The Conservation of Races," in Foner, ed. *Speeches and Addresses*, 73–81.

18. Du Bois, "Address to the Nations of the World," 125.

19. Du Bois, "The Evolution of the Race Problem," in Foner, ed. *Speeches and Addresses*, 201–06.

20. Du Bois, "The Song of the Smoke," in Herbert Aptheker, ed., *Creative Writings by W. E. B. Du Bois: A Pageant, Poems, Short Stories, and Playlets* (White Plains, N.Y.: Kraus Thomson, 1985), 10.

21. W. E. B. Du Bois, *The Suppression of the African Slave-Trade to the United States of America 1638–1870* (Baton Rouge: Louisiana State University Press, 1969), 199.

22. W. E. B. Du Bois, *The Philadelphia Negro: A Social Study* (New York: Schocken, 1967), 2–3.

23. W. E. B. Du Bois, "The Souls of Black Folk," *Independent* 57 (November 17, 1904): 1152.

24. Arnold Rampersad, *The Art and Imagination of W. E. B. Du Bois* (Cambridge, Mass.: Harvard University Press, 1976), 229.

25. W. E. B. Du Bois, *John Brown* (New York: International Publishers, 1962), 7.

26. W. E. B. Du Bois, *Darkwater: Voices from Within the Veil* (New York: Schocken, 1969), 29–42.

27. Du Bois, *Dusk of Dawn*, 134.